# Prefabricated and Modular Steel Structures

# Prefabricated and Modular Steel Structures

Guest Editors

**Enfeng Deng**
**Xuechun Liu**
**Hongfei Chang**
**Liang Zong**
**Jiadi Liu**
**Ke Cao**
**Qi An**
**Xun Zhang**

 Basel • Beijing • Wuhan • Barcelona • Belgrade • Novi Sad • Cluj • Manchester

*Guest Editors*

Enfeng Deng
Zhengzhou University
Zhengzhou
China

Xuechun Liu
Beijing University of
Technology
Beijing
China

Hongfei Chang
China University of Mining
and Technology
Xuzhou
China

Liang Zong
Tianjin University
Tianjin
China

Jiadi Liu
Tianjin University
Tianjin
China

Ke Cao
Chongqing University
Chongqing
China

Qi An
Qingdao University of
Technology
Qingdao
China

Xun Zhang
Zhengzhou University
Zhengzhou
China

*Editorial Office*
MDPI AG
Grosspeteranlage 5
4052 Basel, Switzerland

This is a reprint of the Special Issue, published open access by the journal *Buildings* (ISSN 2075-5309), freely accessible at: https://www.mdpi.com/journal/buildings/special_issues/1946T6X887.

For citation purposes, cite each article independently as indicated on the article page online and as indicated below:

Lastname, A.A.; Lastname, B.B. Article Title. *Journal Name* **Year**, *Volume Number*, Page Range.

**ISBN 978-3-7258-2855-5 (Hbk)**
**ISBN 978-3-7258-2856-2 (PDF)**
https://doi.org/10.3390/books978-3-7258-2856-2

© 2025 by the authors. Articles in this book are Open Access and distributed under the Creative Commons Attribution (CC BY) license. The book as a whole is distributed by MDPI under the terms and conditions of the Creative Commons Attribution-NonCommercial-NoDerivs (CC BY-NC-ND) license (https://creativecommons.org/licenses/by-nc-nd/4.0/).

# Contents

**Yan Wang, Zhuyu Huang and Qi An**
Analysis of Seismic Performance and Applicable Height of a Cooperative Modular Steel Building
Reprinted from: *Buildings* 2024, 14, 678, https://doi.org/10.3390/buildings14030678 . . . . . . . 1

**Xiao-Meng Dai, Liang Zong, Yang Ding, Hao-Wen Zhang and Feng-Wei Shi**
Seismic Behavior of Demountable Self-Lock Joint for Middle Column Connection in Modular Steel Construction
Reprinted from: *Buildings* 2024, 14, 275, https://doi.org/10.3390/buildings14010275 . . . . . . . 24

**Chengyu Li, Cong Luo and Aizhu Zhu**
Experimental Study on Seismic Behavior of Steel Column Base Connections with Arc End-Plates Slip-Friction
Reprinted from: *Buildings* 2022, 12, 2012, https://doi.org/10.3390/buildings12112012 . . . . . . 46

**Bin Yao, Yu Shi, Weiyong Wang, Qiang Wang and Zhiyou Hu**
Flexural Behavior of Cold-Formed Steel Composite Floor Infilled with Desert Sand Foamed Concrete
Reprinted from: *Buildings* 2023, 13, 1217, https://doi.org/10.3390/buildings13051217 . . . . . . 61

**Lianghui Li, Shaochun Ma, Peng Bao and Hao Wang**
Effect of Hidden Column Type on Seismic Performance of the Insulated Sandwich Wall Panel Joints with Ceramsite Concrete Layer
Reprinted from: *Buildings* 2022, 12, 2214, https://doi.org/10.3390/buildings12122214 . . . . . . 84

**Zhansheng Liu and Sen Lin**
Digital Twin Model and Its Establishment Method for Steel Structure Construction Processes
Reprinted from: *Buildings* 2024, 14, 1043, https://doi.org/10.3390/buildings14041043 . . . . . . 101

**Cheng-Yu Li, Fan Wang and Ai-Zhu Zhu**
Seismic Performance of H-Shaped Steel Column with Replaceable Slip Friction Joints
Reprinted from: *Buildings* 2022, 12, 2240, https://doi.org/10.3390/buildings12122240 . . . . . . 118

**Quan Li, Zhe Liu, Xuejun Zhou and Zhen Wang**
Experimental Study and Finite Element Calculation of the Behavior of Special T-Shaped Composite Columns with Concrete-Filled Square Steel Tubulars under Eccentric Loads
Reprinted from: *Buildings* 2022, 12, 1756, https://doi.org/10.3390/buildings12101756 . . . . . . 138

**Yanxiang Yan, Yu Yan, Yansong Wang, Heng Cai and Yaorui Zhu**
Seismic Behavior of UHPC-Filled Rectangular Steel Tube Columns Incorporating Local Buckling
Reprinted from: *Buildings* 2023, 13, 1028, https://doi.org/10.3390/buildings13041028 . . . . . . 166

**Yan Lin, Zhijie Zhao, Xuhui Gao, Zhen Wang and Shuang Qu**
Behavior of Concrete-Filled U-Shaped Steel Beam to CFSST Column Connections
Reprinted from: *Buildings* 2023, 13, 517, https://doi.org/10.3390/buildings13020517 . . . . . . . 185

**Jingjing Zhang, Chao Liu, Jianning Wang, Xuguang Feng and Huanqin Liu**
Experimental Study on Flexural Performance of Precast Prestressed Concrete Beams with Fiber Reinforcement
Reprinted from: *Buildings* 2023, 13, 1982, https://doi.org/10.3390/buildings13081982 . . . . . . 207

Article

# Analysis of Seismic Performance and Applicable Height of a Cooperative Modular Steel Building

Yan Wang, Zhuyu Huang and Qi An *

School of Civil Engineering, Qingdao University of Technology, Qingdao 266520, China; yanwang2010803@163.com (Y.W.); 17866828258@163.com (Z.H.)
* Correspondence: anqi@qut.edu.cn

**Abstract:** As an innovative building system, the modular steel structure demonstrates a high degree of industrialization and assembly efficiency. However, no linkage exists between the components of modular units, leading to issues such as diminished load capacity and excessive steel usage in modular construction. In order to tackle these challenges, finite element numerical simulations are employed to examine the inter-column connectors and the cooperative modular steel buildings. This simulation calculates the initial stiffness across various degrees of freedom in these connectors. In addition, it analyzes the displacement response, changes in internal forces, and height of cooperative modular steel structures under varying seismic precautionary intensities. The results revealed that cooperative modular steel buildings substantially improve overall stiffness and lateral performance compared to their non-cooperative counterparts. There is a maximum reduction in the inter-story displacement angle of up to 36.1%, and the maximum reduction of the top displacement can reach 16.2%. This enhancement also increases structural stiffness, a shortened natural vibration period, and an augmented bottom shear force. Based on these findings, it is advised that the height of cooperative modular steel buildings should not exceed 21 m at 7 degrees (0.10 g), 21 m at 7 degrees (0.15 g), and 12 m at 8 degrees (0.20 g).

**Keywords:** modular steel building; self-locking; inter-column connector; seismic performance; applicable height

**Citation:** Wang, Y.; Huang, Z.; An, Q. Analysis of Seismic Performance and Applicable Height of a Cooperative Modular Steel Building. *Buildings* **2024**, *14*, 678. https://doi.org/10.3390/buildings14030678

Academic Editor: Daniele Perrone

Received: 23 December 2023
Revised: 17 January 2024
Accepted: 27 February 2024
Published: 4 March 2024

**Copyright:** © 2024 by the authors. Licensee MDPI, Basel, Switzerland. This article is an open access article distributed under the terms and conditions of the Creative Commons Attribution (CC BY) license (https://creativecommons.org/licenses/by/4.0/).

## 1. Introduction

In the context of China's vigorous promotion of building industrialization, along with industrial transformation and upgrading, prefabricated buildings are undergoing new upgrades. As an emerging form of prefabricated construction, modular building boasts high industrialization, superior engineering quality, and rapid construction speed. Existing modular steel buildings typically achieve module connections through corner connection nodes. Scholars worldwide have devised various corner connection nodes, analyzing their mechanical properties to ensure reliable connections between modular units [1–3]. Lawson et al. [4] designed a single bolted connector, welding a joint plate at the module column's end, setting construction holes simultaneously, and using high-strength bolts to unite the upper and lower modules. This joint, constructed outside the structure, does not interfere with interior decoration, but hole openings reduce the column end's stiffness. Liu et al. [5] introduced a new modular inner sleeve connection node, facilitating horizontal and vertical connections between modules. However, this node requires welding, increasing the on-site workload and hindering assembly construction. Chen et al. [6] proposed a self-locking inter-module connection based on a locking concept, preserving modular units' integrity and interior decoration. They indicated that this node exhibits excellent hysteresis performance and moment transfer capabilities, but its multiple mechanical components can lead to performance instability. Existing structural systems, connected by corner nodes, lack effective connections between modular unit columns. Each column operates independently, unable to form a cooperative working mode, leading to insufficient structural integrity, low load capacity, high steel consumption, and elevated costs. Hence, developing a cooperative force mode between modular units to enhance modular steel building integrity and load capacity is imperative.

Some scholars have investigated these issues. Palazzo et al. [7] suggested a novel energy-dissipating column design using X-shaped steel strips made from low-yield point steel to connect columns, thereby improving lateral resistance in horizontal directions. However, this connection requires considerable on-site work, conflicting with modular buildings' rapid construction ethos. Sharafi et al. [8] achieved a partial connection between modular unit beams using sawtooth connectors, facilitating cooperative force to some extent. As a unidirectional force transmission mode, this connector cannot support three-way force transmission and has questionable structural reliability. Yang et al. [9] explored a structural approach combining steel plate column-column and bolted beam-beam with backing plates, analyzing its seismic performance. They demonstrated significant improvements in rigidity, load capacity, and seismic performance after combining steel modular components. However, this method requires disrupting the envelope structure of modular units for assembly space. Xu et al. [10] used bolt connectors for connecting channel steel modular beams of adjacent units. They indicated that beam load capacity can increase by 50–90.5% post-combination. However, this method, necessitating the destruction of the modular units' enclosure, suits only non-closed sections. Addressing issues in existing modular steel buildings, such as poor integrity, low loading capacity, high steel usage, and cost, An et al. [11,12] proposed a self-locking inter-column connector enabling reliable connections between horizontally adjacent modules. This connector, simple in structure and requiring no extra construction space, supports rapid assembly. Under the premise of maintaining modular unit integrity, the inter-column connectors facilitate cooperative work between horizontally adjacent modular unit columns, boosting load capacity and enhancing structural integrity.

In this paper, an innovative cooperative modular steel building system is proposed based on the self-locking inter-column connector [11]. However, the stress principle of the collaborative stress modular steel structure is different from that of the conventional modular structure, and the research results of the conventional module structure cannot be directly applied to the new system. Research into the seismic mechanism and applicable height of cooperative modular steel buildings remains limited, posing challenges for engineering applications. Modular steel-structured buildings generally have problems such as small overall stiffness and poor structural displacement response in high-intensity areas. With the increase in floors, the inter-story displacement angle is also at risk of increasing. An excessive inter-story displacement angle will not only cause a large floor tilt angle and affect the normal use of the building but also cause vertical loads to have a large overturning moment on the structure, affecting structural safety. In order to overcome these challenges, this study investigates the seismic performance and applicable height of cooperative modular steel buildings through finite element analysis.

## 2. Cooperative Modular Steel Building System

The cooperative modular steel building, comprising modular units connected with inter-column connectors and an inner sleeve connector node [6], is depicted in Figure 1. The inter-column connector is a mortise-and-tenon structure consisting of two parts: a concave connector and a convex connector. The concave connector includes a trapezoidal chute and holes for the sliding blocks, while the convex connector comprises a trapezoidal member, a connecting backplane, a spring, and sliding blocks.

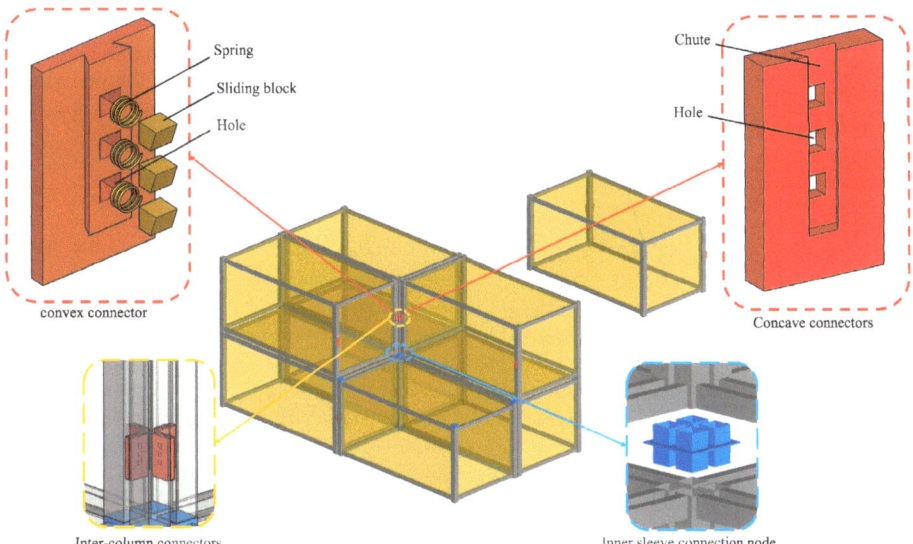

**Figure 1.** Cooperative modular steel building.

Figure 2 illustrates the assembly process of the inter-column connector. The concave connector is welded to modular column A, and the convex connector is welded to modular column B in the factory. At the construction site, modular unit A is hoisted into place, followed by modular unit B to the specified position, allowing the trapezoidal component of the convex connector to insert into the trapezoidal chute of the concave connector. The sliding blocks would be squeezed and then ejected during the slow descent of modular unit B. The connection is considered complete only when the lock is fully engaged and the trapezoidal member of the convex connector slides to the end of the trapezoidal chute of the concave connector. This involves the convex connector descending along the vertical direction with modular unit B until these conditions are met.

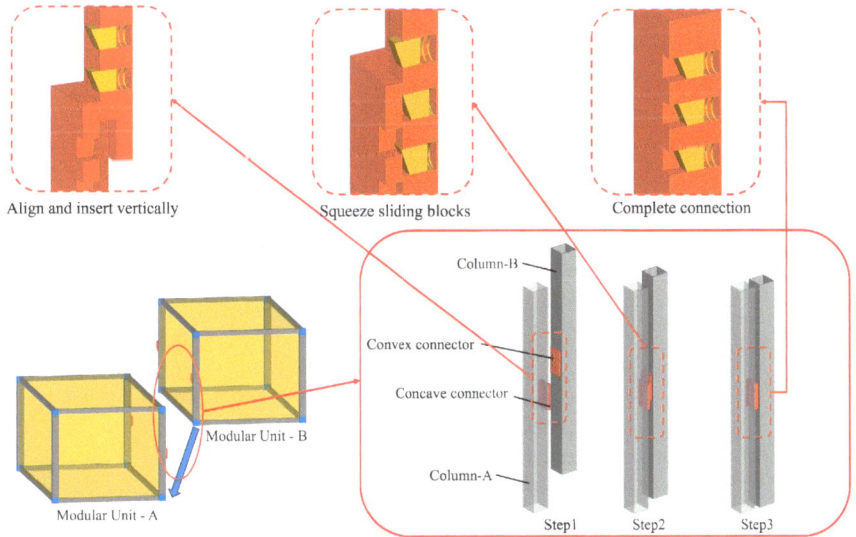

**Figure 2.** Connection process of the modular unit columns with an inter-column connector.

## 3. Initial Stiffness of the Inter-Column Connector

The inter-column connectors transfer shear force, bending moment, and axial force between the modular columns. This section investigates the initial stiffness of each degree of freedom of the inter-column connector to perform the equivalent connection of the inter-column connector in MIDAS/Gen.

*3.1. Finite Element Simulation Scheme and Parameter Design*

3.1.1. Element Selection and Material Constitutive Relationship

The inter-column connector is modeled and analyzed using ABAQUS. Each component in the model is assigned the element type C3D8R (eight-node linear solid element). The same force is applied to the convex connector along the Z direction, and the final displacement of the convex connector at different mesh densities is observed, as shown in Figure 3. The calculation indicates that the final displacement changes little when the mesh density is less than 1 mm. In order to ensure accuracy and convergence, the mesh size is set at 1 mm. Q355 steel is selected as the material. The material property of all components in the connector is set to be elastoplastic. Young's modulus and Poisson's ratio are assigned values of 210 GPa and 0.3, respectively. The yield strength is 355 MPa, and the ultimate strength is 470 MPa. Considering the hardening stage, the bilinear kinematic hardening model is selected as the constitutive relation, obeying the Von Mises yield criterion.

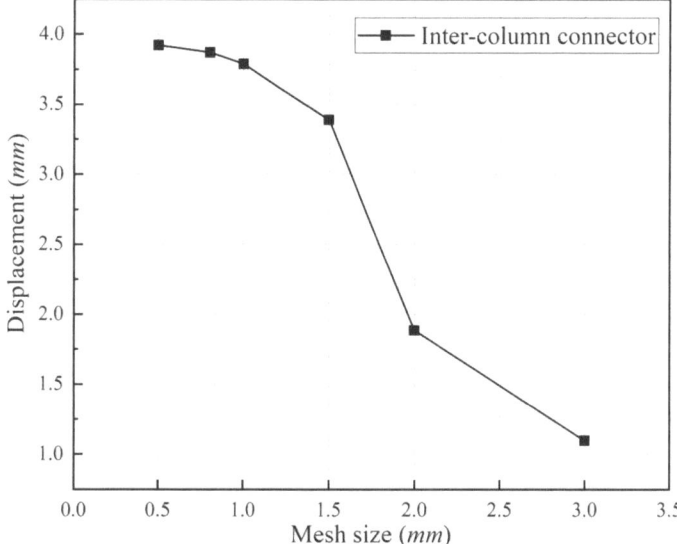

**Figure 3.** The change in the final displacement of the convex connector with the change in mesh density.

3.1.2. Contact Setting, Boundary Conditions, and Loading Regime

The concave and convex connectors are prepared according to the steel structure design standard (GB50017-2017) [13], including shot blasting treatment. The contact between these connectors is configured as a surface-to-surface contact. For the contact property, the contact in the normal direction is set as hard contact, while the tangential direction is established as frictional contact with a friction coefficient of 0.4. Only hard contact is made between the hole and the sliding block. The backplane of the concave connector is fixed, whereas the backplane of the convex connector releases in-plane degrees of freedom in the loading direction and applies a displacement load at the coupling point RP1 on the back of the convex connector, as shown in Figure 4.

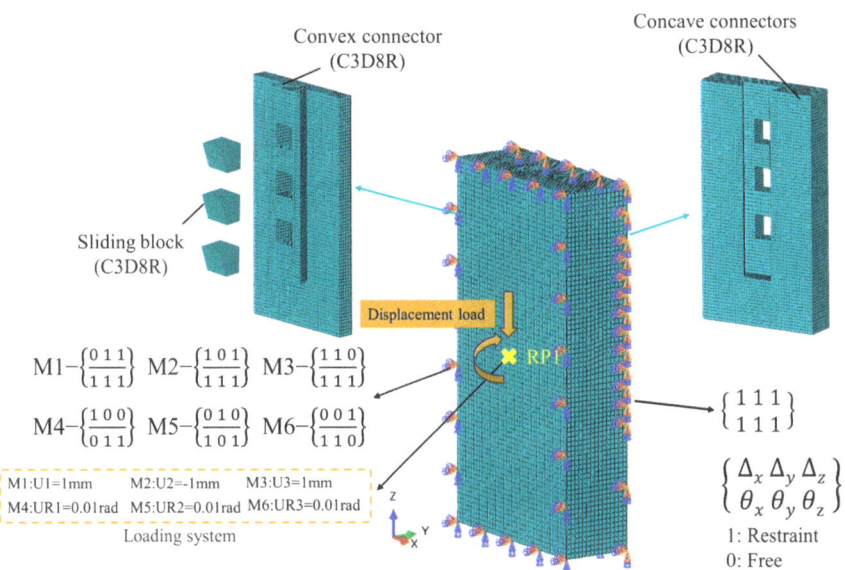

**Figure 4.** A finite element model of an inter-column connector.

### 3.1.3. Parameter Design

A total of six inter-column lateral connector models are designed, as shown in Table 1. Models M1–M3 are employed to calculate the translational stiffness of the connectors in the x, y, and z directions, respectively. Models M4–M6 determine the rotational stiffness in the Rx, Ry, and Rz directions. All numerical models are the same size, and their specific dimensions are detailed in Figure 5.

**Table 1.** Model parameter design.

| Model Parameter | Load Direction | Load Displacement |
|---|---|---|
| M1 | U1 | 1 mm |
| M2 | U2 | −1 mm |
| M3 | U3 | 1 mm |
| M4 | UR1 | 0.01 rad |
| M5 | UR2 | 0.01 rad |
| M6 | UR3 | 0.01 rad |

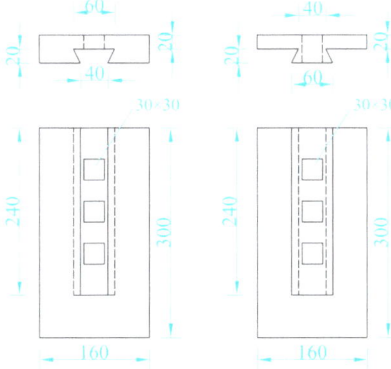

**Figure 5.** Dimensions of an inter-column connector.

## 3.2. Analysis Results

The farthest point method [14] is employed to process the data, with the initial stiffness of each degree of freedom of the inter-column connector presented in Table 2.

**Table 2.** The initial stiffness of each degree of freedom of the inter-column connector.

| Direction of Freedom | Initial Stiffness |
| --- | --- |
| Dx | $4309.1 \times 10^3$ kN/m |
| Dy | $3543.5 \times 10^3$ kN/m |
| Dz | $2556.3 \times 10^3$ kN/m |
| Rx | 47,541.4 kN·m/rad |
| Ry | 77,080.9 kN·m/rad |
| Rz | 1123.8 kN·m/rad |

## 4. Seismic Performance of a Cooperative Modular Steel Building

### 4.1. Seismic Fortification Intensity and Load Parameter Setting

According to the code for seismic design of buildings (GB 50011-2010) [15] and the code for load of building structures (GB 50009-2012) [16], building calculation parameters are designed and selected as follows: The structure's service life is 50 years, the safety grade is two, and the building type is class C. The seismic fortification intensity is considered between 7 and 8 degrees, with basic earthquake accelerations of 0.10, 0.15, and 0.20 g, respectively. The building falls into the second earthquake group, with a site category of class III and a characteristic period of 0.55 s. The essential wind pressure is set at 0.45 kN/m², the primary snow pressure at 0.15 kN/m², and the ground roughness at class C, considering load conditions and combinations under constant, live, wind, and earthquake loads.

### 4.2. Modeling Scheme and Parameter Design

#### 4.2.1. Modeling Scheme

In this section, MIDAS/Gen is employed to model and analyze a modular steel building. In order to ensure the safety and stability of the modular steel building, the following numerical modeling methods are used: The beam-column joints of the module unit are all set as rigid joints. The connection between modular units involves extending the beam-column joints of the upper and lower parts of the module upward and downward to a short column, simulating the vertical connection of the joints. Similarly, the beam-column joints of the module extend a short beam to adjacent modular units to simulate the horizontal connections. The intersection points of the short columns are designated as rigid, as are the intersection points of the short beams, as depicted in Figure 6. Due to an uneven distribution of stiffness in the modular building, where internal stiffness is greater than peripheral stiffness, several supports are strategically placed outside the building to increase the torsional stiffness of the structure. Unlike conventional steel frame structures, which often assume a rigid floor, the modular building exhibits small gaps between units and lacks cooperative work between beams, making it imperative to consider the influence of these gaps on structural force transmission. The results have shown significant deviations between the rigid and elastic floor assumptions, as referenced in [17]. The elastic floor assumption is the preferred calculation method to accurately represent the actual forces in the modular steel frame structure.

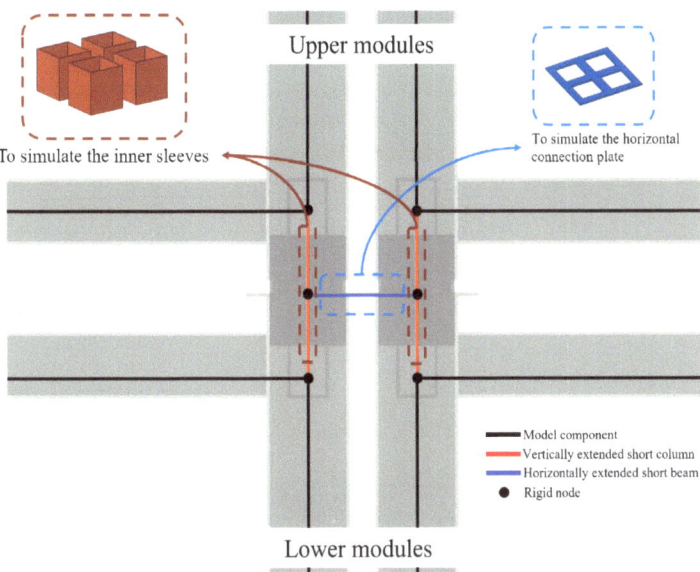

**Figure 6.** The connection mode of vertical modular units in MIDAS/Gen.

A spring connection is established in MIDAS/Gen, which inputs the initial stiffness values of each degree of freedom for the equivalent connection of the inter-column connectors. When the arrangement number is 1, it is positioned at the midpoint of the modular column, and when the arrangement number is 2, it is placed at the one-third and two-thirds points of the column, as shown in Figure 7.

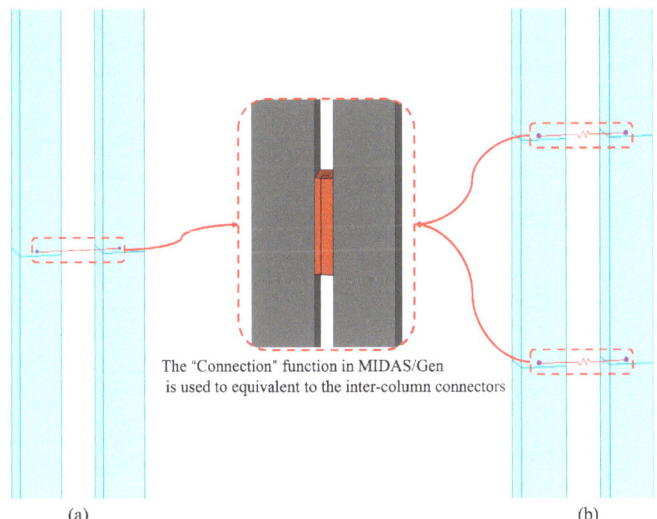

**Figure 7.** The connection mode of the horizontal modular unit in MIDAS/Gen: (**a**) The number of arrangements is one; (**b**) The number of arrangements is two.

Figure 8 presents the plan layout of the cooperative modular steel building. The standard floor measures 35.6 m in length and 15.2 m in width, with the five-story building totaling 15.3 m in height and each floor being 3 m high. As illustrated in Figure 9, modular units are categorized into three types based on structural form, with their dimensions and the components' section dimensions and floor parameters detailed in Table 3.

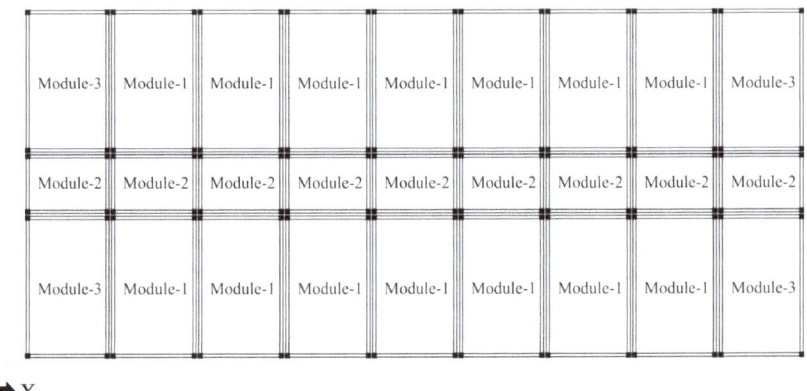

**Figure 8.** Cooperative modular steel building standard floor layout.

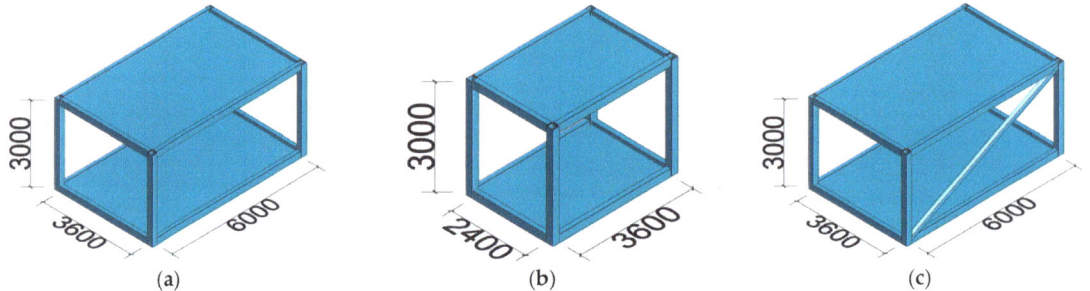

**Figure 9.** Types of modular units: (**a**) Module-1; (**b**) Module-2; (**c**) Module-3.

**Table 3.** Structural section size.

| Type of Member | Section Dimensions (mm) | Materials Chosen |
| --- | --- | --- |
| Modular columns | 200 × 200 × 8 | Q345 |
| Floor beams | 220 × 140 × 6 | Q345 |
| Ceiling beams | 150 × 100 × 6 | Q345 |
| Support | 140 × 140 × 4 | Q235 |
| Ceiling | 20 (board thickness) | C30 |
| Floor | 120 (board thickness) | C30 |

4.2.2. Parameter Design

(1) Response spectrum analysis

A total of nine models are designed for response spectrum analysis to explore the displacement response of modular steel buildings under different seismic design intensities before and after cooperative force. The parameter design is shown in Table 4.

Table 4. Model parameters of response spectrum analysis.

| Model Number | Seismic Fortification Intensity | Number of Inter-Column Connectors |
| --- | --- | --- |
| RSA-7-0 | 7 degrees (0.10 g) | 0 |
| RSA-7-1 | 7 degrees (0.10 g) | 1 |
| RSA-7-2 | 7 degrees (0.10 g) | 2 |
| RSA-7.5-0 | 7 degrees (0.15 g) | 0 |
| RSA-7.5-1 | 7 degrees (0.15 g) | 1 |
| RSA-7.5-2 | 7 degrees (0.15 g) | 2 |
| RSA-8-0 | 8 degrees (0.20 g) | 0 |
| RSA-8-1 | 8 degrees (0.20 g) | 1 |
| RSA-8-2 | 8 degrees (0.20 g) | 2 |

Note: The first number, "RSA", represents the response spectrum analysis, the second represents the seismic design intensity level, and the third represents the number of inter-column connectors.

(2) Time history analysis

Seismic wave selection

According to standard GB 50011-2010 [15], two natural waves, Elcent–h and RH2TG055, and an artificial seismic wave are selected. These waves undergo amplitude modulation and are presented in Figure 10, and their maximum seismic acceleration values under different earthquake intensities are presented in Table 5. The waves are validated against the structural base shear result and deemed suitable for dynamic time-history analysis of modular steel buildings.

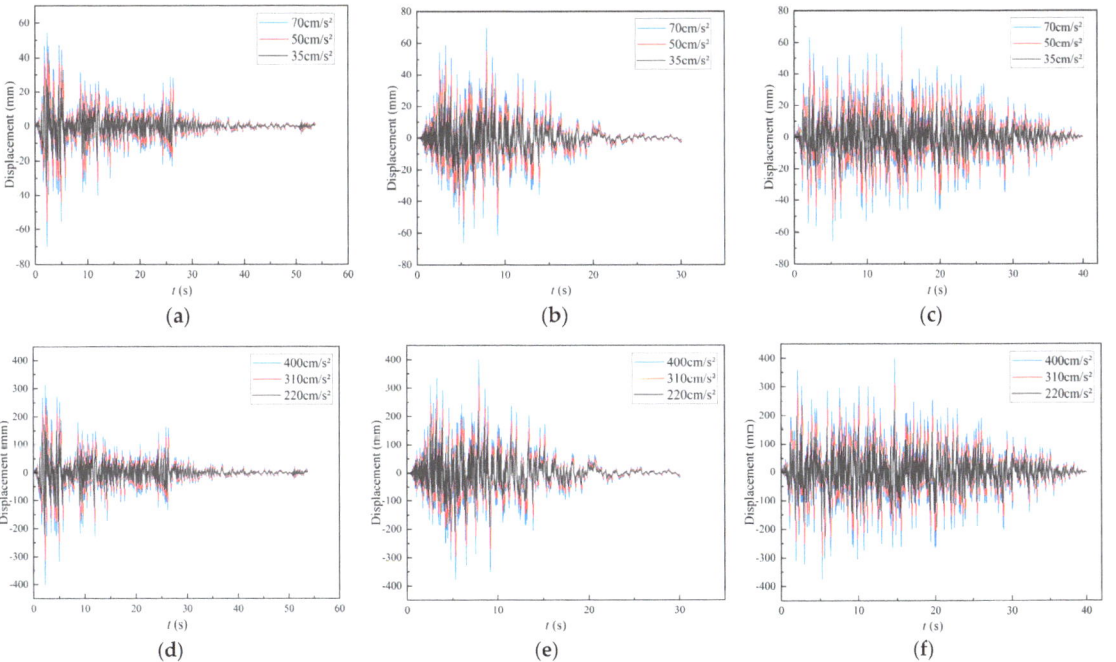

Figure 10. Time history curve of seismic wave: Frequent earthquake: (a) Elcent–h; (b) RH2TG055; (c) Artificial. Rare occurrence earthquake: (d) Elcent–h; (e) RH2TG055; (f) Artificial.

**Table 5.** Model parameters of time history analysis.

| Model Number | Seismic Wave Number | Maximum Value of the Seismic Acceleration (cm/s²) | Number of Inter-Column Connectors | Model Number | Seismic Wave Number | Maximum Value of the Seismic Acceleration (cm/s²) | Number of Inter-Column Connectors |
|---|---|---|---|---|---|---|---|
| ETA-EL-35-0 | EL | 35 | 0 | EPTA-EL-220-0 | EL | 220 | 0 |
| ETA-EL-35-1 | EL | 35 | 1 | EPTA-EL-220-1 | EL | 220 | 1 |
| ETA-EL-35-2 | EL | 35 | 2 | EPTA-EL-220-2 | EL | 220 | 2 |
| ETA-RH-35-0 | RH | 35 | 0 | EPTA-RH-220-0 | RH | 220 | 0 |
| ETA-RH-35-1 | RH | 35 | 1 | EPTA-RH-220-1 | RH | 220 | 1 |
| ETA-RH-35-2 | RH | 35 | 2 | EPTA-RH-220-2 | RH | 220 | 2 |
| ETA-AW-35-0 | AW | 35 | 0 | EPTA-AW-220-0 | AW | 220 | 0 |
| ETA-AW-35-1 | AW | 35 | 1 | EPTA-AW-220-1 | AW | 220 | 1 |
| ETA-AW-35-2 | AW | 35 | 2 | EPTA-AW-220-2 | AW | 220 | 2 |
| ETA-EL-55-0 | EL | 55 | 0 | EPTA-EL-310-0 | EL | 310 | 0 |
| ETA-EL-55-1 | EL | 55 | 1 | EPTA-EL-310-1 | EL | 310 | 1 |
| ETA-EL-55-2 | EL | 55 | 2 | EPTA-EL-310-2 | EL | 310 | 2 |
| ETA-RH-55-0 | RH | 55 | 0 | EPTA-RH-310-0 | RH | 310 | 0 |
| ETA-RH-55-1 | RH | 55 | 1 | EPTA-RH-310-1 | RH | 310 | 1 |
| ETA-RH-55-2 | RH | 55 | 2 | EPTA-RH-310-2 | RH | 310 | 2 |
| ETA-AW-55-0 | AW | 55 | 0 | EPTA-AW-310-0 | AW | 310 | 0 |
| ETA-AW-55-1 | AW | 55 | 1 | EPTA-AW-310-1 | AW | 310 | 1 |
| ETA-AW-55-2 | AW | 55 | 2 | EPTA-AW-310-2 | AW | 310 | 2 |
| ETA-EL-70-0 | EL | 70 | 0 | EPTA-EL-400-0 | EL | 400 | 0 |
| ETA-EL-70-1 | EL | 70 | 1 | EPTA-EL-400-1 | EL | 400 | 1 |
| ETA-EL-70-2 | EL | 70 | 2 | EPTA-EL-400-2 | EL | 400 | 2 |
| ETA-RH-70-0 | RH | 70 | 0 | EPTA-RH-400-0 | RH | 400 | 0 |
| ETA-RH-70-1 | RH | 70 | 1 | EPTA-RH-400-1 | RH | 400 | 1 |
| ETA-RH-70-2 | RH | 70 | 2 | EPTA-RH-400-2 | RH | 400 | 2 |
| ETA-AW-70-0 | AW | 70 | 0 | EPTA-AW-400-0 | AW | 400 | 0 |
| ETA-AW-70-1 | AW | 70 | 1 | EPTA-AW-400-1 | AW | 400 | 1 |
| ETA-AW-70-2 | AW | 70 | 2 | EPTA-AW-400-2 | AW | 400 | 2 |

Note: The first number, "ETA", denotes the elastic time history analysis, and the "EPTA" represents the elastoplastic time history analysis. The second number indicates the selected seismic wave ("EL" for Elcent–h wave, "RH" for RH2TG055 wave, and "AW" for artificial seismic wave). The third number signifies the maximum value of the seismic acceleration, while the fourth number corresponds to the number of inter-column connectors.

A total of 54 models are designed, comprising 27 for elastic time-history analysis and 27 for elastic-plastic time-history analysis. The specific parameters are shown in Table 5.

*4.3. Calculation Results*

4.3.1. Natural Vibration Characteristics

Figure 11 illustrates the first three vibration modes of the modular steel building. The figure reveals that the initial vibration mode of the model is X-translational, followed by the Y-translational mode, and the third mode is torsional. All models consider the first 35 orders of vibration modes. The modal mass participation ratio of all models in the first 35 orders of vibration modes in the X, Y, and Z directions reached 99.9%. Taking RSA-7-0 as an example, from the perspective of the first 10 vibration modes, the participation mass coefficient of the vibration mode in the X direction is 82.56, the Y direction is 81.99, and the Z direction is 81.96. The participation mass coefficient of the vibration mode in the X translation is the largest. Other models show similar laws. Table 6 compares the natural vibration periods of different models. The natural vibration period characteristics of all models demonstrate a consistent trend: as the number of connectors increases, the fundamental period of the structure diminishes. This decrease suggests that introducing inter-column connectors enhances structural stiffness and reduces the fundamental period.

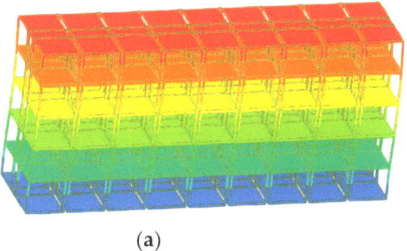 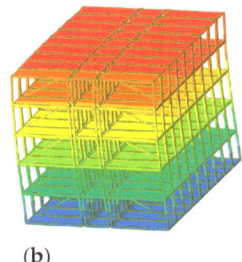 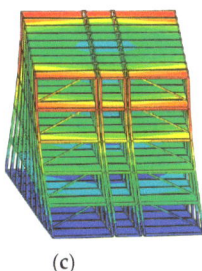

(a) (b) (c)

**Figure 11.** Comparison of the first three modes of the structure: (**a**) The first vibration mode: translation in the X-direction; (**b**) The second vibration mode: translation in the X-direction; (**c**) The third vibration mode: torsion.

**Table 6.** Structural natural vibration period of different models.

| Seismic Fortification Intensity | Model Number | Natural Vibration Period (s) |
| --- | --- | --- |
| 7 degrees (0.10 g) | RSA-7-0 | 0.830 |
| | RSA-7-1 | 0.659 |
| | RSA-7-2 | 0.636 |
| 7 degrees (0.15 g) | RSA-7.5-0 | 0.830 |
| | RSA-7.5-1 | 0.659 |
| | RSA-7.5-2 | 0.636 |
| 8 degrees (0.20 g) | RSA-8-0 | 0.830 |
| | RSA-8-1 | 0.659 |
| | RSA-8-2 | 0.636 |

4.3.2. Response Spectrum Analysis

Table 7 presents the peak displacement of each numerical model in the X and Y directions under frequent earthquakes, with the inter-story displacement angle depicted in Figure 12. Under three design intensities, the maximum inter-story displacement angle of the building occurs in the second story. With a seismic fortification intensity of 8 degrees (0.20 g) and an increase in number of connectors from zero to one, the top displacement decreases from 28.32 mm to 23.72 mm, a reduction of 16.2%, and the maximum decrease in inter-story displacement angle is 36.1%. Increasing the number of connectors from one to two results in a maximum top displacement reduction of 2.1% and a maximum inter-story displacement angle reduction of 13.1%. The inter-story displacement angles on the fourth and fifth floors of the cooperative modular steel building are larger than those in the non-cooperative modular building. This is because the cooperative force between the modular components increases the overall structural stiffness, resulting in increased base shear and significantly higher shear force at the top floor, thereby elevating the inter-story displacement.

The T/CECS 507-2018 *Technical specification for steel modular buildings* [18] stipulates that the inter-story displacement angle of the modular building under frequent earthquake loads should be less than height/300, and the elastic-plastic inter-story displacement angle of the modular building under rare earthquakes should be less than height/50. The inter-story displacement angles of all numerical models remain within the limit (≤story height/300) specified in T/CECS 507-2018. The lateral stiffness of the building in the Y-direction is significantly enhanced due to the transverse support in the modular building, resulting in smaller top displacement and inter-story displacement angles in the Y-direction compared to the X-direction. When the design seismic fortification intensity is 7 degrees (0.10 g) and 7 degrees (0.15 g), the building's displacement response exhibits a similar pattern to that at 8 degrees (0.20 g). The findings indicate that increasing the number of inter-column connectors from zero to one for modular steel buildings significantly improves lateral performance. However, after achieving cooperative force in the modular components, the impact of adding more inter-column connectors on enhancing lateral performance becomes relatively less pronounced.

**Table 7.** Top displacement of modular steel buildings with different seismic fortification intensities.

| Seismic Fortification Intensity | Model Number | Top Displacement (mm) | |
|---|---|---|---|
| | | X-Direction | Y-Direction |
| 7 degrees (0.10 g) | RSA-7-0 | 14.16 | 10.77 |
| | RSA-7-1 | 11.86 | 9.90 |
| | RSA-7-2 | 11.62 | 9.65 |
| 7 degrees (0.15 g) | RSA-7.5-0 | 21.24 | 16.15 |
| | RSA-7.5-1 | 17.79 | 14.85 |
| | RSA-7.5-2 | 17.43 | 14.47 |
| 8 degrees (0.20 g) | RSA-8-0 | 28.32 | 21.53 |
| | RSA-8-1 | 23.72 | 19.80 |
| | RSA-8-2 | 23.24 | 19.29 |

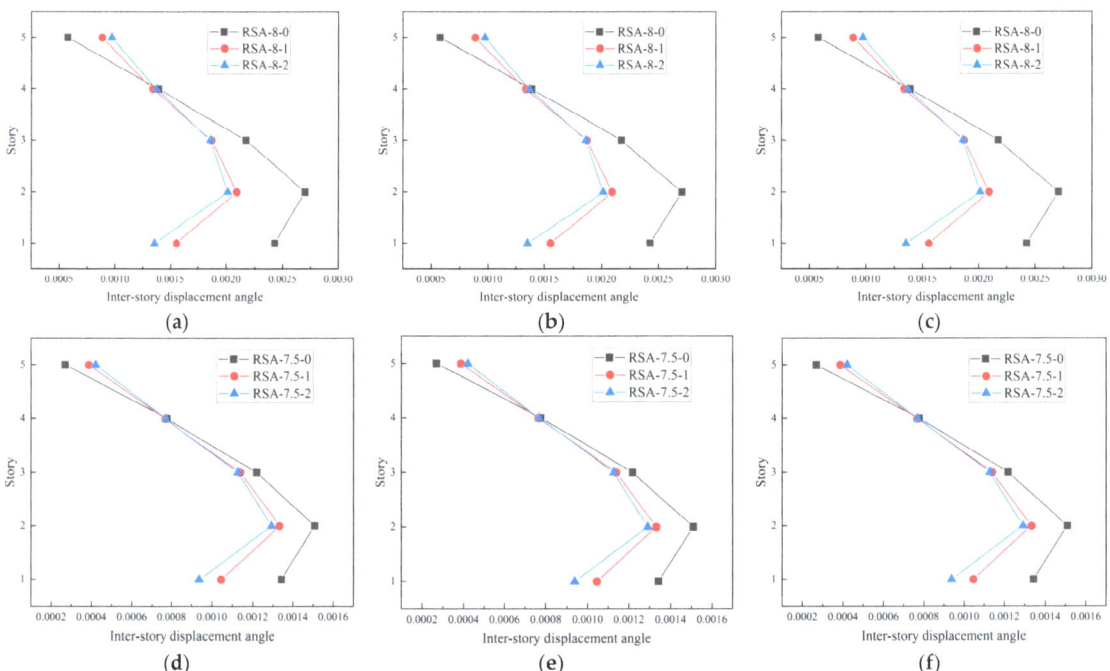

**Figure 12.** Inter-story displacement angle of a modular steel building with different seismic fortification intensities: (**a**) 7-degree (0.10 g) in the X-direction; (**b**) 7-degree (0.15 g) in the X-direction; (**c**) 8-degree (0.20 g) in the X-direction; (**d**) 7-degree (0.10 g) in the Y-direction; (**e**) 7-degree (0.15 g) in the Y-direction; (**f**) 8-degree (0.20 g) in the Y-direction.

4.3.3. Elastic Time History Analysis

The inter-story displacement of 27 numerical models under various earthquake peak accelerations is depicted in Figures 13–15. The maximum inter-story displacement angle for all numerical models occurs on the second floor. In the cooperative modular steel building, the inter-story displacement angle at the bottom story is substantially reduced compared to that in the non-cooperative modular steel building. This reduction is attributed to the building's lateral support, which increases the lateral stiffness in the Y-direction, consequently diminishing the inter-story displacement angle in this direction compared to the X-direction. The displacement response of the numerical models using elastic time-history analysis parallels the results from the response spectrum analysis.

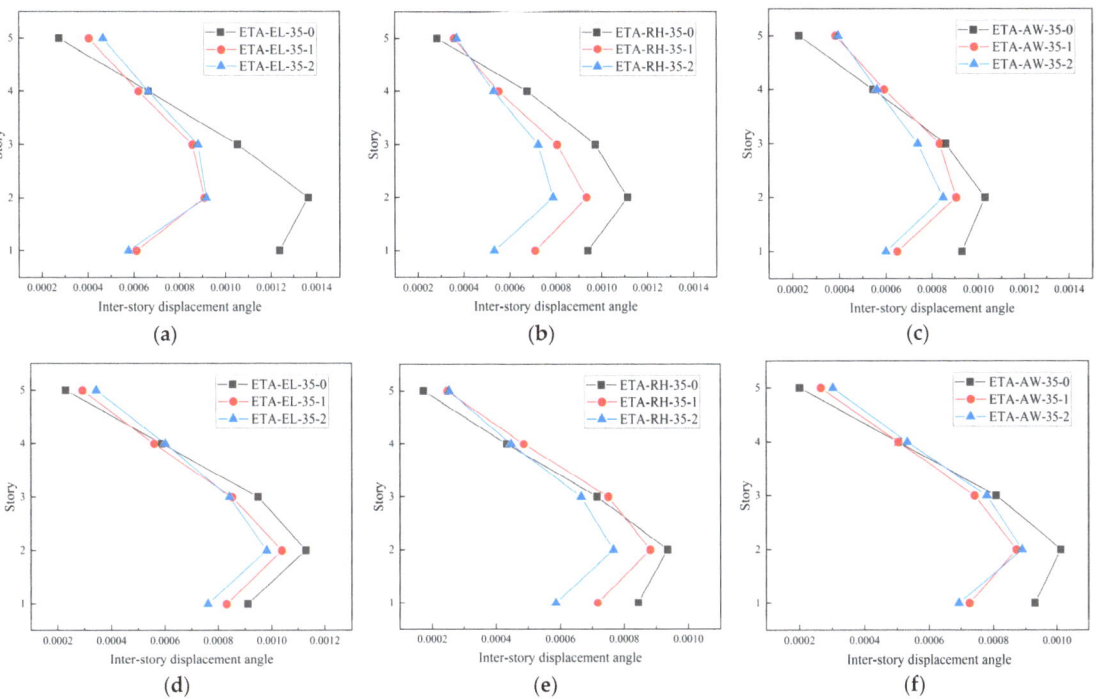

**Figure 13.** The inter-story displacement angle of the modular steel building when the peak acceleration of the earthquake is 35 cm/s$^2$: (**a**) Elcent–h wave in the X-direction; (**b**) RH2TG055 wave in the X-direction; (**c**) Artificial wave in the X-direction; (**d**) Elcent–h wave in the Y-direction; (**e**) RH2TG055 wave in the Y-direction; (**f**) Artificial wave in the Y-direction.

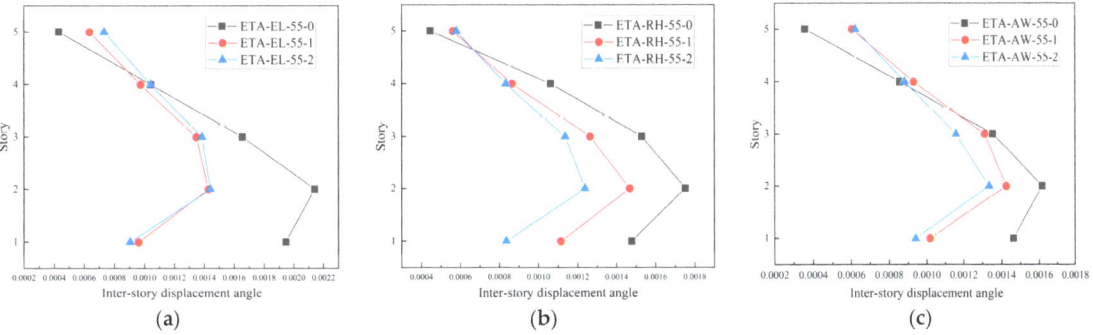

**Figure 14.** *Cont.*

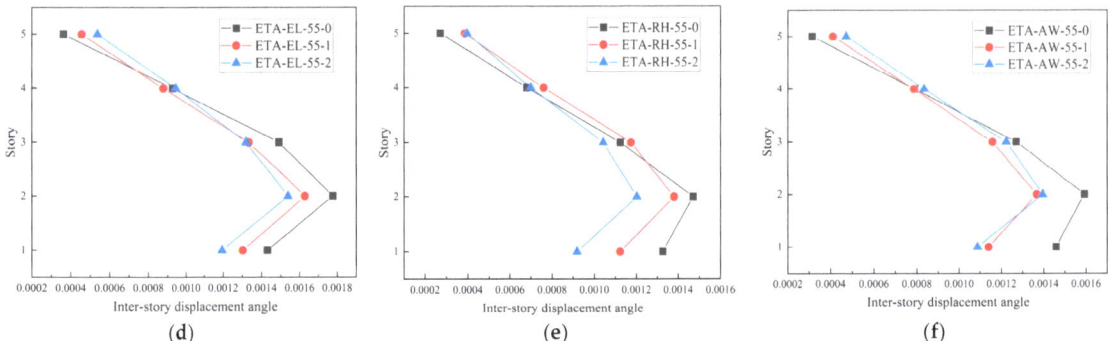

**Figure 14.** The inter-story displacement angle of the modular steel building when the peak acceleration of the earthquake is 55 cm/s$^2$: (**a**) Elcent–h wave in the X-direction; (**b**) RH2TG055 wave in the X-direction; (**c**) Artificial wave in the X-direction; (**d**) Elcent–h wave in the Y-direction; (**e**) RH2TG055 wave in the Y-direction; (**f**) Artificial wave in the Y-direction.

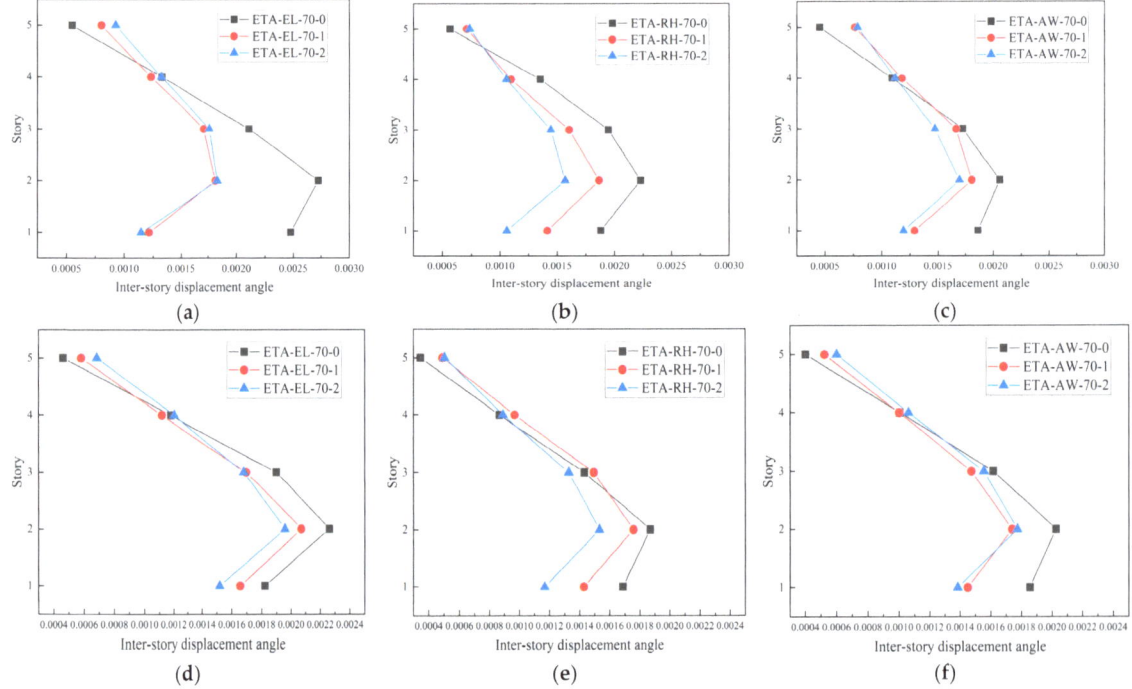

**Figure 15.** The inter-story displacement angle of the modular steel building when the peak acceleration of the earthquake is 70 cm/s$^2$: (**a**) Elcent–h wave in the X-direction; (**b**) RH2TG055 wave in the X-direction; (**c**) Artificial wave in the X-direction; (**d**) Elcent–h wave in the Y-direction; (**e**) RH2TG055 wave in the Y-direction; (**f**) Artificial wave in the Y-direction.

4.3.4. Elastoplastic Time History Analysis

The elastic-plastic time-history analysis of modular steel buildings focuses on the top displacement, inter-story displacement angle, and base shear in the X-direction. This analysis compares the variation in the structural response of the modular steel building under rare earthquakes, both before and after the application of cooperative forces.

(1) Top displacement time histories

Displacement time histories in the X-direction at the top, as illustrated in Figures 16–18, are compared under different seismic peak accelerations. It is evident from the diagrams that achieving cooperative force in the modular steel building markedly reduces the maximum top displacement.

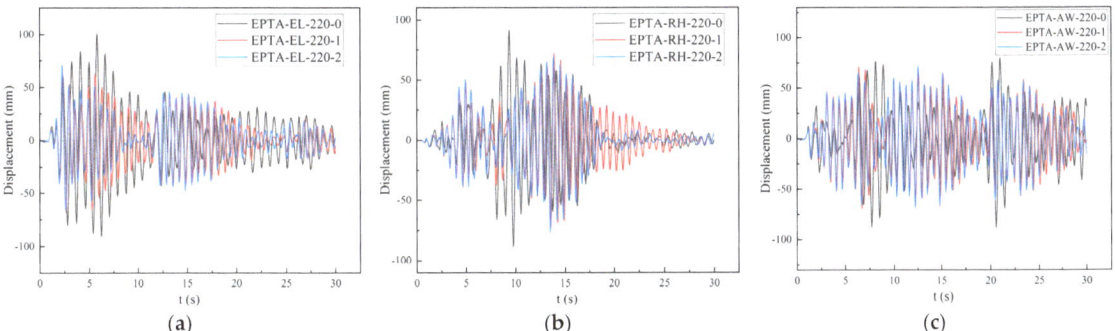

**Figure 16.** The top displacement of the modular steel building when the seismic peak acceleration is 220 cm/s$^2$: (**a**) Elcent–h; (**b**) RH2TG055; (**c**) Artificial.

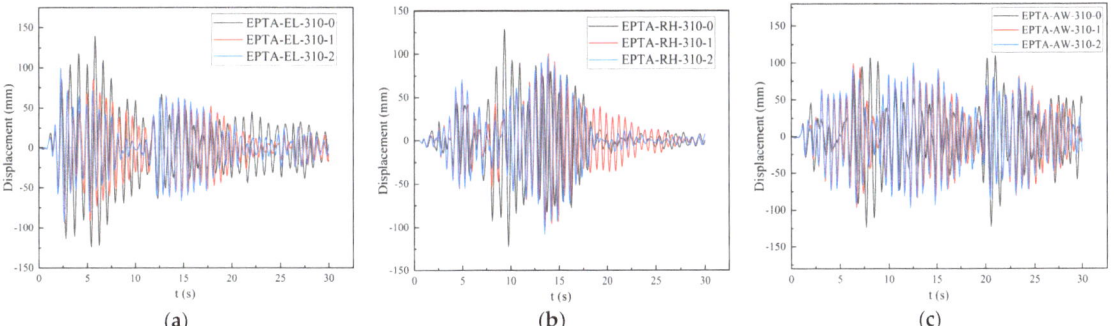

**Figure 17.** The top displacement of the modular steel building when the seismic peak acceleration is 310 cm/s$^2$: (**a**) Elcent–h; (**b**) RH2TG055; (**c**) Artificial.

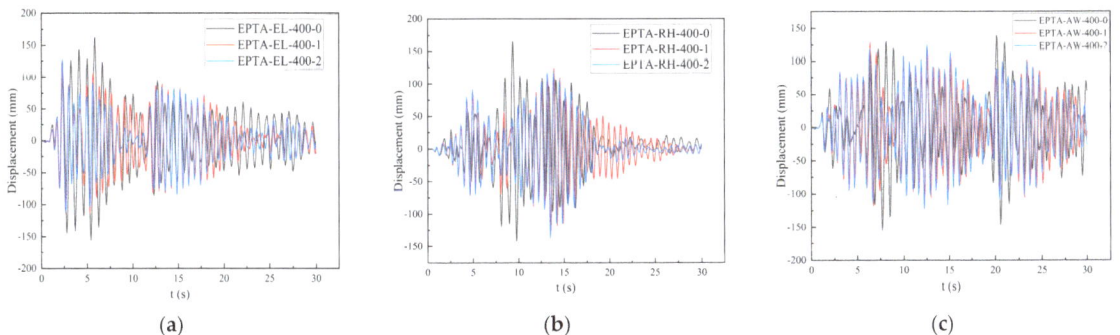

**Figure 18.** The top displacement of the modular steel building when the seismic peak acceleration is 400 cm/s$^2$: (**a**) Elcent–h; (**b**) RH2TG055; (**c**) Artificial.

(2) inter-story displacement angle

Figures 19–21 display the inter-story displacement angle of the model under diverse seismic waves. When subjected to seismic waves with varying seismic peak accelerations, the structural model remains within the 1/50 limit for the inter-story displacement angle as specified in the standard [18]. In contrast to its non-cooperative counterpart, the cooperative modular steel building exhibits reduced inter-story displacement in the weak story, thereby enhancing the building's safety in rare earthquakes and more easily conforming to the standard requirements.

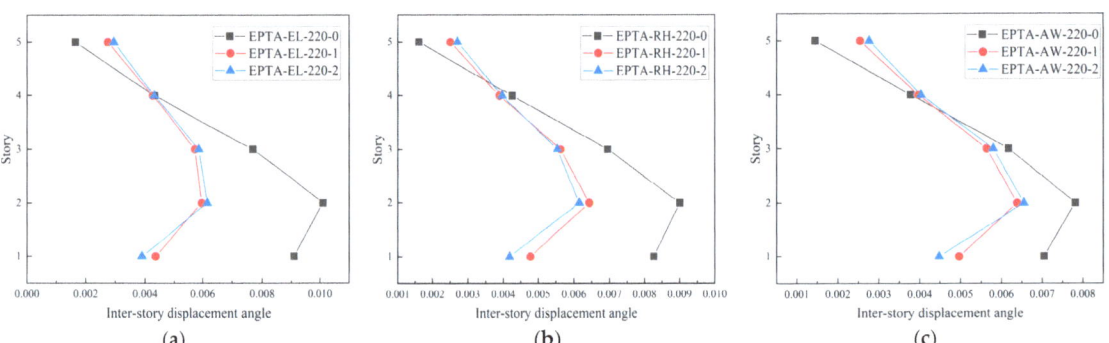

**Figure 19.** The inter-story displacement angle of the modular steel building when the peak acceleration of the earthquake is 220 cm/s$^2$: (**a**) Elcent–h; (**b**) RH2TG055; (**c**) Artificial.

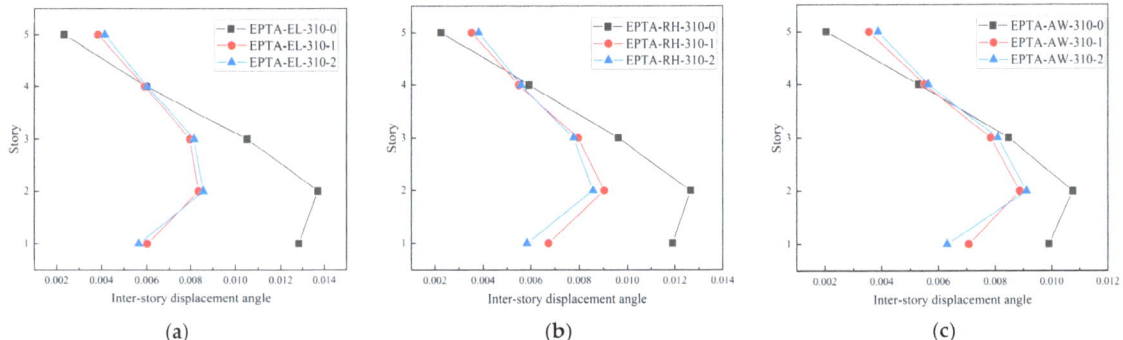

**Figure 20.** The inter-story displacement angle of the modular steel building when the peak acceleration of the earthquake is 310 cm/s$^2$: (**a**) Elcent–h; (**b**) RH2TG055; (**c**) Artificial.

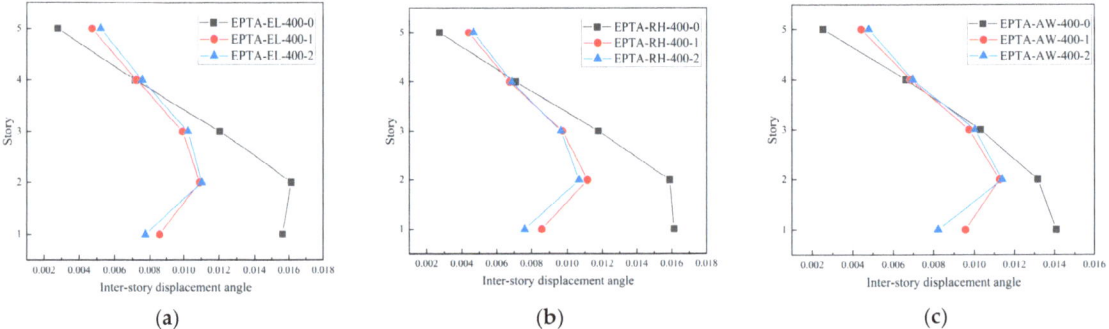

**Figure 21.** The inter-story displacement angle of the modular steel building when the peak acceleration of the earthquake is 400 cm/s$^2$: (**a**) Elcent–h; (**b**) RH2TG055; (**c**) Artificial.

(3) Base shear

The base shear time histories for each numerical model under different rare seismic waves are shown in Figures 22–24. Under the influence of seismic waves with varied seismic peak accelerations, the cooperative modular steel building demonstrates an increased base shear trend compared to the non-cooperative building. This increase can be attributed to improved structural stiffness, a result of the collaborative efforts of modular unit columns, which reduces the natural vibration period. As the period decreases, the seismic influence coefficient escalates, amplifying the earthquake-induced base shear force.

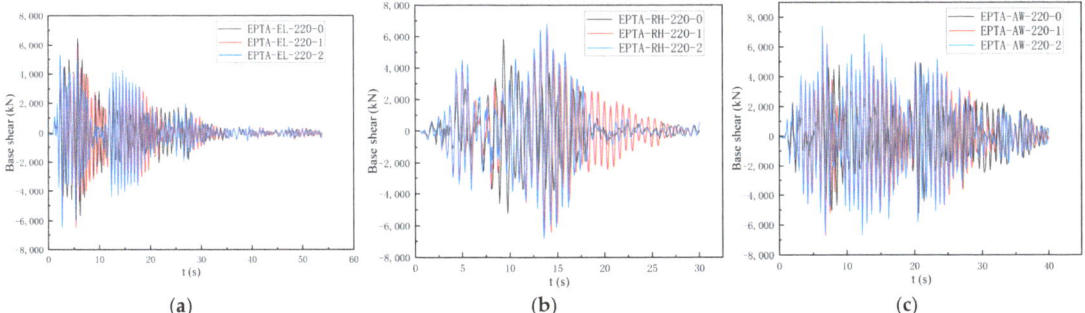

**Figure 22.** The base shear of the modular steel building when the peak acceleration of the earthquake is 220 cm/s$^2$: (**a**) Elcent–h; (**b**) RH2TG055; (**c**) Artificial.

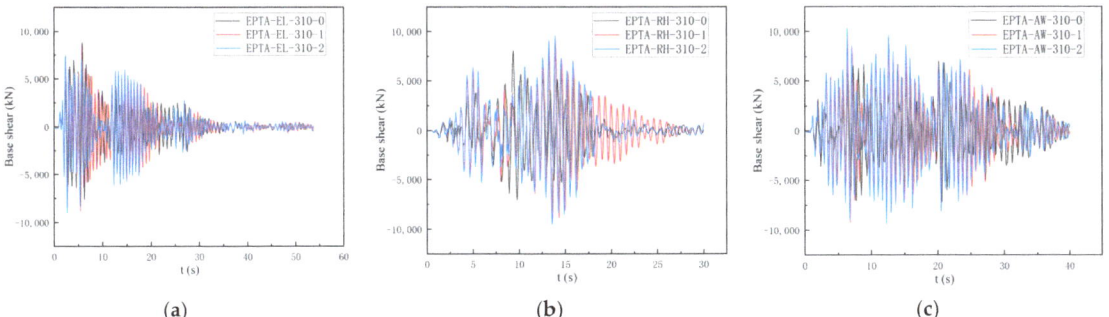

**Figure 23.** The base shear of the modular steel building when the peak acceleration of the earthquake is 310 cm/s$^2$: (**a**) Elcent–h; (**b**) RH2TG055; (**c**) Artificial.

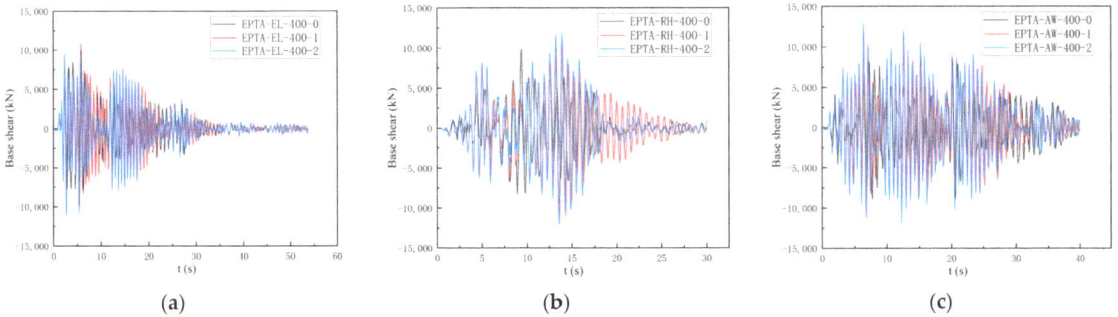

**Figure 24.** The base shear of the modular steel building when the peak acceleration of the earthquake is 400 cm/s$^2$: (**a**) Elcent–h; (**b**) RH2TG055; (**c**) Artificial.

## 5. Applicable Height

### 5.1. Modeling Scheme

According to the T/CECS 507-2018 *technical specification for steel structure modular buildings* [18], *GB 50011-2010* Code for Seismic Design of Buildings [15], and *GB 50009-2012* Load Code for the design of building structures [16], this section mandates that the elastic inter-story displacement angle of 1/300 under frequent earthquakes is the limit value, and the maximum stress ratio of components should be less than 0.85. This study explores the variation in the modular steel building system's calculation results under synergistic force, considering changes in seismic fortification intensity and building height. The seismic fortification intensity is examined in three scenarios: 7 degrees (0.10 g), 7 degrees (0.15 g), and 8 degrees (0.20 g). The module type and layout are depicted in Figure 25. The seismic period reduction factor is set at 0.7. The modular unit size, component section size, and floor parameters used are consistent with those in Chapter 4.

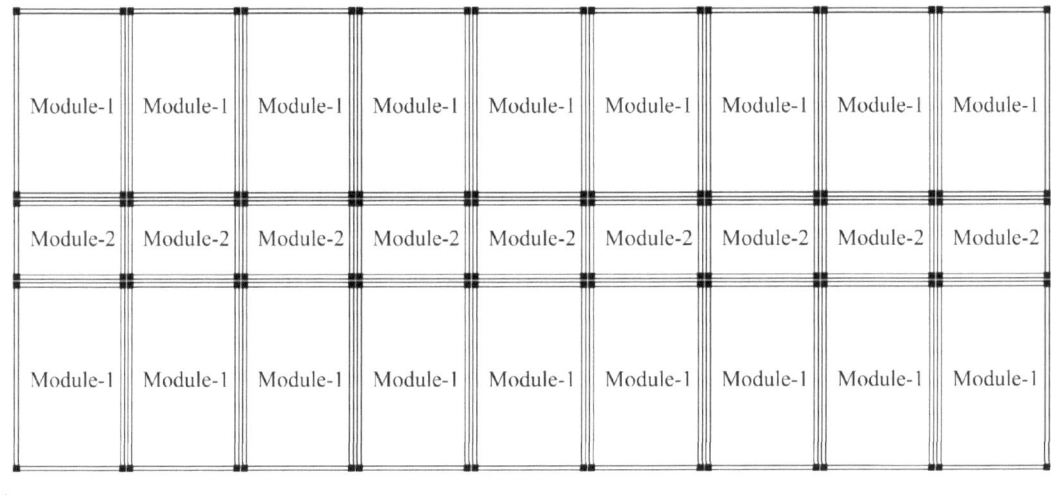

**Figure 25.** Modular steel building standard-story module layout.

### 5.2. Parameter Design

In this section, a total of six models are designed to explore the applicable height range of cooperative modular steel buildings in different seismic fortification intensity areas. The numerical model parameters are detailed in Table 8.

**Table 8.** Model parameters suitable for height analysis.

| Model Number | Seismic Fortification Intensity | Number of Inter-Column Connectors |
|:---:|:---:|:---:|
| HA-7-1 | 7 degrees (0.10 g) | 1 |
| HA-7.5-1 | 7 degrees (0.15 g) | 1 |
| HA-8-1 | 8 degrees (0.20 g) | 1 |
| HA-7-2 | 7 degrees (0.10 g) | 2 |
| HA-7.5-2 | 7 degrees (0.15 g) | 2 |
| HA-8-2 | 8 degrees (0.20 g) | 2 |

Note: The first number, "HA", represents the height analysis, the second number represents the seismic design intensity, and the third number represents the number of inter-column connectors.

## 5.3. Applicable Height

Figures 26 and 27 reveal that the inter-story displacement angle of model HA-7-1 does not exceed the 1/300 limit when its height is eight stories. However, the maximum stress ratio of the component surpasses the 0.85 threshold. Similarly, for model HA-7.5-1 (an eight-story building), its inter-story displacement angle remains within acceptable limits, but its maximum stress ratio exceeds the predefined value. When the HA-8-1 model (a six-story building) is analyzed, its inter-story displacement angle exceeds the allowable value, while at the height of five stories, its maximum stress ratio does not meet the established requirements.

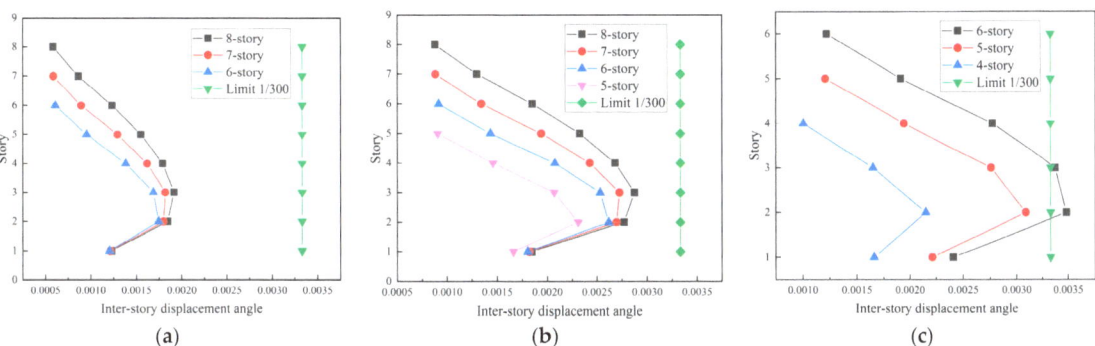

**Figure 26.** Variation of interlayer displacement angle when the number of connectors is one: (**a**) HA-7-1; (**b**) HA-7.5-1; (**c**) HA-8-1.

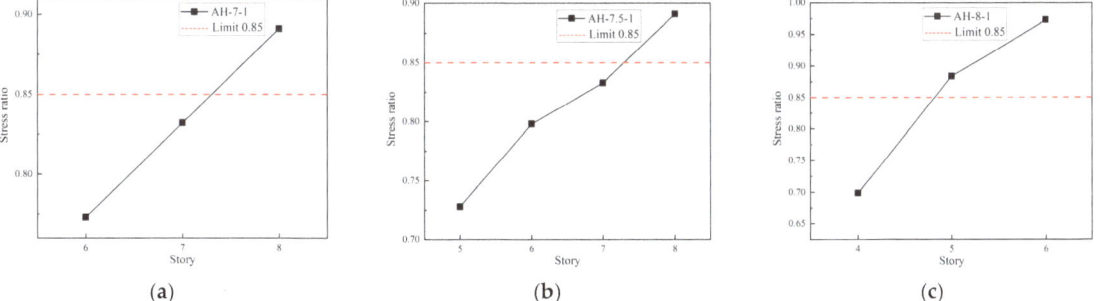

**Figure 27.** Variation of the maximum stress ratio when the number of connectors is one: (**a**) HA-7-1; (**b**) HA-7.5-1; (**c**) HA-8-1.

Figures 28 and 29 indicate that for HA-7-2 with eight stories, the component's maximum stress ratio surpasses the limit. This trend is also evident in HA-7.5-2, with eight stories, where the maximum stress ratio exceeds the set threshold. Moreover, when HA-8-2 comprises only six stories, both the maximum stress ratio and the inter-story displacement angle of the component exceed their respective limits. Additionally, with a five-story configuration, the component exhibits a maximum stress ratio of 0.852, failing to comply with the specified limits. The analysis suggests that in fortification intensities ranging from level 7 to level 8, controlling the story count in cooperative modular steel buildings primarily depends on managing the component's maximum stress ratio. Under identical seismic fortification intensity and story count conditions, increasing the number of connectors can effectively reduce the maximum stress ratio.

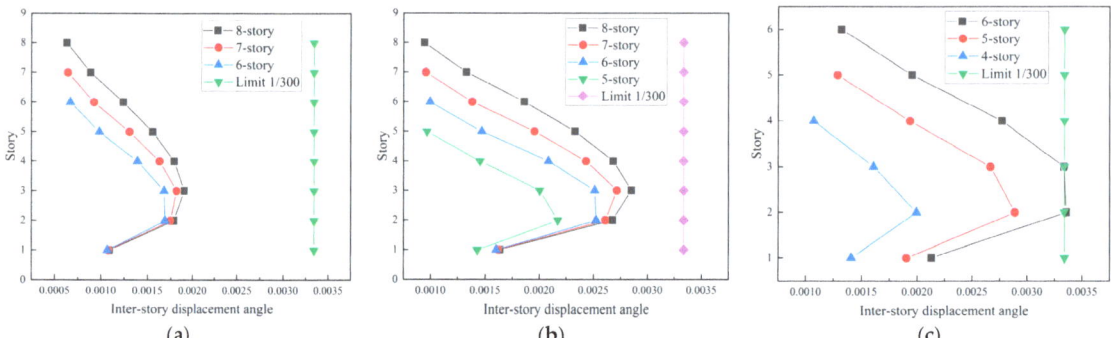

**Figure 28.** Variation of interlayer displacement angle when the number of connectors is two: (**a**) HA-7-1; (**b**) HA-7.5-1; (**c**) HA-8-1.

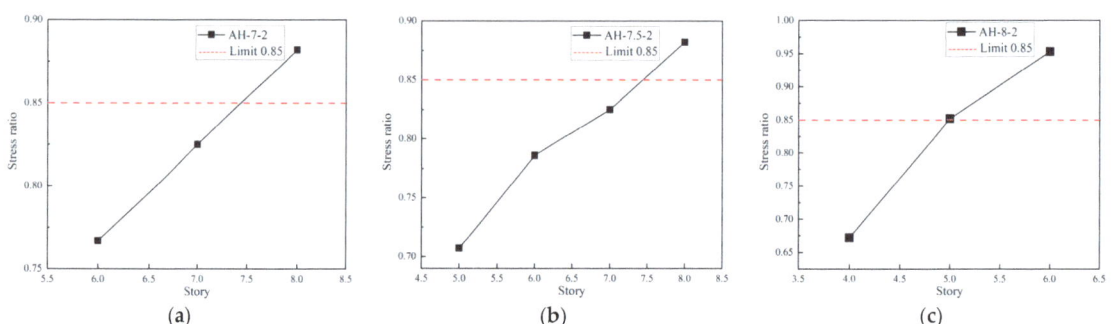

**Figure 29.** Variation of the maximum stress ratio when the number of connectors is two: (**a**) HA-7-1; (**b**) HA-7.5-1; (**c**) HA-8-1.

The scope of application for the modular steel building system under each seismic fortification intensity is detailed in Table 9, and the maximum applicable height of the modular steel building stipulated in the T/CECS 507-2018 *technical specification for steel structure modular buildings* [18] is detailed in Table 10. The comparison shows that under the same seismic fortification intensity, the cooperative modular steel building has a higher building height.

**Table 9.** The maximum applicable height of the cooperative modular steel building system.

| Number of Inter-Column Connectors | Seismic Fortification Intensity | Number of Stories | Applicable Height (m) |
| --- | --- | --- | --- |
| 1 | 7 degrees (0.10 g) | 7 | 21 |
|   | 7 degrees (0.15 g) | 7 | 21 |
|   | 8 degrees (0.20 g) | 4 | 12 |
| 2 | 7 degrees (0.10 g) | 7 | 21 |
|   | 7 degrees (0.15 g) | 7 | 21 |
|   | 8 degrees (0.20 g) | 4 | 12 |

Table 10. The maximum applicable height of the modular steel building stipulated in the T/CECS 507-2018 *technical specification for steel structure modular buildings* [18].

| Seismic Fortification Intensity | Number of Stories | Applicable Height (m) |
|---|---|---|
| 7 degrees (0.10 g) | 3 | 9 |
| 7 degrees (0.15 g) | 3 | 9 |
| 8 degrees (0.20 g) | 1~2 | 3~6 |

## 6. Conclusions

This study numerically investigates the lateral performance and applicable height of modular steel buildings with inter-column connectors. Within the study context, the influence of the number of connectors and type of seismic action on the lateral performance and applicable height of the structure is analyzed. The following conclusions are drawn:

(1) The finite element simulation is conducted to analyze the inter-column connector, and the initial stiffness of the six degrees of freedom of the connector is calculated. The results indicate that the inter-column connectors can effectively transmit the internal force generated by the work between modular unit columns.

(2) Design a five-story modular steel building and carry out finite element modeling. Compare and analyze the cooperative modular steel building and the non-cooperative modular steel building, and perform response spectrum analysis, elastic time history analysis, and elastic-plastic time history analysis. After sorting out and analyzing, the following main conclusions are drawn:

1. The calculation results show that the inter-story displacement angle at the bottom of the cooperative modular steel building and the displacement of the top story of the building are smaller than those of the non-cooperative modular steel building. The maximum reduction of the inter-story displacement angle can reach 36.1%, and the maximum reduction of the top displacement can reach 16.2%, indicating that the modular building of the cooperative force has better lateral performance.

2. Under the same seismic action, compared with the non-cooperative modular steel building, the base shear of the cooperative modular steel building is larger, indicating that the overall stiffness of the structure has increased.

3. Compared with the non-cooperative modular steel building, the cooperative steel building has better displacement response and greater structural safety redundancy under rare earthquakes, which provides a new idea and scheme for the promotion of modular steel buildings in earthquake-prone areas.

(3) The finite element analysis of the cooperative modular steel building is carried out. Considering the change in seismic fortification intensity and the number of stories, the displacement response and internal force change of the cooperative modular steel building system are observed. After analysis and comparison, the applicable height range of the system is obtained. The results show that, compared with the non-cooperative modular steel building in the same seismic intensity area, the number of building layers in the cooperatively stressed modular steel structure is higher. It is recommended that the cooperative modular steel building height be 21 m when the seismic fortification intensity is 7 degrees (0.10 g), 7 degrees (0.15 g) is 21 m, and 8 degrees (0.20 g) is 12 m.

The research results provide important implications for design practice and future research on modular steel buildings. Specifically, based on the newly proposed inter-column connector, this paper studies the improvement of the lateral resistance and applicable height of the cooperative steel modular building compared with the non-cooperative modular steel building, which provides a new method for the popularization and application of the modular building in high-intensity areas. At the same time, the inter-column connector also provides valuable references for the connection design of other modular buildings.

However, since the results of this study were obtained in the context of a five-story steel modular building with a typical plan, changing the type of module unit, building height, plane layout, and building geometry may affect some structural response analysis results.

These changes can be resolved in future research. In addition, under the action of horizontal seismic force, the relative shear displacement between adjacent modular columns is small. Therefore, the elastic stage of the inter-column connector is considered conservatively in this paper. In future research, the contribution of the plastic stage of the connectors to the lateral resistance of the whole structure should also be considered. In addition, the influence of foundation vibration isolation technology on the seismic performance of modular buildings can also be considered [19,20]. The finite-element analysis method can be further improved and structurally analyzed by using meshless approaches that are more generalized than the finite-element method [21,22]. Furthermore, we investigated the free lateral and transverse vibrations of bidirectionally modular beams interconnected by lateral and transverse springs in the framework of the nonlocal elasticity theory. The theory mentioned above is more general than that of classical elasticity theory, which is commonly utilized for structural analyses of macrosystems [23,24].

**Author Contributions:** Conceptualization, methodology, and funding acquisition, Y.W. and Q.A.; project administration, Y.W. and Q.A.; analysis, Q.A. and Z.H.; writing—original draft, Z.H.; writing—review and editing, Q.A.; All authors have read and agreed to the published version of the manuscript.

**Funding:** The project received financial support from the National Natural Science Foundation of China (grant numbers 52208175 and 52078258). All statements, results, and conclusions are those of the researchers and do not necessarily reflect the views of these foundations.

**Data Availability Statement:** The data presented in this study are available on request from the authors. The data are not publicly available due to privacy.

**Acknowledgments:** The authors also sincerely thank the anonymous reviewers for their insightful comments and suggestions.

**Conflicts of Interest:** The authors declare that they have no known competing financial interests or personal relationships that could have appeared to influence the work reported in this paper.

## References

1. Sha, X.; Liu, X.; Wang, Y.; Zeng, M. The development status and trend of modular steel structure system. *Ind. Build.* **2023**, 1–19. Available online: https://kns.cnki.net/kcms/detail/11.2068.TU.20230314.1308.003.html (accessed on 6 November 2023). (In Chinese)
2. Tian, X.; Liu, X.; Liu, Y.; Chen, Y.; Liu, Y. Research progress of connection joints between modules of column-bearing modular steel structure buildings. *Dev. Build. Steel Struct.* **2022**, *24*, 197–205. (In Chinese)
3. Yang, C.; Xu, B.; Xia, J.; Chang, H.; Chen, X.; Ma, R. Mechanical Behaviors of Inter-Module Connections and Assembled Joints in Modular Steel Buildings: A Comprehensive Review. *Buildings* **2023**, *13*, 1727. [CrossRef]
4. Lawson, M.; Ogden, R.; Goodier, C. *Design in Modular Construction*; CRC Press: Boca Raton, FL, USA, 2014; ISBN 0-415-55450-0.
5. Liu, M.Y.; Wang, Y.; Jia, S.S. Study on mechanical properties of new modular steel frame plate inner sleeve connection joint. *Steel Struct.* **2018**, *33*, 1–5+10. (In Chinese)
6. Chen, Z.; Wang, J.; Liu, J.; Khan, K. Seismic Behavior and Moment Transfer Capacity of an Innovative Self-Locking Inter-Module Connection for Modular Steel Building. *Eng. Struct.* **2021**, *245*, 112978. [CrossRef]
7. Palazzo, B.; Castaldo, P.; Marino, I. The Dissipative Column: A New Hysteretic Damper. *Buildings* **2015**, *5*, 163–178. [CrossRef]
8. Sharafi, P.; Mortazavi, M.; Samali, B.; Ronagh, H. Interlocking System for Enhancing the Integrity of Multi-Story Modular Buildings. *Autom. Constr.* **2018**, *85*, 263–272. [CrossRef]
9. Yang, C.; Xu, Y.C.; Ou, J.P. The frame structure and seismic performance analysis of column-column and beam-beam assembled steel module column-column and beam-beam combined structures. *Seism. Eng. Eng. Vib.* **2022**, *42*, 34–45.
10. Xu, B.; Xia, J.; Chang, H.; Ma, R.; Zhang, L. A Comprehensive Experimental-Numerical Investigation on the Bending Response of Laminated Double Channel Beams in Modular Buildings. *Eng. Struct.* **2019**, *200*, 109737. [CrossRef]
11. An, Q.; Wang, Y.; Wang, X. Study on the load capacity of self-locking cooperative force column of steel structure in modular building. *Ind. Build.* **2023**, 1–13. Available online: https://kns.cnki.net/kcms/detail/11.2068.TU.20230411.1319.002.html (accessed on 3 June 2023). (In Chinese)
12. Qi, A.; Yan, W. Module Building Steel Structure Column Lateral Connection Node and Module Building Steel Structure. CN202122127830.9, 3 September 2021. (In Chinese).
13. *GB 50017-2017*; Standard for Design of Steel Structures. China Architecture & Building Press: Beijing, China, 2017. (In Chinese)
14. Feng, P.; Qiang, H.; Ye, L. The definition and discussion of the "yield point" of materials, components, and structures. *Eng. Mech.* **2017**, *34*, 36–46.
15. *GB 50011-2010*; Code for Seismic Design of Buildings. China Architecture & Building Press: Beijing, China, 2010. (In Chinese)

16. *GB 50009-2012*; Load Code for the Design of Building Structures. China Architecture & Building Press: Beijing, China, 2012. (In Chinese)
17. Chen, R.; Qiu, C.; Hao, D. Design and analysis of multi-story steel structure module. *Build. Struct.* **2019**, *49*, 59–64+18. (In Chinese)
18. *T/CECS 507-2018*; Technical Specification for Steel Modular Buildings. China Planning Press: Beijing, China, 2018. (In Chinese)
19. Charmpis, D.C.; Komodromos, P.; Phocas, M.C. Optimized earthquake response of multi-storey buildings with seismic isolation at various elevations. *Earthq. Eng. Struct. Dyn.* **2012**, *41*, 2289–2310. [CrossRef]
20. Forcellini, D.; Kalfas, K.N. Inter-story seismic isolation for high-rise buildings. *Eng. Struct.* **2023**, *275*, 115175. [CrossRef]
21. Kiani, K.; Nikkhoo, A.; Mehri, B. Parametric analyses of multispan viscoelastic shear deformable beams under excitation of a moving mass. *J. Vib. Acoust.* **2009**, *131*, 051009. [CrossRef]
22. Kiani, K.; Nikkhoo, A.; Mehri, B. Assessing dynamic response of multispan viscoelastic thin beams under a moving mass via generalized moving least square method. *Acta Mech. Sin.* **2010**, *26*, 721–733. [CrossRef]
23. Kiani, K. Axial buckling analysis of vertically aligned ensembles of single-walled carbon nanotubes using nonlocal discrete and continuous models. *Acta Mech.* **2014**, *225*, 3569–3589. [CrossRef]
24. Kiani, K. Nonlocal free dynamic analysis of periodic arrays of single-walled carbon nanotubes in the presence of longitudinal thermal and magnetic fields. *Comput. Math. Appl.* **2018**, *75*, 3849–3872. [CrossRef]

**Disclaimer/Publisher's Note:** The statements, opinions and data contained in all publications are solely those of the individual author(s) and contributor(s) and not of MDPI and/or the editor(s). MDPI and/or the editor(s) disclaim responsibility for any injury to people or property resulting from any ideas, methods, instructions or products referred to in the content.

*Article*

# Seismic Behavior of Demountable Self-Lock Joint for Middle Column Connection in Modular Steel Construction

Xiao-Meng Dai [1], Liang Zong [2,3,*], Yang Ding [2,3], Hao-Wen Zhang [2] and Feng-Wei Shi [2]

[1] China Railway Construction Bridge Engineering Bureau Group Corporation, Ltd., Tianjin 300300, China; raptor616888964@126.com
[2] School of Civil Engineering, Tianjin University, Tianjin 300072, China; dingyang@tju.edu.cn (Y.D.); haowenzhang158@outlook.com (H.-W.Z.); shifengwei@tju.edu.cn (F.-W.S.)
[3] Key Laboratory of Coast Civil Structure Safety, Ministry of Education, Tianjin University, Tianjin 300072, China
* Correspondence: zongliang@tju.edu.cn

**Abstract:** The use of modular steel construction (MSC) achieves a minimum of on-site work and the potential for removability and reuse. In order to realize the overall disassembly of module buildings and the rapid off-site reconstruction after disassembly, special requirements are put forward for the joints of MSCs. The existing joints of MSCs have some problems, such as the difficulty in the erection of the joints for middle column connection and their inability to be reused. In order to solve these key technical problems, an improved version of the demountable self-locking joint is proposed based on the previous plug-in self-locking joint. For this new type of joint, a full-scale test consisting of four specimens was carried out. The results of functional tests verify that the joint has good demountability. The seismic behavior of the joint under seismic load was investigated by cyclic loading tests. Then, finite element (FE) models were developed and validated through the test results. The results of finite element parameter analysis show that joint boxes are very important to the initial stiffness of this kind of joint, but the thickness of the joint box and the diameter of the stud have little influence on the seismic behavior of the joint.

**Keywords:** full-scale tests; seismic behavior; modular steel construction; finite analysis; column-beam joint

## 1. Introduction

Modular steel construction (MSC) has been used widely due to its exceptional advantages: minimum of on-site work, and higher construction speed and qualities. Different from other types of construction, modular steel construction is highly integrated prefabricated. Due to these features, MSCs are an ideal construction for emergency situations (e.g., emergency hospital centers). Structural components and building services, i.e., electrics, pipelines, and decorations, are integrated into room modules, which are the basic units of modular steel construction. Each room module combines structural and architectural functioning, e.g., a living room module, a bathroom module, or a staircase. These room modules are off-site prefabricated and can be replaced easily. This feature of MSC provides the potential for removability and reuse. Thus, MSC can be adapted to temporary and movable buildings.

The connecting joints of modular steel construction are very different from that of regular steel structures [1]. Figure 1 compares the joints in a regular structure and MSC. In joints of a regular structure, there are four beams and one continuous column. In joints of MSC, the numbers are sixteen and eight. Additional special requirements should be fulfilled for the MSC joints: good cooperation with other installed structure components and building services, minimum need of construction spaces and time, and potential to be demounted. Joints with mechanical connections are recommended due to good detachability. One of the key issues of MSC joints is the operation spaces for installation or uninstallation. As shown in Figure 2, there are three types of joints for modular steel construction, i.e., side, corner, and middle joints. Among these joints, the side and corner joints will not be limited by operation spaces. But for the middle joints, there is no access from outside. As the walls, doors, floors, and ceilings were installed before the assembling, there are no operation spaces for the connection of joints.

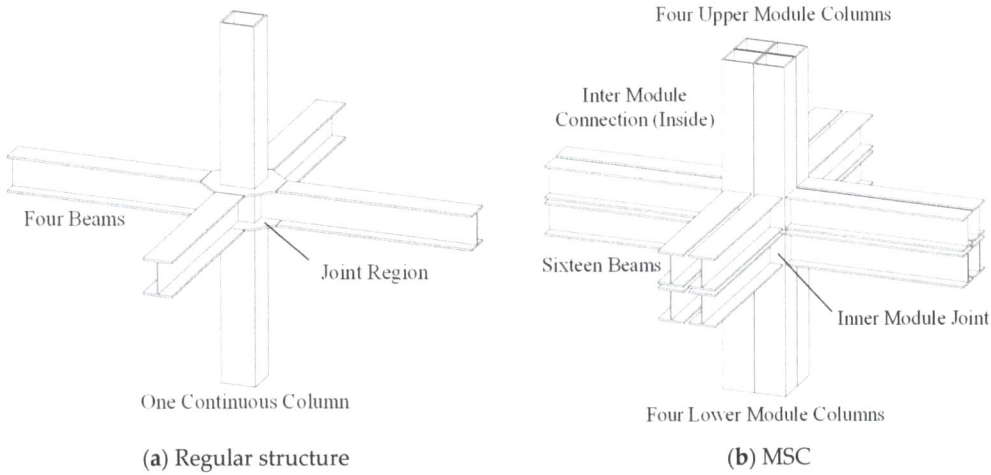

**Figure 1.** Comparison of joints in regular structure and MSC.

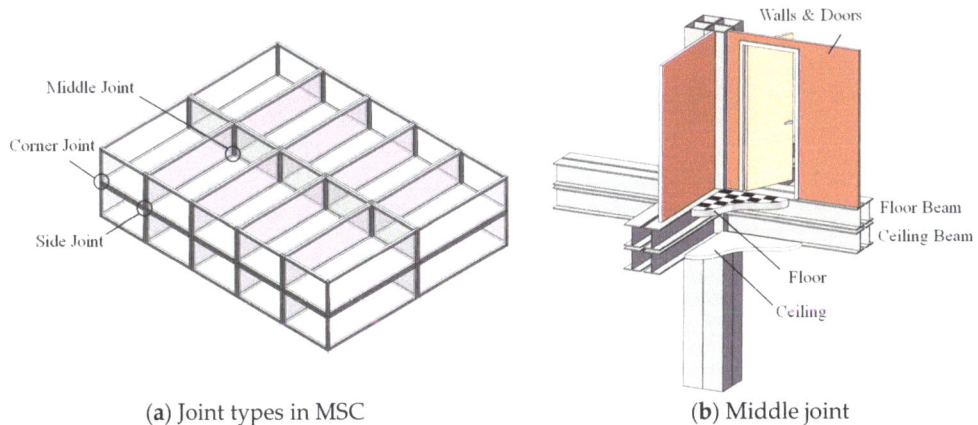

**Figure 2.** Joint in modular steel construction.

Previous research has provided various types of mechanical-connecting joints for modular steel construction. Lawson proposed bolt-connecting joints for a square hollow section or open section column, as shown in Figure 3a [2]. These types of joints can be used as side or corner joints for modular steel construction, but cannot be used as middle joints. The end plates of the upper and lower module columns are connected with bolts. For square hollow section columns, access holes are set for installation or uninstallation. Chen developed bolt-connecting joints with a plug-in for square hollow section columns [3,4]. These types of joints can be used as middle or side joints for modular steel construction. Upper and lower modules are connected by long penetrating bolts at the end of the beams. A plug-in component is set between the upper and lower square hollow section columns.

The vertical load cannot be transferred between the upper and lower columns directly. Moreover, the penetrating long bolts will interfere in the installation of other structure components, e.g., wall plates. Ding developed blind bolt-connecting joints with a plug-in for square hollow section columns, as shown in Figure 3b. These types of joints can be used as side joints for modular steel construction, but cannot be used as middle joints. Similar to the joints of Chen, a plug-in component is set between the upper and lower square hollow columns. The columns are connected to the plug-in component with blind bolts, which only require one-side operation. Though many other joints were proposed, analyzed, and tested, the problems of joints for modular steel construction still exist [5–9]. Joints for modular steel construction still need to be improved.

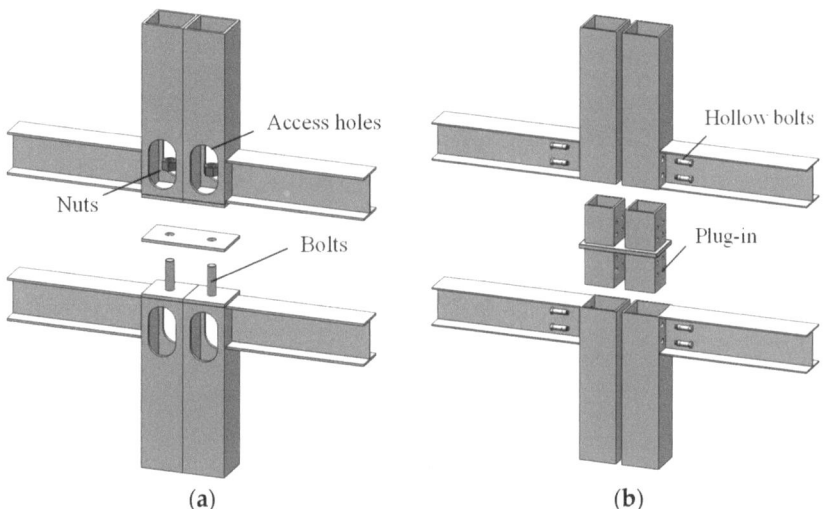

**Figure 3.** Previous joints for MSC: (**a**) Lawson [2]. (**b**) Ding [10].

The most common modular buildings also include the steel frame modular, which consists of the full length of beams and girders, and column ends and requires beam-column bolt connections at each floor. Chen developed a new type of f site-bolted assembled joint for prefabricated modular H-shaped steel-beam-column joints [11]. The assembly diagram of joints is shown in Figure 4a. The developed joint assembles the columns and beams at the connector region through on-site bolting of the column base plate and beams' splice plate, avoiding direct welding of the structural components to each other. Du proposed a beam-through moment-resisting joint for H-section (wide-flange) beams and columns that can be prefabricated [12]. The joints erect an entire floor by bolting the upper-level columns to the lower-level beams, as shown in Figure 4b. With this type of beam-through beam-column joint, it is feasible to offset columns on adjacent floors and increase the flexibility and versatility of the framing plan layout.

Self-lock joints for modular steel construction were proposed to solve this middle joint connection issue [13]. These self-lock joints need no operation spaces during both the connection and disconnection processes, and can be demounted easily due to the unlocking device. Meanwhile, the joints have no interruptions with other integrated structural components and services, and no limitations to sections of beams or columns. Thus, this type of joint can be used as a middle joint for modular steel construction.

Although more and more new modular joints have been developed in recent years, there are still considerable difficulties in realizing the overall disassembly of module buildings and the rapid off-site reconstruction after disassembly. In this follow-up research, the self-lock plug-in connector was improved. A set of unlocking devices was added for easier disconnection of the joint. This improvement could increase the speed of the demountable function for the joints, which helps to further realize the overall disassembly of module buildings. A full-scale test consisting of four specimens is reported in the following part of this paper. The demounting processes of the joints were verified through a functional test. Then, the full-scale specimens were applied with cyclic load to investigate the seismic behavior. Finite element (FE) models of these novel joints were developed and validated with the test results. Parameter analysis was conducted based on the FE models.

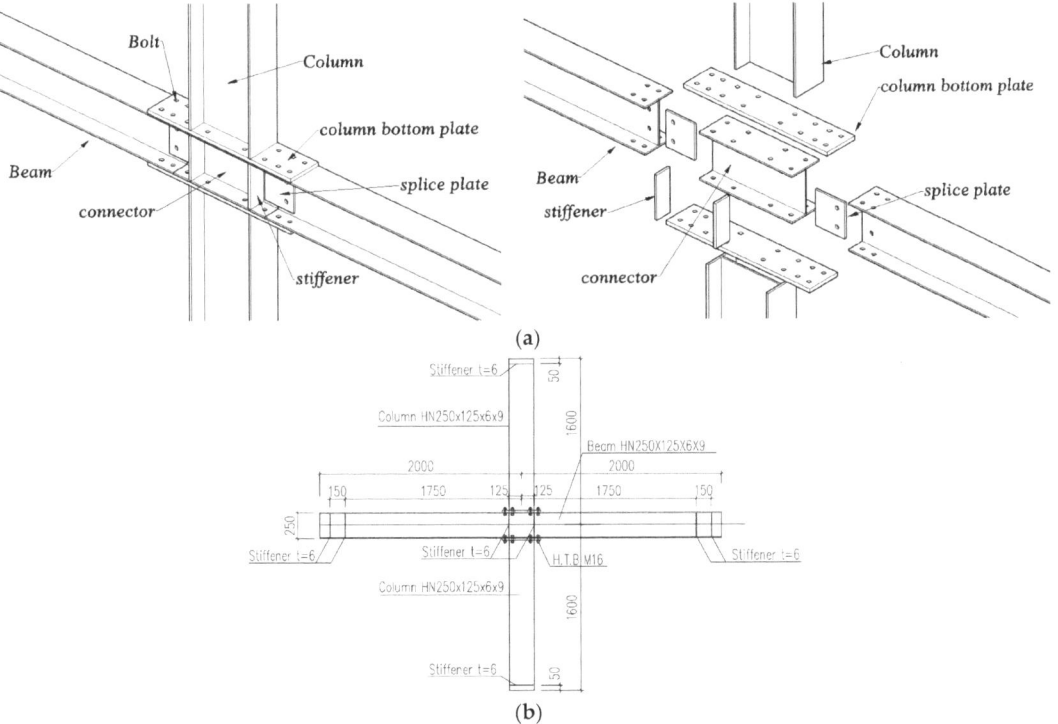

**Figure 4.** Joints for steel frame modular: (**a**) Chen [11]. (**b**) Du [12].

## 2. Mechanism of Self-Lock Joint

### 2.1. Self-Lock Connector and Unlocking Device

The key components of the novel joint are a self-lock connector and an unlocking device. This connector is developed based on the previous self-lock plug-in connector and a set of unlocking devices is added [14]. The unlocking device is an additional device that provides an easy way to demount and reuse the room module in modular steel construction. The mechanism of the connector is shown in Figure 5. Components of this connector can be divided into two sets: unlocking components (Component 1–3) and self-lock connecting components (Component 4–15). The key components of this connector are an unlocking hydraulic jack (1), safe spring (4), acting spring (6), trigger block (7), sleeve (12), cone-shaped latches (13), and stud (15). The unlocking hydraulic jack is integrated into this connector and can be powered by an external hydraulic pump, which is not shown in the figure. The safe and action springs are pre-compressed to certain compressive forces, respectively. The cone-shaped latches consist of four cone-shaped quarter orientation components. The inner surface of the cone-shaped latches is fabricated with ring-teeth and the outer surface is a cone surface. A trigger block is set between the four cone-shaped latches before connecting. As the diameter of the trigger block is higher than the diameter of the inner hole of the latches, the closing trend of the cone-shaped latches is blocked.

The sleeve is a circle-shaped component, with a step on the outer surface to hold the acting spring. The inner surface of the sleeve is the cone surface, which can fit with the cone-shaped latches. The stud is a rod with ring-teeth and is fixed on the top surface of the lower module column. The pull side of the ring-teeth on the stud fit tightly with that on the cone-shaped latches. A clearance is set to allow machining errors and dust. The working process can be divided into these four phases below.

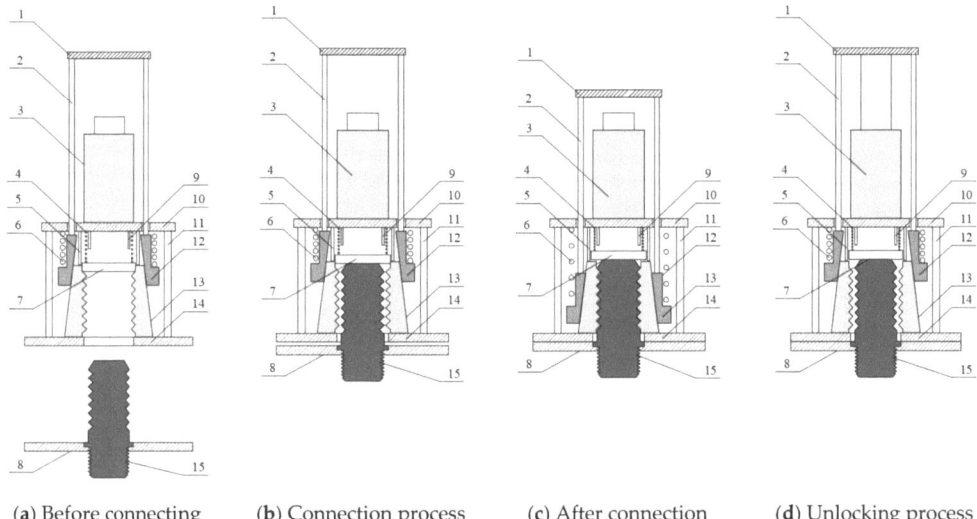

(a) Before connecting    (b) Connection process    (c) After connection    (d) Unlocking process

**Figure 5.** Mechanism of self-lock connector and unlocking device: 1—unlock plate, 2—unlock bar, 3—unlock hydraulic jack, 4—safe spring, 5—outer barrel, 6—action spring, 7—trigger block, 8—top surface of the lower module column, 9—inner barrel, 10—locating plate, 11—locating screw, 12—sleeve, 13—cone—shaped latches, 14—bottom surface of upper module column, 15—stud.

Figure 5a shows the phase before connecting. The sleeve and cone-shaped latches are compressed by the action spring. The closing trend of the cone-shaped latches is still blocked by the trigger plate. The spacing between the latches is larger than the diameter of the stud and allows the stud to plug in.

During the connection process, the upper module is placed onto the lower module so that the stud is plugged into the spacing of the cone-shaped latches, as shown in Figure 5b. The stud pushes the trigger plate out of the cone-shaped latches. Without the trigger block, the sleeve moves under the compressive force of the action spring and forces the latches to close. The ring-teeth on the stud and the cone-shaped latches fit tightly. Machining errors can be eliminated automatically due to the wedging effect.

Figure 5c shows the working phase after connection. After the connection is made, this connector can resist the pull force. The pull force can be transferred through the ring-teeth on the stud and the cone-shaped latches. Because the angle of the cone surfaces between the sleeve and the cone-shaped latches is smaller than the friction angle of the steel material, the connector is friction-locked and will not come loose. Thus, the separation between the upper and lower modules is prevented and the pull force is transferred.

Figure 5d shows the unlocking process of the connector. When it is necessary to disconnect the upper and lower modules, the unlocking device is needed. The unlocking hydraulic jack is powered by an external pump and the piston of the jack extends. The piston pushes the unlocking plate and drives the sleeve to move upward. Without the constraint of the sleeve, the cone-shaped latches can be open. The stud can be pulled out and the connector is unlocked. After the unlocking process, the connector can be reset and will be functional.

## 2.2. Demountable Self-Lock Joint in Modular Steel Construction

The demountable self-lock joint can be used as corner, side, and middle joints in modular steel construction, as shown in Figure 6. Joint boxes are set at the corners of each module and are welded to beams and columns. The stud is fixed on the top surface of the lower module column while the other components of the self-lock connector are set inside the joint box. A soft hydraulic tube is integrated into the joint. One end of the tube is connected to the unlocking hydraulic jack, the other end is set outside of the joint in case of the unlocking process. For side and middle joints, a connecting plate is needed to connect the two (for side joint) or four (for middle joint) modules in the same story, as shown in Figure 6b,c. Matching holes are fabricated on the connecting plate to allow the studs through. The connecting plate is bolted on the top surfaces of lower module joint boxes. The sunk bolts are used to flatten the top surface of the connecting plate.

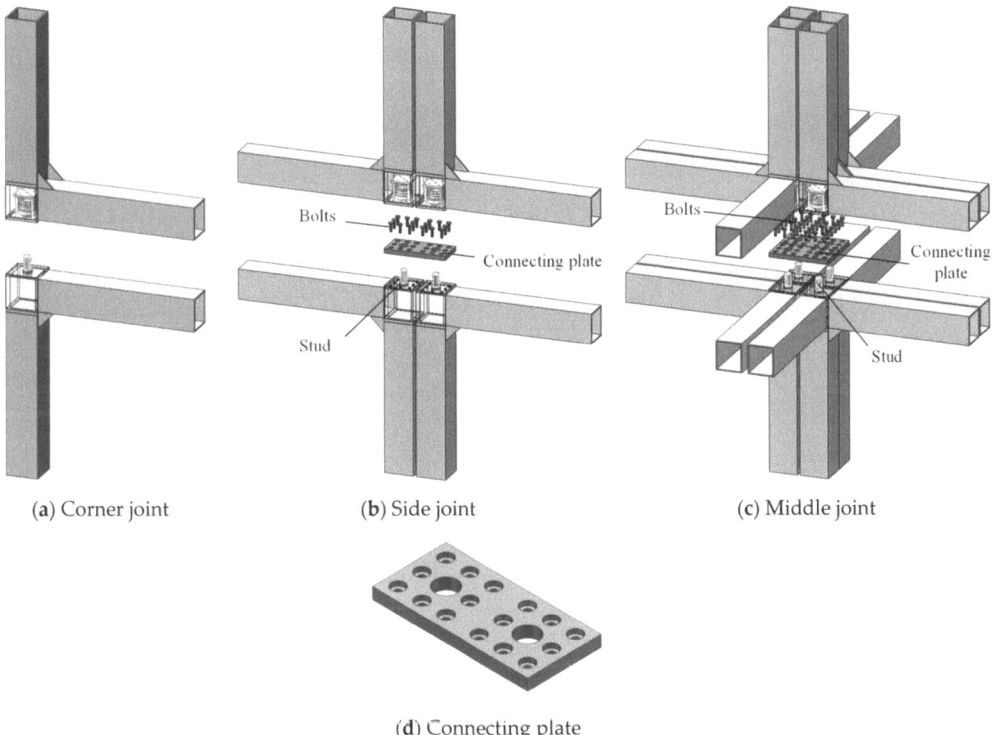

**Figure 6.** Self-lock joints for modular steel construction.

With this novel joint, the modular steel construction can be assembled or disassembled by a crane. Room modules can be piled up or removed as containers. Compared with previous joints, the characteristics of the novel joint include:

(a) No extra operation spaces are needed during the construction. The connecting process is performed automatically during the piling up of the modules. The on-site work is minimized. Thus, this novel joint provides an easy solution for middle joints of modular steel construction.
(b) The unlocking device of this joint provides exceptional detachability and interchangeability. Room modules can be easily detached and reused on another site. Thus, resources can be saved and the disruption to the environment can be minimized.

(c) No limitations to sections of beams or columns are needed. This joint can be adapted to beams and columns with various types of sections. The choices of the beam and column sections are flexible.

## 3. Experimental Program

### 3.1. Specimen Design

The seismic behavior of T-shaped specimens has been tested in previous research [13]. This paper focused on the effect of unlocking devices and combined effect of cross-shaped joint specimens. A test on four full-scale specimens was conducted. Figure 7 and Table 1 shows the details of the specimens. These specimens can be divided into two groups. The specimens TS-1 and TS-2 were T-shaped specimens to investigate the effect of the unlocking devices. Specimen TS-1 was defined as a contrast specimen while specimen TS-2 was defined as a demountable specimen. For specimen TS-2, a set of unlocking devices was integrated and a 110 × 120 mm maintenance opening was set on the joint boxes, as shown in Figure 7c. The hydraulic tube that was connected to the unlocking jack extended to the outside and could be connected to a hydraulic pump. TS-3 and TS-4 were cross-shaped joint specimens to investigate the combined effect in middle joints. The difference between the two cross-shaped specimens was the thickness of the connecting plates, i.e., 20 mm (TS-3) and 30 mm (TS-4). The column and beam sections of the specimens were square hollow sections: 200 × 200 × 10 (column), 200 × 180 × 8 (floor beam), and 200 × 180 × 6 (ceiling beam). The thickness of the joint boxes was set as 20 mm to ensure their strength and stiffness. Rib stiffeners were added at the corners.

**Table 1.** Specimens of Demountable Self-Lock Joint.

| Specimen No. | Joint Type | Shape | Thickness of Connecting Plate (mm) | Remarks |
|---|---|---|---|---|
| TS-1 (Contrast) | Corner joint | T-shape | - | - |
| TS-2 | Corner joint | T-shape | - | Unlocking device |
| TS-3 | Side Joint | Cross-shape | 20 | - |
| TS-4 | Side Joint | Cross-shape | 30 | - |

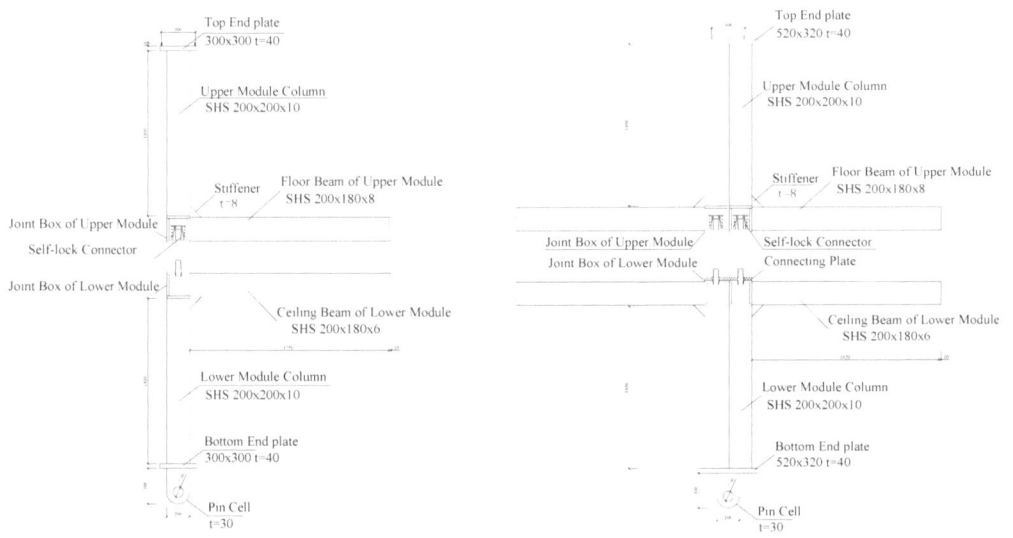

(a) T-shaped specimens      (b) Cross-shaped specimens

**Figure 7.** Cont.

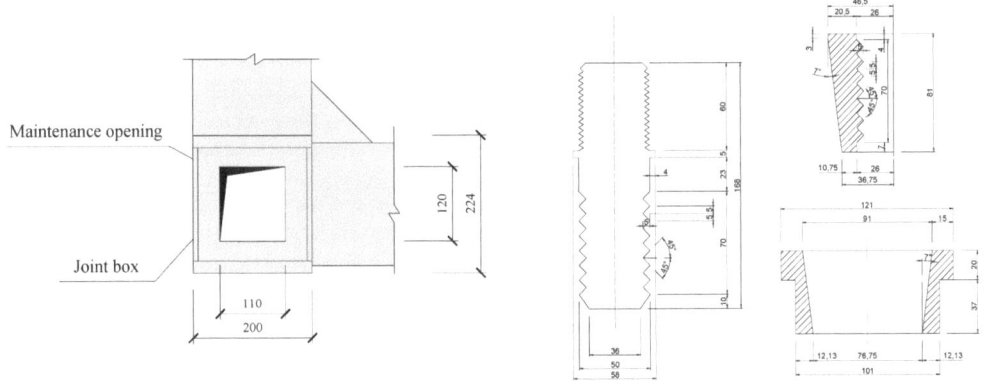

(c) Maintenance opening on TS-2          (d) Details of connector

**Figure 7.** Design of self-lock joints (mm).

The mechanical properties of the specimen were tested before the experimental study. Most components of the self-lock connector, including stud, sleeve, and cone-shaped latches, were fabricated with U20452 (45#) class steel. Columns, beams, and joint boxes were welded with a Q345B class steel plate. Coupon tests were performed according to Chinese standard GB/T 228.1-2010 [14]. Engineering tensile stress–strain curves are given in Figure 7. The results are listed in Table 2, showing the mechanical properties of the steel were qualified according to the Chinese standard GB/T 699-2015 and GB/T 1591-2018 [15,16].

**Table 2.** Mechanical Properties.

| Parts | Steel Grade | Elastic Modulus (N/mm$^2$) | Yield Strength (N/mm$^2$) | Ultimate Strength (N/mm$^2$) | Ultimate Strain | Elongation (%) |
|---|---|---|---|---|---|---|
| Connector components | U20452 (45#) | 193.3 | 441.3 | 553.7 | 0.170 | 30.6 |
| Steel plate | Q345B | 195.8 | 393.8 | 523.5 | 0.192 | 33.8 |

*3.2. Experimental Program*

The function of demounting was validated before loading the program. Figure 8 shows the demounting process of the specimen TS-2, which was equipped with an unlocking device. As shown in Figure 8a, the initial status of the specimen TS-2 was a whole. The extended hydraulic pipe, which was connected to the unlocking hydraulic jack in the joint box, was powered by an external pump. The unlocking device was activated and the connection was loosed. The upper module component could be lifted up by a crane, as shown in Figure 8b. The self-lock connector and the unlocking device were reset through the maintenance opening on the joint box and re-functioned after the reset. The specimen was re-connected, as shown in Figure 8c.

The setup of the loading program is shown in Figure 9. The testing devices and facilities included reaction wall, constraint frame, bottom base, reaction frames, and hydraulic jacks. The constraint frame was fixed on the side surface of the reaction walls with four 80 mm diameter bolts. The specimens were constrained at the end of the constraint frame. The bottom base was fixed on the ground and was pin-connected to the specimens. Only displacements were constrained while the rotations were not at the top or bottom of the specimens. A hydraulic jack was placed on the top surfaces of the specimens to provide vertical load during the loading program. The axial force hydraulic jack was supported by a reaction frame, which was not shown in Figure 9a. An axial force of 150 kN (for T-shaped specimens) or 300 kN (for cross-shaped specimens) was applied and kept during the loading program. The nominal axial compression ratio of the columns was kept as 0.05. Two loading hydraulic jacks (one for T-shaped specimens) were fixed on the ground to apply load on the ends of the specimen beams. For cross-shaped specimens (TS-3 and TS-4), the load on the beams was rotational symmetric. As the floor and ceiling beams worked separately in practical construction, a special loading cell was designed to simulate the working conditions of the beams [17]. This loading cell released the horizontal displacements and constrained the vertical displacements at the ends of the beams. Thus, the combined effect of the two beam sections was avoided and the beams could work separately.

(**a**) Initial

(**b**) During demounting

(**c**) After re-connecting

**Figure 8.** Unlocking process of specimen (TS-2).

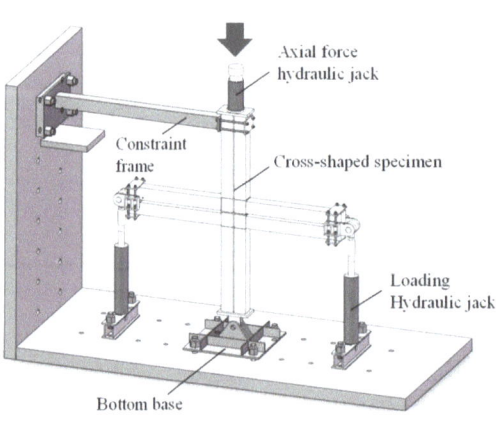

(**a**) Loading device     (**b**) Measurement

**Figure 9.** Test setup.

Displacement-controlled cyclic load was applied to the ends of the specimen beams according to standard ATC-24 [18], as shown in Figure 10. The yield displacement $\Delta_y$ was predicted as 30 mm before the test. Two cycles were loaded in each loading step except the yield phase. During the yield phase, three cycles were loaded at loading steps of 30, 45, and 60 mm.

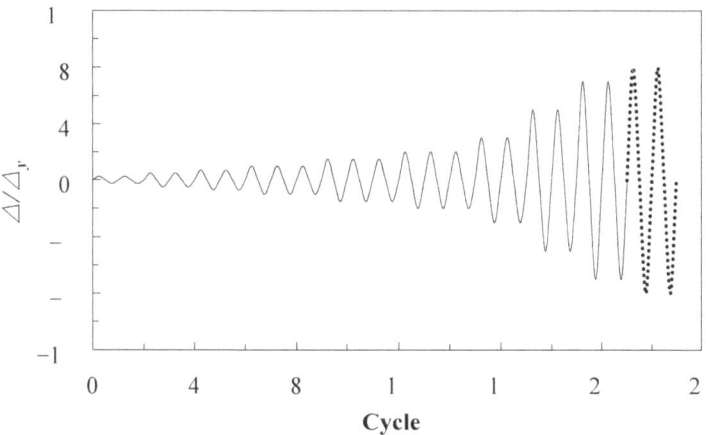

Figure 10. Cyclic loading protocol.

The measurement of the specimens is shown in Figure 9b. The axial and cyclic loads were measured by dynamic force sensors that were integrated into the hydraulic jacks. Seven linear variable differential transformers (LVDTs) were set to measure the vertical and horizontal displacements of the specimens. LVDT 1 and 2 were placed to measure the vertical displacement of the beam ends. They were also the control displacements during the loading program. Two pairs of LVDTs were set near the root of the beams and columns. LVDT 3 and 4 measured the vertical displacements of the right floor beam. LVDT 5 and 6 measured the horizontal displacements of the upper module column. With these two pairs of displacements, rotations of the beam and column sections at the root could be calculated. Strains on the specimens were measured by strain gauges.

## 4. Result and Discussion

### 4.1. General Behavior

#### 4.1.1. T-Shaped Demountable Specimens (TS-1 and TS-2)

Seismic behavior of the contrast specimen TS-1 was reported in reference [13]. Moment–drift ratio curves of T-shaped specimens (TS-1 and TS-2) is shown in Figure 11. Compared with specimen TS-1, the demountable specimen TS-2 had a lower stiffness due to its opening on the joint box. The elastic stiffness of specimen TS-2 was lower than that of specimen TS-1 by 15%. During the first cycle of the loading step (drift ratio = 1.67%), paint wrinkled at the root of the ceiling beams. The moment–drift ratio curve bent slightly. A residual deformation of 1.1 mm was observed after the third cycle of this loading step. When the drift ratio reached 2.50%, i.e., point A in the moment–drift ratio curves, a continual sizzle sound was heard. Micro-cracks were observed at the corners of the ceiling beam section. The position of the cracks was just outside the stiffeners. Paint peeled off from the beam webs and flanges. After the drift ratio reached 3.33%, i.e., point B in the curves, local buckling occurred at the root of the ceiling beam. The flanges buckled inward while the webs buckled outward. The cracks extended on the ceiling beam, causing fractures at the corners of the beam. Figure 12a shows the extended cracks on the specimen beam. When the drift ratio reached 5.00%, the moment reached the maximum at point C and began to decrease. The maximum strengths of these specimens were close. The difference was not more than 10%. As the damage on the beam accumulated, the plastic hinge was observed at the root of the ceiling beam. Slight local buckling was observed on the floor beam. After the drift ratio reached 6.67%, the ceiling beam was close to failure and lost most of its bearing capacity. Most of the load was taken by the floor beam. The local buckling on the floor beam was significant, as shown in Figure 12b. No cracks were observed on the floor beam. Rotation between the upper and lower modules occurred. A gap occurred on the original tight compressed surfaces of the joint boxes. As shown in Figure 12c, one side of the surface was compressed while the other side was open. These two sides switched with each other under the cyclic load. The upper and lower module columns were not in a straight line anymore, as shown in Figure 12d. The maximum angle between the upper and lower module columns was about 3.5°. When the drift ratio approached 8.33%, the cracks expanded with a loud noise. The load decreased to 85% of its maximum and the loading process was terminated.

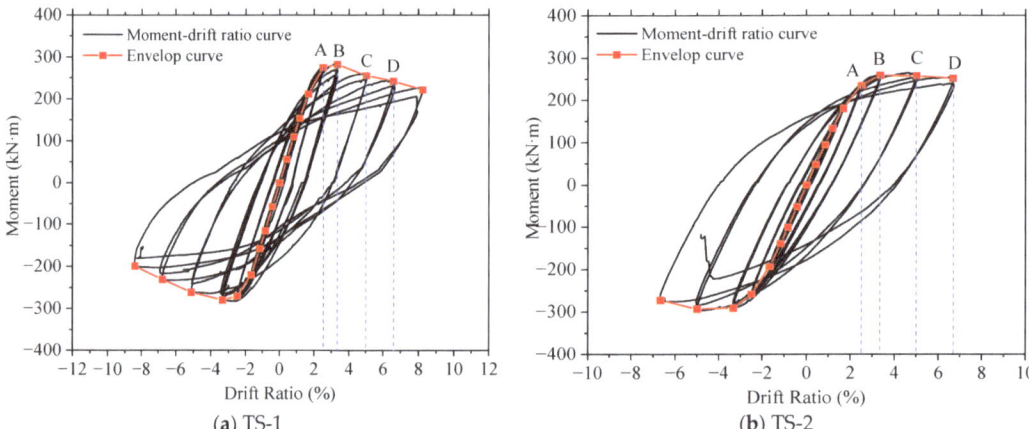

**Figure 11.** Moment–drift ratio curves of T-shaped specimens (TS-1 and TS-2).

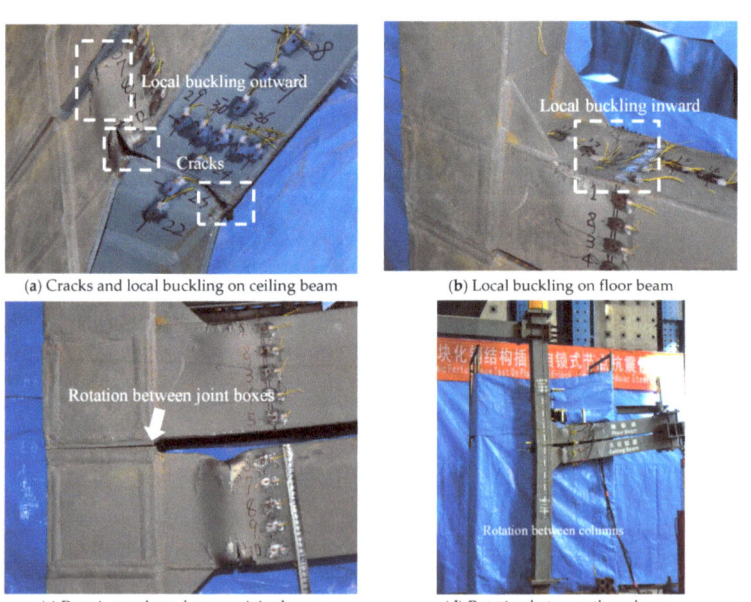

**Figure 12.** Observations of the T-shaped specimens (TS-1 and TS-2).

The failure mode of these T-shaped specimens was the failure of the ceiling beams. The cracks at the corners of the ceiling beam section extended while the flanges and webs buckled. The position of the failure was at the root of the beam, just outside of the stiffeners. The floor beam was less damaged due to its thickness (8 mm vs. 6 mm). The columns and the joint boxes were elastic during the whole loading program.

4.1.2. Cross-Shaped Specimens (TS-3 and TS-4)

In general, the observations of the cross-shaped specimens were rotational symmetric. Local buckling, cracks, and plastic hinges were observed on both floor and ceiling beams, as shown in Figure 13a,b. The cracks penetrated the whole flange of the section. During the loading program, no relative rotation occurred between the upper and lower joint boxes, as shown in Figure 13c. The original compressed surfaces remain tight and no gap occurred. Figure 13d shows that the upper and lower columns were in a straight line. No defamations were observed on the connecting plate. Moment-drift ratio curves of the cross-shaped specimens (TS-1 and TS-2) are shown in Figure 14. According to the comparison between Figures 14a and 14b, the differences between specimens TS-3 and TS-4 were insignificant during the loading program, indicating that the seismic behavior of the specimens was not controlled by the thickness of the connecting plate. The failure mode of the cross-shaped specimens was the fracture of floor and ceiling beams. The fracture position was just outside of the stiffeners, the same as that in T-shaped specimens.

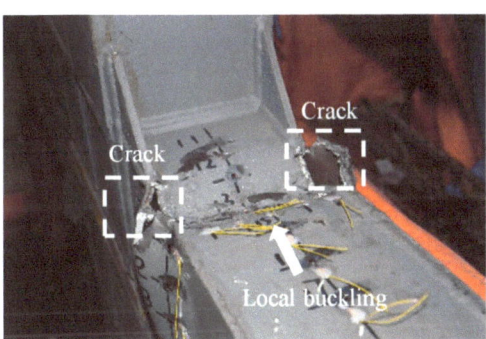

(a) Cracks and local buckling on floor beam

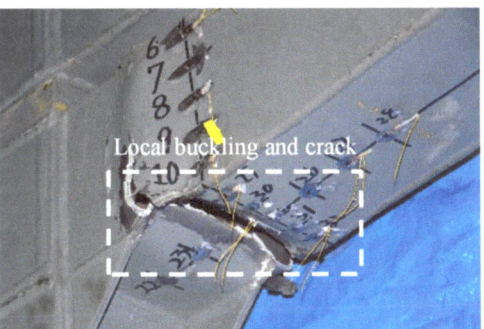

(b) Cracks and local buckling on ceiling beam

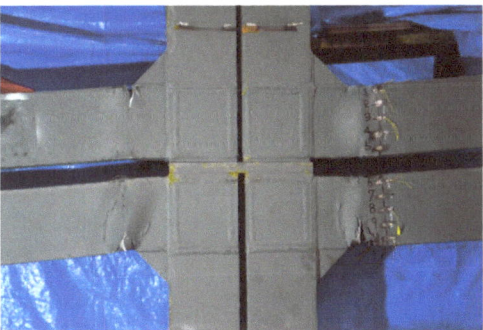

(c) Joint region

(d) Columns were in straight line

**Figure 13.** Observations of the Cross-shaped specimens (TS-3 and TS-4).

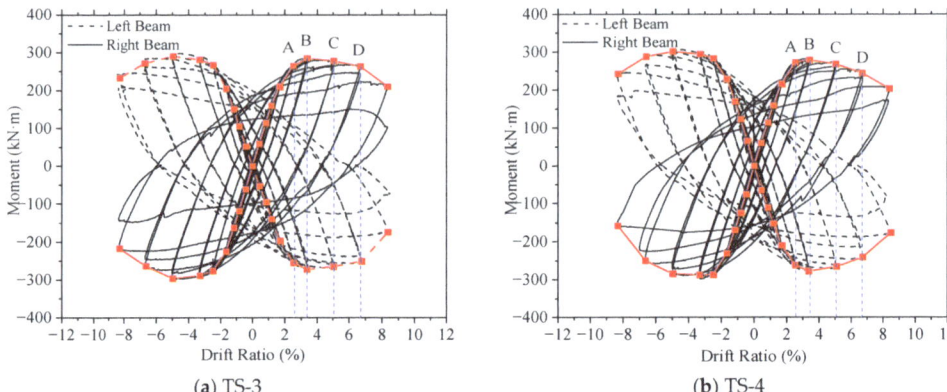

(a) TS-3    (b) TS-4

**Figure 14.** Moment-drift ratio curves of the cross-shaped specimens (TS-1 and TS-2).

*4.2. Strength, Stiffness and Ductility*

The moment–rotation envelop curves of the specimens are shown in Figure 15. The rotation was gained through the rotations of floor beam root and column root on the right side, which was measured by LVDT 3–6. Thus, the effect of the beam and column deformation can be eliminated. The stiffness of the specimens is between 0.5 EI/L and 8 EI/L. Moreover, the strength of the joints is higher than that of the floor and ceiling beams. Thus, these types of joints can be defined as semi-rigid full-strength joints [19].

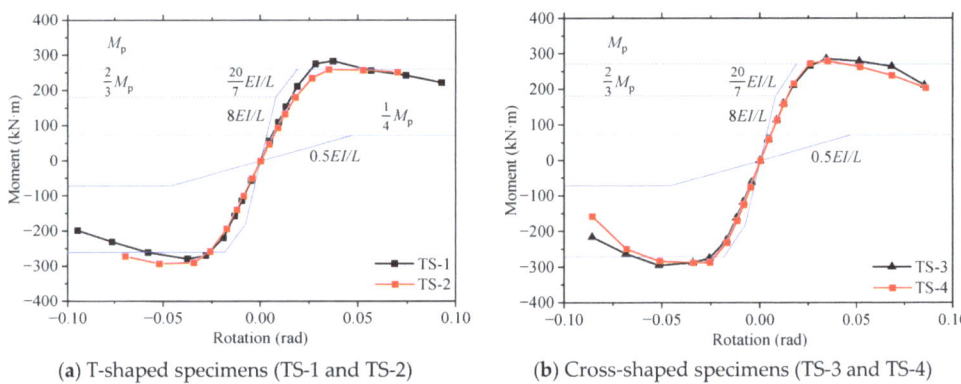

(a) T-shaped specimens (TS-1 and TS-2)    (b) Cross-shaped specimens (TS-3 and TS-4)

**Figure 15.** Moment-rotation envelop curves.

Two pairs of comparisons (TS-1 vs. TS-2, TS-3 vs. TS-4) are made, as shown in Figure 15a,b. The results show that the strength difference of the specimens was insignificant (lower than 8%). This indicates that the factor of unlocking the device and connecting plate will not affect the strength of the joints. The reason is that the failure mode of the joints is the fracture of the beams. As the strength of the joint region is much higher than that of the beam sections, the failure always occurs on the sections of the beam root. Thus, the failure mode is determined by the bending strength of beam sections.

The stiffness is calculated through the slope of the moment–drift ratio envelop curves, as shown in Figure 16. The stiffness curves are convex in shape. Also, comparisons of the specimens are made to investigate the effect of the factors. As shown in Figure 16a, the stiffness of specimen TS-1 is higher than that of the specimen TS-2 by about 15%. This is due to the opening on the joint box of the specimen TS-2. As the opening is essential for the reset of the unlocking device, it can be concluded that the factor of the unlocking device will weaken the stiffness of the joint. Figure 16b shows the comparisons of four curves, i.e., both sides of specimen TS-3 and TS-4. These curves are in good coincidence and are symmetric in shape. That indicates that the thickness of the connecting plate does not affect the stiffness of the joint. It can also be concluded that the behavior of the joints is symmetric.

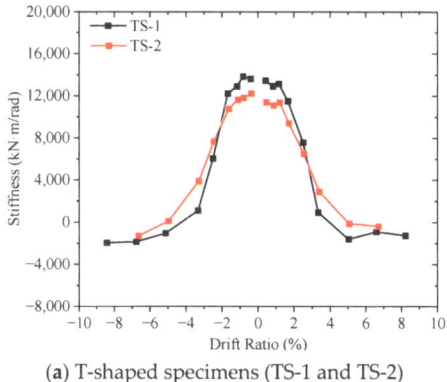
(a) T-shaped specimens (TS-1 and TS-2)

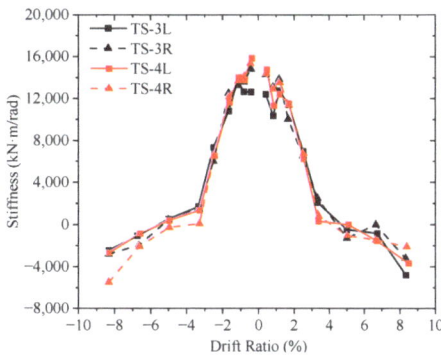
(b) Cross-shaped specimens (TS-3 and TS-4)

**Figure 16.** Stiffness degradation curves.

The angular displacement ductility coefficient ($\mu$) is defined as the ratio between the failure inter-story drift ratio and the yielding inter-story drift ratio, as given in Equation (1).

$$\mu = \frac{\theta_y}{\theta_u} \quad (1)$$

Table 3 shows the ductility of the specimens. The ductility coefficients of the specimens are about 2.5–3.1. The results show that all the joints have good ductility. The ductility of the specimen TS-2 is lower than that of TS-1. This is due to the higher yield drift ratio of specimen TS-2. The lower stiffness of specimen TS-2 results in higher yield displacement. Meanwhile, the ultimate drift ratio is mainly determined by the beam section for these specimens. Thus, the ductility coefficient of specimen TS-2 is higher than that of the contrast specimen. For cross-shaped specimens, the effect of the connecting plate is insignificant.

**Table 3.** Strength and Ductility Coefficient.

|      |       | Yield Strength (kN·m) | | Maximum Strength (kN·m) | | Yield Drift Ratio (%) | Ultimate Drift Ratio (%) | Ductility Coefficient |
|------|-------|----------|----------|----------|----------|------|------|------|
|      |       | Positive | Negative | Positive | Negative |      |      |      |
| TS-1 |       | 269.6    | 262.4    | 283.0    | 279.4    | 2.39 | 6.75 | 2.82 |
| TS-2 |       | 253.0    | 260.5    | 270.9    | 278.6    | 2.66 | 6.67 | 2.50 |
| TS-3 | Left  | 254.9    | 271.4    | 271.6    | 290.7    | 2.52 | 7.22 | 2.87 |
|      | Right | 261.2    | 269.6    | 285.5    | 295.8    | 2.42 | 7.44 | 3.07 |
| TS-4 | Left  | 255.6    | 270.1    | 279.3    | 294.7    | 2.22 | 7.18 | 3.23 |
|      | Right | 262.1    | 268.9    | 280.1    | 287.1    | 2.28 | 6.68 | 2.93 |

### 4.3. Energy Dissipation

Energy dissipation performance is usually evaluated by hysteretic energy dissipation and equivalent viscous damping coefficient, as given in Equations (2) and (3).

$$E = \frac{S_{(ABC+CDA)}}{S_{(OBE+ODF)}} \quad (2)$$

$$\xi_{eq} = \frac{E}{2\pi} \quad (3)$$

where $S_{(ABC+CDA)}$ and $S_{(OBE+ODF)}$ are the area enclosed by the hysteretic loop and the summation of the triangle areas OBE and ODF, respectively. An idealized hysteresis loop is shown in Figure 17.

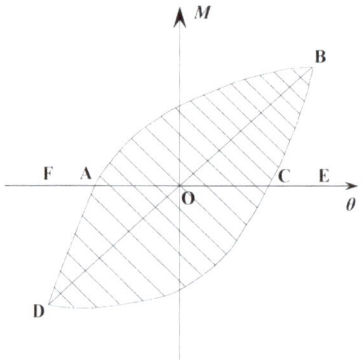

**Figure 17.** Idealized hy.teretic loop.

A comparison is made between specimens TS-1 and TS-2 in Figure 18a,b. Before the yield drift ratio, hysteretic energy dissipation of both specimens is almost none. The difference between the two specimens is almost ignorable. After the yield ratio, the equivalent viscous damping coefficient of TS-1 is higher than that of specimen TS-2 by 10–15%. This can also be due to the weakened stiffness of TS-2. Figure 18c,d compare the four curves of both sides of TS-3 and TS-4. The result shows a good coincidence of these curves, indicating that the factor of the connecting plate thickness can be ignored.

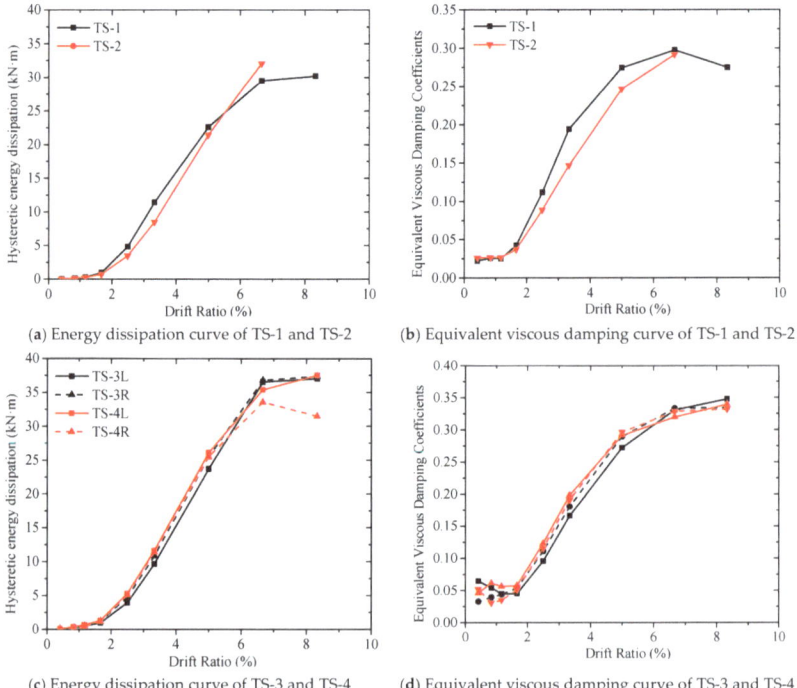

(**a**) Energy dissipation curve of TS-1 and TS-2

(**b**) Equivalent viscous damping curve of TS-1 and TS-2

(**c**) Energy dissipation curve of TS-3 and TS-4

(**d**) Equivalent viscous damping curve of TS-3 and TS-4

**Figure 18.** Energy dissipation of the specimens.

## 5. Numerical Analysis

For further investigation of the self-lock joints, finite element (FE) models were developed and numerical analysis was conducted based on commercial software ABAQUS (Ver.6.13).

### 5.1. Geometry, Material Properties, and Boundary Condition

The geometry of the FE models was based on the specimens above, as shown in Figure 19. These models consist of most parts of the specimens, including beams, columns, joint boxes, and connectors. Details of the connectors were also considered, including ring-teeth and cone surfaces. An opening was set on the joint box to simulate the weakening effect of the self-lock device. All components of the FE models were modeled with solid element C3D8R. In order to balance the computational efficiency and convergence, different mesh sizes are set for different parts of the joints: 40.0 mm for the module column, 20.0 mm for the floor and ceiling beam, 20.0 mm for the side of the node box, and 10.0 mm for the bottom plate where the self-locking connector is inserted. The mesh size for inserting the self-locking connector is the smallest, the mesh size of the sleeve is 8.0 mm, the mesh size of the insert rod and the taper card is 5.0 mm, and the mesh size of the ring tooth part is encrypted to 2.0 mm.

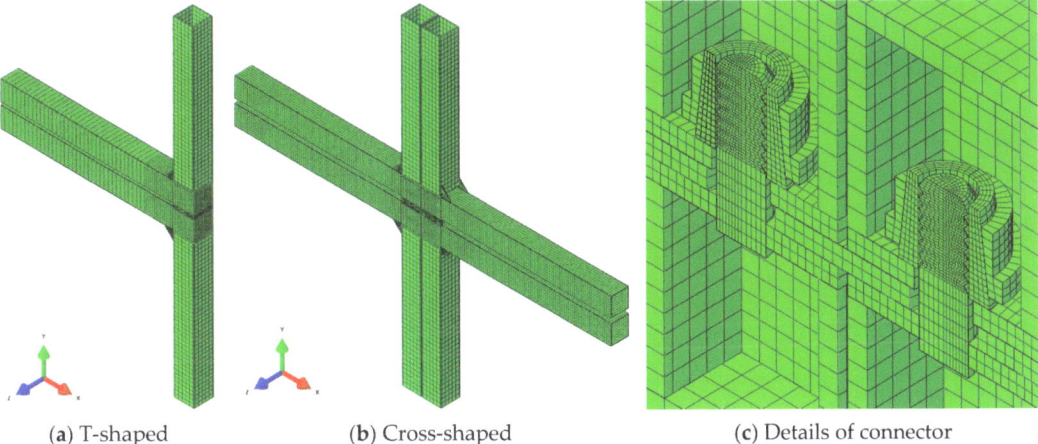

(a) T-shaped     (b) Cross-shaped     (c) Details of connector

**Figure 19.** FE models of self-lock joint.

The constraints of these parts were simulated based on the real condition. In an upper or lower module, beam, column, and stiffeners were tie-connected to the joint box to simulate the welding. But the interface between the upper and lower joint boxes was not tied. Instead, a surface contact pair was set to simulate the separation and slide of the interface. The normal behavior of the contact pair was set as the hard contact while the tangential behavior was set as the frictional contact. Based on previous research, the friction coefficient was set as 0.15 in this paper. Similar contact pairs were also set on the ring-teeth and cone surfaces of the connector.

The boundary condition of the FE models was also based on the experimental study. As shown in Figure 19, displacement constraints were applied at the top and bottom of the FE models. At the bottom of the lower column, Ux, Uy, and Uz displacement constraints were applied. At the top of the upper column, Ux and Uz displacement constraints were applied while Uy was released. A constant axial force was applied on the top of the models. The cyclic load was applied at the beam ends according to ATC-24. The rotations of the beam and column ends were not restricted. Uy displacement constraints were applied to the beam ends to prevent the out-of-plane rotation of the models.

The material properties were set based on the coupon test results above, as shown in Table 4 and Figure 20. Elastoplastic properties were applied to the FE meshes. To simulate the behavior under cyclic load, kinematic hardening was set for material properties.

**Table 4.** Material Properties of FE Models.

| Parts | Elastic Modulus (N/mm$^2$) | Yield Strength (N/mm$^2$) | Ultimate Strength (N/mm$^2$) |
|---|---|---|---|
| Connector components | 200.0 | 441.3 | 553.7 |
| Steel plate | 200.0 | 393.8 | 523.5 |

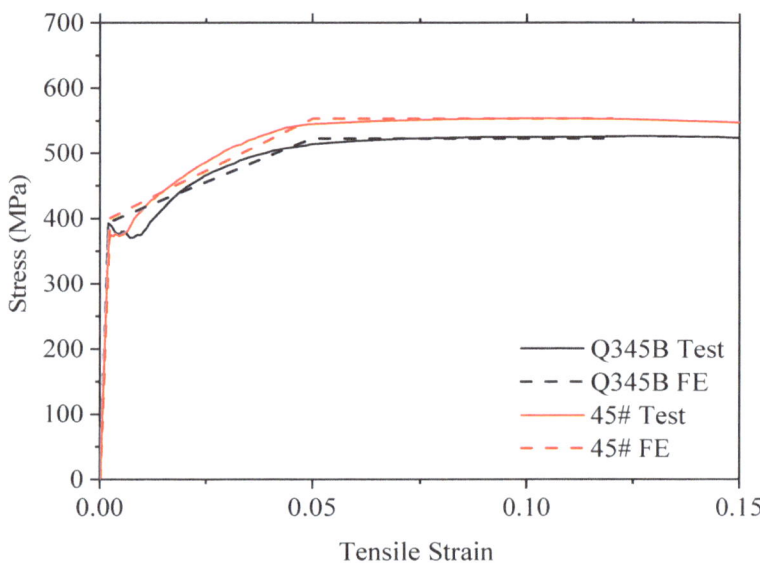

**Figure 20.** Elastoplastic material properties for FE models.

## 5.2. Validation

The FE models were analyzed with an implicit solver and the analysis results were validated with the test results. Figure 21 shows the validation of moment–drift ratio curves. In general, the FE curves fit well with the test ones. The hysteresis loops of FE and test curves are close except for the loops near the ultimate point. At the elastic and yield phases, the hysteresis loops of FE and test curves are in good agreement. During the strengthening phase, the loops of FE results are thinner than the test ones. This is due to the simplified model of elastoplastic material properties. As fractures are not considered in the FE material properties, the cracks on the beam sections cannot be simulated correctly. This results in the difference between the last loops.

Table 5 shows the strength and initial stiffness of FE and test results. The yield strength, maximum strength, and initial stiffness of the FE results fit well with the test ones. The maximum error of these important features was about 5.3%, which is acceptable to the authors.

Figure 22 shows the key observations on FE models and test results. The buckling and deformation at the root of the beams are simulated correctly. The high-stress areas in FE models, as shown as the grey-colored areas in Figure 22a,c, are the exact fractured areas in the test specimens. These indicate that the FE models are effective and can simulate the behavior of the novel self-lock joints correctly.

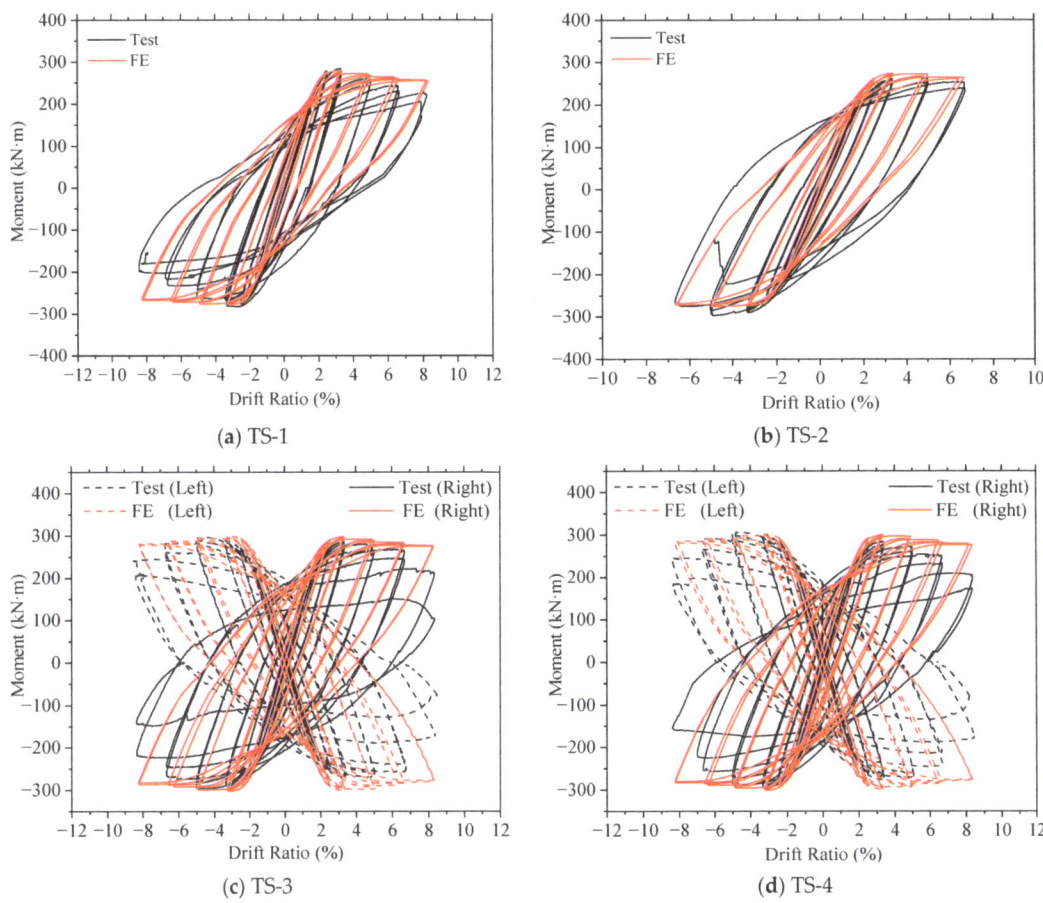

**Figure 21.** Validation of FE results.

**Table 5.** Comparison of Strength and Stiffness in FE and Test Results.

| No | Yield Strength | | | Maximum Strength | | | Initial Stiffness | | |
|---|---|---|---|---|---|---|---|---|---|
| | FE Result (kN·m) | Test Result (kN·m) | Error (%) | FE Result (kN·m) | Test Result (kN·m) | Error (%) | FE Result (kN·m/rad) | Test Result (kN·m/rad) | Error (%) |
| TS-1 | 271.2 | 266.0 | 2.0 | 279.4 | 281.2 | 0.6 | 13,395 | 13,543 | −1.1 |
| TS-2 | 262.7 | 256.8 | 2.3 | 274.6 | 274.8 | <0.1 | 12,262 | 11,855 | +3.4 |
| TS-3 | 273.8 | 264.2 | 3.4 | 297.9 | 285.9 | 4.2 | 13,868 | 13,596 | +2.0 |
| TS-4 | 270.7 | 265.1 | 2.1 | 301.4 | 287.6 | 5.0 | 13,997 | 14,780 | −5.3 |

### 5.3. Parameter Analysis

For further investigation of the seismic behavior of this type of joint, twenty FE models were developed to evaluate the factors that may affect the performance. Several inner-module and inter-module factors are considered, including the thickness of the side and end plate of joint boxes, the diameter of the stud, the unlocking device, and the inner plate, as shown in Figure 23. Table 6 shows the details of the FE models. Considering the "Strong joint" principle, the thickness of the joint region should not be lower than the thickness of columns and beams. In this case, the minimum thickness of the joint region is set as 10 mm.

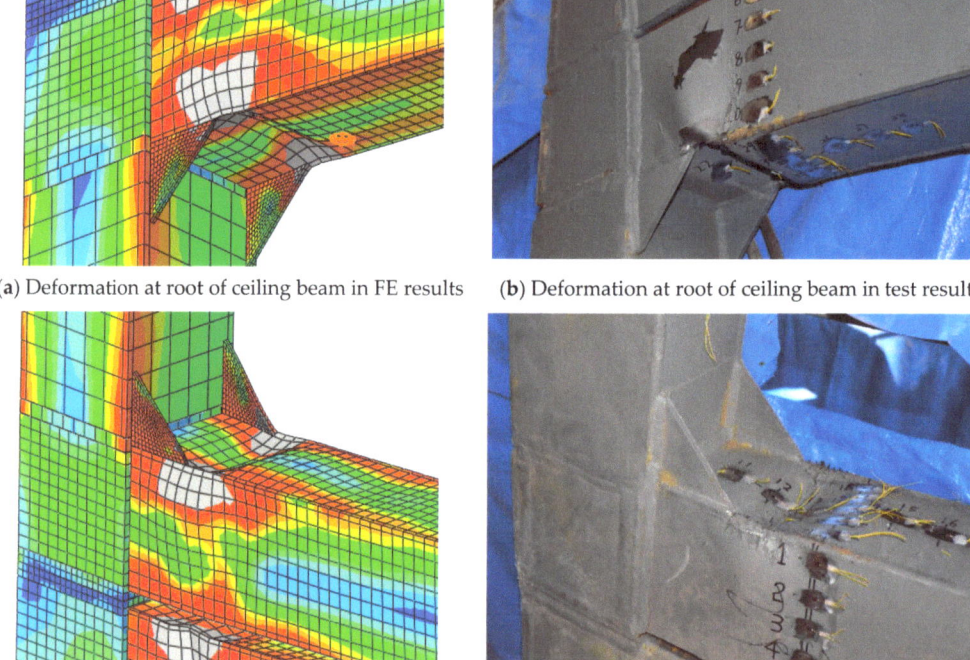

(a) Deformation at root of ceiling beam in FE results  
(b) Deformation at root of ceiling beam in test results  
(c) Deformation at root of floor beam in FE results  
(d) Deformation at root of floor beam in test results  

**Figure 22.** Observations on FE models and test specimens.

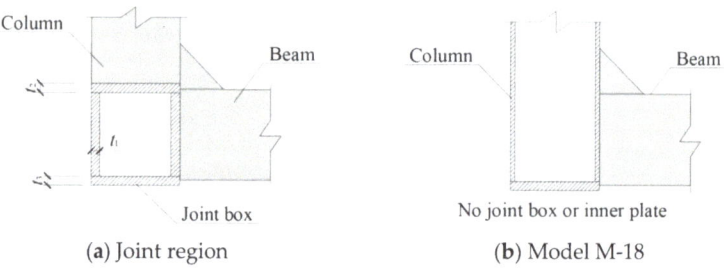

(a) Joint region  (b) Model M-18

**Figure 23.** Joint region of the FE models.

The results show that all models exhibit similar yield and maximum strength except for model M-18. The thickness of the joint boxes and the diameter of the stud do not affect the strength of the joint significantly. As shown in Figure 24, yield the strength remains at about 260–270 kN·m while the thickness of the joint box changes. The reason is that the failure mode of the joint is buckling at the root of the beam. The strength joint is determined by the beam sections instead of joint boxes. The model M-18 is a joint model without joint boxes. The beams are directly welded to the square hollow section columns. The yield and maximum strength of M-18 is lower than that of other models by about 10%. Figure 25 compares the deformation on models M-6 and M-18. The side thickness of the joint boxes in model M-6 is 10.0 mm, which is the same as the thickness of the column in model M-18. The failure mode of this model is due to the failure of the column. Plastic out-of-plane deformation occurs at the root of the column. Also, the initial stiffness of the model is lower.

This indicates that the joint boxes are essential for this type of joint. Joints that welded the beams directly to the columns are not recommended.

**Table 6.** Details of FE Models.

| No | $t_1$ (mm) | $t_2$ (mm) | $t_3$ (mm) | D (mm) | Unlocking Device | Yield Strength (kN·m) | Maximum Strength (kN·m) | Initial Stiffness (kN·m/rad) |
|---|---|---|---|---|---|---|---|---|
| M-1 | 20 | 16 | 16 | 50 | - | 269.8 | 285.0 | 13,834 |
| M-2 | 18 | 16 | 16 | 50 | | 269.5 | 284.5 | 13,724 |
| M-3 | 16 | 16 | 16 | 50 | - | 269.1 | 284.2 | 13,628 |
| M-4 | 14 | 16 | 16 | 50 | | 266.4 | 281.9 | 13,430 |
| M-5 | 12 | 16 | 16 | 50 | - | 264.9 | 280.0 | 13,265 |
| M-6 | 10 | 16 | 16 | 50 | - | 262.9 | 278.1 | 13,063 |
| M-7 | 16 | 16 | 16 | 50 | Yes | 263.8 | 282.0 | 12,288 |
| M-8 | 16 | 20 | 16 | 50 | - | 269.6 | 283.8 | 13,726 |
| M-9 | 16 | 18 | 16 | 50 | | 269.4 | 284.5 | 13,695 |
| M-10 | 16 | 14 | 16 | 50 | | 268.8 | 284.1 | 13,560 |
| M-11 | 16 | 12 | 16 | 50 | - | 267.8 | 283.7 | 13,531 |
| M-12 | 16 | 10 | 16 | 50 | - | 267.2 | 282.8 | 13,516 |
| M-13 | 16 | 16 | 20 | 50 | - | 269.4 | 284.1 | 13,683 |
| M-14 | 16 | 16 | 18 | 50 | | 269.1 | 284.3 | 13,665 |
| M-15 | 16 | 16 | 14 | 50 | | 269.0 | 284.2 | 13,556 |
| M-16 | 16 | 16 | 12 | 50 | - | 265.5 | 281.1 | 13,452 |
| M-17 | 16 | 16 | 10 | 50 | | 265.8 | 282.4 | 13,383 |
| M-18 | | No joint box | | | - | 235.1 | 255.6 | 12,360 |
| M-19 | 20 | 20 | 20 | 60 | - | 268.2 | 284.3 | 13,656 |
| M-20 | 20 | 20 | 20 | 40 | - | 267.7 | 283.9 | 13,523 |

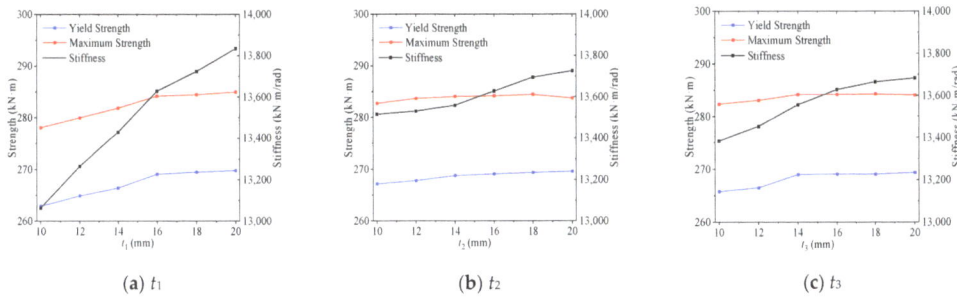

(a) $t_1$     (b) $t_2$     (c) $t_3$

**Figure 24.** Effects of thickness.

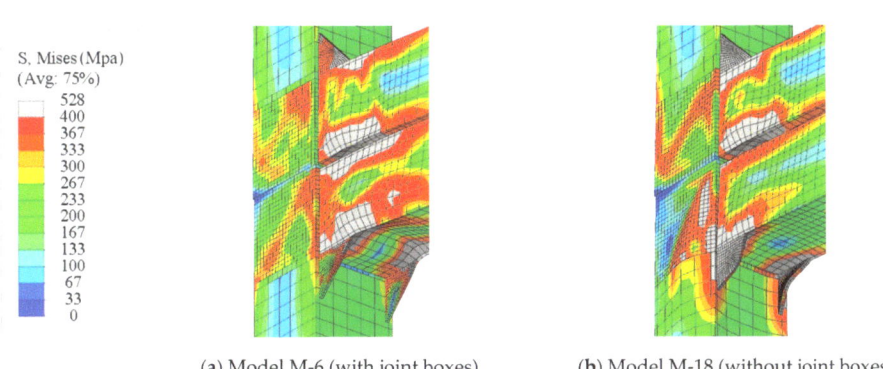

(a) Model M-6 (with joint boxes)     (b) Model M-18 (without joint boxes)

**Figure 25.** Comparison of deformation on model M-6 and M-18.

## 6. Conclusions

A type of self-lock joint for modular steel construction was tested and analyzed in this paper. An experimental study, including functional and cyclic loading tests, was conducted on four full-scale specimens. The finite element (FE) models were developed and validated through the test results. The following conclusions are made based on the test and analysis results.

(a) The demountable function of the self-lock joints was validated through the test program. The results show that the mechanism of the joints works well. The connecting and demounting function of the novel joints can be realized in modular steel construction.

(b) The seismic behavior of the self-lock joints was investigated through experimental study. The results show that these types of novel joints exhibit exceptional seismic behavior, and they can be defined as semi-rigid full-strength joints. The strength of the joint is determined by the beam sections. Due to the maintenance opening on the joint boxes, the unlocking device decreases the stiffness of the joint by 10%, but this does not affect the yield and maximum strength. The thickness of the connecting plate does not affect the seismic behavior of cross-shaped joints.

(c) Numerical analysis was conducted based on the tests. FE models were developed and validated through the test. Comparisons of the load–drift ratio curve, strength, stiffness, and deformation were made between the FE and test results. The comparisons show that the FE result fits well with the test ones. The main conclusions of the parameter analysis show that the absence of the joint box reduces the initial stiffness of the joint, and the thickness of the joint box plate and the diameter of the stud do not significantly affect the strength of the joint. Therefore, for the design of a demountable self-locking joint, it is necessary to set joint boxes. The plate size of the joint box can be considered according to the conventional plate size, that is, not less than the thickness of the beam and column.

**Author Contributions:** Conceptualization, L.Z. and Y.D.; Methodology, X.-M.D. and L.Z.; Validation, X.-M.D.; Formal analysis, X.-M.D. and F.-W.S.; Investigation, L.Z.; Writing—original draft, X.-M.D. and F.-W.S.; Writing—review & editing, H.-W.Z.; Visualization, H.-W.Z.; Funding acquisition, L.Z. and Y.D. All authors have read and agreed to the published version of the manuscript.

**Funding:** This paper is funded by the Natural Science Foundation of Tianjin City (Grant NO. 16PTSYJC00070). This reported research is also sponsored by the National Key Research and Development Program of China (Grant NO. 2018YFC1504303).

**Data Availability Statement:** Data are contained within the article.

**Conflicts of Interest:** Author Xiao-Meng Dai was employed by the company China Railway Construction Bridge Engineering Bureau Group Corporation, Ltd. The remaining authors declare that the research was conducted in the absence of any commercial or financial relationships that could be construed as a potential conflict of interest.

## References

1. Deng, E.F.; Zong, L.; Ding, Y.; Dai, X.M.; Lon, N.; Chen, Y. Monotonic and cyclic response of bolted connections with welded cover plate for modular steel construction. *Eng. Struct.* **2018**, *167*, 407–419. [CrossRef]
2. Lawson, R.M.; Ogden, R.; Goodier, C. *Design in Modular Construction*; CRC Press: Boca Raton, FL, USA, 2014.
3. Chen, Z.H.; Liu, J.D.; Yu, Y.J. Experimental study on interior connections in modular steel buildings. *Eng. Struct.* **2017**, *147*, 625–638. [CrossRef]
4. Chen, Z.; Liu, J.; Yu, Y.; Zhou, C.; Yan, R. Experimental study of an innovative modular steel building connection. *J. Constr. Steel Res.* **2017**, *139*, 69–82. [CrossRef]
5. Lacey, A.W.; Chen, W.; Hao, H.; Bi, K. Structural response of modular buildings—An overview. *J. Build. Eng.* **2018**, *16*, 45–56. [CrossRef]
6. Liu, X.C.; Pu, S.H.; Zhang, A.L.; Xu, A.X.; Ni, Z.; Sun, Y.; Ma, L. Static and seismic experiment for bolted-welded joint in modularized prefabricated steel structure. *J. Constr. Steel Res.* **2015**, *115*, 417–433. [CrossRef]
7. Sanches, R.; Mercan, O.; Roberts, B. Experimental investigations of vertical post-tensioned connection for modular steel structures. *Eng. Struct.* **2018**, *175*, 776–789. [CrossRef]

8. Fest, E.; Shea, K.; Domer, B.; Smith, I.F. Adjustable tensegrity structures. *J. Struct. Eng. ASCE* **2003**, *129*, 515–526. [CrossRef]
9. Du, X.L.; Wang, W.; Chan, T.M. Seismic design of beam-through steel frames with self-centering modular panels. *Eng. Struct.* **2018**, *141*, 179–188. [CrossRef]
10. Dai, X.M. Research on Seismic Behavior and Design Method of Self-Lock Plug-In Joints in Modular Steel Construction. Ph.D. Thesis, Tianjin University, Tianjin, China, 2021.
11. Chen, Z.; Niu, X.; Liu, J.; Khan, K.; Liu, Y. Seismic study on an innovative fully bolted beam-column joint in prefabricated modular steel buildings. *Eng. Struct.* **2021**, *234*, 111875. [CrossRef]
12. Du, H.; Zhao, P.; Wang, Y.; Sun, W. Seismic experimental assessment of beam through beam-column connections for modular prefabricated steel moment frames. *J. Constr. Steel Res.* **2022**, *192*, 107208. [CrossRef]
13. Dai, X.M.; Zong, L.; Ding, Y.; Li, Z.X. Experimental study on seismic behavior of a novel plug-in self-lock joint for modular steel construction. *Eng. Struct.* **2019**, *181*, 143–164. [CrossRef]
14. *GB/T 228.1-2010*; Metallic Materials-Tensile Testing-Part 1: Method of Test at Room Temperature. SAC (Standardization Administration of the People's Republic of China): Beijing, China, 2010. (In Chinese)
15. *GB/T 699-2015*; Quality Carbon Structure Steels. SAC (Standardization Administration of the People's Republic of China): Beijing, China, 2015. (In Chinese)
16. *GB/T 1591-2018*; High Strength Low Alloy Structural Steels. SAC (Standardization Administration of the People's Republic of China): Beijing, China, 2018. (In Chinese)
17. Srisangeerthanan, S.; Hashemi, M.J.; Rajeev, P.; Gad, E.; Fernando, S. Numerical study on the effects of diaphragm stiffness and strength on the seismic response of multi-story modular buildings. *Eng. Struct.* **2018**, *163*, 25–37. [CrossRef]
18. *ATC-24*; Guidelines for Cyclic Seismic Testing of Components of Steel Structures. ATC (Applied Technology Council): Redwood City, CA, USA, 1992.
19. *BS EN 1993-1-8:2005*; Design of Steel Structures—Part 1–8: Design of Joints. CEN (European Committee for Standardization): London, UK, 2005.

**Disclaimer/Publisher's Note:** The statements, opinions and data contained in all publications are solely those of the individual author(s) and contributor(s) and not of MDPI and/or the editor(s). MDPI and/or the editor(s) disclaim responsibility for any injury to people or property resulting from any ideas, methods, instructions or products referred to in the content.

*Article*

# Experimental Study on Seismic Behavior of Steel Column Base Connections with Arc End-Plates Slip-Friction

Chengyu Li [1,2], Cong Luo [1,2] and Aizhu Zhu [3,*]

[1] School of Urban Construction, Wuhan University of Science and Technology, No.947 Qingshan Heping Road, Wuhan 430081, China
[2] Hubei Provincial Engineering Research Center of Urban Regeneration, Wuhan University of Science and Technology, No.947 Qingshan Heping Road, Wuhan 430081, China
[3] School of Civil and Hydraulic Engineering, Huazhong University of Science and Technology, No.1037 Luoyu Road, Wuhan 430074, China
* Correspondence: zhuaizhu1228@hust.edu.cn; Tel.: +86-13545158888

**Abstract:** This paper proposes a new type of steel slip-friction column base connections with arc end-plates. Two arc end-plates of the steel column base, which can slide between each other to some extent, were set at the position where the column base is subject to plastic deformation. Thus, the sliding-friction energy dissipation between the arc end-plates can effectively minimize or eliminate the energy dissipation of the traditional column base connections. Cyclic loading tests were conducted to study the hysteretic performance and energy consumption performance of the proposed connections. Considerations have been given to different axial compression ratios, Belleville springs (Bes), brass plates, and horizontal loading protocols. The test results show no obvious deformation or damage during the radial cyclic loading test. The curve shape of the test measurement approximates a parallelogram, showing good force performance. The proposed connections with the increasing axial compression force can increase the energy dissipation ability and load-carrying capacity. Therefore, the proposed connection has perfect seismic behavior.

**Keywords:** column base connection; slip-friction connection; hysteresis behavior; friction energy dissipation

## 1. Introduction

The steel column base is a vulnerable part of steel structures. In the 1994 Northridge Earthquake [1] in the United States and the 1995 Hanshin Earthquake [2] in Japan, quite a lot of the buildings were damaged or collapsed due to large deformation or damage to the steel column bases. Repairing, dismantling, or even terminating the use of these structures will cause huge losses, economic losses, and negative social impacts. In order to reduce structural damage and the secondary effects of earthquakes, many scholars have begun to focus on the seismic performance of steel column bases. Suzuk et al. [3] carried out tests on conventional column base joints and showed that flexural deformation of conventional column base joints leads to axial shortening of the steel column which in turn leads to a reduction in the bending capacity and axial load-carrying capacity of the steel column. It is therefore necessary to control the damage to the column base connection.

Friction connection is a low-damage connection, SFC (Symmetry Friction Connect) and AFC (Asymmetric Friction Connect) were originally used in beam-column connections [4,5]. By providing friction dampers at the joint instead of the traditional rigid connection, seismic energy is dissipated and damage to the main structure is reduced [6,7]. In recent years, the use of friction mechanisms for column base connections has received attention from scholars. Borzouie et al. [8,9] designed a sliding asymmetric friction connection. Tests have demonstrated that the frictional column base connection shows no significant strength degradation and can achieve low loss performance of the main structure, which can be

widely used in seismic-resistant structures. Liu et al. [10] conducted an experimental study of a new type of elastic rocking (IRR) column with replaceable steel seam dampers. The experimental results showed that the IRR column had good ductility and hysteretic properties, with no significant strength and stiffness degradation, and that the damage was mainly to the dampers. The steel seam dampers can be repaired quickly and the performance after the repair is essentially the same as before the repair. Freddi et al. [11,12] proposed a swaying column base connection with a friction device, which is connected to the foundation by the friction device, and the friction device dissipates energy during the column swaying process so that the main body of the column base remains undamaged. Elettore et al. [13,14] proposed a self-centered lossless column base connection, where the steel column slides. The frictional load generated between the column end and the friction plate dissipates energy to achieve a low and lossless structure. Li et al. [15,16] proposed a new sliding frictional column base connection that achieves a lossless performance of the structure by replacing the energy dissipated by the conventional column base connection with the frictional dissipation between the curved end plates at the column end.

Based on the previous studies [15,16], an innovative kind of steel column base connection with arc end-plates slip-friction was proposed (in Figure 1) to achieve damage-free energy dissipation. This column base connection is composed of the steel column, upper and lower arc end-plates, high-strength bolts, top plate, and base plate. Among them, the upper steel column is welded with the upper arc end-plate and the top plate. The lower steel column is welded with the lower arc end-plate and the base plate, the upper and lower arc end-plates are connected using high-strength bolts. The pre-compression between the upper and lower arc end-plates is produced by applying a pre-tension force to the high-strength bolts. Oblong bolt holes are set in the upper arc end-plate so that the upper part of the connection can rotate about the oblong holes. Circular bolt holes are made in the lower arc end-plate. Because the arc end-plate of the connection is set at the position where the plastic hinge is easy to appear at the bottom of the column. The seismic energy is dissipated by rotating sliding friction instead of consuming the yield energy of traditional members. The main structure remains undamaged, so as to achieve the design goal of undamaged energy consumption. The maximum rotation angle of the connection can be controlled by the size of the oblong bolt hole on the upper arc end-plate. Therefore, the prominent advantage of the proposed connection is that when the arc end-plate of the connection does not slip, the connection is equivalent to the traditional steel column. However, when the connected arc end-plate slides, the seismic energy is dissipated by arc end-plates and the rotational friction between the arc end-plates and bolts. The sliding-friction energy dissipation is used to replace the energy dissipation caused by the material yielding of the traditional connection. The steel column base connections with arc end-plates slip-friction proposed in this paper is a non-damage connection mode applied by SHJ to the column base, the axial compression force can effectively increase the friction force between the arc end-plates of the column base slip friction connection proposed in this paper.

This paper describes an experimental research plan, including eight groups of tests of four full-scale specimens under two loading systems, to study the effects of axial pressure, BeSs, and brass plate on the seismic behavior of steel column base connections with arc end-plates slip-friction.

This paper answers the following questions through eight groups of experimental results:

1. What is the seismic performance of steel column base connections with arc end-plates slip-friction under different parameters?

2. What are the reasons for the column base connection post-sliding loss of bolt pre-tension force? What is the influence of configurations of BeSs in the connection bolt assemblage on maintaining the post-sliding connections' loss of bolt pre-tension force?

3. What is the influence of assembling BeSs and brass plates at the column base connection on the sliding surface wear of the column base connection?

4. After the test, whether the connection meets the requirements of a no-damage design?

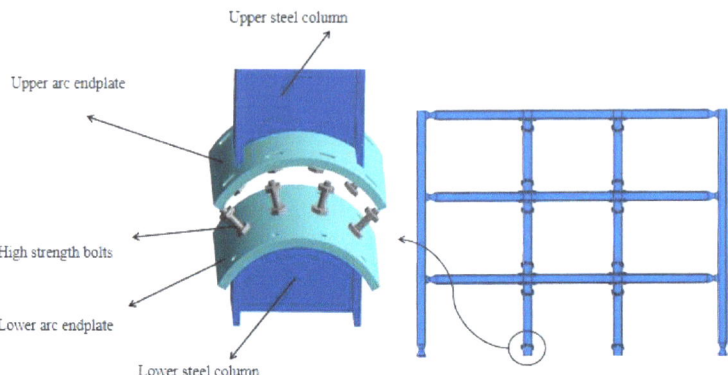

**Figure 1.** Schematic diagram of column base connection.

## 2. Test Description

*2.1. Specimen Design*

The column base connection specimen with arc end-plate slip friction consists of a steel column, upper and lower arc end-plate, high-strength bolts, top plate and base plate. The section dimensions of the steel column are HW 350 mm × 350 mm × 12 mm × 19 mm (as shown in Figures 2 and 3) and the total height of the specimen is 1950 mm. The width (W) of the arc end-plate is 550 mm, the thickness of the arc end-plate is 25 mm and the inner radius (R) is approximately 0.7 H (H is the height of the steel column section, i.e., 350 mm). The slip performance of the column base connection is most stable when the radius of the arc end-plate is 0.7 H [15,16]. The length of the rectangular bolt hole in the upper arc end-plate is 45 mm (Figure 4). The circular bolt holes in the lower arc end-plate have a diameter of 22 mm. The upper and lower arc end-plates are connected using S8.8M20 high-strength bolts and more design details of the connection can also be found in Figure 3. Taking into account the Chinese Code [17], a total of four full-size specimens with sliding friction steel column base connections with arc end-plates were designed to analyze the effects of the axial compression ratio, the setting of belleville springs (Bes) at the bolts, the setting of brass plates between the arc plates and different horizontal load protocols on the force performance of the specimens. The main parameters of the specimens are shown in Table 1. The specimen number H350 indicates the section dimension of the H-beam column. The first number indicates the parameter classification. The second number indicates the different loading regimes, where 1 is a variable amplitude constant loading protocol and 2 is a constant amplitude loading protocol. Two cycles of loading are carried out on each specimen. After the first test, the friction surface of the curved end-plate is cleaned and repaired, and then the second test is conducted. Take H350-1-1 to H350-4-1 as an example. Specimen H350-1-1 is the reference specimen with an axial compression ratio of 0.1 and no bass spring. H350-2-1 and H350-3-1 are set up with a bass spring and axial compression ratios of 0.2 and 0.3, respectively. H350-4-1 is based on H350-3-1 and a brass plate is set up between the curved end plates.

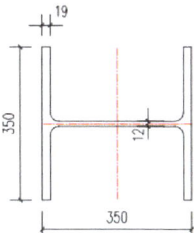

**Figure 2.** Sectional sizes of H-shaped section (unit: mm).

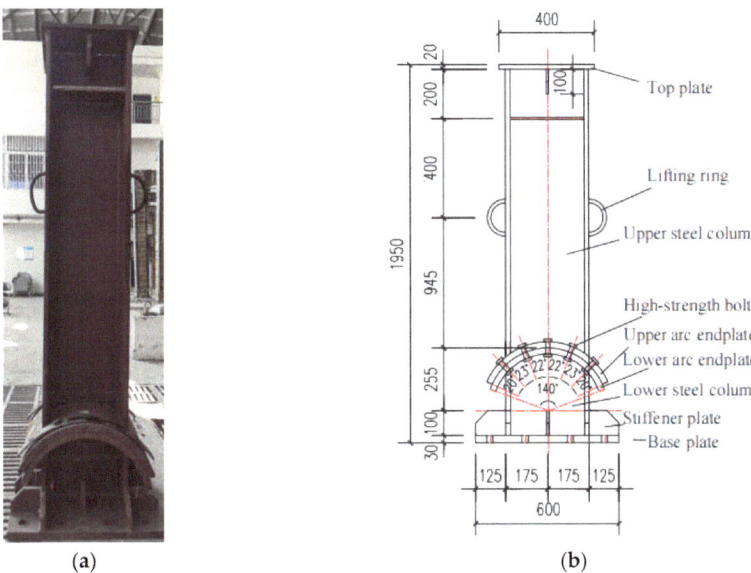

**Figure 3.** Design details of the specimen (unit: mm): (**a**) Specimen; (**b**) Dimensional drawings.

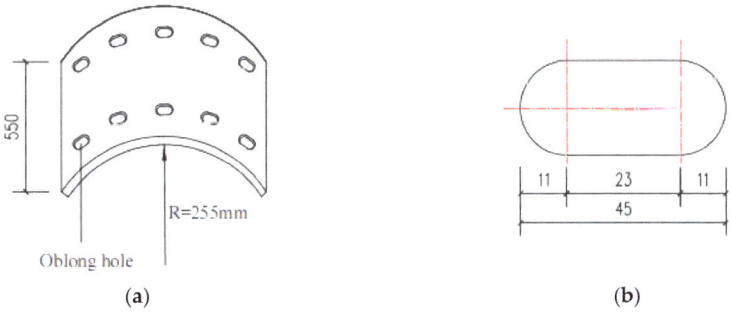

**Figure 4.** Dimensions of the upper arc end-plate: (**a**) the arc end-plate; (**b**) the oblong bolt holes (unit: mm).

Table 1. Parameters of the specimens.

| Specimen | Steel Column Section Size/mm | Axial Compression Ratio n | Washer Type | Whether to Use Brass Plate | Number of High-Strength Bolts | Horizontal Loading System |
|---|---|---|---|---|---|---|
| H350-1-1 | 350 × 350 × 12 × 19 | 0.1 | Ordinary | No | 10 | variable amplitude constant-amplitude loading |
| H350-2-1 | 350 × 350 × 12 × 19 | 0.2 | Bes | No | 10 | |
| H350-3-1 | 350 × 350 × 12 × 19 | 0.3 | Bes | No | 10 | |
| H350-4-1 | 350 × 350 × 12 × 19 | 0.3 | Bes | Yes | 10 | |
| H350-1-2 | 350 × 350 × 12 × 19 | 0.1 | Ordinary | No | 10 | constant-amplitude loading |
| H350-2-2 | 350 × 350 × 12 × 19 | 0.2 | Bes | No | 10 | |
| H350-3-2 | 350 × 350 × 12 × 19 | 0.3 | Bes | No | 10 | |
| H350-4-2 | 350 × 350 × 12 × 19 | 0.3 | Bes | Yes | 10 | |

*2.2. Material Properties and Determination of Anti-Slip Coefficient*

According to the test requirements, the steel used for the sample is Q345B. The material properties of the main parts of the specimen were tested by referring to ng the Chinese Code [18]. The test mechanical properties of steel are reported in Table 2, where $f_y$ and $f_u$ are the yield strength and maximum strength, respectively. $\Delta$ is the elongation. The anti-sliding coefficient of the steel sliding surface of the specimen is measured referring the Chinese Code [19], and the steel friction coefficient is also listed in Table 3, where the friction coefficient $\mu$ is determined by the formula $\mu = N_V/(n_f \cdot \sum P_i)$. $N_V$ is the slip load, $n_f$ is the number of friction surfaces, $\mu$ is the friction coefficient, and $\sum P_i$ is the sum of the measured values of the preload of the high-strength bolt when the specimen slips.

Table 2. Material properties.

| Type | Thickness (Actual Thickness)/mm | $f_y$/MPa | $f_u$/MPa | Elongation $\delta$/% |
|---|---|---|---|---|
| Web | 12(11.9) | 376 | 532 | 29.5 |
| Flange | 19(18.8) | 436 | 537 | 30.7 |
| Arc end-plate | 25(25.1) | 369 | 512 | 23.2 |

Table 3. Friction coefficient of steel sliding surface.

| Type | $\sum P_i$/kN | Sliding Load $N_V$/kN | Friction Coefficient $\mu$ |
|---|---|---|---|
| Single bolt specimen | 125 | 52.4 | 0.42 |
| Four bolts specimen | 500 | 205.6 | 0.41 |

*2.3. Testing Devices and Loading Regimes*

The test loading device is shown in Figure 5 and the column bottom is fixed to the foundation using high-strength bolts. The axial pressure is applied through a hydraulic jack placed at the top of the column. The axial compression ratio can be calculated by the formula, $n = N/(f_y A)$, where N is the axial load, $f_y$ and A are the yield stress of the steel, and the section area of the column, respectively. A stainless-steel sliding bearing with a coefficient of friction of 0.01 is provided between the jack and the reaction beam so that the jack rotates together with the steel column during the stressing process.

The horizontal displacement load is applied through the actuator, the distance between the height of the loading center of the actuator and the center of the inner diameter of the upper curved end-plate is 1600 mm, the maximum stroke of the hydraulic actuator is ±150 mm and the load range is 500 KN. The horizontal loading protocol refers to the Chinese code for the seismic design of buildings [20], and two loading protocols of displacement control method are used. The first loading mode is a constant variable amplitude loading scheme. The specimens are loaded at $0.25\Delta y$, $0.5\Delta y$ and $0.75\Delta y$ before sliding, cycling each stage only once. After the specimen slides, it is changed to equal displacement increment control and loaded according to 1.0Δy, 2.0Δy, 3.0Δy, ... , nΔy. The loading was carried out to 6.0Δy. Each stage was cycled three times (as shown in Figure 6a). Δy is the horizontal loading displacement of the loading center of the electro-hydraulic servo actuator when the arc end-plate of the specimen slides. The second loading method is a constant equal amplitude loading protocol, where the specified displacement Δy2 is given as 5–6 times Δy and the load cycle is repeated 30 times (Figure 6b). The test loading is stopped if the load drops below 85% of the peak load or if the specimen is visibly damaged.

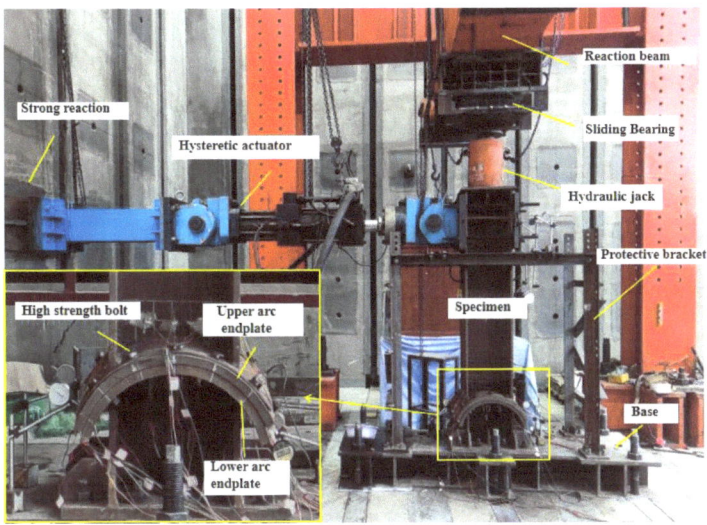

**Figure 5.** Test set-up.

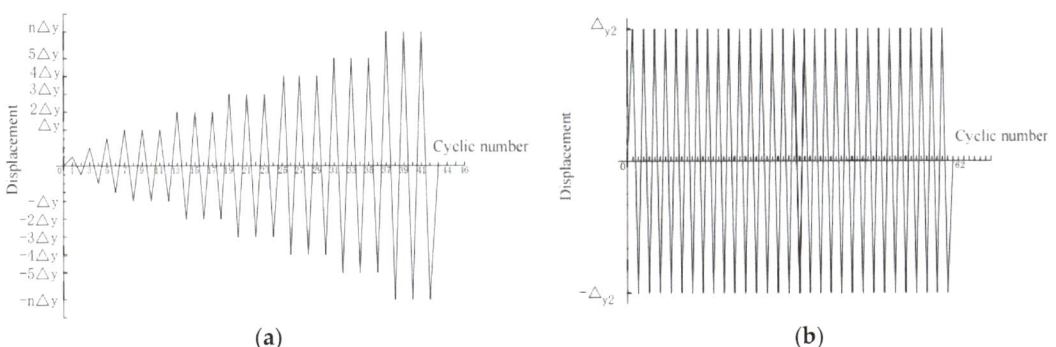

**Figure 6.** Horizontal loading protocol: (**a**) Variable amplitude constant-amplitude loading protocol; (**b**) Constant-amplitude loading protocol.

Before the test begins, the upper and lower arc end-plates should be aligned, and then the bolt preload should be applied to make full contact with the contact surface of the arc end plates. S8.8M20 high-strength bolts are used for this experiment, with a bolt preload of 125 kN, applied through a torque spanner, and a final construction torque of 330 N-m. Before the formal test, the specimen is preloaded and the test device and measuring equipment are checked for normal operation.

## 3. Description and Analysis of Experimental Phenomena

During the test, the specimen experienced two stages, i.e., the elastic stage and the rotational sliding-friction stage. The column base connection proposed in this paper is equivalent to the traditional steel column in the elastic stage. However, the upper and lower arc end-plates of column base connection are equivalent to friction dampers in the arc end-plate sliding-friction stage, in which the friction resistance was used to dissipate energy, in the arc end-plate sliding-friction stage, the specimen made different degrees of sound and vibration. After the test, it was observed that the surface of the arc end-plate had different degrees of abrasion. The specific phenomena and analysis are as follows.

### 3.1. Connection Rotation Slip-Friction

At the initial stage of the loading process, there is no rotation between the arc end-plates. At this time, the test specimen is in a state of elastic stress. When the loading reaches a certain degree, the rotation between the arc end-plates occurs, the static friction between the arc end-plates changes to dynamic friction, and the thrust of the hydraulic actuator decreases instantaneously. In the subsequent continuous loading process, intermittent slip rotation occurs between the arc-shaped end-plates, accompanied by varying degrees of sound and vibration. With the increase in cycle times, the degree of sound and vibration decreases, and the frequency increases. When it is loaded to 5 or 6 times the slip displacement $\Delta y$, the test is completed due to the connection rotation angle reaching 0.05 rad. The appearance of the test piece has no obvious deformation or damage.

### 3.2. The Abrasion of Arc End-Plate

Figure 7 shows the wear of the lower arc end-plates of specimens H350-1-1, H350-2-1 and H350-3-1 at the end of the test after the mixed constant and variable amplitude loading protocol. The arc end-plate of specimen H350-1-1 showed less wear and the wear was mainly distributed between the 1st and 2nd row of bolts from left to right, the 4th and 5th row of bolts, and near the bolt holes as well, as shown in Figure 7a. As the axial compression ratio increases, the area of the lower arc end-plate wear increases, gradually spreading from both sides of the end-plate to the middle area, the wear degree increases, and the grooves on the surface of the arc end-plate further deepen as shown in Figure 7b,c.

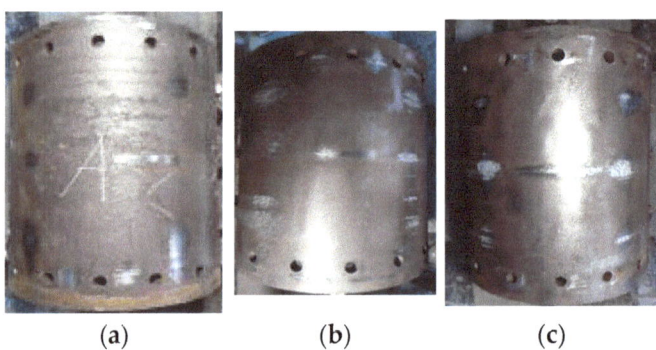

(a)          (b)          (c)

**Figure 7.** Influence of axial compression ratio on wear of lower arc end-plates: (**a**) H350-1-1; (**b**) H350-1-2; (**c**) H350-1-3.

H350-4-1 added a thin brass plate between the arc end-plates based on the test condition of H350-3-1, as shown in Figure 8a. At the end of loading, specimen H350-4-1, the surface of the brass plate in contact with the lower arc end-plate showed uneven plough groove-like wear. The wear was mainly distributed between the 1st and 2nd row of bolts from left to right, and the 4th and 5th row of bolts, as shown in Figure 8b. The lower arc end-plate of specimen H350-4-1 shows less wear than specimen H350-3-1, with a large amount of copper powder adhering to the contact area where the wear is more severe with the brass plate, as shown in Figure 8c. This is mainly because the brass plate material is soft, and the profile material is hard. Under the action of axial compression load and bolt preload, the brass plate is in full contact with the profile and the micro-convexity on the surface of the profile will be embedded in the brass plate. During the loading process, the steel column rotates and the harder micro bumps plough through the softer brass plate, causing eventual ploughing of the brass plate. However, the sound and vibration level of specimen H350-4-1 was louder and more pronounced than that of specimen H350-3-1.

**Figure 8.** Specimen H350-4-1: (**a**) H350-4-1; (**b**) Brass abrasion; (**c**) Abrasion of lower arc end-plate.

As shown in Figure 9, under the constant-amplitude horizontal loading protocol, the sliding abrasion area of the arc-shaped end-plate of the sample is expanded and the abrasion degree is increased. However, the abrasion area and degree near the bolt hole of the arc end-plate increase slightly. It can be seen from Figure 9 that after cyclic loading, a large number of abrasion iron chips are produced.

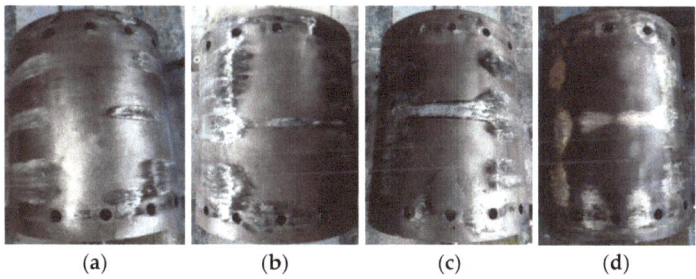

**Figure 9.** Wear on the friction surface of the lower arc end-plate of each specimen under an equal amplitude loading protocol: (**a**) H350-1-2; (**b**) H350-2-2; (**c**) H350-3-2;(**d**) H350-4-2.

As shown in Figure 10, an enlarged view of the abrasion part of the arc end-plate. the steel plate has an obvious convex abrasion when the axial compression ratio equals 0.3 (in Figure 10c). According to the tribology principle [21]: abrasion refers to the surface damage and shedding of two solid surfaces in sliding, rolling, or impact motion. Generally, inter-metal abrasion is divided into abrasive abrasion, adhesive abrasion, surface fatigue abrasion, and corrosion abrasion. In this test, the abrasion between arc end-plates is mainly adhesive wear and abrasive wear. According to the principle of friction [22], the sliding friction between metals is a process of adhesion and sliding alternately, and the friction force is the sum of resistance caused by the Adhesion Effect and Furrow Effect. With the increase in axial pressure, the friction force between sliding interfaces increases, so the Adhesion Effect and Furrow Effect increase, which leads to the serious abrasion of arc end-plates. During the test, a thin brass plate was added between the arc end-plates. Compared with steel plate, the friction force between steel plate and brass plate under the same pressure is less than that between steel plate and steel plate, so the Adhesion Effect and Furrow Effect between steel plate and brass plate are lower than that between steel plate and steel plate. Because of the material properties, the abrasion of the brass plate is greater than that of the steel arc end-plate (shown in Figure 8b).

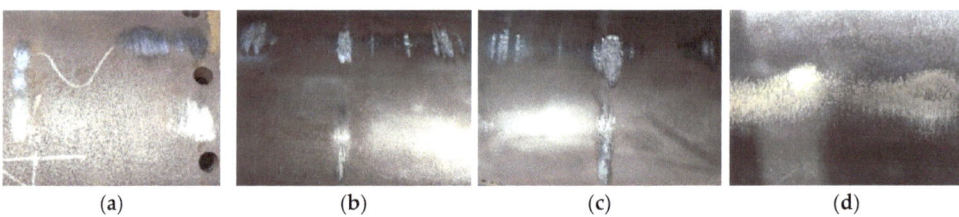

**Figure 10.** Local wear on the friction surface of the lower arc end-plate of each specimen under an equal amplitude loading protocol: (**a**) H350-1-1; (**b**) H350-2-1; (**c**) H350-3-1; (**d**) H350-4-1.

*3.3. Loss of Preload and Deformation of Bolt*

The washers used in the tests were Bes and normal high-strength bolt washers. The high-strength bolts were subjected to a construction torque applied by a torque spanner to produce a preload, with a final construction torque of approximately 330 N.m. The loss of preload after the high-strength bolt test was measured by an ultrasonic measuring device and a torque spanner. Normal high-strength bolt washers were used for specimens H350-1-1 and H350-1-2, where the load-displacement was reset to the initial position at the end of the loading test and the measured loss of construction torque was between 50% and 58.3%. Considering the severe loss of preload, Bes disc spring washers were used in subsequent tests and specimens with Bes disc spring washers showed a loss of construction torque of 0–50%, the extent of the loss of preload is shown in Table 4.

**Table 4.** Pre-tightening force loss of connecting high-strength bolts.

| Specimen I.D. | The Pre-Tightening Force of Bolts after Loading/N m | | | | |
|---|---|---|---|---|---|
| | No.1 Bolt | No.2 Bolt | No.3 Bolt | No.4 Bolt | No.5 Bolt |
| H350-1-1 | 125~150 | 125~150 | 125~150 | 125~150 | 125~150 |
| H350-1-2 | 125~150 | 125~150 | 125~150 | 125~150 | 125~150 |
| H350-2-1 | 225~250 | 225~250 | 225~250 | 225~250 | 225~250 |
| H350-2-2 | 150~175 | 175~200 | 175~200 | 175~200 | 150~175 |
| H350-3-1 | 250~275 | 275~300 | 275~300 | 275~300 | 250~275 |
| H350-3-2 | 175~200 | 175~200 | 200~225 | 175~200 | 175~200 |
| H350-4-1 | 175~200 | 250~275 | 250~275 | 175~200 | 175~200 |
| H350-4-2 | 150~175 | 175~200 | 225~250 | 175~200 | 150~175 |

The main reason for the loss of bolt preload is the interaction of bending moment, shear force and axial force (MVP) for the high-strength bolts connected at the column base proposed in this paper [23]. The friction between the bolt and the bolt hole causes the clamping length of the bolt to become longer, resulting in a decrease in the preload force of the high-strength bolt. At the same time, the interaction of the MVP and the mutual friction between the bolt and the bolt hole leads to the deformation of the bending moment of the high-strength bolt. Another reason for the decrease in the preload force of the high-strength bolts was that the connection of the curved end-plate is an asymmetric friction connection [24]. During the continuous loading test, the upper curved end-plate drove the bolts to rotate together as they turned. The bolt hole on the screw extrusion, shear effect, and the test piece rotation will cause vibration, so that the high-strength bolts loosen, reducing their preload. After the test, the bolt was removed and the bolt was found to be bent and deformed, as shown in Figure 11. Under the same axial pressure, the sliding vibration of specimen H350-4-1 between the connected curved end plates increased by the copper plate was greater than that of specimen H350-3-1, so the preload loss of the connected bolt increased after the copper plate was assembled.

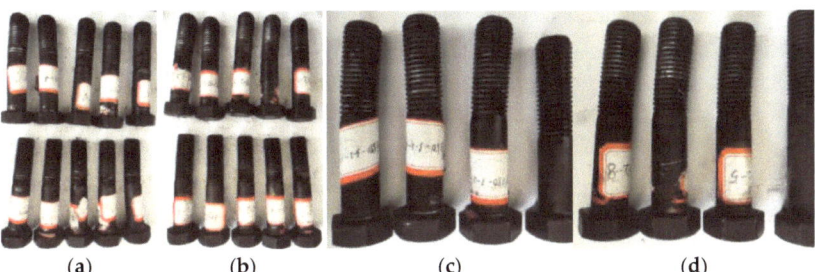

**Figure 11.** High-stre bolt of specimen: (**a**) H350-3-2 (**b**) H350-4-2; (**c**) Bending deformation of No.1, 9 and No.10 ngth bolts of H350-3-2; (**d**) Bending deformation of No. 5, No. 7 and No. 8 bolts of H350-4-2.

## 4. Test Results and Discussion

The hysteresis curve, also known as restoring force curve, is the load-displacement curve of the specimen under cyclic displacement loading. It is the basis for the analysis of specimen stiffness degradation, energy consumption, and seismic performance.

### 4.1. Hysteretic Curve

The Hysteresis curves from the variable amplitude constant-amplitude horizontal loading test were shown in Figure 12. The arc end-plates did not slide relative to each other during the initial loading period. The specimens were in the elastic state before the arc end-plate began to slip. Thus the load-displacement curves were approximated in a straight line. After the arc end-plate of the specimen slides, the slip section appears in the hysteretic curve, with the loading test, the load-displacement hysteretic curve is similar to the parallelogram. From Figure 12, the sliding load of the arc end-plate of the specimen increases with the axial pressure ratio. At the same time, after the circular end-plate slides, the curve slope in the slip stage of the hysteretic curve also increases. After the application of the brass plate, the buffeting amplitude of the specimen in the slip stage of the hysteretic curve increases significantly, the load-carrying capacity decreases, and the curve slope of the slip stage of the hysteretic curve decreases.

The horizontal load of each specimen showed different degrees of jitter, which was due to the influence of the adhesion mechanism and wear mechanism of friction when the objects in contact with each other and squeezed each other showed relative sliding, resulting in an unstable friction coefficient during the sliding process and thus an unstable jitter in the bearing capacity [22]. Compared with specimens H350-2-1 and H350-3-1, the hysteresis curve of specimen H350-1-1 was more dramatic in its jittering phenomenon, and the load showed a huge change when the horizontal displacement was loaded to −30 mm. The main reason for this is that there is a large amount of rust on the frictional contact surface of the specimen, and the sliding mechanism and friction mechanism are more complicated during the stressing process of the specimen. The high horizontal load on the specimen at the beginning of loading is mainly due to the fact that the horizontal load is mainly provided by the axial load and the static friction between the members. After the sliding of the arc end-plates, the static friction between the members turns into dynamic friction and the load-carrying capacity decreases rapidly. As the test progresses, the horizontal load-carrying capacity of the specimen increases. The main reason for this is that the specimen drives the bolts to slide together during the sliding process and a certain degree of tensile action occurs between the specimen and the bolts. On the other hand, errors in the assembly of the specimen prior to the test caused the upper and lower arc plates to not be perfectly aligned. Moreover, due to the complex mechanism of friction, the test piece was not completely reset during the sliding process, and there was an in-plane or out-of-plane deflection, resulting in an increase in the load-bearing capacity of the test piece during the stressing process.

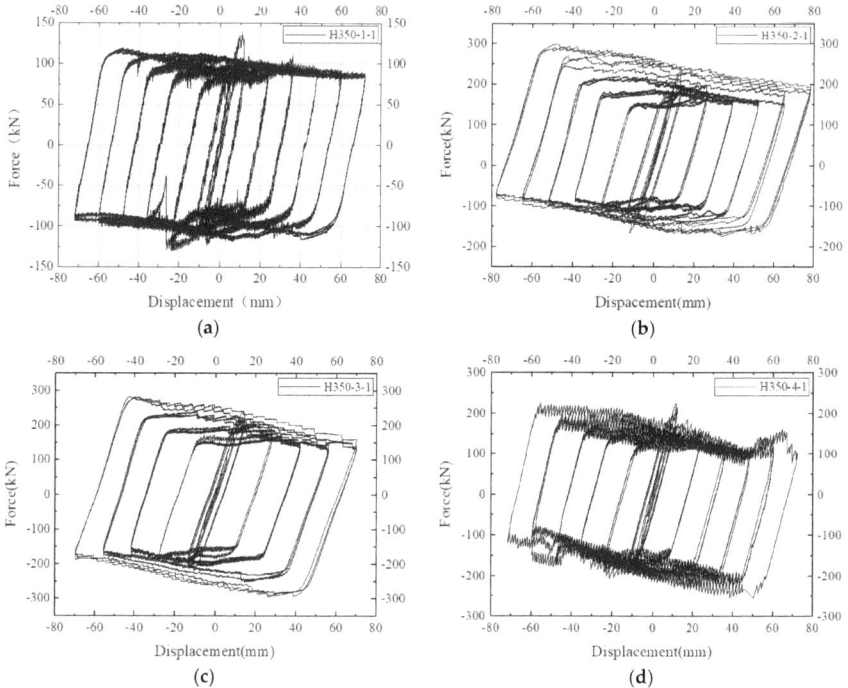

**Figure 12.** Force−displacement curves: (**a**)H350-1-1; (**b**)H350-2-1; (**c**) H350-3-1; (**d**)H350-4-1.

The hysteresis curves from the constant-amplitude horizontal loading test were shown in Figure 13. With the progress of cyclic loading, the horizontal force of the hydraulic actuator continues to decrease. When the test load is cycled to 10 times $\Delta y_2$, the horizontal force decreases more and more slowly. When the load is cycled to 20 times $\Delta y_2$, the decrease in the horizontal force is negligible. The load-carrying capacity of the specimen also decreases more and more slowly. It can also be seen from the figure that the decline rate of the load-carrying capacity of the specimen slows down after using Bes. The reason is the pressure and the Bes reduce the decrease in the pre-tension force of high-strength bolts due to the cyclic loading of large displacement. As the number of cyclic tests increase, the pre-tension force of high-strength bolts continues to decrease. When the test load is cycled to 10 times $\Delta y_2$, the reduction range of the pre-tension force of high-strength bolts decreases, and the supply of pressure between arc end-plates by high-strength bolts continues to decrease. When the load is cycled to 20 times $\Delta y_2$, the decrease in the pre-tension force of high-strength bolts is also negligible. At this time, although the pressure between arc end-plates is provided by axial pressure and the pre-tension force of high-strength bolts, the effect of axial pressure is greater than that of the pre-tension force of high-strength bolts. After adding brass between the arc end-plates, although the load-carrying capacity of the specimen with brass plate is reduced, the decreased rate of the load-carrying capacity of the sample is lower than that of the sample without brass.

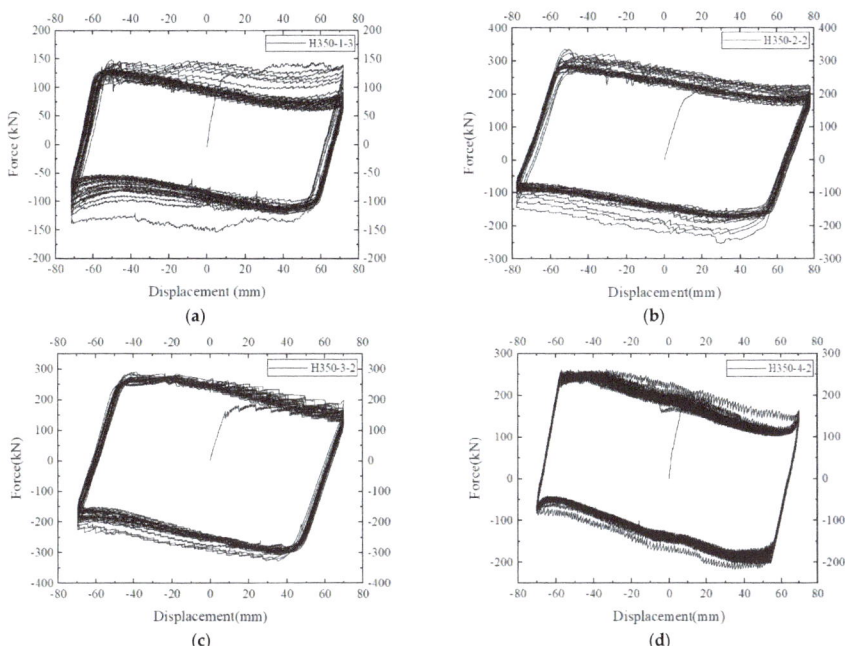

**Figure 13.** Force-displacement curves: (**a**) H350-1-2; (**b**) H350-2-2; (**c**) H350-3-2; (**d**) H350-4-2.

## 4.2. Skeleton Curve

Specimens H350-1-1, H350-2-1, H350-3-1, H350-4-1 were selected for analysis. The force-displacement skeleton curves were shown in Figure 14, and the characteristic values of the skeleton curves were reported in Table 5.

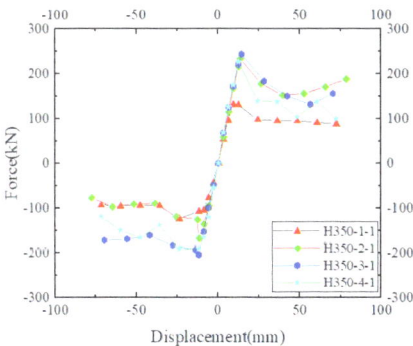

**Figure 14.** Force-displacement skeleton curves.

**Table 5.** Force and displacement at characteristic points of the skeleton curves.

| Specimen I.D. | Slip Threshold $F_y$/kN | Sliding Displacement $\Delta m$/mm |
|---|---|---|
| H350-1-1 | 139.9 | 11.9 |
| H350-2-1 | 233.4 | 12.8 |
| H350-3-1 | 242.8 | 13.6 |
| H350-4-1 | 225.1 | 11.8 |

From Figure 14 and Table 5, the skeleton curves of each specimen at the elastic stage coincide. The slip threshold and slip displacement of the specimen increase with the increase in axial pressure ratio, and the slope of the curve increases in the slip stage. After using the brass plate, the slip threshold and slip displacement of the specimen is reduced.

### 4.3. Stiffness Degradation

Specimens H350-1-1, H350-2-1, H350-3-1, and H350-4-1 were selected for analysis. Figure 15 shows the stiffness degradation curves of the specimens. The secant stiffness K is used to represent the stiffness degradation of the connection. At the initial stage of loading, the arc end-plate of the specimen did not slip, and the stiffness degradation of the connection was insignificant. After the arc end-plate of the connection slipped, the stiffness decreased significantly. Meanwhile, the stiffness degradation slows down gradually when the loading displacement increases. It can also be seen from the figure that the initial stiffness increased along with the increase of the axial compression ratio and the brass plate has no obvious effect on the initial stiffness of the connection when the axial pressure is the same.

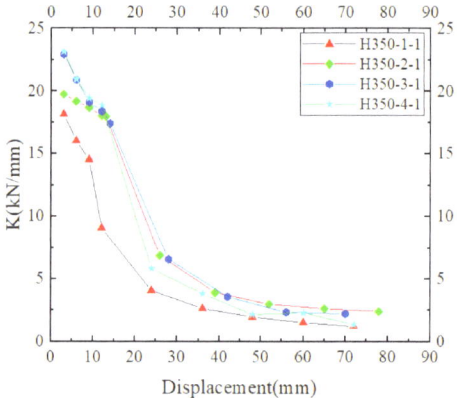

**Figure 15.** Stiffness degradation curves.

### 4.4. Energy Dissipation Behavior

To study the effect of vertical load and other variables on the energy dissipation ability of the connections, the equivalent viscous damping ratio and energy dissipation coefficient were calculated for the column base connections with slip-friction. The energy dissipation coefficient $E_d$ [21,22] is calculated by the following formula,

$$h_e = \frac{1}{2\pi} \cdot E_d \quad (1)$$

Specimens H350-1-1, H350-2-1, H350-3-1, and H350-4-1 were selected for analysis. The calculated $h_e$ and $E_d$ are listed in Table 6. The energy dissipation performance of the connections can be improved due to the application of the brass plates. Loss of the bolt preload can also be reduced by using the Bes, while energy dissipation performance is insignificantly effective. However, the energy dissipation performance of the connection is improved significantly when the vertical pressure increases. From the table, the connections have good energy consumption performance.

Table 6. The equivalent viscous damping ratios and energy dissipation coefficients.

| Specimen I.D. | Equivalent Viscous Damping Ratio/$h_e$ | Energy Dissipation Coefficient/$E_d$ |
| --- | --- | --- |
| H350-1-1 | 0.67 | 4.18 |
| H350-2-1 | 0.81 | 5.08 |
| H350-3-1 | 0.82 | 5.18 |
| H350-4-1 | 0.86 | 5.39 |

## 5. Conclusions

The seismic performance of steel column base connections with arc end-plates slip-friction was studied by conducting the test. The main conclusions are as follows:

(1) The steel column base connection with sliding arc end-plates has a good load-carrying capacity and hysteresis performance. The specimen dissipates seismic energy through the frictional behavior of the upper and lower arc end-plates, achieving a non-destructive performance of the column base connection, and the specimen can be used continuously after bolt replacement.

(2) Axial pressure is beneficial to the connection proposed in this paper. which can improve the load-carrying capacity, energy consumption performance, sliding threshold, and initial stiffness and reduce the loss of the pre-tension force of high-strength bolts.

(3) With the application of brass plate, although the load-carrying capacity of the connection decreases, the energy dissipation performance, Adhesion Effect and Furrow Effect of the steel column-based connection with arc end-plates the sliding-friction has been effectively improved, while the initial stiffness of the connection has no obvious influence.

(4) The use of Bes in connection can reduce the loss of pre-tension force of high-strength bolts, but it cannot avoid the deformation of high-strength bolts and has no significant impact on the seismic performance of the connection.

**Author Contributions:** Conceptualization, C.L. (Chengyu Li) and A.Z.; Methodology, C.L. (Chengyu Li) and A.Z.; Software C.L. (Cong Luo); Validation, C.L. (Chengyu Li) and C.L. (Cong Luo); Formal analysis, C.L. (Cong Luo); Investigation, C.L. (Chengyu Li). and A.Z.; Resources, C.L. (Chengyu Li); Data curation, C.L. (Chengyu Li) and C.L. (Cong Luo); Writing-original draft, C.L. (Cong Luo); Writing-review and editing, C.L. (Chengyu Li); Visualization, C.L. (Cong Luo); Supervision, C.L. (Chengyu Li) and A.Z.; Project administration, C.L. (Chengyu Li); Funding acquisition, C.L. (Chengyu Li). All authors have read and agreed to the published version of the manuscript.

**Funding:** This work was financially supported by the National Natural Science Foundation of China (Granted number: 51878522).

**Institutional Review Board Statement:** Not applicable.

**Informed Consent Statement:** Not applicable.

**Data Availability Statement:** The data presented in this study are available on request from the corresponding author.

**Conflicts of Interest:** The authors declare no conflict of interest.

## References

1. Miller, D.K. Lessons Learned from the Northridge Earthquake. *Eng. Struct.* **1998**, *20*, 249–260. [CrossRef]
2. Mahin, S.A. Lessons from Damage to Steel Buildings during the Northridge Earthquake. *Eng. Struct.* **1998**, *20*, 261–270. [CrossRef]
3. Suzuki, Y.; Lignos, D. Collapse Behavior of Steel Columns as Part of Steel Frame Buildings: Experiments and Numerical Models. In Proceedings of the 16th World Conference on Earthquake Engineering (16WCEE), Santiago, Chile, 9–13 January 2017.
4. Yang, T.S.; Popov, E.P. Experimental and Analytical Studies of Steel Connections and Energy Dissipators. Ph.D. Thesis, University of California, Berkeley, CA, USA, 1995.
5. Hsen-Han, K.; Clifton, C.; Butterworth, J.; MacRae, G.; Gledhill, S.; Sidwell, G. Development of the Self-Centering Sliding Hinge Joint with Friction Ring Springs. *J. Constr. Steel Res.* **2012**, *78*, 201–211.

6. Cavallaro, G.F.; Francavilla, A.B.; Latour, M.; Piluso, V.; Rizzano, G. Cyclic Response of Low Yielding Connections Using Different Friction Materials. *Soil Dyn. Earthq. Eng.* **2018**, *114*, 404–423. [CrossRef]
7. Iyama, J.; Seo, C.Y.; Ricles, J.M.; Sause, R. Self-Centering MRFs with Bottom Flange Friction Devices under Earthquake Loading. *J. Constr. Steel Res.* **2009**, *65*, 314–325. [CrossRef]
8. Borzouie, J.; MacRae, G.A.; Chase, J.G.; Rodgers, G.W.; Clifton, G.C. Experimental studies on cyclic performance of column base weak axis aligned asymmetric friction connection. *J. Constr. Steel Res.* **2015**, *112*, 252–262. [CrossRef]
9. Borzouie, J.; MacRae, G.A.; Chase, J.G.; Rodgers, G.W.; Clifton, G.C. Experimental studies on cyclic performance of column base strong axis–aligned asymmetric friction connections. *J. Struct. Eng.* **2016**, *142*, 04015078. [CrossRef]
10. Liu, X.; Chicchi, R.; Shahrooz, B. An Innovative Resilient Rocking Column with Replaceable Steel Slit Dampers: Experimental Program on Seismic Performance. *Eng. Struct.* **2019**, *183*, 830–840. [CrossRef]
11. Freddi, F.; Dimopoulos, C.A.; Karavasilis, T.L. Rocking damage-free steel column base with friction devices: Design procedure and numerical evaluation. *Earthq. Eng. Struct. Dyn.* **2017**, *46*, 2281–2300. [CrossRef]
12. Freddi, F.; Dimopoulos, C.A.; Karavasilis, T.L. Experimental evaluation of a rocking damage-free steel column base with friction devices. *J. Struct. Eng.* **2020**, *146*, 04020217. [CrossRef]
13. Latour, M.; Rizzano, G.; Santiago, A.; da Silva, L.S. Experimental response of a low-yielding, self-centering, rocking column base joint with friction dampers. *Soil Dyn. Earthq. Eng.* **2019**, *116*, 580–592. [CrossRef]
14. Elettore, E.; Freddi, F.; Latour, M.; Rizzano, G. Design and analysis of a seismic resilient steel moment resisting frame equipped with damage-free self-centering column bases. *J. Constr. Steel Res.* **2021**, *179*, 106543. [CrossRef]
15. Li, C.; Liu, Q.; Li, G. Seismic behavior of steel column base with slip-friction connections. *Materials* **2020**, *13*, 3986. [CrossRef] [PubMed]
16. Li, C.; Lai, Z. Study on Mechanical Performance of Column Base Joint with Slip-Friction Arc Endplates. In *Proceedings of the International Conference on Green Building, Civil Engineering and Smart City*; Springer: Singapore, 2023; pp. 1030–1038.
17. GB 50017–2016; Code for Design of Steel Structures. Ministry of Housing and Urban-Rural Development of China, Architecture & Building Press: Beijing, China, 2015.
18. GB/T 228-2010; Metallic Materials Tensile Test Method at Room Temperature. National Standards of the People's Republic of China, Architecture & Building Press: Beijing, China, 2002.
19. GB 50011–2010; Code for Seismic Design of Buildings. National Standards of the People's Republic of China, Architecture & Building Press: Beijing, China, 2010.
20. JGJ/T 101–2015; Specification of Testing Method for Earthquake Resistant Building. Ministry of Housing and Urban-Rural Development of China, Architecture & Building Press: Beijing, China, 2015.
21. Wen, S.Z.; Huang, P.; Tian, Y.; Ma, L.R. *Principles of Tribology*, 5th ed.; Tsinghua University Press: Beijing, China, 2018.
22. Chouery, K.E.; Kui, F.A.N.; Liang-jiu, J.I.A. State-of-the-art review of symmetric and asymmetric friction connections: Seismic behavior and design methods. *Eng. Mech.* **2021**, *38*, 22–37. [CrossRef]
23. Ramhormozian, S.; Clifton, G.C.; MacRae, G.A.; Davet, G.P.; Khoo, H.-H. Experimental Studies on Belleville Springs Use in the Sliding Hinge Joint Connection. *J. Constr. Steel Res.* **2019**, *159*, 81–94. [CrossRef]
24. Golondrino, J.C.C.; MacRae, G.A.; Chase, J.G.; Rodgers, G.W.; Clifton, G.C. Asymmetric Friction Connection (AFC) design for seismic energy dissipation. *J. Constr. Steel Res.* **2019**, *157*, 70–81. [CrossRef]

*Article*

# Flexural Behavior of Cold-Formed Steel Composite Floor Infilled with Desert Sand Foamed Concrete

Bin Yao [1], Yu Shi [2,3], Weiyong Wang [2,3,*], Qiang Wang [1] and Zhiyou Hu [1]

[1] Guiyang Engineering Corporation Limited of Power China, Guiyang 550081, China; yaobin_gyy@powerchina.cn (B.Y.); wangqiang_gyy@powerchina.cn (Q.W.); hzy931013@163.com (Z.H.)
[2] School of Civil Engineering, Chongqing University, Chongqing 400045, China; shiyu7811@163.com
[3] Key Laboratory of New Technology for Construction of Cities in Mountain Area (Chongqing University), Ministry of Education, Chongqing 400045, China
* Correspondence: wywang@cqu.edu.cn

**Abstract:** Desert sand foamed concrete (DSFC), which offers advantages, such as fire resistance, sound insulation, construction convenience, and environmental benefits, has not been used in cold-formed steel (CFS) composite floors. In this study, four full-scale specimens were designed and tested under four-point bending to investigate the effect of foamed concrete filling and holes. The load–deflection curves and strain distribution at mid-span were measured and analyzed. The experimental results indicated that the failure modes of the CFS composite floors were local buckling at the top flange for specimens without holes and tensile failure at the bottom flange for specimens with holes, respectively, which differed from the web crippling observed in non-composite floors. Moreover, due to the presence of foamed concrete, the flexural stiffness was significantly improved by 117.6% and 73.6% for the specimens without holes and with holes, respectively, while ultimate capacity increased by 224.9% and 121.8%, respectively. Through the nonlinear finite element models validated against experimental results, it was found that the flexural behavior was improved with the increase in CFS thickness and foamed concrete strength. The impact of the holes was not obvious for specimens infilled with holes.

**Keywords:** cold-formed steel; composite floor; flexural behavior; desert sand foamed concrete; four-point bending test

Citation: Yao, B.; Shi, Y.; Wang, W.; Wang, Q.; Hu, Z. Flexural Behavior of Cold-Formed Steel Composite Floor Infilled with Desert Sand Foamed Concrete. *Buildings* **2023**, *13*, 1217. https://doi.org/10.3390/buildings13051217

Academic Editor: Paulo Santos

Received: 14 April 2023
Revised: 29 April 2023
Accepted: 30 April 2023
Published: 5 May 2023

**Copyright:** © 2023 by the authors. Licensee MDPI, Basel, Switzerland. This article is an open access article distributed under the terms and conditions of the Creative Commons Attribution (CC BY) license (https://creativecommons.org/licenses/by/4.0/).

## 1. Introduction

Cold-forming is an industrial process that involves cold-rolling, brake-forming, and bending brake operations to transform flat steel panels into various sections. Due to the effects of cold forming, CFS exhibits significantly higher yield strength. This higher strength allows for thinner section thickness and lower steel consumption. However, thinner sections with lower width-to-thickness ratios increase the possibility of local buckling in compression zones, which can result in reduced cross-sectional area (effective section method) or diminished strength (direct strength method). To address this challenge in CFS floor systems, composite action can be introduced. The material with higher compressive strength in the compression zone can share compressive stress in CFS and also limit local deformation through the coating, infilling, or ample connections.

Concrete is the most commonly used building material due to its outstanding performance, and it was initially considered as a composite material for use in CFS floor systems. Hanaor [1] summarized typical configurations of composite sections and identified the key issue in implementing these designs as ensuring sufficient shear transfer between the concrete slab and the CFS beam. Full-scale experimental results demonstrated higher ductility and capacity than design assumptions. Subsequent studies, including experimental and numerical analyses on various shear connectors, were conducted by M. Hosseinpour et al. [2–4]. The most popular type of CFS floor system at present is the composition among the mortar casting in site, profiled steel plates, and joists or trusses considering the convenience of construction, and studies related to strength, stiffness, and ductility have been published in [5–7]. Meanwhile, compression zones, such as top flanges and top chords, have been embedded in concrete to improve composite action and limit local deformation in various studies [8,9]. All specimens showed similar failure modes with high ductility, namely the tension yielding of bottom flanges or chords.

Wood-based boards, such as oriented strand boards (OSBs), have been used to resist compression in CFS composite floors as structural sheathings, in addition to concrete. Xu et al. [10] investigated the vibration performance of lightweight residential floors supported by CFS C-shape joists sheathed with OSBs, while Zhou et al. [11] focused on flexural capacity and proposed a simplified evaluation method. Kyvelou et al. [12] conducted a series of four-point bending tests to examine the overall behavior and shear transfer mechanisms of self-drilling screws and structural adhesive, while Li et al. [13] proposed a new type of lightweight I-section bamboo–steel composite beam utilizing adhesive bonding.

In recent years, many innovative composite floor systems have been proposed and tested. In addition to mechanical properties, materials now need to fulfill additional functions, such as fire resistance, sound insulation, construction convenience, and environmental benefits. Tian et al. [14] proposed a new lightweight composite floor consisting of CFS trusses and a gypsum-based expanded polystyrene granule mortar (GEPM) slab which simplified floor details, improved sound and vibration absorption performance, and increased fire resistance. Shi et al. [15] applied gypsum-based self-leveling underlayment (GSU) cast on the profiled steel plate to CFS composite floors due to its ease of construction, cost efficiency, non-combustibility, and satisfactory serviceability performance. Wang et al. [6,7] combined CFS trusses with assembled autoclaved lightweight concrete (ALC) slabs to improve the assembly site. The flexural behavior out-of-plane and cyclic behavior in-plane were investigated.

Based on the above studies, an innovative CFS composite floor infilled with desert sand foamed concrete (DSFC) is proposed. Desert sand can be used in civil engineering instead of river sand as an environment-friendly resource with rich reserves. It also has advantages in terms of price and transport, particularly in regions adjacent to deserts. Using desert sand as the fine aggregate of foamed concrete not only reduces costs but also minimizes environmental damage. Extensive basic research achievements [16–21] on desert sand concrete have been published. In this study, DSFC was utilized as a filler to provide constraints for cold-formed thin-walled steel joists, which had lighter self-weight and improved thermal insulation performance. Calcium silicate boards (CSBs) were applied to decrease formwork. Four full-scale specimens were designed to investigate flexural behavior considering the effects of foamed concrete filling and holes, and were loaded through four-point bending tests. Nonlinear finite element models were developed and validated against experimental results. Parametric analyses were conducted by the verified FE models to assess the influences of CFS thickness, foamed concrete strength, and hole spacing.

## 2. Experimental Program

### 2.1. Specimen Details and Fabrication

Four full-scale floor specimens were fabricated to investigate the influences of desert sand foamed concrete filling and holes on flexural behavior. The general information of specimens is listed in Table 1.

Table 1. General information on the floor specimens.

| Specimen | Span (mm) | Width (mm) | Height (mm) | Component |
|---|---|---|---|---|
| CF-1 |  |  | 180 | CFS joists + CSBs |
| CF-2 | 3200 | 1800 | 180 | CFS joists + CSBs + DSFC |
| CF-3 |  |  | 200 | CFS joists with holes + CSBs |
| CF-4 |  |  | 200 | CFS joists with holes + CSBs + DSFC |

All specimens were 3200 mm long and 1800 mm wide with a 600 mm joist spacing. The joists with a section of C160 × 60 × 20 × 1.2 mm (height × width × lip length × thickness) were framed into an 1800 mm long U160 × 60 × 1.2 mm (height × width × thickness) CFS U-shape rim track at each end, and were fastened by ST4.8 self-drilling screws with an edge distance of 30 mm. To avoid possible local failure of end supports under a concentrated reaction, CFS stiffeners with a section of C100 × 55 × 20 × 1.2 mm were fastened to the web at each end of the joists with six ST4.8 screws. In addition, lateral bracing with a section of C160 × 60 × 20 × 1.2 mm was arranged at the trisection point and connected to the joists by ST4.8 screws and CFS angle steel. The general configuration of CFS framing is illustrated in Figure 1, while connection details are shown in Figure 2.

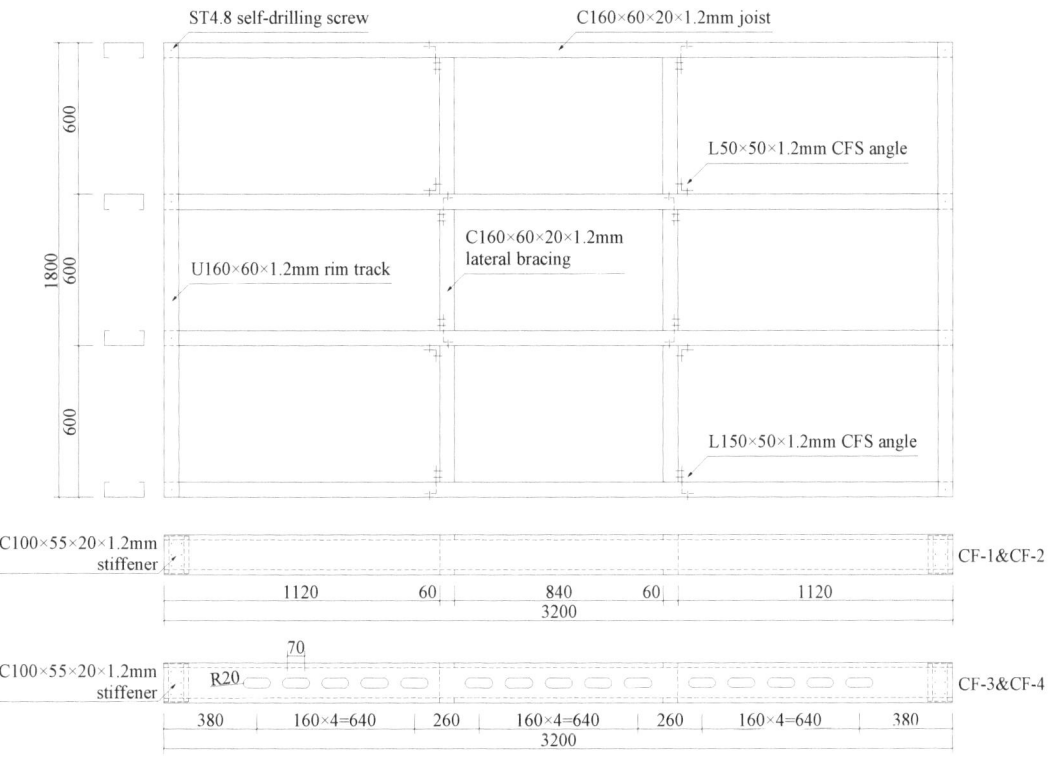

**Figure 1.** General configuration of CFS framing (unit: mm).

The layouts of CSBs and self-drilling screws are depicted in Figure 3. The section details of the specimens are shown in Figure 4. For specimens CF-1 and CF-2, CSBs were placed on both the top and bottom flanges and connected using ST4.8 self-drilling screws with a spacing of 140–150 mm. For specimens CF-3 and CF-4, CSBs were only placed on the bottom flanges to serve as formwork. DSFC was cast in and covered the top flange up to 30 mm. It should be noted that 10 × 10 × 1 mm steel wire meshes were embedded at the middle position of the top 30 mm DSFC to limit crack expansion.

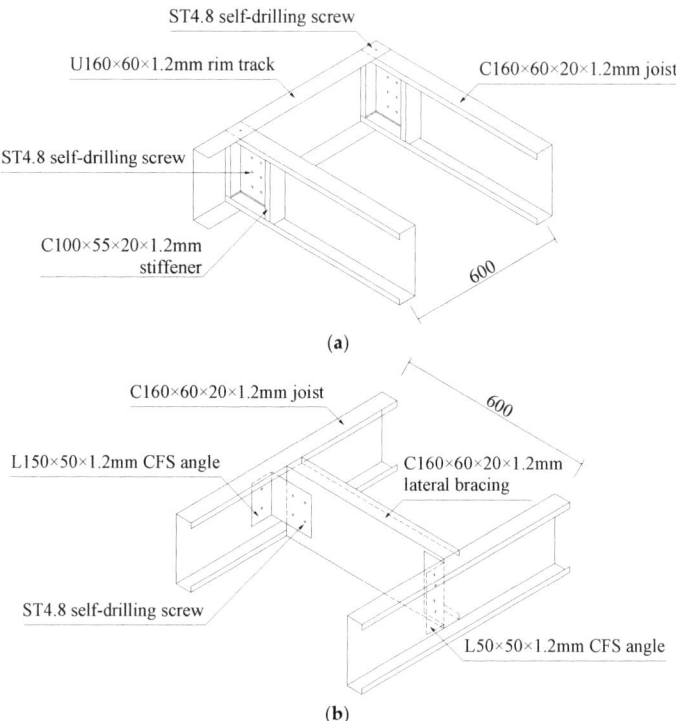

**Figure 2.** Connection details (unit: mm). (**a**) Web stiffener at each end of the joists; (**b**) lateral bracing at the trisection point.

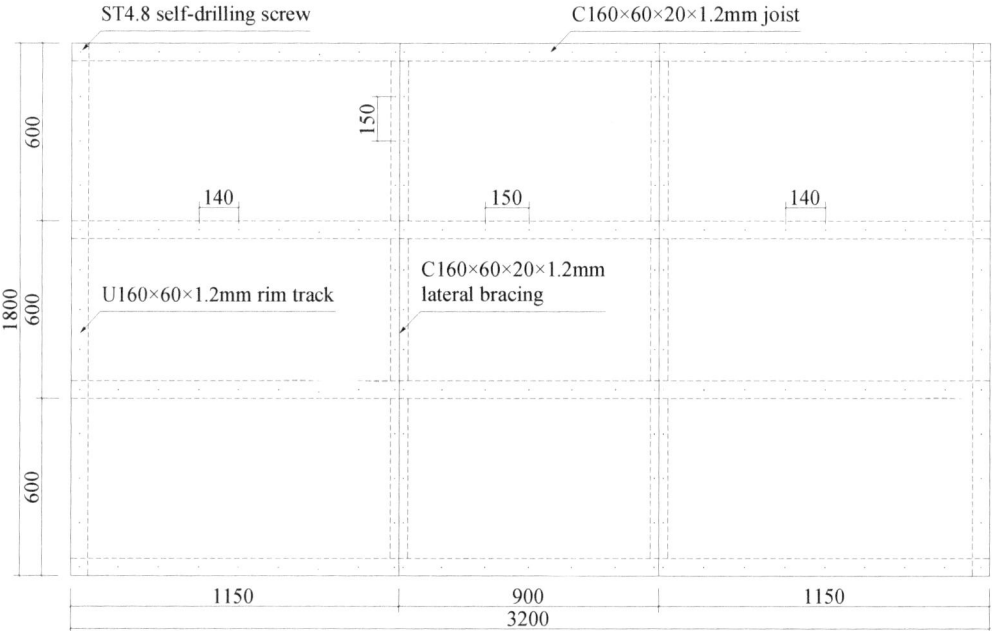

**Figure 3.** Layouts of the CSBs and self-drilling screws (unit: mm).

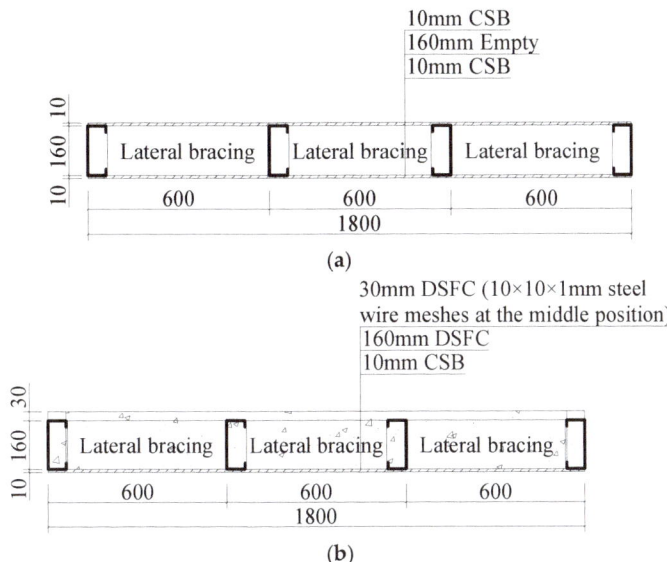

**Figure 4.** Section details of specimens (unit: mm). (**a**) CF-1 and CF-3; (**b**) CF-2 and CF-4.

## 2.2. Material Properties

The material property test process is shown in Figure 5. The material properties of the LQ550 cold-formed thin-walled steel were determined through metallic material tensile tests in accordance with GB/T 228.1-2021 [22]. Three coupons were tested, and stress–strain curves are shown in Figure 6, while the results are presented in Table 2. It is obvious that LQ550 cold-formed thin-walled steel, as a high-strength material, exhibited minimal strain hardening and poor ductility.

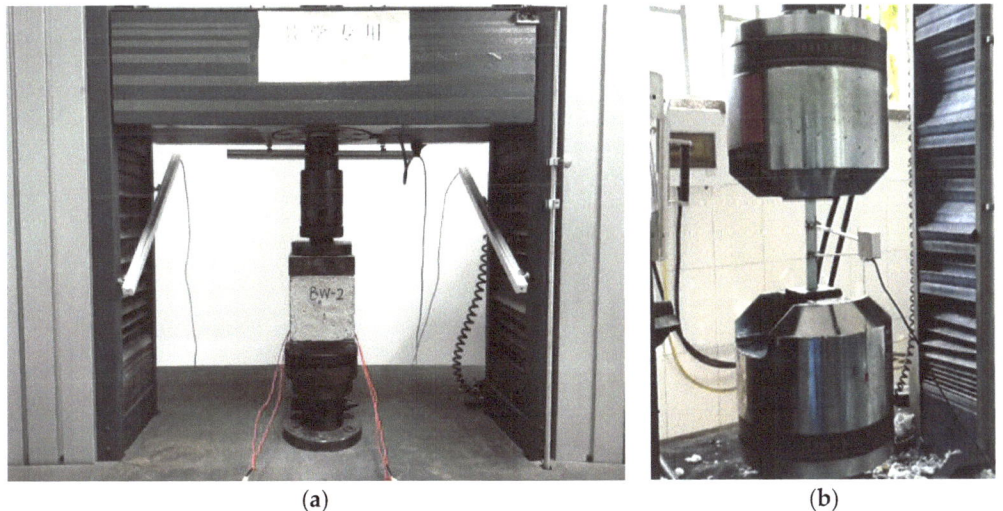

**Figure 5.** Material properties test. (**a**) Compression test; (**b**) tensile test.

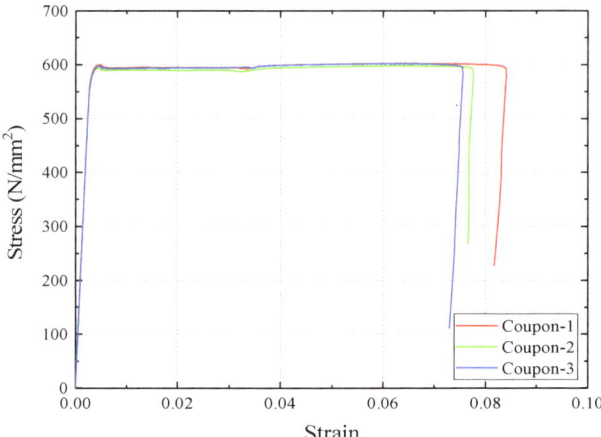

**Figure 6.** Stress–strain curves of LQ550 CFS.

**Table 2.** Properties of the CFS.

| Thickness (mm) | Elastic Modulus (MPa) | Yield Stress (MPa) | Ultimate Stress (MPa) | Elongation (%) |
|---|---|---|---|---|
| 1.2 | $2.12 \times 10^5$ | 594.36 | 601.75 | 16.1 |

Desert sand has a smaller particle size than natural river sand and manufactured sand. Desert sand from Lingshou County in Hebei Province was selected for this study, and its gradation is listed in Table 3. The mix proportions of the foamed concrete are listed in Table 4, where the cement was PO 42.5 ordinary Portland cement with a water–cement ratio of 0.28; the polycarboxylic high-efficiency water-reducing agent was used with a solid-liquid ratio of 0.4; the foaming agent used is the plant-based concrete foaming agent; polypropylene fiber with a volume ratio of 0.1% (0.9 kg/m$^3$) was added to limit the shrinkage of foamed concrete and improve its bonding behavior with cold-formed thin-walled steel. The mechanical properties of the DSFC were obtained based on JG/T 266-2011 [23]. Three $100 \times 100 \times 100$ mm cubic coupons were reserved during casting and cured under the same environment. Density, compression strength, and elastic modulus were measured, and the results are listed in Table 5. The material properties of the CSBs were obtained from the test report provided by the manufacturer, and summarized in Table 6.

**Table 3.** Gradation of desert sand.

| Particle size (μm) | 600 | 300 | 150 | <150 |
|---|---|---|---|---|
| Residue on sieve (%) | 24.4 | 23.4 | 49.2 | 3.0 |

**Table 4.** Mix proportion of foamed concrete.

| Cement (g) | Desert Sand (g) | Water (g) | Foam Volume (L) | Water-Reducing Agents (g) | Polypropylene Fiber (g) | Water-Cement Ratio |
|---|---|---|---|---|---|---|
| 450 | 150 | 126 | 1 | 3.6 | 0.9 | 0.28 |

**Table 5.** Properties of the DSFC.

| Density (kg·m$^{-3}$) | Compressive Strength (MPa) | Elastic Modulus (MPa) |
|---|---|---|
| 1042.0 | 4.80 | 3243.3 |

**Table 6.** Properties of the CSBs.

| Thickness (mm) | Density (g·cm$^{-3}$) | Flexural Strength (MPa) |
|---|---|---|
| 10.0 | 1.32 | 11.9 |

*2.3. Test Set-Up and Procedure*

In this study, two concentrated loads were applied at one-third of the span length to induce a pure bending moment on the mid-span of the composite floor for investigating its flexural behavior. The test set-up is shown in Figure 7. Steel blocks and steel beams were used as rigid supports, with hinge supports fixed on top to achieve simply supported boundary conditions. The specimen was supported on hinge supports at both ends, with a support length of 3000 mm. The loading width was controlled by shims to be 100 mm. A hydraulic jack was used for loading. Reaction forces were provided by the portal steel frame, and load distribution was achieved through spreader beams and hinges.

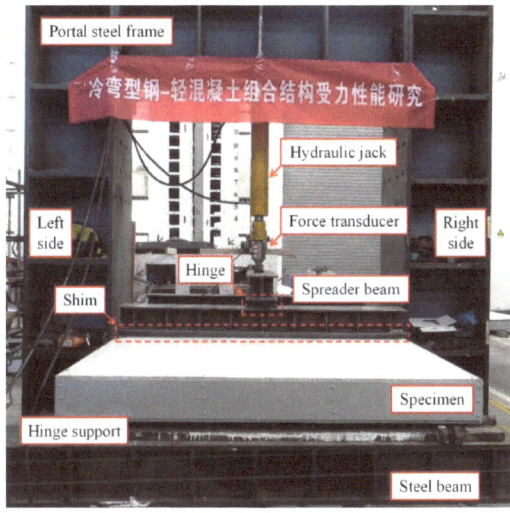

(**a**)

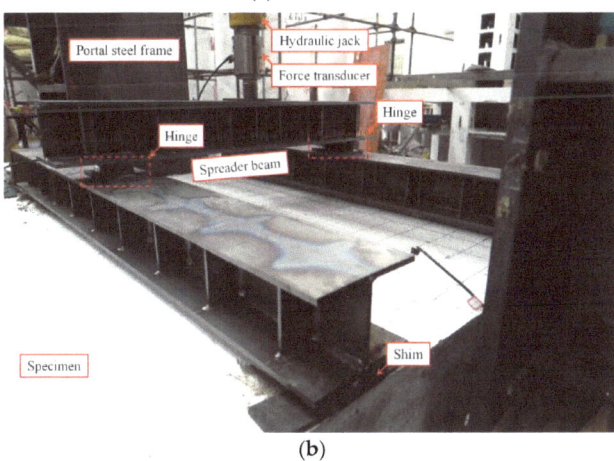

(**b**)

**Figure 7.** Test set-up. (**a**) Front view; (**b**) details.

The layout of transducers is illustrated in Figure 8. Considering the symmetry of the composite floor, the linear variable differential transformers (LVDTs) D1–D3 were used to measure the deflection of the composite floor within the half-span range. D1 and D2 were placed at the mid-span, while D3 was placed at the one-third span. Strain gauges G1–G11 were used to measure the strain distribution at the mid-span section of the composite floor to analyze the stress distribution of the maximum bending moment section and to verify whether the plane section assumption was valid.

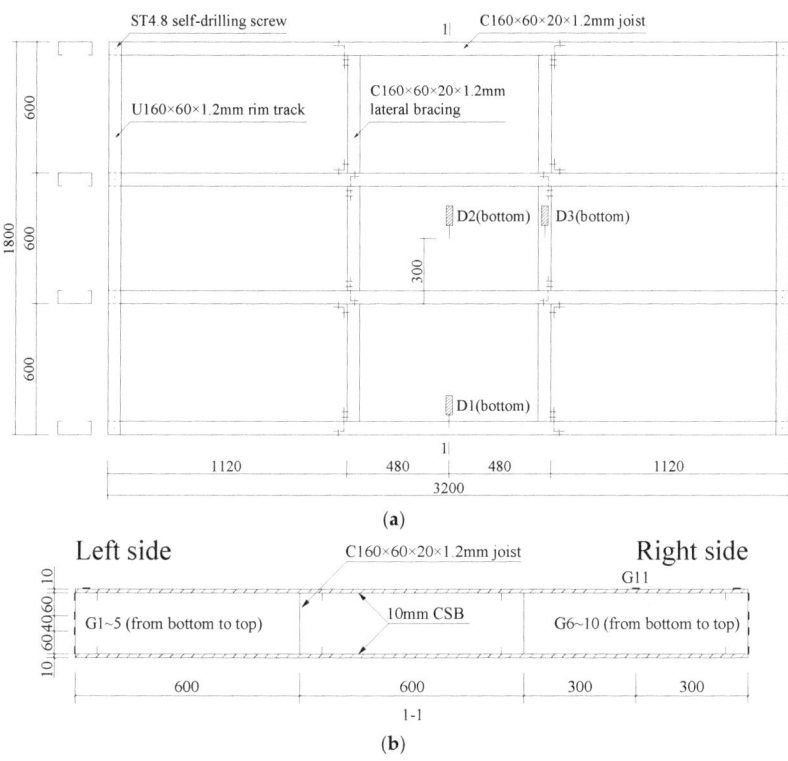

**Figure 8.** Layout of transducers (unit: mm). (**a**) LVDTs; (**b**) strain gauges.

Preloading is a very important part of the experiment, which can ensure full and tight contact between the device and specimen. It can also be used to test the reliability of the equipment and check whether the measuring instruments are working properly. In this study, preloading was carried out at a speed of 5 kN/min and unloaded when it reached 20 kN. The formal loading was performed in stages, with a loading increment of 10 kN at a speed of 5 kN/min. After the loading was completed, the load was held for 3 min. When the load reached its peak and stopped increasing, the loading controlled by displacement continued at a speed of 0.5 mm/min until the load dropped to 80% of the peak load, and then the loading was stopped.

## 3. Experimental Results and Discussion

### 3.1. Failure Phenomena and Modes

#### 3.1.1. CF-1

During the initial loading stage, there was no apparent experimental phenomenon. When loaded up to 30 kN, corner cracks appeared at the screw connections of the joint between the bottom CSBs (Figure 9a). At 42.6 kN, obvious local crippling occurred in the right CFS joist under the spreader beam, and the top CSB was crushed (Figure 9b), while the edge of the bottom CSB was pulled off (Figure 9c). At the same time, local failure occurred in the CSB at the mid-span top screw connections (Figure 9d). As the subsequent loading under displacement control progressed, the above damage and failures further intensified.

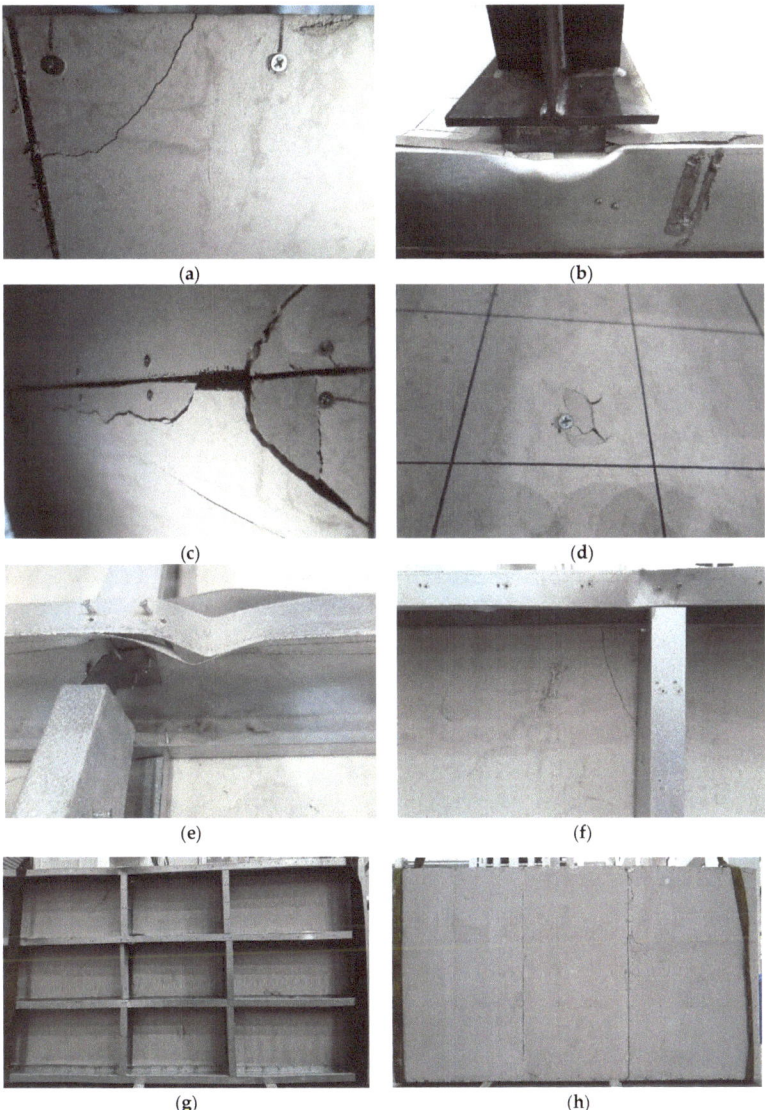

**Figure 9.** Failure phenomena of CF-1; (**a**) Corner cracks; (**b**) web crippling and CSB crushing; (**c**) edge fracture; (**d**) connection failure; (**e**) tearing; (**f**) local buckling; (**g**) failure form of CFS frame; (**h**) failure form of bottom CSB.

After the test, the top CSB was removed, and the deformation of the CFS joists was observed. It was found that the right joist broke the restraint of the single-sided CSB, causing web crippling. The middle joists were constrained by CSBs on both sides and had poor ductility due to the LQ550 grade and thin wall, which caused insufficient coordination of section deformation and resulted in tearing at the cold-formed position under the loading point (Figure 9e). Meanwhile, slight local buckling of the compression flange occurred at other sections (Figure 9f). The final failure forms of the cold-formed thin-walled steel joists and the bottom CSB are shown in Figure 9g,h, respectively. The failure mode of specimen CF-1 was web crippling and tearing of the steel joists under the loading point, which belongs to instability failure.

3.1.2. CF-2

During the initial loading stage, there was no apparent experimental phenomenon. When loaded up to 60 kN, cracks appeared around screw connections (Figure 10a); when loaded up to 80 kN, the cracks extended to both sides and connected (Figure 10b). At the same time, there were obvious tensile cracks in the bottom CSB (Figure 10c); when loaded up to 90 kN, the cracks further developed, and the bottom CSB gradually stopped working.

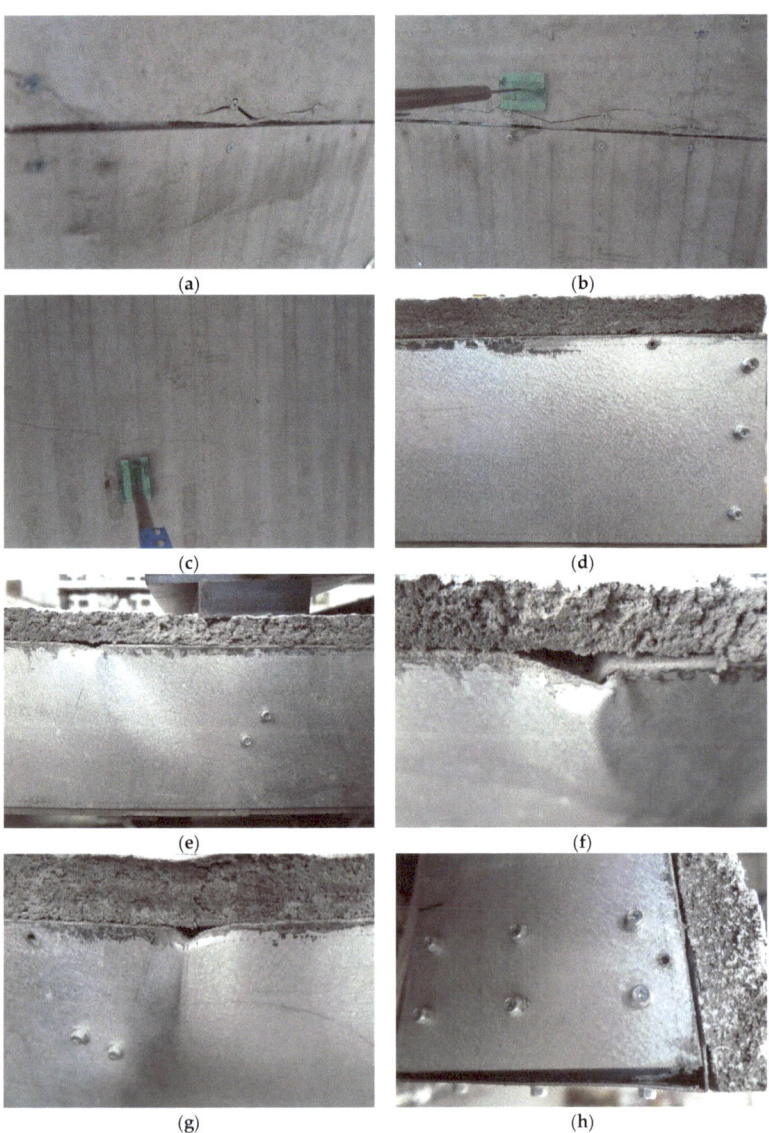

**Figure 10.** *Cont.*

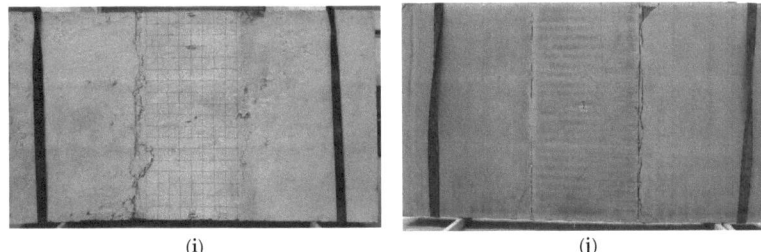

|   (i)   |   (j)   |

**Figure 10.** Failure phenomena of CF-2; (**a**) Cracks around screws; (**b**) extension of cracks; (**c**) joint cracks; (**d**) separation between CFS and DSFC; (**e**) local buckling (left-side); (**f**) tearing and crushing of DSFC under flange; (**g**) local buckling (right-side); (**h**) bulging of rim track; (**i**) failure form of DSFC; (**j**) failure form of bottom CSB.

When loaded up to 130 kN, separation occurred between the flange of CFS joists and DSFC at the end position (Figure 10d); when loaded up to 138.3 kN, local buckling occurred on the left CFS joist outside the loading point (Figure 10e). As the subsequent loading under displacement control progressed, the left-side local buckling further intensified, and the foamed concrete under the flange was crushed, resulting in tearing at the cold-formed position (Figure 10f). Meanwhile, local buckling occurred on the right CFS joist under the loading point (Figure 10g). The natural bonding effect between the foamed concrete and joists was completely lost, causing bulging of the rim track (Figure 10h). The final failure forms of the foamed concrete and the bottom CSB are shown in Figure 10i,j, respectively.

The failure mode of specimen CF-2 was local buckling and tearing of the compression side of CFS joists, which belongs to instability failure.

3.1.3. CF-3

During the initial loading stage, there was no apparent experimental phenomenon. When loaded up to 40 kN, corner cracks appeared at the screw connections of the joint between the bottom CSBs (Figure 11a). When loaded up to 50 kN, elastic buckling deformation occurred throughout the entire length of the CFS joists (Figure 11b); when loaded up to 60 kN, the buckling deformation intensified (Figure 11c).

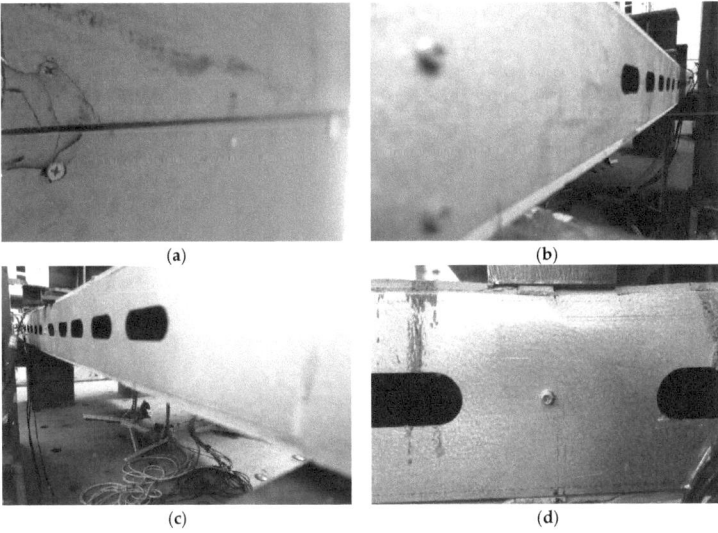

**Figure 11.** *Cont.*

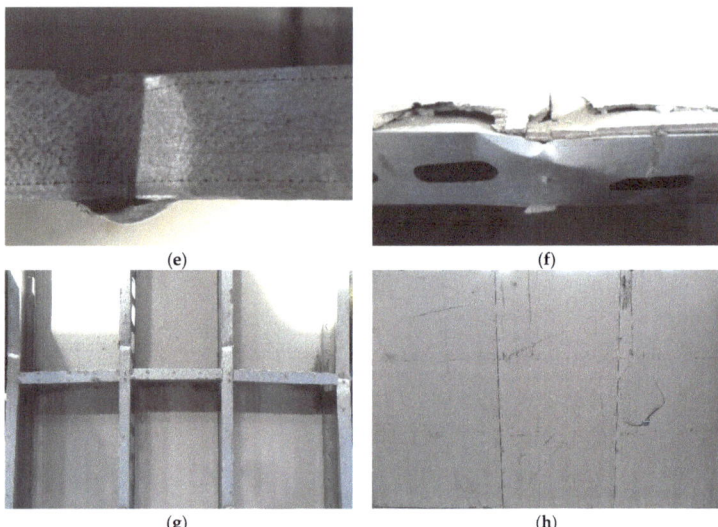

**Figure 11.** Failure phenomena of CF-3; (**a**) Corner cracks; (**b**) local buckling (left-side); (**c**) local buckling (right-side); (**d**) web crippling; (**e**) tearing; (**f**) web crippling and CSB crushing; (**g**) failure form of CFS frame; (**h**) failure form of bottom CSB.

When loaded up to 64.8 kN, local crippling occurred under the loading point of the CFS joist (Figure 11d). As the subsequent loading under displacement control progressed, the web crippling further intensified, resulting in the tearing of the CFS at the cold-formed position (Figure 11e) and crushing of the CSB under the spreader beam (Figure 11f). The final failure forms of the cold-formed thin-walled steel joists and the bottom CSB are shown in Figure 11g,h, respectively.

The failure mode of specimen CF-3 was web crippling and tearing of the steel joists under the loading point, which is the same as specimen CF-1 and belongs to instability failure.

3.1.4. CF-4

During the initial loading stage, there was no apparent experimental phenomenon. When loaded up to 70 kN, there was an obvious separation between the web of the CFS and foamed concrete (Figure 12a); when loaded up to 100 kN, two joint cracks appeared in the bottom CSB, and cracks around screws were observed (Figure 12b).

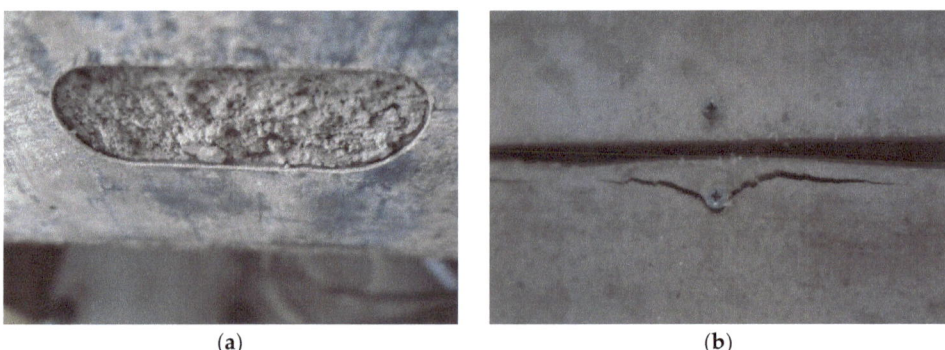

**Figure 12.** *Cont.*

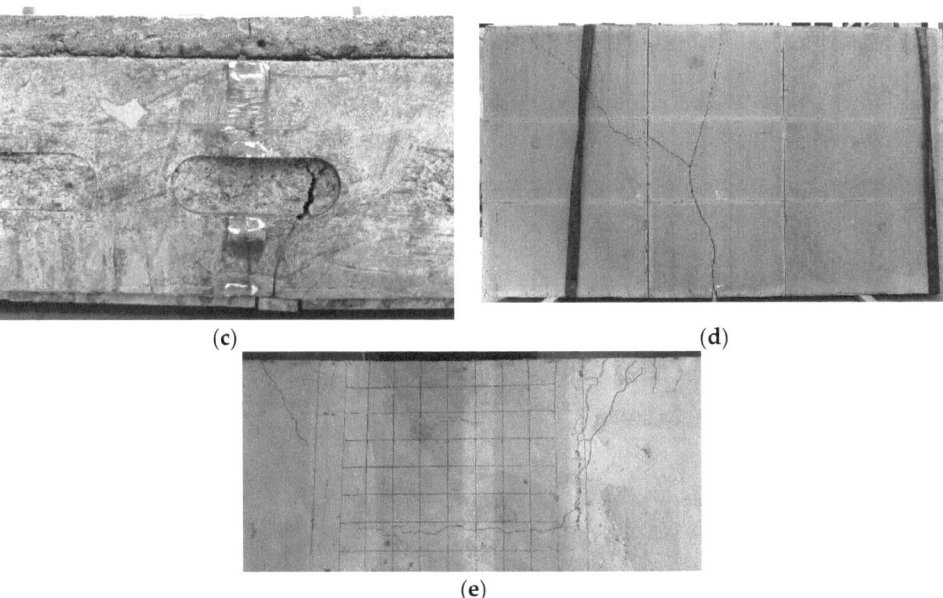

**Figure 12.** Failure phenomena of CF-4; (**a**) separation between CFS and DSFC; (**b**) cracks around screws; (**c**) tensile fracture of CFS and DSFC; (**d**) joint cracks; (**e**) arched cracks.

When loaded up to 143.6 kN, the section from the bottom flange to the hole edge of the right-side CFS joist at the mid-span position broke with a sudden "bang" sound (Figure 12c). Correspondingly, the upper web had slight outward bulging, and the lower foamed concrete had obvious tensile cracks (Figure 12c). At the same time, the bottom CSB panel broke completely, with the main crack forming a "Y" shape (Figure 12d). It should be noted that due to the poor ductility of the LQ550 grade cold-formed thin-walled steel, uniform distribution of the load cannot be achieved through section plasticity development, resulting in only one-sided CFS joist breaking, tilting of the composite floor, and arched cracks appearing on the top surface (Figure 12e).

The failure mode of the specimen CF-4 was tensile fracture of the CFS joists at the mid-span, which belongs to strength failure and also exhibits obvious brittle failure characteristics.

3.1.5. Comparison and Discussion

The experimental results indicated that the failure modes of the CFS composite floors were local buckling at the top flange for specimens without holes and tensile failure at the bottom flange for specimens with holes, respectively, which differed from the web crippling observed in non-composite floors. The reasons why foamed concrete improved the flexural behavior of composite floors result from two aspects. The first is the compression effect of foamed concrete, while the second is the restraining effect. For specimens without holes, the tensile capacity of the bottom flange was greater than the buckling capacity of the compressed flange. For specimens with holes, the weakening of the cross-section led to the fracture of the bottom flange before the buckling of the compression flange, and its failure mode was similar to that of a reinforced concrete slab.

*3.2. Load vs. Mid-Span Deflection Curves*

The relations between the load and mid-span deflection of composite floors are shown in Figure 13. Several important parameters that merit attention are summarized and listed in Table 7, where the slope $K$ at the allowable deflection $L/250$ [24] is defined as the flexural stiffness, and the corresponding load $F_{250}$ is defined as the normal use load. In addition, the peak load is represented by $F_p$, and the corresponding deflection is represented by $\Delta_p$. Based on the comparison of the load–deflection curves and characteristic parameters for each specimen, the following conclusions can be drawn:

(1) The introduction of foamed concrete filling significantly enhanced the flexural stiffness and ultimate capacity of the floor. The flexural stiffness $K$ increased by 117.6% and 73.6% for the specimens without holes and with holes, respectively, while $F_p$ increased by 224.9% and 121.8%, respectively.

(2) The specimens without holes (CF-1 and CF-2) displayed a more gradual decrease in bearing capacity after reaching the peak load, indicating better ductility. For specimen CF-2, the foamed concrete was compressed and compacted after reaching the peak load, which showed good ductility, and the load dropped sharply until the compression strain was too large and the CFS buckled and failed.

(3) The presence of holes increased the ultimate capacity of the composite floor. For the specimens without foamed concrete filling (CF-1 and CF-3), $F_p$ increased significantly by up to 52.2%. In general, the presence of holes weakens the cross-section of the CFS joists, reducing their capacity regardless of whether the final failure mode is local buckling or web crippling under the loading point. However, due to the high strength and poor ductility of the LQ550 grade cold-formed thin-walled steel used in this study, the deformation of CFS sections without holes was limited, and a tearing failure occurred at the cold-formed position before the full development of deformation. For the specimens infilled with foamed concrete (CF-2 and CF-4), $F_p$ only increased by 3.9%. The presence of holes improved the bond–slip behavior between foamed concrete and CFS, increasing the degree of composite action and making better use of the compression strength of the foamed concrete. However, the presence of holes also weakened the web section, causing a tensile fracture of the steel joist from the bottom flange to the hole edge, resulting in a strength failure. Consequently, the impact of holes on the ultimate capacity of specimens infilled with foamed concrete was not significant.

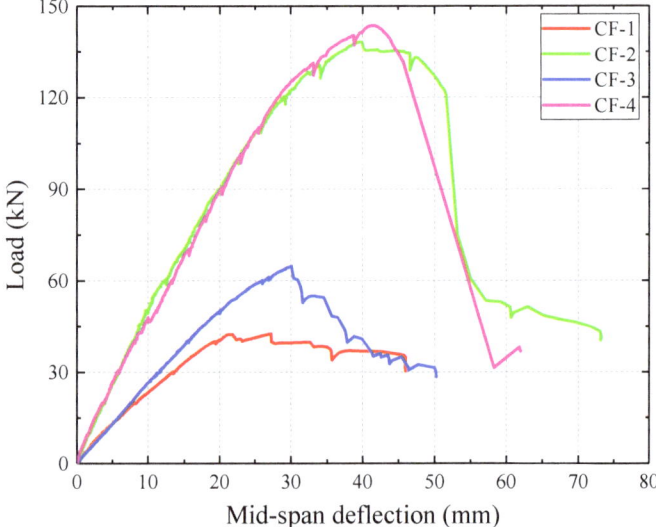

**Figure 13.** Load–deflection curves.

Table 7. Parameters summarized from test results.

| Specimen | L/250 (mm) | K (kN/mm) | $F_{250}$ (mm) | $F_p$ (kN) | $\Delta_p$ (mm) |
|---|---|---|---|---|---|
| CF-1 |    | 2.27 | 27.35 | 42.55 | 27.22 |
| CF-2 | 12 | 4.94 | 59.33 | 138.25 | 39.77 |
| CF-3 |    | 2.61 | 31.43 | 64.76 | 30.06 |
| CF-4 |    | 4.53 | 54.45 | 143.64 | 41.50 |

*3.3. Strain Distribution at Mid-Span Section*

The strain distribution of the side sections at mid-span for each specimen is summarized in Figure 14. The following conclusions can be drawn by observing the mid-span strain distribution:

(1) Foamed concrete was effective in constraining the buckling deformation of cold-formed steel. For the specimens without foamed concrete filling (CF-1 and CF-3), the CFS satisfied the plane section assumption during the initial loading stage ($\Delta = L/250$; $\Delta = L/200$). As the load approached the ultimate capacity ($\Delta = L/150$), abnormal tensile strains occurred at the height of 110 mm due to local buckling deformation that caused outward bulging. When load reached the peak ($\Delta = \Delta_p$), very large compressive strains occurred at the height of 110–170 mm due to the web crippling failure. For the specimens infilled with foamed concrete (CF-2 and CF-4), the foamed concrete prevented web crippling failure and effectively constrained the buckling deformation of CFS joists throughout the entire length, so that the CFS satisfied the plane section assumption during the entire loading process.

(2) Self-drilling screws had difficulty in achieving effective load transfer and coordinated deformation between the CSB and CFS. By comparing the strains at the CFS web (height of 170 mm) and the top surface of the CSB (height of 180 mm) for specimens CF-1 and CF-3, it can be found that as the load increased, the compressive strain of the CFS kept increasing, while the compressive strain of the CSB remained almost unchanged at a low level. Instead, local damage occurred at the stress concentration point where the self-drilling screws were connected to the CSB. This indicated that self-drilling screw connections struggled to achieve effective load transfer and coordinated deformation between the CSB and CFS.

(3) Partial composite action was achieved by the bonding effect between foamed concrete and CFS. By comparing the strains at the CFS web (height of 170 mm) and the top layer of the foamed concrete (height of 200 mm) for specimens CF-2 and CF-4, it can be found that as the load increased, the compressive strain of the CFS and the foamed concrete both kept increasing. For the specimen without holes (CF-2), the strain growth of the foamed concrete was relatively low, and only partial coordinated deformation was achieved. Moreover, the degree of composite action significantly decreased in the later loading stage due to the separation between the foamed concrete and CFS. For the specimen with holes (CF-4), the enhancement from the bond–slip behavior under holes resulted in a higher growth rate in the foamed concrete strain throughout the entire loading process, achieving fully coordinated deformation, and the section basically satisfied the plane section assumption.

(4) The strain distribution on the left and right sides of the CF-1 specimen was significantly different, which is consistent with its failure mode of only right-side crippling and buckling of the CFS joist.

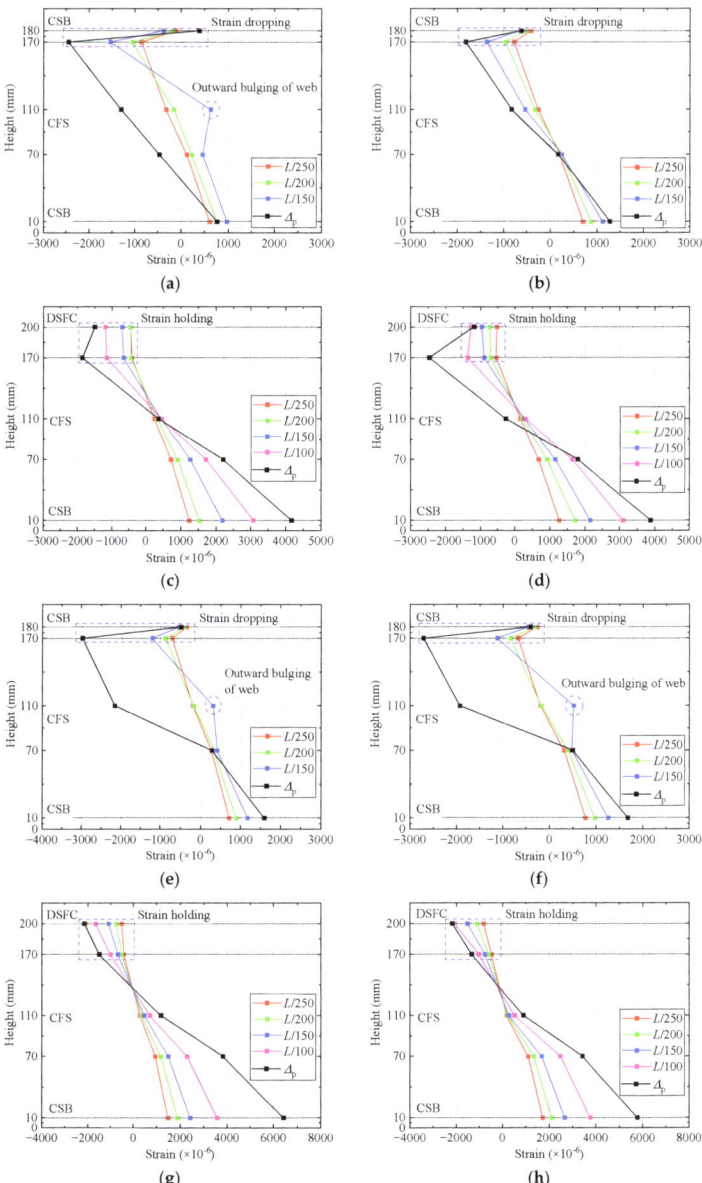

**Figure 14.** Strain distribution at mid-span; (**a**) CF-1 (right-side); (**b**) CF-1 (left-side); (**c**) CF-2 (right-side); (**d**) CF-2 (left-side); (**e**) CF-3 (right-side); (**f**) CF-3 (left-side); (**g**) CF-4 (right-side); (**h**) CF-4 (left-side).

## 4. Nonlinear Finite Element Analysis

### 4.1. Finite Element Modeling

In this study, three-dimensional nonlinear finite element (FE) models of specimens CF-2 and CF-4 were established by using the software ABAQUS to conduct intensive research on the flexural behavior of CFS composite floor infilled with DSFC, while specimens CF-1 and CF-3 were not under consideration due to the difficulty in considering the impact of tearing damage. This model only consisted of CFS framing and DSFC, while, owing to the negligible structural performance, CSB, steel wire meshes, and self-drilling screws were omitted to improve computing efficiency. CFS framing was simulated by the four-node shell element (S4R) due to the negligible effect in the thickness direction compared to the whole plane, while DSFC was simulated by the eight-node solid element (C3D8R). It is best to be an integer multiple of the mesh size of the embedded region for the mesh size of the host region to achieve reliable computational accuracy and efficiency. Therefore, the mesh size of the CFS framing and DSFC were both set as 30 mm.

The material properties adopted in the FE model were obtained from the material test results discussed previously. The isotropic elastic–plastic material model and bi-linear constitutive model were adopted on CFS. The yield strength, elastic modulus, and Poisson's ratio of CFS were 594.36 N/mm$^2$, 2.12 × 10$^5$ N/mm$^2$ and 0.3, respectively. A ductile damage model was applied to simulate the response of CFS. Moreover, the yield strength and elastic modulus of the DSFC were 4.80 N/mm$^2$ and 3243.3 N/mm$^2$, respectively. The Concrete Damaged Plasticity (CDP) model available in ABAQUS was used to simulate the response of DSFC. The relevant parameters are referred to [25] and listed in Table 8.

**Table 8.** Parameters of the CDP model.

| Dilation Angle | Flow Potential Eccentricity | $f_{b0}/f_{c0}$ | K | Viscosity Parameter |
|---|---|---|---|---|
| 30° | 0.1 | 1.16 | 0.6667 | 0.0005 |

Note: $f_{b0}/f_{c0}$ = ratio of the initial equi-biaxial compressive yield stress to initial uniaxial compressive yield stress; K = the ratio of the second stress invariant on the tensile meridian.

The embedded element technique was used to model the bonding contact between CFS and DSFC. The simply supported boundary conditions were adopted by restraining the corresponding displacements of the rim track bottom flange in the x, y, and z directions at one support, and restraining the displacements in the y and z directions at the other support. In addition, two rigid plates coupled by a reference point were built to apply load controlled by displacement to zones under the spreader beams, and a general contact interaction procedure was used with normal behavior ("hard" formulation) to avoid intrusion between units. Figure 15 illustrated the details of the FE model.

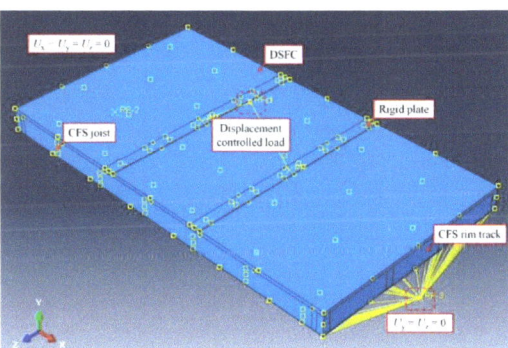

**Figure 15.** Details of the FE model.

*4.2. Verification of Finite Element Model*

Load–deflection curves obtained from tests and simulations are presented in Figure 16. The simulated ultimate capacity of specimens CF-2 and CF-4 are 136.97 kN and 138.28 kN, respectively, exhibiting a remarkable agreement with test results of 138.25 kN and 143.64 kN with the error of 0.9% and 3.7%, respectively. Moreover, the flexural stiffness of FE models is basically consistent with the experimental results within the error of 4.0%. Significant disparities between the simulation and experimental results in the descent section of load–deflection curves are revealed in Figure 16, and the simulation results show stronger ductility with a slow dropping because the actual failure modes of the specimens CF-2 and CF-4 involve the large deformation and fracture, which need to define more complex parameters to simulate the removal of failed elements. However, the descent stage is not the point of this study, so it is unnecessary to increase modeling difficulty and computational expense.

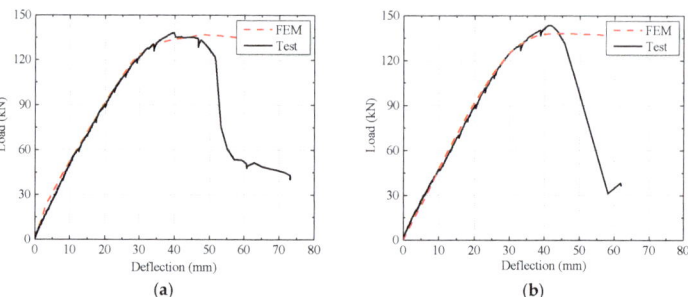

**Figure 16.** Comparison of load–deflection curves; (**a**) CF-2; (**b**) CF-4.

Stress distribution contours and comparisons with experimental phenomena are presented in Figure 17. Although the buckling deformation or fracture of the CFS is not demonstrated, the stress at the failure position has reached the ultimate value, which indirectly verifies that the failure mode of the simulation is consistent with tests.

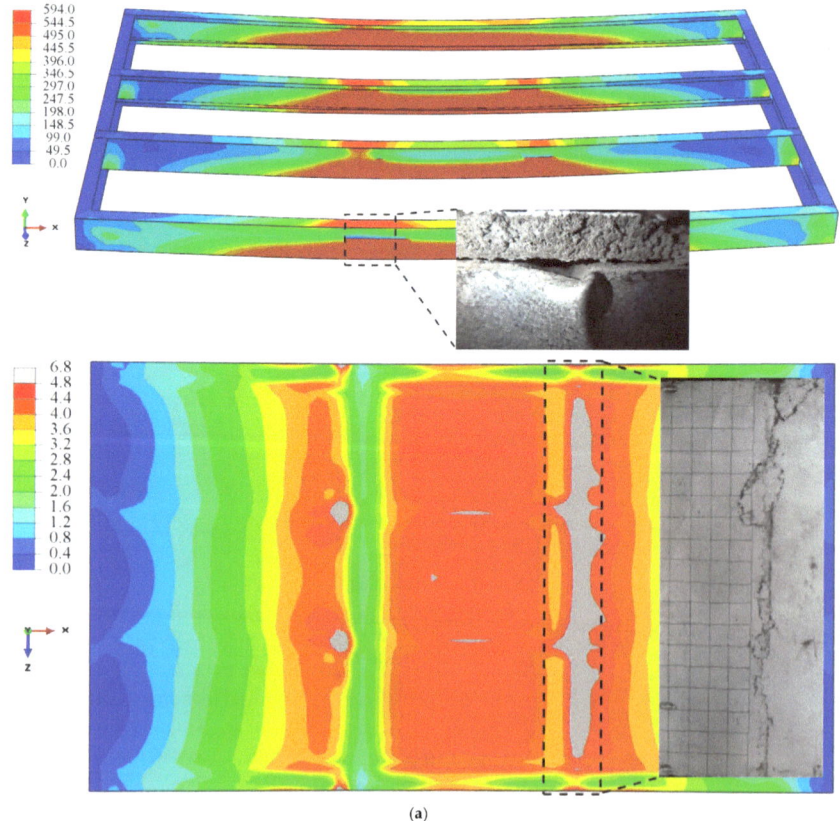

(**a**)

**Figure 17.** *Cont.*

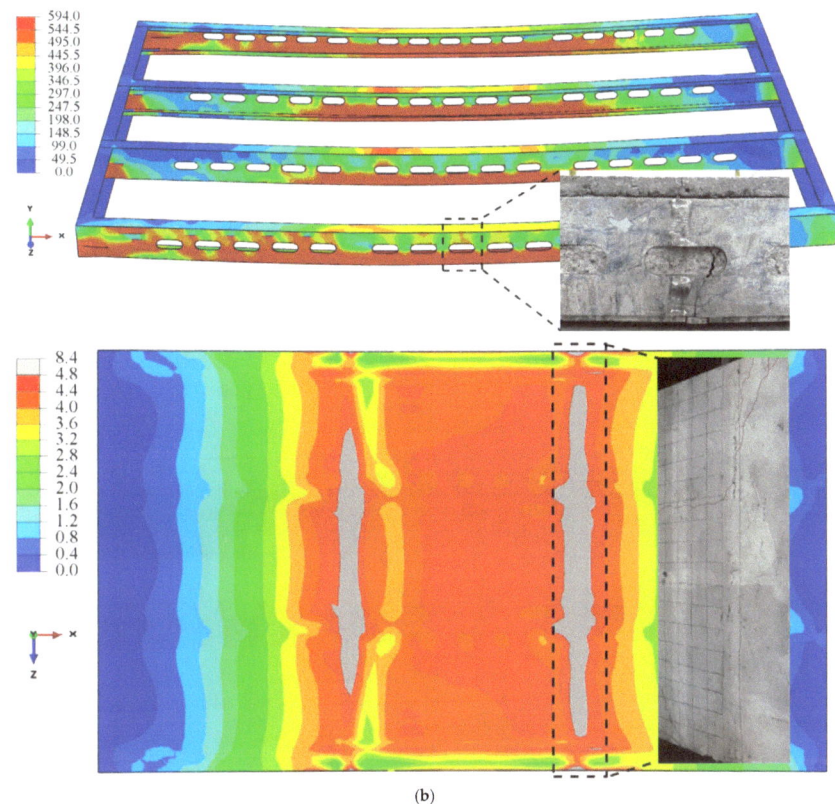

**Figure 17.** Stress distribution contours of the FE models (unit: MPa); (**a**) CF-2; (**b**) CF-4.

*4.3. Parametric Analyses*

To explore the effects of material and geometrical parameters on the flexural behavior of CFS composite floor, parametric studies were conducted by FE modeling. In this parametric study, the CFS joist thickness ($t$), foamed concrete strength ($f_c$), and hole spacing ($s$) were focused on. The flexural stiffness $K$ and ultimate capacity $F_p$ were analyzed and compared. It is worth noting that the change in density caused by the strength change in foamed concrete was not considered in this study, because of the uncertainty of the density–strength relationship.

4.3.1. Influence of CFS Thickness

The flexural behavior of the composite floor associated with the variation in the CFS thickness, as obtained from the FE modeling, is presented in Table 9 and Figure 18. When the CFS thickness increased from 1.2 to 1.8 mm, the corresponding enhancements of all specimens were nearly 30% for flexural stiffness and 40% for ultimate capacity, respectively. The increase in the thickness resulted in a significant improvement in the flexural stiffness and ultimate capacity of the composite floors. For cold-formed thin-walled steel, there was a very complex nonlinear relationship between thickness and effective section area. However, due to the adequate constraints of foamed concrete, full section efficiency was achieved, so that a clear linear relationship between thickness and flexural behavior was observed.

Table 9. Parametric analyses.

| Specimen | $K_{FE}$ | $R_{K,t}$ | $R_{K,fc}$ | $F_{p,FE}$ | $R_{F,t}$ | $R_{F,fc}$ |
|---|---|---|---|---|---|---|
| CF-1.2t-4.8fc | 5.00 | 1.00 | 1.00 | 136.97 | 1.00 | 1.00 |
| CF-1.5t-4.8fc | 5.67 | 1.13 | \ | 162.32 | 1.19 | \ |
| CF-1.8t-4.8fc | 6.34 | 1.27 | \ | 187.51 | 1.37 | \ |
| CF-1.2t-6.4fc | 5.33 | \ | 1.07 | 148.80 | \ | 1.09 |
| CF-1.2t-8.0fc | 5.60 | \ | 1.12 | 158.85 | \ | 1.16 |
| CF-160s-1.2t-4.8fc | 4.71 | 1.00 | 1.00 | 138.28 | 1.00 | 1.00 |
| CF-160s-1.5t-4.8fc | 5.68 | 1.21 | \ | 167.50 | 1.21 | \ |
| CF-160s-1.8t-4.8fc | 6.28 | 1.33 | \ | 196.52 | 1.42 | \ |
| CF-160s-1.2t-6.4fc | 5.06 | \ | 1.07 | 148.06 | \ | 1.07 |
| CF-160s-1.2t-8.0fc | 5.42 | \ | 1.15 | 157.16 | \ | 1.14 |
| CF-320s-1.2t-4.8fc | 4.98 | 1.00 | 1.00 | 139.78 | 1.00 | 1.00 |
| CF-320s-1.5t-4.8fc | 5.80 | 1.16 | \ | 168.72 | 1.21 | \ |
| CF-320s-1.8t-4.8fc | 6.44 | 1.29 | \ | 197.83 | 1.42 | \ |
| CF-320s-1.2t-6.4fc | 5.34 | \ | 1.07 | 150.23 | \ | 1.07 |
| CF-320s-1.2t-8.0fc | 5.63 | \ | 1.13 | 158.98 | \ | 1.14 |

Note: CF-160s-1.2t-4.8fc represents the specimen with a 160 mm hole spacing, 1.2 mm CFS thickness, and 4.8 N/mm² foamed concrete strength. $K_{FE}$ is the predicted flexural stiffness from FE analysis. $R_{K,t}$ and $R_{K,fc}$ are the corresponding ratios considering the influence of thickness and foamed concrete strength, respectively. $F_{p,FE}$ is the predicted ultimate capacity from FE analysis. $R_{F,t}$ and $R_{F,fc}$ are the corresponding ratios considering the influence of thickness and foamed concrete strength, respectively.

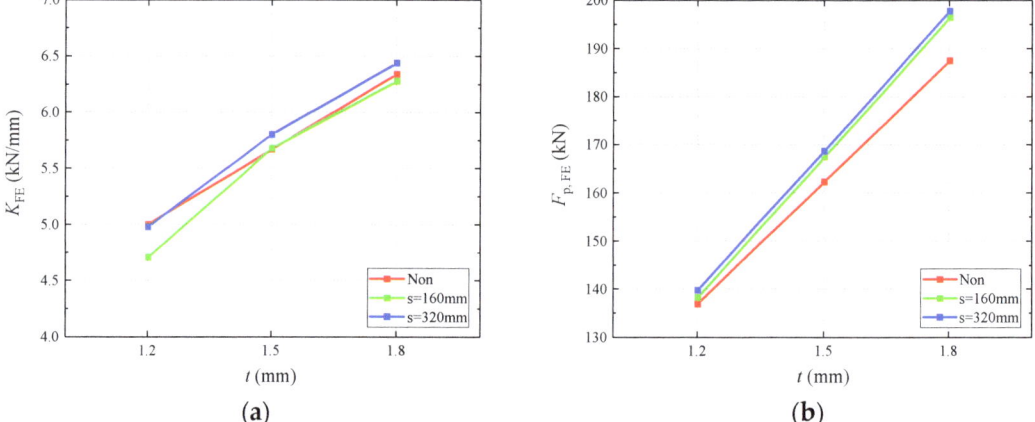

Figure 18. Influence of CFS thickness and hole spacing; (a) $K_{FE}$—$t$; (b) $F_{p,FE}$—$t$.

4.3.2. Influence of Foamed Concrete Strength

As indicated in Table 9 and Figure 19, the increase in the strength of foamed concrete resulted in improvements in both the stiffness and flexural capacity of the composite floor. The improvement in foamed concrete strength made the neutral axis move upward, increased the modulus of the flexural section, and improved the flexural behavior; on the other hand, it also improved the restraint effect on the local buckling of CFS joists. Regardless of the hole spacing, both the flexural stiffness and ultimate capacity were enhanced by nearly 15% when the foamed concrete strength increased from 4.8 to 8.0 kN/mm².

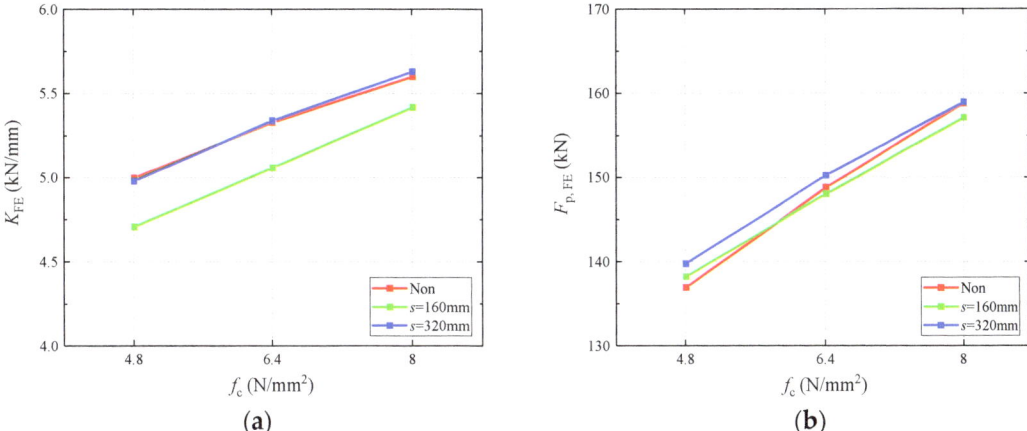

**Figure 19.** Influence of foamed concrete strength and hole spacing; (**a**) $K_{FE}$—$f_c$; (**b**) $F_{p, FE}$—$f_c$.

### 4.3.3. Influence of Hole Spacing

To investigate the influence of hole spacing on the flexural behavior of composite floors, the results obtained from the FE modeling are presented in Table 9 and Figures 18 and 19. Generally, the flexural behavior of CFS joists with un-stiffened holes will be greatly weakened compared to the joists without holes, due to the reduction in web stability [26–29]. In this study, the influence of hole spacing on flexural behavior was not significant on the whole. The holes enhanced the bond–slip behavior of the interface between the CFS and foamed concrete but weakened the section and changed the failure mode.

## 5. Conclusions

In this paper, the experimental investigation on the four full-scale specimens to determine the flexural behavior of cold-formed steel composite floors infilled with desert sand foamed concrete was presented. Then, the finite element models of the composite floor were established and validated with the test results followed by parametric analyses on CFS thickness, foamed concrete strength, and hole spacing. Based on the experimental and numerical results, the following conclusions were obtained:

(1) For specimens without foamed concrete filling, the failure mode was web crippling of cold-formed thin-walled steel joists under concentrated loads. The presence of holes weakened the section stiffness, allowing the deformation of LQ550 steel to fully develop. For specimens infilled with foamed concrete, the presence of holes changed the failure mode from tensile fracture to local buckling of CFS and crushing of constrained foamed concrete.

(2) Foamed concrete resisted compression in the compression zone and effectively constrained the buckling deformation of cold-formed thin-walled steel to improve the bearing capacity and stiffness of the composite floor.

(3) Self-drilling screw connections struggled to achieve effective load transfer and coordinated deformation between CSB and CFS. The bonding effect between DSFC and CFS achieved partial composite action, and the degree of composite action increased with the improvement in the bond–slip behavior from holes.

(4) The flexural behavior was improved with the increase in CFS thickness and foamed concrete strength. The impact of the holes was not obvious for specimens infilled with holes.

## 6. Future work

Based on the current research in this paper, it was found that foamed concrete can effectively improve the flexural behavior of the composite floor, because of the compression and restraint effects. Next, how to quantitatively consider the contribution of these two effects to the flexural capacity will be the focus of future work, including the estimate of the degree of composite action and the rectification of the effective width of compression plates. The final aim is to obtain a reliable design method for CFS composite floor infilled with foamed concrete.

**Author Contributions:** Writing—original draft, B.Y.; Investigation, Y.S.; Supervision, W.W.; Formal analysis, Q.W.; Validation, Z.H. All authors have read and agreed to the published version of the manuscript.

**Funding:** This research was funded by Guiyang Engineering Corporation Limited of Power China grant number [YJZD2019-01].

**Data Availability Statement:** The data presented in this study are available on request from the corresponding author.

**Conflicts of Interest:** The authors declare no conflict of interest.

## References

1. Hanaor, A. Tests of composite beams with cold-formed sections. *J. Constr. Steel Res.* **2000**, *54*, 245–264. [CrossRef]
2. Hosseinpour, M.; Zeynalian, M.; Ataei, A.; Daei, M. An experimental study on structural performance of U-shaped shear connector in composite cold-formed steel floor joists. *Eng. Struct.* **2021**, *249*, 113379. [CrossRef]
3. Hosseinpour, M.; Zeynalian, M.; Ataei, A.; Daei, M. Push-out tests on bolted shear connectors in composite cold-formed steel beams. *Thin-Walled Struct.* **2021**, *164*, 107831. [CrossRef]
4. Hosseinpour, M.; Zeynalian, M.; Daei, M.; Ataei, A. Numerical study on behavior of bolted shear connector used in composite cold-formed steel beams. *Thin-Walled Struct.* **2022**, *177*, 109377. [CrossRef]
5. Hsu, C.-T.T.; Punurai, S.; Punurai, W.; Majdi, Y. New composite beams having cold-formed steel joists and concrete slab. *Eng. Struct.* **2014**, *71*, 187–200. [CrossRef]
6. Zhang, Z.; Wang, J.; Xiao, Y.; Wang, W. Experimental and analytical assessments on flexural behaviour of CTLST composite beams. *Thin-Walled Struct.* **2019**, *138*, 15–31. [CrossRef]
7. Wang, J.; Wang, W.; Xiao, Y.; Guo, L. Cyclic behavior tests and evaluation of CFS truss composite floors. *J. Build. Eng.* **2020**, *35*, 101974. [CrossRef]
8. Lakkavalli, B.S.; Liu, Y. Experimental study of composite cold-formed steel C-section floor joists. *J. Constr. Steel Res.* **2006**, *62*, 995–1006. [CrossRef]
9. Güldür, H.; Baran, E.; Topkaya, C. Experimental and numerical analysis of cold-formed steel floor trusses with concrete filled compression chord. *Eng. Struct.* **2021**, *234*, 111813. [CrossRef]
10. Xu, L.; Tangorra, F. Experimental investigation of lightweight residential floors supported by cold-formed steel C-shape joists. *J. Constr. Steel Res.* **2007**, *63*, 422–435. [CrossRef]
11. Zhou, X.; Shi, Y.; Xu, L.; Yao, X.; Wang, W. A simplified method to evaluate the flexural capacity of lightweight cold-formed steel floor system with oriented strand board subfloor. *Thin-Walled Struct.* **2018**, *134*, 40–51. [CrossRef]
12. Kyvelou, P.; Gardner, L.; Nethercot, D.A. Composite Action Between Cold-Formed Steel Beams and Wood-Based Floorboards. *Int. J. Struct. Stab. Dyn.* **2015**, *15*, 1540029. [CrossRef]
13. Li, Y.; Shan, W.; Shen, H.; Zhang, Z.-W.; Liu, J. Bending resistance of I-section bamboo–steel composite beams utilizing adhesive bonding. *Thin-Walled Struct.* **2015**, *89*, 17–24. [CrossRef]
14. Tian, L.-M.; Kou, Y.-F.; Hao, J.-P.; Zhao, L.-W. Flexural performance of a lightweight composite floor comprising cold-formed steel trusses and a composite mortar slab. *Thin-Walled Struct.* **2019**, *144*, 106361. [CrossRef]
15. Shi, Y.; Yang, K.; Guan, Y.; Yao, X.; Xu, L.; Zhang, H. The flexural behavior of cold-formed steel composite beams. *Eng. Struct.* **2020**, *218*, 110819. [CrossRef]
16. Guettala, S.; Mezghiche, B. Compressive strength and hydration with age of cement pastes containing dune sand powder. *Constr. Build. Mater.* **2011**, *25*, 1263–1269. [CrossRef]
17. Luo, F.J.; He, L.; Pan, Z.; Duan, W.H.; Zhao, X.L.; Collins, F. Effect of very fine particles on workability and strength of concrete made with dune sand. *Constr. Build. Mater.* **2013**, *47*, 131–137. [CrossRef]
18. Bouziani, T. Assessment of fresh properties and compressive strength of self-compacting concrete made with different sand types by mixture design modelling approach. *Constr. Build. Mater.* **2013**, *49*, 308–314. [CrossRef]
19. Yan, W.; Wu, G.; Dong, Z. Optimization of the mix proportion for desert sand concrete based on a statistical model. *Constr. Build. Mater.* **2019**, *226*, 469–482. [CrossRef]
20. Zhang, M.; Zhu, X.; Shi, J.; Liu, B.; He, Z.; Liang, C. Utilization of desert sand in the production of sustainable cement-based materials: A critical review. *Constr. Build. Mater.* **2022**, *327*, 127014. [CrossRef]
21. Shi, Z. Green manufacturing of silicate materials using desert sand as a raw-material resource. *Constr. Build. Mater.* **2022**, *338*, 127539. [CrossRef]

22. GB/T 228-2021; Metallic Materials-Tensile Testing at Ambient Temperature. China Architecture & Building Press: Beijing, China, 2021. (In Chinese)
23. JG/T 266-2011; Foamed Concrete. Standards Press of China: Beijing, China, 2011. (In Chinese)
24. JGJ/T 421-2018; Technical Standard for Cold-Formed Thin-Walled Steel Multi-Storey Residential Buildings. China Architecture & Building Press: Beijing, China, 2018. (In Chinese)
25. Dai, S.; Zuo, Y.; Zhao, X.; Li, P. Research on effect of axial compression ratio on lightweight steel-foam concrete shear wall. *Earthq. Resist. Eng. Retrofit.* **2021**, *43*, 32–36. (In Chinese)
26. Yu, C. Cold-formed steel flexural member with edge stiffened holes: Behavior, optimization, and design. *J. Constr. Steel Res.* **2012**, *71*, 210–218. [CrossRef]
27. Zhao, J.; Sun, K.; Yu, C.; Wang, J. Tests and direct strength design on cold-formed steel channel beams with web holes. *Eng. Struct.* **2019**, *184*, 434–446. [CrossRef]
28. Chen, B.; Roy, K.; Uzzaman, A.; Lim, J.B. Moment capacity of cold-formed channel beams with edge-stiffened web holes, un-stiffened web holes and plain webs. *Thin-Walled Struct.* **2020**, *157*, 107070. [CrossRef]
29. Chen, B.; Roy, K.; Fang, Z.; Uzzaman, A.; Chi, Y.; Lim, J.B. Web crippling capacity of fastened cold-formed steel channels with edge-stiffened web holes, un-stiffened web holes and plain webs under two-flange loading. *Thin-Walled Struct.* **2021**, *163*, 107666. [CrossRef]

**Disclaimer/Publisher's Note:** The statements, opinions and data contained in all publications are solely those of the individual author(s) and contributor(s) and not of MDPI and/or the editor(s). MDPI and/or the editor(s) disclaim responsibility for any injury to people or property resulting from any ideas, methods, instructions or products referred to in the content.

*Article*

# Effect of Hidden Column Type on Seismic Performance of the Insulated Sandwich Wall Panel Joints with Ceramsite Concrete Layer

Lianghui Li [1], Shaochun Ma [1,2,*], Peng Bao [1,2] and Hao Wang [1]

1. School of Civil Engineering and Architecture, Henan University, Kaifeng 475004, China
2. Kaifeng Research Center for Engineering Repair and Material Recycle, Henan University, Kaifeng 475004, China
* Correspondence: scma@vip.henu.edu.cn

**Abstract:** Ceramsite concrete, with its advantages such as excellent long-term durability and thermal insulation properties, is suitable to be utilized as precast sandwich wall panels. While the lack of assessment of the seismic performance of such wall panel joints has been studied. Therefore, an experimental program was carried out to investigate and improve the seismic performance of the new type of wall panel joints. The seismic performances of the specimens were experimentally evaluated, including failure mode, loading and deformation capacity, ductility, the strain of vertically distributed steels, stiffness, and energy dissipation. The insulated sandwich wall panel joints have good seismic performance shown by the quasi-static test. The ductility coefficient of all specimens was greater than 3. The structure of the control group specimen presented a better match in stiffness, bearing capacity, ductility, and energy dissipation. The sleeve connection confirmed that the integrity of the joint, and the L-shaped hidden column could improve the ductility coefficient and equivalent viscous damping coefficient by about 4.2%. The results can promote the research of such wallboard system. This design approach of sandwich wall panel joints with lightweight concrete is broadly applicable to the exploration of more types of energy-saving wallboard systems.

**Keywords:** precast wall panel joint; sleeve joint; seismic performance; L-shaped hidden column; quasi-static test

**Citation:** Li, L.; Ma, S.; Bao, P.; Wang, H. Effect of Hidden Column Type on Seismic Performance of the Insulated Sandwich Wall Panel Joints with Ceramsite Concrete Layer. *Buildings* **2022**, *12*, 2214. https://doi.org/10.3390/buildings12122214

Academic Editors: Enfeng Deng, Xuechun Liu, Hongfei Chang, Liang Zong, Jiadi Liu, Ke Cao, Qi An, Xun Zhang and Tiago Miguel Ferreira

Received: 20 October 2022
Accepted: 12 December 2022
Published: 13 December 2022

**Publisher's Note:** MDPI stays neutral with regard to jurisdictional claims in published maps and institutional affiliations.

**Copyright:** © 2022 by the authors. Licensee MDPI, Basel, Switzerland. This article is an open access article distributed under the terms and conditions of the Creative Commons Attribution (CC BY) license (https://creativecommons.org/licenses/by/4.0/).

## 1. Introduction

The assembled concrete structure has been attractive and supportable from many governments as its advantages in terms of high industrialization, high product quality, and good environmental protection. Figure 1 summarized the literature with precast concrete as a keyword in each country in recent years. Due to the increased quotations abruptly from 2015 to 2021, which reflected that the assembled concrete structure had become a popular research topic. Currently, there is more attention on the seismic performance of wall panels in the assembled concrete structure, and it has been highlighted the need to improve their thermal properties. For example, Cong [1] focused on improving the fire resistance of wall panels to obtain better thermal insulation properties. Chikun [2] tried to utilize lightweight concrete to prepare structural wall panels. Thus, it is inevitable to improve thermal performance and develop the precast wall panels as well as wall panel joints in further work.

There are two methods to enhance the thermal performance of the precast wall panel joints. Firstly, the wall panel joints are equipped with insulation layers (e.g., internal, external, and sandwich insulation). Secondly, the materials of the joints show excellent thermal performance. Ceramsite concrete has high specific strength, low apparent density, and good thermal insulation properties, to present significant advantages as a material for wall panel joints [3]. Whereas sintered fly ash ceramsite concrete also has notable long-term durability and economic and environmental benefits [4,5]. Owing to the closed pore structures for sintered fly ash ceramsite, it would be potential to improve the long-term durability of ceramsite concrete results from the crystallization pressure generated by ice or sulfate attack. The ceramic particles would absorb water in the early stage of cement hydration and release during the cement hardening process, which can promote the degree of hydration and strengthen the bonding properties of the aggregate and cementitious materials. Thus, it provides excellent long-term durability for ceramsite concrete [6–10]. Generally, ceramsite concrete could be utilized in energy-efficient wall panel joints. For instant, Ma and co-workers reported the applications of assembled composite panels [11,12], ceramsite concrete combined with a sandwich insulation layer exhibited good thermal and seismic performance, and met the requirements of multifunctional wall panels. The temperature distribution and heat flux density of the inner surface and outer surface of the wallboard are analyzed by numerical simulation, which proves that the wallboard has good thermal performance [13]. However, the research on assembled ceramsite concrete sandwich composite wall panels still have not formed a system yet. And the joints of wall panels are the key to determining the integrity, safety, and reliability of assembled concrete structures. To optimize an appropriate structural form and prove the seismic performance of the joints is essential to develop such prefabricated assembled concrete structures.

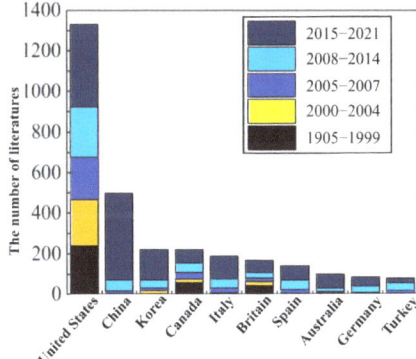

**Figure 1.** Literature Statistics of Prefabricated Concrete Structures in Various Countries.

The connection of vertical distributed steels is a crucial factor so to affecting their seismic performance [14–16]. Several literature have confirmed the excellent integrity and seismic performance of precast shear walls via using sleeve connections [17–19]. Khaled et al. [14] compared the seismic performance tests of shear walls with different types of steel connections. The results proved that the best seismic performance of the specimens with grouted sleeve connections and shear connectors was achieved, while bolted connections were not a good choice. Qian Jieru et al. [20] demonstrated the effect of different connection methods of vertical reinforcement on the seismic performance of precast shear wall specimens. The results showed that the energy dissipation capacity and the ultimate displacement angle of the specimens with sleeve connections were better than others. Therefore, it is feasible to use sleeve connections for vertical reinforcement in assembled wall panel joints.

On the other hand, some literature reported that utilizing various strength measurements such as concealed bracing, hidden columns, and steel trusses to ensure that energy-efficient wall panel joints possess good seismic performance. All these measurements could improve the lateral force resistance of wall panel joints [21–24]. The literature [25] compared the effect of section steel hidden column and channel steel hidden column on the seismic performance of ceramsite concrete wall panels and found that the type of hidden column had a significant effect on the seismic performance of the wall panels. However, the wall panel and the main structure are connected by bolt, which is more suitable for assembled steel structures. The boundary members have a significant influence on the working performance of wall panel joints, and there are few studies on the effect of different types of hidden columns on ceramsite concrete sandwich wall panel joints.

Herein, we proposed a new type of composite sandwich wall panel joint and aimed to investigate and improve the seismic performance of the joints. Two types of ceramsite concrete sandwich L-shaped composite joints were designed in this study. Ceramsite concrete as the structural layer material and polystyrene panels as the sandwich insulation layer, which was combined into a sandwich web by tension bars. The test program was composed of the test group and the control group. Specimens of the test group are composed of sandwich webs and a rectangular hidden column. The specimen of the control group is designed as an L-shaped hidden column and uses the grouted sleeve connections to connect the vertical distribution steels. The failure character, the strain of reinforcement, hysteresis curve, skeleton curve, stiffness degradation, energy dissipation capacity, and ductility of the specimen are investigated through the quasi-static test. Subsequently, the seismic performance of different types of specimens is evaluated according to the results to optimize the ideal construction formation of the joints. Consequently, it provided theoretical support for the application of assembled ceramsite concrete sandwich composite wall panel system and provide directions for more research on assembled concrete structures.

## 2. Materials and Methods

Quasi-static test is the most commonly used method to evaluate the seismic performance of structural members. Therefore, this paper mainly evaluates the influence of different factors on the seismic performance of joints by quasi-static test. Moreover, the mechanical tests of the materials used in the joint specimens are carried out, including the compressive test of ceramsite concrete and the tensile test of steel bar and sleeve. Based on the properties of the material used in the test, this paper can more accurately discuss the seismic performance of the specimen.

*2.1. Experimental Parameters and Plan*

Two groups of specimens were proposed in this study. The test group investigated the seismic performance of ceramsite concrete sandwich composite joints. Three specimens, L−1, L−2, and L−3 (cast-in-place joints with the rectangular hidden column), were designed. The control group tried to figure out the influence of the connection method between the vertical reinforcement and the hidden column construction on the seismic performance of wall slab joints. Therefore, TL−1 was assembled by sleeve connections and the L-shaped hidden column. The two groups of specimens were subjected to the quasi-static test, and the seismic performance of the specimens was evaluated by analyzing the damage characteristics, including loading and deformation capacity, ductility, and energy dissipation capacity.

*2.2. Test Specimen*

1. Cast-in-place joints with the rectangular hidden column (L−1, L−2, and L−3): The load beam, the hidden column, sandwich webs, and the base beam were cast into the whole. The dimension of the sandwich webs is 582.5 mm (length) × 240 mm (width) × 1280 mm (height). The section of the hidden column is 240 mm × 240 mm. Figures 2 and 3 are the schematic representation of the specimen size, arrangements of rebars, and connections in the specimens. Rebars of C8 (strength level is HRB400 and the diameter is 8 mm) are employed as distributed rebars with a spacing of 150 mm (C8@150), distributed in the structural layer on both sides of the web. The rebars of HPB300 strength level are used as tie bars in the sandwich webs. All longitudinal rebars of the webs were anchored to the base beam.
2. Assembled joint with L-shaped hidden column (TL−1): The load beam and the sandwich webs were cast together. The base beam was prefabricated separately. Then,

the vertical distributed reinforcement in the webs and the rebars reserved on the base beam, which were connected by GTZB4-14-B semi-grouted sleeves. The L-shaped hidden column was employed between the webs of the specimen. The dimension of the sandwich webs is 240 mm (width) × 450 mm (length) × 1280 mm (height). Rebars of C8 are used as distributed rebars with a spacing of 150 mm (C8@150), distributed in the structural layer on both sides of the web. The rebars of HPB300 strength level were used as tie bars in the sandwich webs. The horizontally distributed rebars in the webs extend into the hidden column.

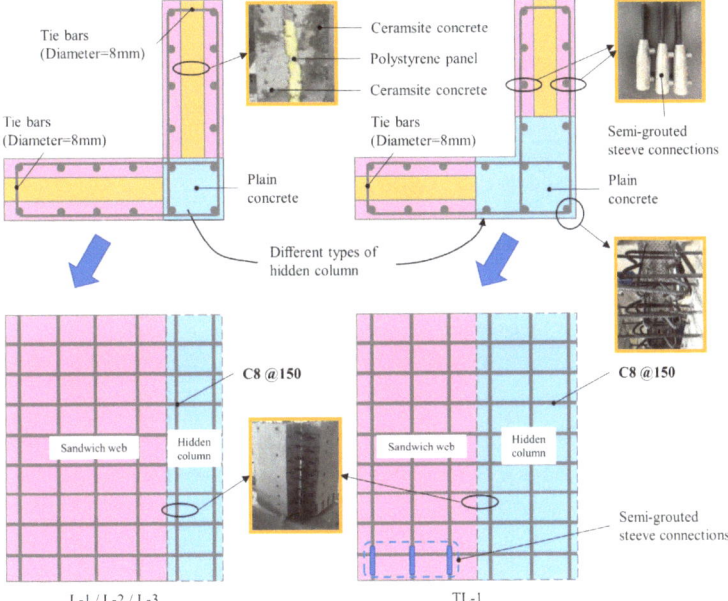

Figure 2. Geometric size and rebar arrangement of the specimens. (Unit of mm).

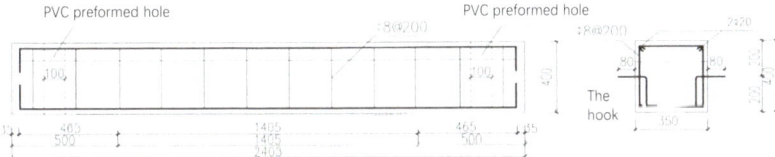

Figure 3. Geometric size and rebar arrangement of the base beam. (Unit of mm).

### 2.3. Material Properties

The HRB400 strength level was used for the distributed rebars with a diameter of 8 mm. The yield strength ($f_y$) and ultimate strength ($f_u$) were 464 MPa and 646 MPa, respectively. The tensile properties of the HRB400 strength level rebars with diameters of 12 mm, 14 mm, and 20 mm are listed in Table 1. Three standard cubic specimens (size of 100 mm × 100 mm × 100 mm) of plain concrete and ceramsite concrete were reserved for compressive tests during the joint casting. The results of the compressive test are listed in Table 2. Additionally, the properties of semi-grouted sleeves, ceramsite, and polyphenyl plates are shown in Tables 3–5.

**Table 1.** The tensile properties of reinforcements.

| Specimen | Diameter (mm) | The Yield Strength (MPa) | The Ultimate Strength (MPa) | Section Elongation (%) |
|---|---|---|---|---|
| A1 |   | 450 | 625 | 22 |
| A2 | 8 | 455 | 660 | 24 |
| A3 |   | 485 | 655 | 24.5 |
| B1 |   | 475 | 600 | 23 |
| B2 | 12 | 465 | 600 | 21.2 |
| B3 |   | 452 | 580 | 23 |
| C1 |   | 445 | 570 | 22 |
| C2 | 14 | 455 | 580 | 21.5 |
| C3 |   | 458 | 588 | 22.5 |
| D1 |   | 455 | 620 | 23 |
| D2 | 20 | 450 | 620 | 23.5 |
| D3 |   | 485 | 630 | 23.5 |

**Table 2.** Compressive test results.

| Materials | Specimens | Curing Time (d) | Failure Load (kN) | Compressive Strength (Mpa) |
|---|---|---|---|---|
| The plain concrete | TA-1 | 28 | 393.4 | 37.6 |
|  | TA-2 | 28 | 389.4 | 37.1 |
|  | TA-3 | 28 | 391.7 | 37.2 |
| The ceramsite concrete | CA-1 | 28 | 196.4 | 19.2 |
|  | CA-2 | 28 | 195.7 | 18.5 |
|  | CA-3 | 28 | 203.6 | 19.3 |

**Table 3.** The properties of semi-grouted sleeves.

| Sleeve Type | Yield Strength MPa | Ultimate Strength MPa | Yong's Modulus $\times 10^5$ N/m² | Elongation | Failure Mode |
|---|---|---|---|---|---|
| TT-1 | 508.34 | 655 | 2.06 | 6.1% | Tensile damage |
| TT-2 | 511.34 | 632 | 2.06 | 5.6% | Tensile damage |
| TT-3 | 531.74 | 654 | 2.06 | 5.9% | Tensile damage |

**Table 4.** The properties of polyphenyl plates.

| Thermal Conductivity | Fire-Resistance Rating | Water Absorption % | Density kg/m³ | Elastic Modulus (MPa) |
|---|---|---|---|---|
| 0.030 | B1 | 0.5 | 27 | 83 |

**Table 5.** The properties of ceramsite particles.

| Type | Particle Diameters (mm) | Porosity (%) | Apparent Density (kg/m³) | Water Absorption (1 h) (%) |
|---|---|---|---|---|
| fly ash ceramsite | 3–10 | 36 | 2329 | 9.41 |

## 2.4. Loading Plan

The quasi-static test was carried out in the civil and architectural laboratory of Henan University. The loading device was mainly divided into 200 T range hydraulic jacks for vertical loading and 100 T range transverse jacks for transverse loading, and the connection method is shown in Figure 4.

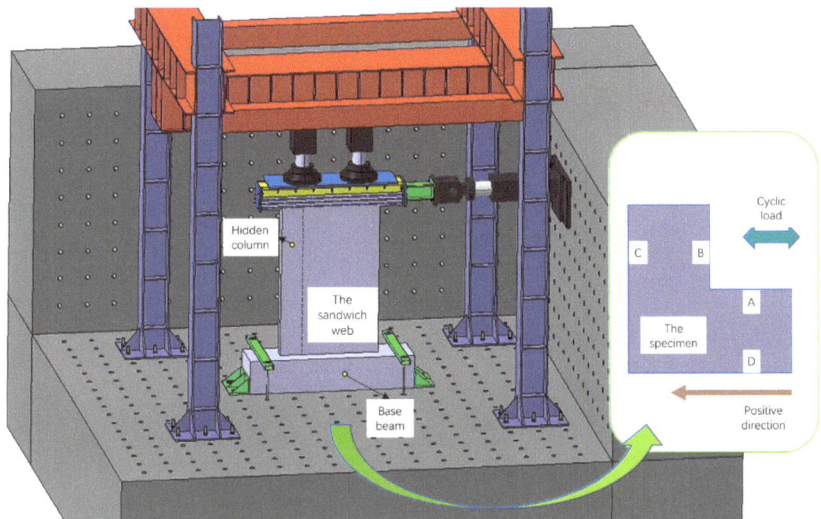

**Figure 4.** Test setup.

2.4.1. Vertical Loading

An axial force was utilized on top of the specimen to simulate the load from the superstructure by a vertical actuator. An L-shaped steel beam with sufficient stiffness was placed between the vertical actuator and the loading beam. The size of the steel beam was the same as that of the loading beam to simulate the uniform load applied by the superstructure to the joint. Moreover, a sliding roller was placed between the steel beam and the vertical actuator to reduce the error caused by the slip between the steel beam and the actuator. The magnitude of the force applied during preloading is 40% of the full load vertical force, and then the vertical pressure was increased to full load and maintained until the end of the test when the test officially started.

2.4.2. Horizontal Loading

According to JGJ/T 101-2015, prior to the formal test, the specimen should be preloaded in the horizontal direction to reduce the error caused by inelastic deformation (preload did not allow damage to the specimens). The loading system of the test should be determined according to the specimen and the research purpose. The loading system should ensure that each loading level standards are consistent, and a reasonable loading spectrum should be selected according to the actual situation and test characteristics. The loading time of each load level input in this test was consistent with the unloading time around 30 s. The loading curve is shown in Figure 5. When the bearing capacity of the specimen decreases to 85% of the peak load, the test stopped.

*2.5. Measuring Instrument Arrangement*

Two external displacement meters were set up. The height of the displacement meter was 1/3 of the height of the specimen and 1/2 of the height of the specimen, respectively, to confirm that the specimen keeps laterally during the loading process. Prior to the sleeve grouting, strain gauges (numbered x) were set on the surface of the vertical reinforcement. After the sleeve grouting, strain gauges (numbered $T_x$) were set on the surface of the sleeve to observe the strain of the sleeve and the reinforcement inside the sleeve after grouting.

Consequently, the intelligent crack width gauge was used to record and measure the width of the crack. The layout details of all test instruments are shown in Figure 6.

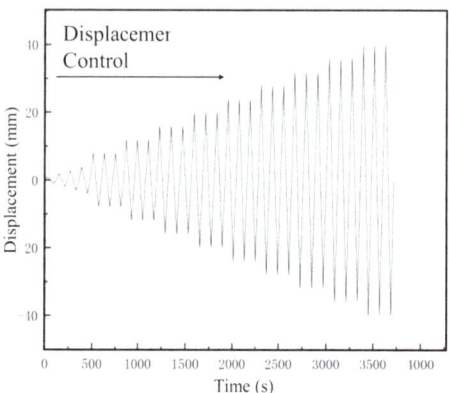

**Figure 5.** The loading rules.

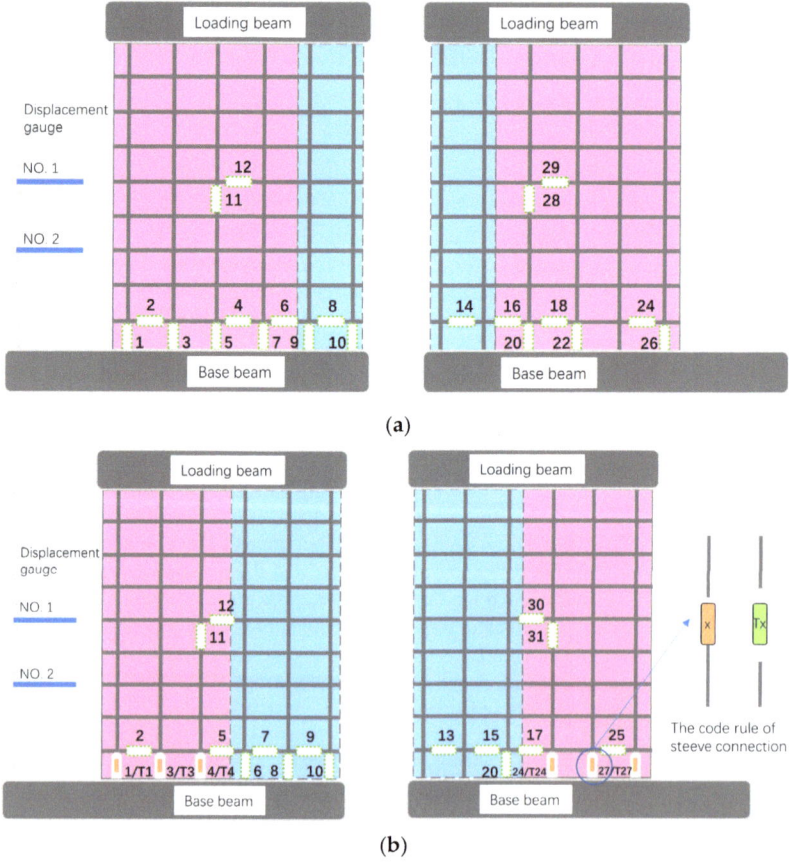

**Figure 6.** Measuring Instruments for the specimens. (**a**) The specimens L−1, L−2 and L−3. (**b**) The specimens TL−1.

## 3. Results and Discussion
### 3.1. Failure Characteristics

The failure characteristics and crack distribution can reflect the influence of different design parameters on the failure mode of the wallboard. The failure process of the test group represented by L−1 is as follows: horizontal cracks firstly appeared in the middle of the web of specimen A, then cross-oblique cracks appeared and extended to the uncracked part. The length of oblique cracks was short but dense. Consequently, the concrete at the corner of the web was crushed, and the steel bar was buckled. The failure process of TL−1 was similar to that of L−1, but the final failure characteristics were slightly different. Horizontal cracks firstly appeared on the surface of A, and then cross cracks, while no oblique cracks through the wall surface were obtained, and the bottom of the specimen damage was not serious. Thus, the overall stiffness of TL−1 with an L-shaped hidden column is stronger, which significantly improved the lateral force resistance of the whole specimen. The strengthening effect of sleeves on vertical steel bars improved the restraint capacity of the wallboard and effectively suppressed the development of cracks.

Figure 7 shows the final crack distribution and concrete damage pattern. The damage phenomenon and the crack distribution indicate that L−1 and TL−1 are typical bending-shear failures. The bending-shear cracks are mainly distributed on the webs. The cracking characteristics on the hidden column are mainly bending cracks, and extending in a horizontal direction. For TL−1, the grouted interface at the bottom of the wall did not appear a large slip at the end of the experiment, mainly resulting from the effect of the reinforced hidden column. The cracks of specimen TL−1 are distributed more evenly, and the damage to the hidden column is not serious.

### 3.2. Hysteretic Curve

The hysteresis curve directly demonstrates the deformation characteristics, stiffness degradation, and energy dissipation of the wallboard under repeated loads [26]. In Figure 8, the hysteresis curves of the two groups of specimens were roughly consistent with the same failure development law. At the initial loading stage, the specimen was in the elastic stage, the approximately linear curve appeared, and the hysteresis loop area was small with continuous loadings. The specimen was altered from the elastic stage to the plastic stage. The hysteresis curve would bend to the displacement axis, and the development trend was inverse 'S' shape, showing an obvious pinch phenomenon. The hysteresis loop area was increasing, and the residual deformation was accumulating. Finally, the bearing capacity of the specimens slightly decreased after reaching the peak, and there was no apparent mutation.

The specimens L−1, L−2, L−3 show no typical brittle failure, but the loading capacity is different under positive and negative loading directions due to the influence of the rectangular hidden column and L-shaped joint. This phenomenon is obvious in specimens L−2 and L−3. The specimen TL−1 is a precast panel joint with an L-shaped hidden column, which connected the base beam with semi-grouted sleeve connections, so the loading capacity is smaller than that of L−1, L−2, L−3. Because the wobble performance of TL−1 is much better, the ultimate displacement is larger than that of L−1, L−2, L−3.

Compared the hysteresis curves of the two groups of specimens, the two groups of specimens had different degrees of pinching. The kneading results were caused by the excessive stiffness change of the specimen under low cyclic loading. After forward unloading, the crack of ceramsite concrete could not be closed in time with reduced bending stiffness, mainly provided by the steel bar. In the later stage of reverse loading, it helped the crack of ceramsite concrete to close, and the stiffness of the specimen increased generally. The difference was that TL−1 has better energy dissipation performance as the strengthening of stiffness by L-shaped hidden columns. Therefore, the restoring force of the hysteresis curve under positive and reverse loads was similar, while the curves of the three specimens in the first group couldn't show the familiar characteristics. Due to the limitation of test conditions, the influence of more factors on the seismic performance of joints can be explored by numerical simulation in the later stage, and the accuracy of the computer model can be verified by comparing the results of hysteresis curves.

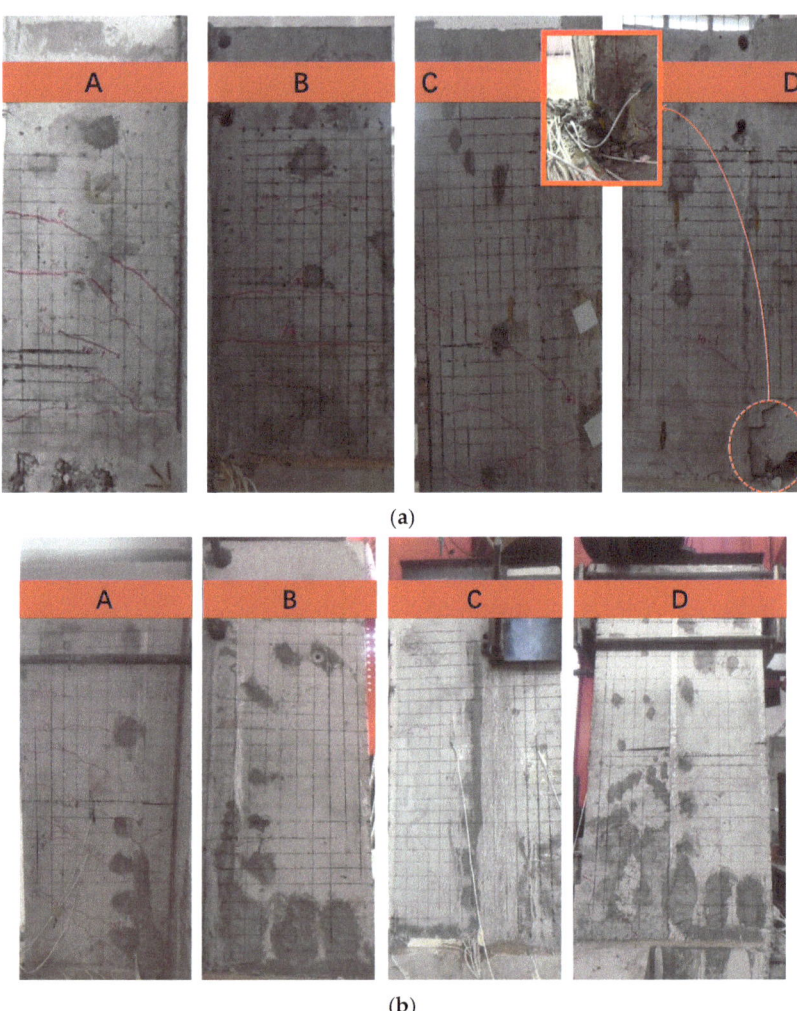

**Figure 7.** The failure model of the specimens. (**a**) The failure model of specimen L−1. (**b**) The failure model of specimen TL−1.

*3.3. Skeleton Curve*

The skeleton curve is an outer envelope obtained by sequentially connecting the peak load points loaded at each stage of the tension or compression side on the hysteresis curve, reflecting the relationship between the force and deformation of the component at each stage [27]. The skeleton curves of the two groups of specimens showed that the specimens matched with ductile structures [28], and the trend of the curves with barely differences. The stress process could be summarized into three stages: the elastic stage, the strengthening stage, and the failure stage.

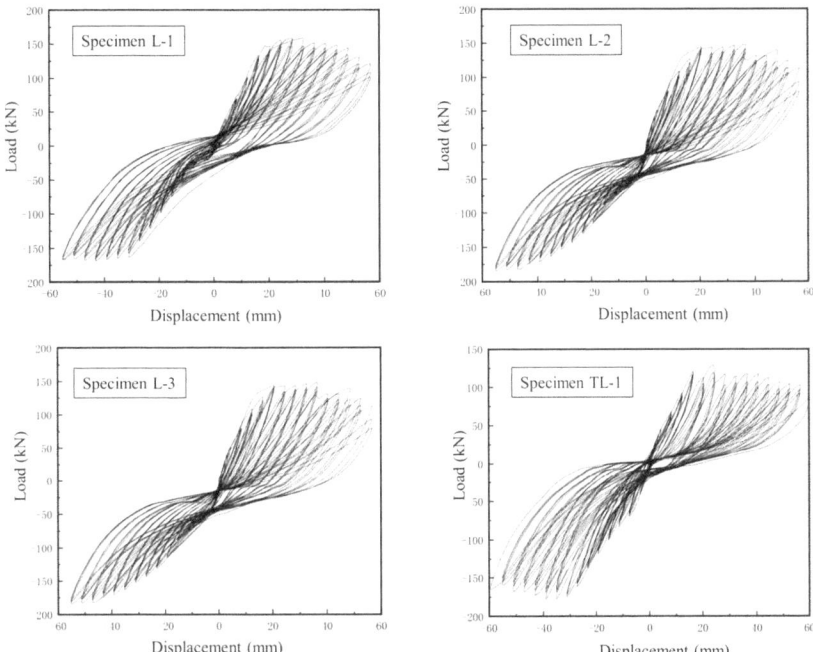

**Figure 8.** Hysteretic Curve.

Combined with the results of feature points, the influence of the connection form of vertical steel bars and the structure of hidden columns on the working performance of wall panel joints could be quantified. As shown in Table 6, the joint strengthening with the L-shaped hidden column enhances the crack load by 15.3% to 21.7%, and the yield, peak, and ultimate load of the specimen TL−1 are slightly lower than those of L−1/L−2/L−3. However, the specimen TL−1 shows a better deformation capacity. The deformations of the specimens L−1/L−2/L−3 in the direction of positive and negative loading have a large gap. This result is consistent with what the hysteresis curve shows. This phenomenon is caused by the sandwich structure of the webs. However, the specimen TL−2 with semi-grouted sleeve connections did not show such behavior, reflecting that the L-shaped hidden column could enhance the integrity of the precast joint to some degree. Generally speaking, the performance of TL−2 is better than that of L−1/L−2/L−3, which indicates that the type of hidden column and assembly methods are feasible and effective.

**Table 6.** Feature point parameters.

| Model | Loading Direction | Cracking Point | | Yield Point | | Peak Point | | Limit Point | |
|---|---|---|---|---|---|---|---|---|---|
| | | Cracking Load /kN | Cracking Displacement /mm | Yielding Load /kN | Yielding Displacement /mm | Peak Load /kN | Peak Displacement /mm | Extreme Load /kN | Extreme Displacement /mm |
| L−1 | Positive | 33.3 | 3.5 | 102.1 | 13.1 | 152.3 | 27.3 | 151.2 | 48.9 |
| | Negative | 38.7 | 3.7 | 73.8 | 12.2 | 178.0 | 40.3 | 177.6 | 50.3 |
| L−2 | Positive | 49.9 | 3.3 | 108.0 | 13.1 | 153.4 | 27.6 | 158.3 | 48.6 |
| | Negative | 36.9 | 3.5 | 71.1 | 12.8 | 176.1 | 43.3 | 175.4 | 49.3 |
| L−3 | Positive | 33.1 | 3.5 | 102.3 | 13.1 | 152.3 | 27.3 | 150.2 | 48.9 |
| | Negative | 38.6 | 3.6 | 73.1 | 12.0 | 178.2 | 40.3 | 177.6 | 50.3 |
| TL−1 | Positive | 38.4 | 4.1 | 86.3 | 14.3 | 132.6 | 30.3 | 112.2 | 54.6 |
| | Negative | 47.1 | 4.2 | 87.5 | 14.9 | 175.6 | 41.1 | 148.8 | 54.7 |

It can be seen from Figure 9 and Table 6 that the sleeve form and hidden column had less effects on the specimen's bearing capacity prior to the displacement reaching 20 mm. After reaching 20 mm, the plastic deformation capacity of the specimen with an L-shaped hidden column was higher than that of the specimen with a rectangular hidden column under the same displacement, but the bearing capacity was reduced. In Tables 3–8, the ultimate displacement of the specimen TL−1 was 8.7%, 11%, and 8.7%, which were higher than that of the three specimens of the test group. The peak load of specimen TL−1 was 1.4%, 0.3%, and 1.5% lower than that of the three specimens in the test group. Therefore, the connection between the anisotropic hidden column and the sleeve had a minimal reduction in the bearing capacity of the wallboard, but it efficiently improved deformability and presented better seismic performance.

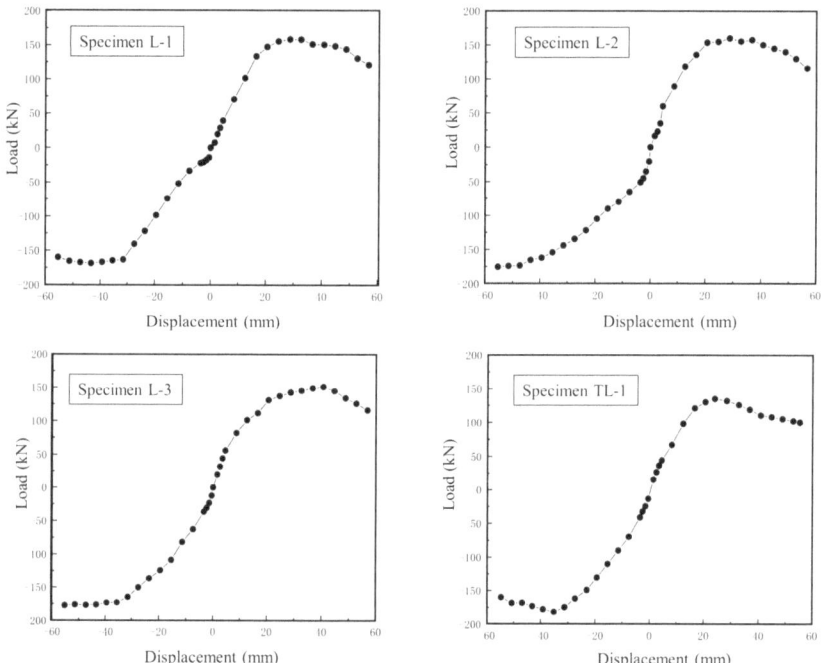

**Figure 9.** Skeleton Curve.

**Table 7.** Equivalent viscosity coefficient.

| Specimen Number | Cracking Point | Yield Point | Peak Point | Limit Point |
| --- | --- | --- | --- | --- |
| L−1 | 0.0927 | 0.1033 | 0.1096 | 0.1216 |
| L−2 | 0.0932 | 0.1023 | 0.1116 | 0.1235 |
| L−3 | 0.0927 | 0.1033 | 0.1096 | 0.1216 |
| TL−1 | 0.0994 | 0.1082 | 0.1203 | 0.1267 |

**Table 8.** Ductility coefficient.

| Model | L−1 | L−2 | L−3 | TL−1 |
| --- | --- | --- | --- | --- |
| μ | 3.73 | 3.7 | 3.73 | 3.81 |

### 3.4. Energy Dissipation Capacity

The energy dissipation capacity of the specimens is evaluated by an equivalent viscous coefficient. Table 7 shows the equivalent viscous damping coefficients of the cracking load point, yield point, peak point, and limit point in the negative loading process measured by the test (the calculation formula is as follows 1, the diagram shown in Figure 10). The equivalent viscosity coefficient of the specimen had the linear correlation with the energy dissipation performance of the specimen [29,30].

$$h_{eq} = \frac{1}{4\pi} \times \frac{E_{DISS}}{E_{STO}} \quad (1)$$

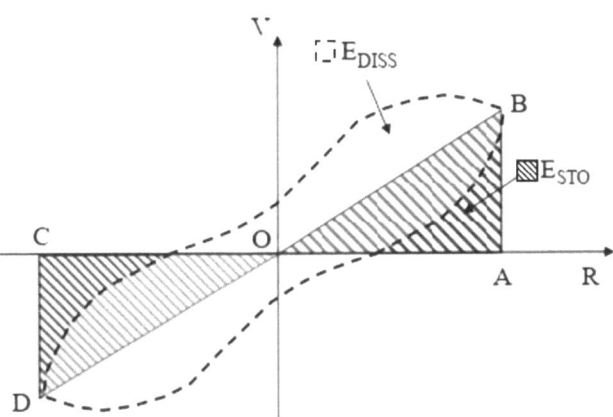

**Figure 10.** Calculation diagram of the equivalent viscous damping coefficients.

Comparing the two groups of specimens, it can be seen that the equivalent viscous damping coefficient of all specimens will increase with the load, which demonstrates that the energy dissipation capacity is constantly improving. The equivalent viscous damping coefficient of the test group L−1, L−2, and L−3 specimens kept increasing after the peak point, which led to the specimens still having a certain energy dissipation capacity after reaching the ultimate bearing capacity, and no brittle failure occurred. Moreover, the equivalent viscous damping coefficient of the TL−1 specimen was greater than that of the test group L−1, L−2, and L−3 specimens, indicating that the L-shaped hidden column is beneficial to improve the energy dissipation performance of the specimen, and the energy dissipation performance of the TL−1 specimen is better.

### 3.5. Ductility

Ductility is the deformation ability of the wallboard from the beginning of yield to the maximum bearing capacity or after reaching the maximum bearing capacity without pronounced decline. The yield displacement is calculated by the general yield bending moment method [31]. The ultimate displacement was the corresponding displacement value when the maximum bearing capacity in the positive direction of the specimen decreases to 85%. The calculation of the ductility coefficient is shown in Formula 2, and the ductility coefficient is shown in Table 8.

$$\mu = \frac{\Delta u}{\Delta y} \quad (2)$$

where: $\triangle u$-the ultimate displacement of the specimen at the time of damage. $\triangle y$-yield displacement at yielding.

It can be seen from Table 8 that the ductility coefficient μ of all specimens under the positive loading direction is greater than 3, reflecting that the wall panel joints have good ductility. On the other hand, the ductility of the TL−1 specimen is greater than that of the rectangular concealed column specimen. The ductility coefficient of the TL−1 specimen is 2.1%, 3% and 2.1% higher than that of L−1, L−2, L−3 respectively, which indicates that the L-shaped hidden column is beneficial to improve the deformation capacity of joints. That is consistent with the analysis results of energy dissipation capacity.

## 3.6. Rigidity Degeneration

Stiffness degradation presents the decrease of stiffness with the increase of structural plasticity after the development of cracks in concrete structures and reflects the ability of concrete structures to absorb and dissipate energy under earthquake action [31]. The stiffness algorithm of the specimen at different stages was shown in Formula 3. Through the above formula, the stiffness corresponding to each stage of each specimen could be calculated and made into a stiffness degradation curve, as shown in Figure 11.

$$K_i = \frac{(|+F_i| + |-F_i|)}{(|+X_i| + |-X_i|)} \qquad (3)$$

where: $F_i$-the peak point load in the positive direction during the loading of the i-th level.-$F_i$-the peak point load in the negative direction during the loading of the i-th level.

$X_i$-the displacement of the peak point in the positive direction during the i-th cycle.

$-X_i$-the displacement of the peak point in the second direction during the i-th cycle.

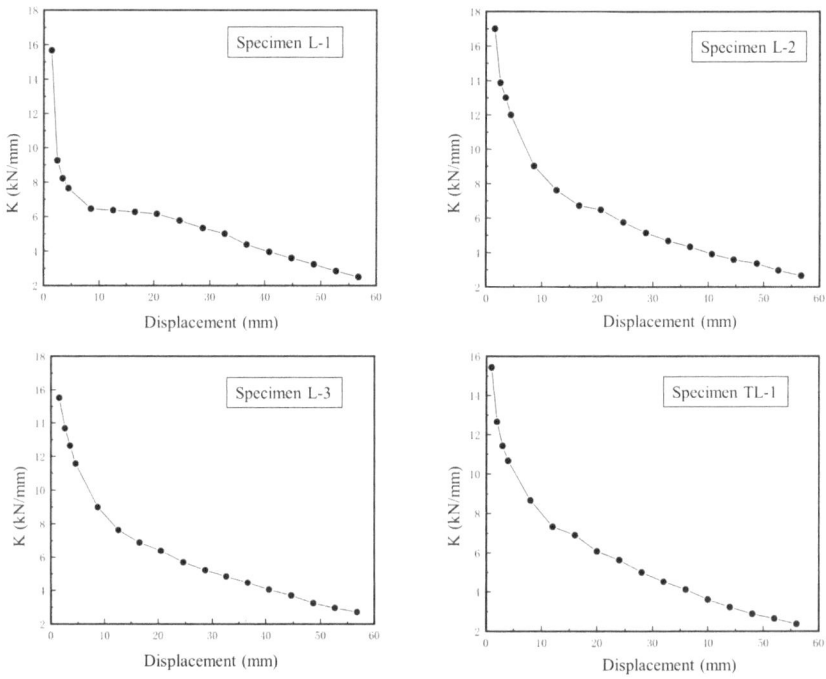

**Figure 11.** The stiffness degradation of the specimen.

The stiffness degradation of the specimen represents the stability of the mechanical performance of the specimen. In Figure 11, the stiffness of the two specimens decreased steadily with the accumulation of damage after cracking without a sudden drop, and the seismic performance was good. In the initial stage, the specimens of the rectangular hidden column have obvious stiffness degradation, and the stiffness reduction of the L-shaped hidden column is relatively small. After the cracking of ceramsite concrete, the horizontal connection part of the rectangular hidden column produces horizontal slip, which leads to a slower stiffness degradation rate than TL−1. In the later stage of the test, the changing trend and change rule of the two joints are similar.

## 3.7. Strain Analysis of Longitudinal Bar

The strain of the longitudinal reinforcement of the cast-in-place specimen at the key positions 1,4,24 and 27 with L−1 since the micro-strain after the yield of the steel bar was too large in Figure 12. The steel bar strain was no longer increased. And the failure of L−1 started from the outermost web and developed inward. After the web lost most of its bearing capacity, the flange plate and the joint began to bear the force together, and the flange plate failure extended from the outermost to the inward. Finally, the joint kept working.

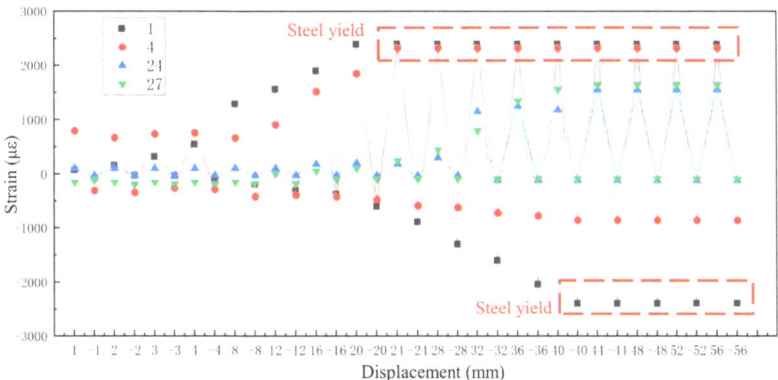

**Figure 12.** The Strain of longitudinal bar.

The strain of the vertical distributed steel at the strain gauges 1,4,8,24,27 and T1, T24, and T27 positions of TL−1 are shown in Figure 13. By comparing the strain curves of the strain gauges T1 and 1, it is not difficult to find that the tensile strain at the sleeve is much smaller than the vertical steel bar spliced inside it. This shows that the sleeve can effectively connect the precast panel joint and the base beam, and help the vertical reinforcement bear part of the tensile force. Given the results of strain gauge records of No.1 and No.4, the tensile stress of the vertical steel bar located outside the web is larger than that of the vertical steel bar located in the center. However, the trend of the strain recorded by the two strain gauges is consistent. This result is consistent with the trend of specimen L−1. No.8 strain gauge is located in the interior of the concealed column, and its strain trend is consistent with No.1, reflecting that the horizontal distribution steel bars extending to the interior of the concealed column can make the integrity of the joint better. No.24 and No.27 strain gauges are located in the B−C sandwich web, which is perpendicular to the loading direction, so the change of strain is different from No.1 and No.4. The maximum value recorded by No.24 strain gauge is much larger than that of No.27, which may be due to the fact that No.24 strain gauge is close to the L-shaped hidden column and the stiffness of the hidden column is large. No.24 bears more tension.

Overall, the vertical reinforcement strain in the two specimens has similar rules. The yielding sequence of the vertical steel bars of L−1 and TL−1 specimens is from the outermost steel bar to the hidden column. Moreover, the web and flange longitudinal reinforcement of the two specimens has yielded prior to the vertical reinforcement in the hidden column reaching the yield strain. Although the vertical reinforcement of the TL−1 specimen is connected by a sleeve, where the reinforcements at T4 and T1 showed different strains resulted in the sleeve helping to bear part of the external load. On the other hand, the strain value of the steel bar in the sleeve has a better performance compared with that of the specimen L−1, which also showed from the side that the L-shaped hidden column strengthens the stiffness of the core area of the joint, which increases the load distributed by the outer vertical steel bar, so the strain also increases accordingly. Because the strain gauge is fragile, prone to failure, the latter can establish a computer model to verify the results.

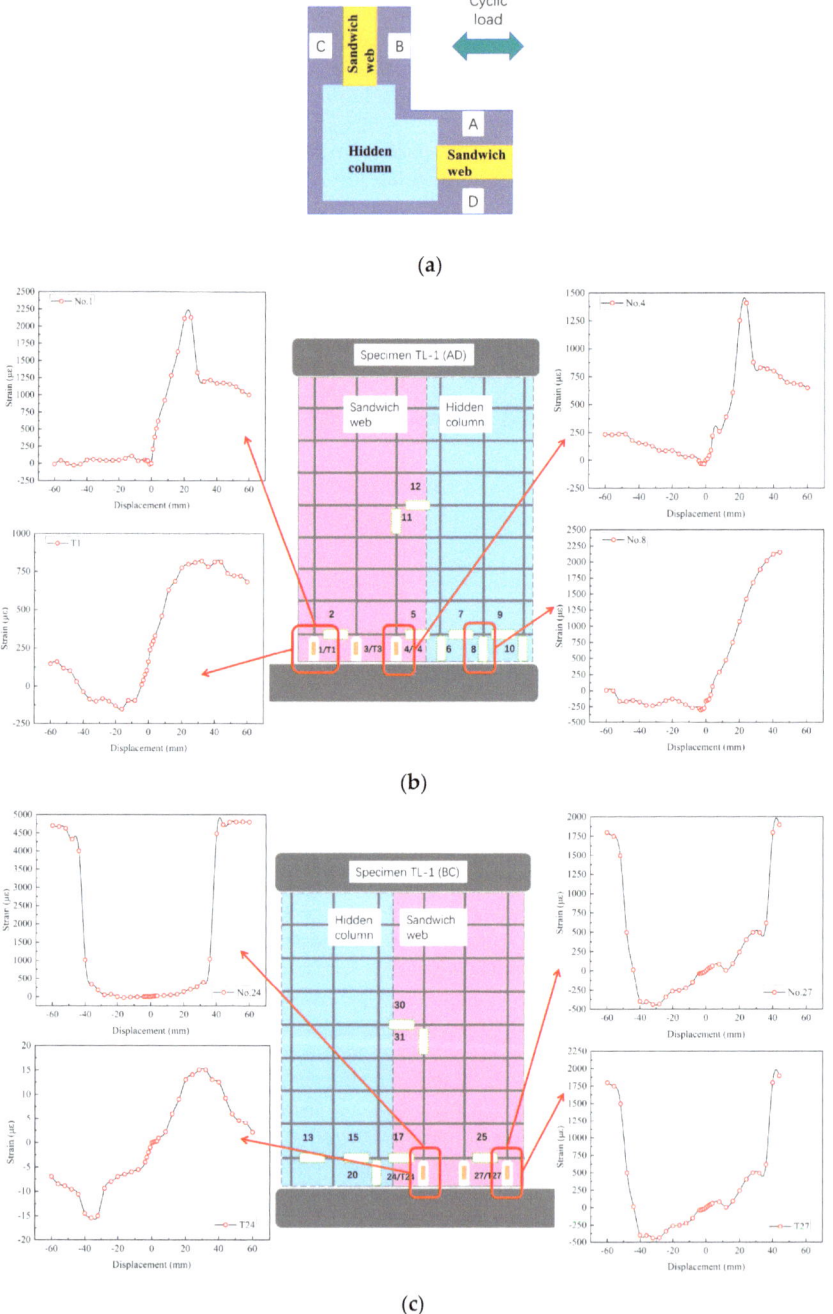

**Figure 13.** The Strain of longitudinal bar. (**a**) The loading direction. (**b**) The AD web of the joint. (**c**) The BC web of the joint.

## 4. Conclusions

In this study, firstly, the specimen design and material test of two groups of joint specimens were carried out. Finally, through the low cyclic loading test, the failure mode, hysteresis curve, skeleton curve, stiffness degradation, ductility, energy dissipation capacity, and steel stress and strain of different specimens under low cyclic loading are obtained. By analyzing the experimental data, the main conclusions are as follows:

1. The failure process of the two groups of specimens remains the same, while the degree of damage is different. The specimen firstly appears horizontal cracks in the A plane, followed by the formation of the X-shaped cross-crack, until the end of the wall appears plastic hinge and component damage. The TL−1 specimen with sleeve connection and special-shaped hidden column has less cracking on the BC wall, and the corner hinge is not obvious, while the integrity of the ordinary rectangular hidden column specimen is better, and there is a lot of cracking on the four walls.
2. Both specimens showed good seismic performance. According to the hysteresis curve, it could be seen that both groups of specimens have a ductile failure, and the stiffness degradation was stable under low-cycle reciprocating cyclic loading. And under large displacement, the energy dissipation capacity of the specimen provided an excellent performance.
3. The ultimate bearing capacity of the three specimens with rectangular hidden columns was higher, and the equivalent viscosity coefficient still increased in the limit state, that is, the energy dissipation performance was improved, and the toughness of the specimens was good. The ultimate displacement of the specimen with sleeve connection and special-shaped hidden column is larger, and the equivalent viscosity coefficient of each stage of the specimen is greater than that of the rectangular hidden column specimen, that is, the energy dissipation performance is better.
4. Sleeve connection would reduce the integrity of the specimen, and the bearing capacity at a small discount, but could significantly improve the toughness of components. Moreover, the ductility of the wall was significantly improved by increasing the area of the hidden column and enhancing the lateral stiffness of the wall. Therefore, it was more rational to design L-type ceramsite concrete sandwich composite joints by sleeve connection and special-shaped hidden column.
5. The control group specimen presented a better match in stiffness, bearing capacity, ductility, and energy dissipation. The test results can provide technical support for the application of the insulated sandwich wall panel joints with ceramsite concrete layer, and lay a foundation for the design of other sandwich panel joints.

However, there are still many factors that are not considered in the design of the joints. Future research could continue to validate the outcomes based on numerical simulation method and establishing the relationship between material microstructure and macroscopic seismic performance of the joints. And the thermal performance of the joint can be tested to further verify its energy-saving effect.

**Author Contributions:** Writing—original draft preparation, L.L. & H.W., writing—review and editing, S.M.; supervision, P.B. All authors have read and agreed to the published version of the manuscript.

**Funding:** This research was funded by China Postdoctoral Science Foundation funded project (No. 2018M632805), Key scientific and technological project of Henan Province (No. 212102310932), Key scientific and technological project of Kaifeng City (No. 2001010).

**Data Availability Statement:** All data, models, and code generated or used during the study appear in the published article.

**Conflicts of Interest:** The authors declare no conflict of interest.

# References

1. Zeng, C.; Wang, Z.; Chen, J.; Wang, D. Fire Resistance of an Assembled Integrated Enclosure Panel System. *Buildings* **2022**, *12*, 1582. [CrossRef]
2. Zhang, C.; Ding, K.W.; He, S. Seismic Performance of Panel Connectors with Steel Frame Based on Autoclaved Lightweight Concrete (ALC). *Buildings* **2022**, *12*, 372. [CrossRef]

3. He, S.; Yan, H. Application Status and Technology Research of Energy-efficient Shear Wall in China. *Mater. Rev.* **2018**, *11*, 1910–1915.
4. Chen, Y.; Zhu, L.; Zhang, S.; Ye, P.; Wu, H. Failure Mechanism and Strength Criterion of Fly Ash Ceramsite Concrete Under Triaxial Compression. *J. Chin. Ceram. Soc.* **2022**, *50*, 2196–2204. [CrossRef]
5. Shi, Y.; Zhu, J.; He, D.; Luo, X.; Wu, T.; Du, S. Effect of Mineral Admixture on Mechanical Properties and Cracking Tendency of Concrete. *J. Chin. Ceram. Soc.* **2019**, *47*, 1605–1610.
6. Youm, K.; Moon, J.; Cho, J.Y.; Kim, J.J. Experimental study on strength and durability of lightweight aggregate concrete containing silica fume. *Constr. Build. Mater.* **2016**, *114*, 517–527. [CrossRef]
7. Zhang, S.; Cao, K.; Wang, C.; Wang, X.; Wang, J.; Sun, B. Effect of silica fume and waste marble powder on the mechanical and durability properties of cellular concrete. *Constr. Build. Mater.* **2020**, *241*, 117980. [CrossRef]
8. Mu, L.; Li, S.; Feng, J.; Yang, J. Study on Effect of Prewet Aggregate on Performance of Ceramsite Concrete. *China Concr. Cem. Prod.* **2019**, 66–69.
9. Shi, Y.; Bai, H.; Li, J. Lytag concrete antifreeze performance study. *Concrete* **2016**, *11*, 86–89.
10. Liu, W. Preparation of Non-Fired Fly Ash Ceramsite and Research on Ceramsite Lightweight Aggregate Concrete. Master's Dissertation, Heifei University of Technology, Hefei, China, 2021.
11. Ma, S.; Li, L.; Bao, P. Seismic Performance Test of Double-Row Reinforced Ceramsite Concrete Composite Wall Panels with Cores. *Appl. Sci.* **2021**, *11*, 2688. [CrossRef]
12. Ma, S.; Fang, H. Research on Seismic Test and Calculation Model for Improving Factor of Composite Board with Heat Preservation Function. *Adv. Civ. Eng.* **2021**, *2021*, 5546387. [CrossRef]
13. Han, X. Performance Analysis of Ceramsite Concrete Sandwich Insulation Composite Wallboard. Master's Dissertation, Henan University, Henan, China, 2017.
14. Soudki, K.A.; Rizkalla, S.H.; Leblanc, B. Horizontal Connections for Precast Concrete Shear Walls Subjected to Cyclic Deformations Part 1: Mild Steel Connections. *PCI J.* **1995**, *40*, 78–96. [CrossRef]
15. Soudki, K.A.; Rizkalla, S.H.; Daikiw, R.W. Horizontal Connections for Precast Concrete Shear Walls Subjected to Cyclic Deformations Part 2: Prestressed Connections. *PCI J.* **1995**, *40*, 82–96. [CrossRef]
16. Soudki, K.A.; West, J.S.; Rizkalla, S.H.; Blackett, B. Horizontal Connections for Precast Concrete Shear Wall Panels Under Cyclic Shear Loading. *PCI J.* **1996**, *41*, 64–80. [CrossRef]
17. Einea, A.; Yamane, T.; Tadros, M.K. Grout-Filled Pipe Splices for Precast Concrete ConstructION. *PCI J.* **1995**, *40*, 82–93. [CrossRef]
18. Alias, A.; Zubir, M.A.; Shahid, K.A.; Rahman, A.B. Structural Performance of Grouted Sleeve Connectors with and without Transverse Reinforcement for Precast Concrete Structure. *Procedia Eng.* **2013**, *53*, 116–123. [CrossRef]
19. Ling, J.H.; Rahman, A.B.; Ibrahim, I.S.; Hamid, Z.A. Behaviour of grouted pipe splice under incremental tensile load. *Constr. Build. Mater.* **2012**, *33*, 90–98. [CrossRef]
20. Qian, J.; Yang, X.; Qin, H.; Peng, Y.; Zhang, J.; Li, J. Tests on seismic behavior of pre-cast shear walls with various methods of vertical reinforcement splicing. *J. Build. Struct.* **2011**, *32*, 51–59.
21. Wu, Y.; Yang, W.; Xiao, Y. Seismic behavior of high strength concrete composite walls with embedded steel truss. *J. Constr. Steel Res.* **2016**, *118*, 180–193. [CrossRef]
22. Liao, F.; Han, L.; Tao, Z. Performance of reinforced concrete shear walls with steel reinforced concrete boundary columns. *Eng. Struct.* **2012**, *44*, 186–209. [CrossRef]
23. Ji, X.; Sun, Y.; Qian, J.; Lu, X. Seismic behavior and modeling of steel reinforced concrete (SRC) walls. *Earthq. Eng. Struct. Dyn.* **2015**, *44*, 955–972. [CrossRef]
24. Sritharan, S.; Aaleti, S.; Henry, R.S.; Liu, K.-Y.; Tsai, K.-C. Precast concrete wall with end columns (PreWEC) for earthquake resistant design. *Earthq. Eng. Struct. Dyn.* **2015**, *44*, 2075–2092. [CrossRef]
25. Guo, X. Research on Shear Behavior and Damage Performance of Prefabricated Wall Panel with Concealed Brace. Ph.D. Thesis, South China University of Technology, Guangzhou, China, 2020.
26. Sun, Y.P.; Cai, G.C.; Takeshi, T. Seismic Behavior and Performance-Based Design of Resilient Concrete Columns. *Appl. Mech. Mater.* **2013**, *438–439*, 1453–1460. [CrossRef]
27. Hany, M.; Seif, E.; Khaled, G. In-Plane Seismic Performance of Fully Grouted Reinforced Masonry Shear Walls. *J. Struct. Eng.* **2017**, *143*, 04017254.
28. Yuan, W. Seismic Performance and Evaluation Method of Earthquake Resilient Shear Walls. Ph.D. Thesis, Southwest Jiaotong University, Chengdu, China, 2019.
29. Lu, Z.; Wang, Y.; Li, J.; Wang, L. Experimental study on seismic performance of L-shaped insulated concrete sandwich shear wall with a horizontal seam. *Struct. Des. Tall Spec. Build.* **2018**, *28*, e1551. [CrossRef]
30. Lu, X.; Yang, J. Seismic behavior of T-shaped steel reinforced concrete shear walls in tall buildings under cyclic loading. *Struct. Des. Tall Spec. Build.* **2015**, *24*, 141–157. [CrossRef]
31. Wu, Q.; Li, G.; Li, M.H.; Luo, Y. An Experimental Study on Mechanical Properties of Concrete-Filled Steel Tube (CFST) Key-Connected Prefabricated Wall and Column. *Adv. Steel Constr.* **2020**, *16*, 206–215.

*Article*

# Digital Twin Model and Its Establishment Method for Steel Structure Construction Processes

Zhansheng Liu [1,2,*] and Sen Lin [1,2]

1 Faculty of Architecture, Civil and Transportation Engineering, Beijing University of Technology, Beijing 100124, China
2 Key Laboratory of Urban Security and Disaster Engineering of Ministry of Education, Beijing University of Technology, Beijing 100124, China
* Correspondence: liuzhansheng@bjut.edu.cn

**Abstract:** At present, the informatization level in the construction process of steel structures is relatively low. Meanwhile, digital twin technology, with better interactive features, provides a new development direction for the intelligent construction of steel structures. Therefore, this paper introduces the concept of a digital twin into the steel structure construction process, analyzes the connotation and characteristics of the digital twin model, and proposes the digital twin model architecture for steel structure construction processes. Furthermore, a method for establishing a digital twin model for steel structure construction processes is presented, which includes three stages: the acquisition and transmission of physical space data, the construction of a digital twin virtual model, and information exchange in the digital twin model. Based on these concepts, this paper describes a digital twin system architecture for the steel structure construction process from the perspective of data flow in the digital twin model. Finally, with the application of information technology in the steel structure construction process of the university park library project in Xiongan New Area and the reconstruction and expansion project of the Nanchong Gaoping airport, the digital twin model and its establishment method methods are analyzed practically and demonstrated effectively in this study.

**Keywords:** digital twin; steel structure; construction process; intelligent construction

**Citation:** Liu, Z.; Lin, S. Digital Twin Model and Its Establishment Method for Steel Structure Construction Processes. *Buildings* **2024**, *14*, 1043. https://doi.org/10.3390/buildings14041043

Academic Editors: Francisco López-Almansa and Nerio Tullini

Received: 31 January 2024
Revised: 26 March 2024
Accepted: 3 April 2024
Published: 8 April 2024

**Copyright:** © 2024 by the authors. Licensee MDPI, Basel, Switzerland. This article is an open access article distributed under the terms and conditions of the Creative Commons Attribution (CC BY) license (https://creativecommons.org/licenses/by/4.0/).

## 1. Introduction

### 1.1. Background

The rapid development of information technology has had a profound impact on society and has greatly improved the informatization level of all industries. However, compared to other industries, the construction industry has one of the lowest levels of informatization [1,2]. In recent years, many countries have attached great importance to the application of information technology in the construction industry and have issued relevant policies for its promotion [3]. Under the current circumstances, in order to better improve the informatization and intelligence level of the construction process and meet the needs of modern society, intelligent construction has become a new trend in the development of the construction industry [4,5]. Digital twin technology provides a new method for the realization of intelligent construction [6].

Driven by social development and industrial demand, steel structure buildings progressively highlight the advantages of a high degree of industrialization, low-carbon environmental protection, and recyclable utilization, have become a pivotal building form for adapting to the industrialization and green development of buildings, which have developed speedily and are getting increasingly extensively used in various large public buildings. Therefore, it is imperative to integrate digital twins and information technology into the construction process of steel structures, leverage the advantages of new technologies, and change the traditional construction mode. This article focuses on the construction process of steel structures, proposes a digital twin model for the construction process of steel structures, and analyzes its establishment method, targeting the construction practice cases of large public buildings in China.

## 1.2. Literature Review

Many theoretical methods for the application of information technology in the construction process and the implementation of intelligent construction have been researched around the world. Fan et al. [7] proposed a definition of intelligent construction, discussed its main characteristics, and studied the characteristic representation method and reward mechanism of the closed-loop control state of intelligent construction. Mao et al. [8] proposed a theoretical framework and studied the kernel logic of data-driven models for intelligent construction. Based on the internet configuration and physical information systems, Niu et al. [9] proposed a theoretical framework for intelligent construction using means such as technical analysis and case studies. In recent years, many information technologies have been applied in the construction process of buildings, including BIM, the Internet of Things [10], artificial intelligence technology [11], and so on. BIM technology, as a key foundational technology for the development of architecture in the intelligent construction industry, has been deeply researched in the field of architectural applications. It is also widely used in many environments, such as visual display, collision detection [12], construction simulation [13], engineering quantity calculation [14], and normalization examination [15], among others. Yang et al. [16] proposed a BIM model for the entire informatization process of steel structure dismantling and used the moving wedge matrix method to formulate and optimize dismantling plans. For the assembly process during the steel structure construction stage, Wang et al. [17] proposed a steel structure virtual assembly framework based on BIM technology, established a virtual assembly program prototype of the steel structure, and achieved the two basic functions of geometric detection and assembly detection. The Internet of Things is considered the evolution of the internet. Multiple devices are associated with each other in real time through unique identifiers (UIDs) to better facilitate the interaction of data among them [18]. In building construction, the Internet of Things can realize the collection and transmission of massive data, such as the equipment and environment in the construction process, and achieve real-time control of the construction site. Artificial intelligence technology is an important aspect of the "intelligence" in intelligent construction. Based on intelligent algorithms, artificial intelligence technology analyzes the massive data generated in the construction process, then carries out intelligent analysis, prediction, and other functions of the construction process [19]. With the rapid development of various information technologies, the integration and application of information technology has become a new trend. At present, a variety of information technologies are applied in the field of engineering construction, such as BIM + 3D laser scanning [20], BIM + VR [21], BIM + GIS [22], AI + IoT [23], and so on.

With the proposal of the development of intelligent construction strategies in various countries, the proposal of intelligent construction theory, and the integrated application of BIM, the Internet of Things, and other information technologies in building construction, the integration of digital twin technology and the building construction process has been remarkably promoted [5]. Digital twin technology, with its high-fidelity simulation of the real world and realization of intelligent closed-loop control through virtual–real interactions, has received extensive attention and gradually become a research hotspot [24]. The concept of digital twin technology was first proposed by Professor Michael Grieves in 2002 [25], and it was initially applied in the aerospace field [26]. Subsequently, due to the high-fidelity dynamic simulation characteristics, the research and application of digital twin technology have gradually expanded to many industries, such as machinery, manufacturing [27], medical [28], agriculture [29], power generation [30], ecological environment [31], and so on. Tao et al. [32,33] proposed a five-dimensional digital twin structure model, studied the interaction theory and key technologies of digital twin models, and provided a new framework for the application of digital twin technology in other industries. Digital twin technology is a digital mapping of physical entities, providing a transformation of the foundation of traditional construction modes in the construction industry [34]. Liu et al. [35] introduced digital twin technology into the construction industry, established an application framework of digital twin technology in the field of intelligent construction, and applied digital twin technology for the intelligent monitoring of the stress state during the tensioning process of pre-stressed steel structures. Pan et al. [36] took project management in the process of intelligent construction as a research object and proposed a closed-loop digital twin framework integrating BIM, IoT, and data mining. Wang et al. [37] constructed a digital twin system architecture for pre-fabricated building products and elaborated on its related supporting technologies and implementation methods. Regarding building operation and maintenance, Zhao et al. [38] proposed the theory of an intelligent building operation and maintenance system construction combining digital twin technology with machine learning, explained the fusion mechanism for the digital twin technology and machine learning, and proposed a construction method for a building operation and maintenance system based on digital twin technology. Based on the concept of digital twins, Torzoni et al. [39] proposed a prediction method for the health monitoring and maintenance of civil engineering structures.

*1.3. Research Gaps and Organizational Structures*

As mentioned above, various information technologies have been widely used in construction processes, but most of them are single-point applications. Digital twin technology provides a new framework for the integration and application of various information technologies in the process of building construction and the realization of intelligent construction. At present, the study and application of digital twins is mainly focused on manufacturing, machinery, and other fields [40]. In the field of architecture, scholars in the field of civil engineering have carried out corresponding research and explorations and have proposed digital twin application frameworks for pre-fabricated buildings, building operation and maintenance, and so on. However, for the construction process of steel structures, establishing a digital twin model is still in the exploration stage. Digital twin models can combine and express the information of various elements of the steel structure construction process in a virtual space. Furthermore, according to the actual needs of the steel structure construction process, the construction process of the steel structure can be analyzed and simulated in the virtual space, providing a reference for the real steel structure construction process.

Intelligent construction is a new development direction for steel structure construction processes, and the integration and application of various information technologies provide a basis for the development of intelligent construction. Thus, this paper introduces the concept of digital twin models in the construction process of steel structures. First, the connotation and characteristics of the digital twin model for steel structure construction processes are analyzed in Section 2. Then, in Section 3, a digital twin model architecture for the steel structure construction process is proposed. Based on this, in Section 4, through the integration of perception technology, the Internet of Things, and other technologies, an establishment method for a digital twin model of the steel structure construction process is proposed. Finally, the applications of information technology in the construction of steel structures for the university park library project in the Xiongan New Area and the reconstruction and expansion project of the Nanchong Gaoping airport are used as examples, in order to analyze the digital twin model of the steel structure construction process.

## 2. Connotation and Characteristics of a Digital Twin Model for Steel Structure Construction

The connotation of the digital twin model for steel structure construction processes is to integrate the digital twin and various building information technologies. Based on the elements used in an actual steel structure construction scenario, various information perception and transmission technologies are used to collect information about each element during the construction process, form the digital twin data, and establish a virtual digital model for each construction element and its related activities. Furthermore, under certain rule constraints, digital twin data is processed according to the real construction process in the virtual space. Finally, through the information platform, guidance, management, and control of the construction process of steel structures can be achieved in the real space. The digital twin model of the steel structure construction process integrates information technologies such as digital twin, intelligent algorithm, Internet of Things, and so on, and it conspicuously demonstrates multiple characteristics such as multiple dimensions, intelligence, high integration level, real-time performance, and interactivity.

(1) Multiple dimensions. Due to the complexity of the construction process of steel structures, which involve multiple elements and diverse demands, a digital twin model of steel structure construction is established in multiple dimensions. According to its spatial dimensions, the digital twin model of steel structure construction can be divided into the component level, unit level, and structural level. According to its application function dimension, it can also be divided into the cost dimension, schedule dimension, quality dimension, and so on.

(2) Intelligence. The digital twin model of the steel structure construction process integrates multiple information technologies and intelligent algorithms. Intelligence is the specific embodiment and an inherent requirement of the value of digital twin models. Intelligence refers to the intelligence of the physical entities of the mechanical equipment used during the construction process, such as the intelligent welding of steel components. Additionally, digital twin models have the general capabilities of self-perception, learning, analysis, and mutual control.

(3) High integration level. A construction digital twin model is a model that integrates various types of information, such as personnel information, mechanical information, steel component information, environmental information, and so on. This information comprises a large amount of data and a variety of data types. The digital twin model cannot meet various functional requirements for the construction process without transforming and integrating these various types and large amounts of data such that they can be better utilized.

(4) Real-time performance. The construction period of steel structures is short, and the information changes quickly. The digital twin virtual model is a mapping of the physical entities and, so, the information in the digital twin virtual space also changes rapidly in real time. The steel structure digital twin model obtains relevant information based on the actual construction needs, processes the information according to the corresponding mechanisms, and provides timely data analysis results for the construction process.

(5) Interactivity. Digital twin technology consists of a physical space, a virtual space, and information exchange between these two spaces. The essence of digital twin technology is to depict a physical space through a virtual space. Based on continuously generated real-time twin data, digital twin models construct and present physical entities in the real world through the use of information technology platforms, such as BIM and virtual reality, allowing information exchange between the physical space and virtual space to be achieved.

## 3. Digital Twin Model for Steel Structure Construction Processes

Based on the concept of digital twin technology and the characteristics of steel structure construction, the establishment of a digital twin model for steel structure construction processes must follow certain principles. First, a digital twin model should be established to meet the needs of the steel structure construction project. Before establishing a digital twin model, it is necessary to fully analyze the construction needs and establish digital twin models with different levels and functions according to different needs, in order to describe the characteristics of the different levels and dimensions in the steel structure construction process. Second, while meeting real construction needs, digital twin models should be as simple as possible to avoid unnecessary resource consumption.

Based on the characteristics and application requirements of the digital twin model in the construction process, and according to the concept of the five-dimensional digital twin model [32], digital twin technology is introduced into the construction process of steel structures. A digital twin model architecture for steel structure construction processes is proposed, which includes five parts: physical spatial entities, virtual twin models, data centers, functional applications, and information links, as shown in Equation (1). The architecture diagram is shown in Figure 1.

$$DT_{sc} = \{PE, VM, DC, FA, IL\} \quad (1)$$

where $DT_{sc}$ is the digital twin model framework and physical spatial entity for the construction process of steel structures; $PE$ is the physical spatial entity; $VM$ is the virtual twin model; $DC$ is the data center; $FA$ is the functional application; and $IL$ is the information link.

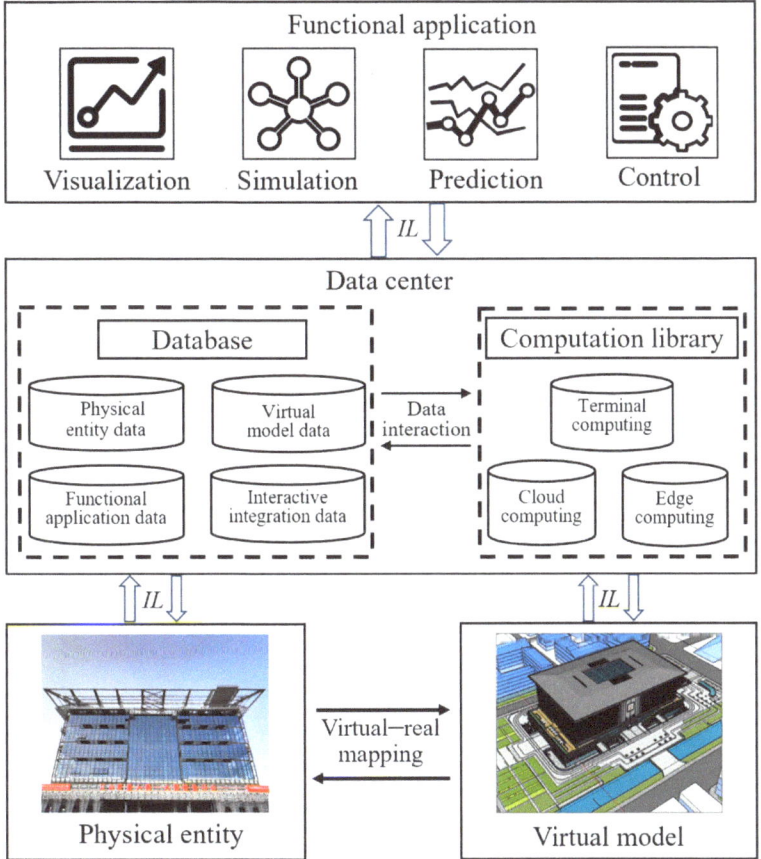

**Figure 1.** Digital twin model of the steel structure construction process.

Physical entities. The physical entities are the elements related to construction, such as personnel, machinery, components, environment, and so on. The physical entity is the cornerstone of the digital twin model and the object that the digital twin model serves.

Virtual model. The virtual model refers to the establishment of a digital model at the geometric, physical, behavioral, and rule levels, based on data from the construction process in a physical space. Through the interconnection and collaboration of various virtual models, a digital representation of the construction process of steel structures in a physical space can be achieved. With the accumulation of data, the accuracy of virtual models continues to improve and continuously approaches the real construction process in the physical space.

Data center. The data center consists of two parts: a database and a computation library. The function of the database is to provide storage for the operation data of the digital twin model. The computation library has a large number of algorithms and high computing power, providing support for the data processing of digital twin models. The data center controls the operation of the entire digital twin model through the storage and analysis of data. Due to the complexity of the construction process and the involvement of multiple elements, the data of the digital twin model are characterized by multiple data types and a large volume. The data of digital twin models can be divided into physical entity data, virtual model data, functional application data, and interactive integration data, according to their source [41], and can also be divided into static data and dynamic data from a temporal perspective.

Functional application. The functional application provides corresponding functions based on the specific construction needs. When a demand is initiated during the construction process, an in-depth analysis of the digital twin model in the construction process is carried out, relying on the data, computing power, and algorithm support of the data center. Functions such as the visual presentation, analysis, prediction, and control of the construction process are performed, and decisions are made that help the project personnel in the construction process.

Information link [31]. The information link refers to the interaction channel between the information and the resources of each module in the entire digital twin model [17]. The implementation of information links requires high-speed and stable communication networks (e.g., 5G, WiFi) to achieve the interconnection and exchange of information and resources among the various modules of the digital twin. The information link for the digital twin model of a steel structure construction process should also include a mapping method from the physical entities to the virtual entities, such as BIM models established through drawings and actual engineering situations.

## 4. Establishment Method for Digital Twin Model of the Steel Structure Construction Process

Based on the digital twin model architecture for steel structure construction processes, the establishment of a digital twin model includes three stages: the acquisition and transmission of physical space data, the construction of a digital twin virtual model, and information exchange in the digital twin model [42]. The acquisition and transmission of physical space data refers to the acquisition and transmission of relevant information about various elements of the construction process of steel structures in a physical space to a virtual space. Establishing virtual twin models involves creating digital models for the various construction elements of steel structures at the four levels of geometry, physics, behavior, and rules, and associating them with the physical space to form a multi-dimensional digital twin virtual model [43]. Based on digital twin theory, information exchange in the digital twin model allows for the combination of the various modules of the model, establishing closed-loop control of the digital twin model. The digital twin system provides technical support for the implementation of various processes in establishing the digital twin model, integrates specific functional modules, and provides a platform for project-related personnel to interact with the digital twin model. The establishment method for a digital twin model of a steel structure construction process is shown in Figure 2.

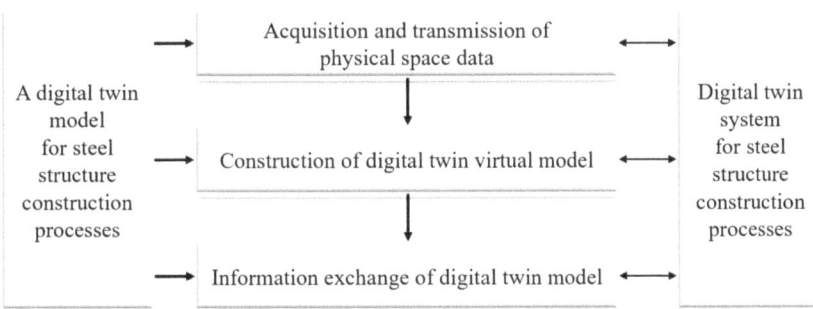

**Figure 2.** Operational flow of digital twin model.

*4.1. Acquisition and Transmission of Physical Space Data*

Data are the key to connecting the physical entity part with the digital twin virtual part. The acquisition of data for the various elements in the steel structure construction process is a primary issue in the application of digital twin technology. In the process of steel structure construction, the physical space data collection system is complex and dynamic, comprising the physical entity part and the data acquisition and transmission parts. Through comprehensively obtaining data on the various elements of the construction process, restoration of the physical space can be maximized in the virtual space. According to engineering practices [44], the physical space data of a steel structure construction process include the personnel, mechanical equipment, steel components, and environment (Equation (2)).

$$DT_{PS} = \{P_P, P_E, P_S, P_M\} \qquad (2)$$

where $DT_{PS}$ represents the set of physical space information, $P_P$ represents the set of personnel information, $P_E$ represents the set of mechanical equipment information, $P_S$ represents the information set of the steel components, and $P_M$ represents the set of environmental information.

The construction element information includes the number, size, shape, material, stress, and so on; the mechanical equipment information includes their function, location, status, and so on; the personnel information includes the personnel's numbers, positions, job types, and so on; and the environmental information includes the temperature, humidity, visibility, and so on.

Data acquisition modes include tag reading, sensor sensing, platform input, and other methods. For the acquisition of personnel information, their location information can be located in real time through smart helmets. Job types, numbers, and other personnel information can be entered into the digital twin system through platform input and matched with the other personnel information. Environmental information can be detected on the construction site through sensor devices and transmitted to the digital twin platform through the network. The information acquisition of the steel components is mainly achieved through reading RFID tags and information from sensors. During the construction process, the components will be used in different construction processes, such that the information on the components will change with the progress of the construction process. Regarding the change in information of the construction process components, the editable nature of their labels can be used to modify their information. Due to the complexity of the construction process, various types of construction machinery and equipment are required. To ensure that information is captured in real time during the construction process, an embedded information acquisition system is used to obtain real-time information on the current status of the machinery and equipment. According to a certain transmission protocol, the transmission of physical spatial information utilizes communication technology to transfer data from a data source to a database, mainly through network modules [6]. The processes for the acquisition and transmission of physical space data to the digital twin model during the steel structure construction process are depicted in Figure 3.

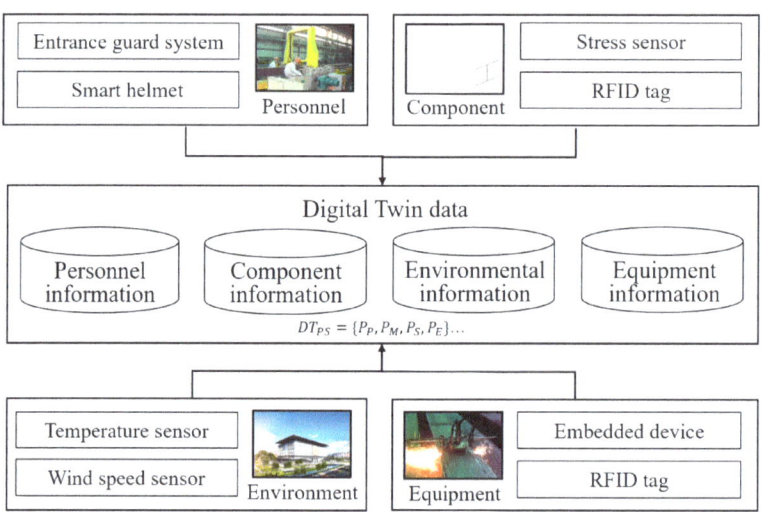

Figure 3. Acquisition and transmission of physical space data.

*4.2. Construction of the Digital Twin Virtual Model*

A digital twin virtual model is the concrete presentation of multi-source heterogeneous data in a virtual space. After the acquisition and transmission of the physical space data, it is necessary to analyze and process the acquired data to achieve high-fidelity simulation of the physical entities. According to the implementation logic of the digital twin virtual model, the virtual model carries out the establishment and association integration of the virtual model at the four levels of geometry, physics, behavior, and rules [41]. As a virtual digital mirror of the physical space, the digital twin virtual model reflects the real steel structure construction process of the physical space. After the acquisition and transmission of the physical space data, the data are processed, and a virtual model is established to realize the high-fidelity simulation of the physical space. Based on the implementation logic of the virtual model, the mathematical language expression of the virtual model is shown in Equation (3).

$$VM = \{V_G, V_P, V_B, V_R\} \qquad (3)$$

where $VM$ is the digital twin virtual model of the steel structure construction process, and $V_G, V_P, V_B, V_R$ represent virtual models at the four levels of geometry, physics, behavior, and rules, respectively.

The geometry model is a virtual representation of the geometric attributes of a physical entity, such as its geometric size, shape, and position. In comparison, the physics model is a virtual expression of the information that reflects the physical properties of an entity collected by means of sensor perception and two-dimensional code reading. The rule model provides a constraint rule corresponding to the reality for the establishment and operation of the virtual model according to the current standards and construction schemes. The behavior model integrates geometric, physical, and rule models and makes a corresponding response to the actual situation of the construction process driven by the construction demand. The four models at different levels work together to construct a digital twin virtual model for steel structure construction processes. The construction of a digital twin virtual model is shown in Figure 4.

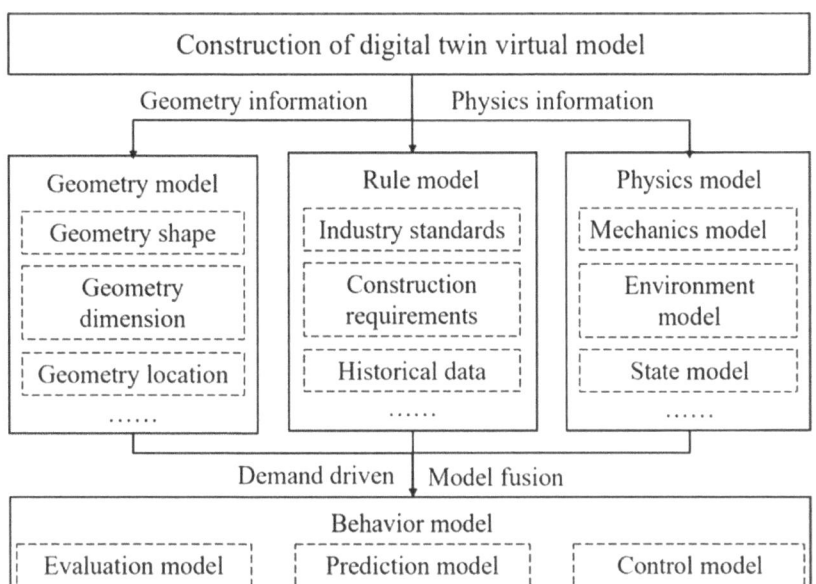

**Figure 4.** Construction of a digital twin virtual model.

*4.3. Information Exchange of Digital Twin Model*

The information exchange of the digital twin model in the steel structure construction process is achieved through data collection, transmission, analysis, and application [45]. According to the requirements of the construction process, the data from the physical space of the construction site are collected and transmitted to the virtual space through sensors and other methods, allowing for the operation of the digital twin model. Additionally, virtual spaces rely on the high computing power and algorithms of computing libraries to analyze and process data, and they provide corresponding functional support according to the actual construction needs of the physical space to support progress and decision making in steel structure construction processes.

Information exchange within the virtual space mainly occurs among the data center, virtual models, and functional modules. The data center provides data storage and algorithmic support for digital twin models, stores and processes multi-source heterogeneous data from the physical space, drives the modeling, updating, and simulation of virtual models, and supports the operation of the functional modules. The operation of its various modules is achieved through exchanging information within the digital twin model, thus forming closed-loop control of the digital twin, as shown in Figure 5. The various modules of the digital twin model are connected using Internet of Things technology, and based on a high-speed, stable, and low-latency data transmission protocol, a bidirectional data transmission channel is established between the physical space and the virtual space, completing the virtual–real interaction.

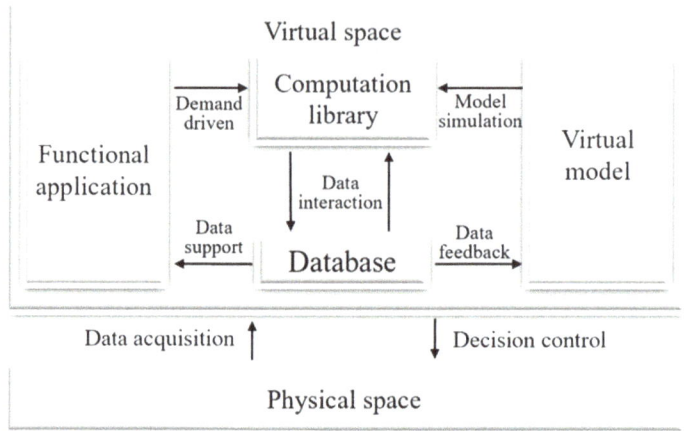

**Figure 5.** Information exchange of the digital twin model.

*4.4. Operation of Digital Twin System in Steel Structure Construction Process*

Operating the digital twin model in the steel structure construction process requires the collaboration of multiple information technologies. Using digital platform functions, such as data processing, parameter modeling, and intelligent analysis, digital twin models provide intelligent functional support for the construction process of steel structures, including visual presentation, construction simulation, intelligent welding, personnel management, environmental monitoring, and so on. In order to achieve the flow of information between various modules of the digital twin model in the steel structure construction process and to drive the operation of the digital twin model, support for the steel structure construction digital twin system is required, which includes a perception layer, transmission layer, data layer, terminal layer, and user layer, as shown in Figure 6.

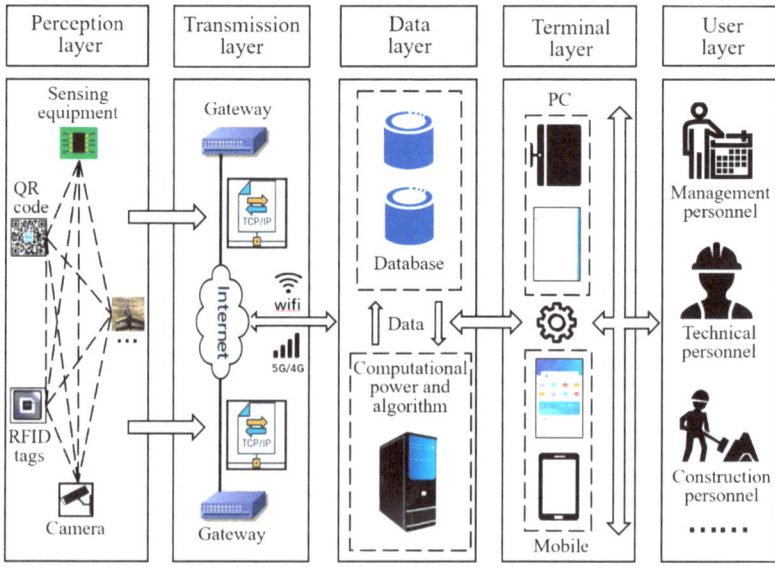

**Figure 6.** Digital twin system platform for the steel structure construction process.

Perception layer. The perception layer is the foundation for achieving information exchange between the physical and virtual spaces in digital twin models. As the construction process progresses, digital twin systems continuously generate multi-source heterogeneous data. Therefore, it is necessary to apply corresponding methods to perceive the data. Commonly used perception methods include QR code reading, sensor perception, and so on. For construction plans and other information, the corresponding data can be directly reflected in the data layer through platform input.

Transmission layer. The role of the transport layer is to transfer the data obtained by the perception layer to the database for management. The transport layer first processes the multi-source heterogeneous data obtained from sensors, videos, and so on, and relies on gateways to convert the data into a format that the server can receive. The data are then transmitted to the data layer through networks (e.g., wireless networks, mobile networks). Due to the characteristics of digital twin technology, the transmission network of the transport layer needs to have specific characteristics, such as fast speed and strong stability.

Data layer. The main function of the data layer is to store and analyze data, which is the key to ensuring the efficient operation of the digital twin model. Massive multi-source heterogeneous data from the physical entities and digital twin virtual models are transmitted to the data layer. The data layer improves the accuracy, completeness, and uniformity of the data through pre-processing them so they can be efficiently analyzed.

Terminal layer. The terminal layer relies on terminal devices and provides functional applications for the steel structure construction process based on the data analysis results of the data layer. The terminal layer is user-oriented and feeds back the operation process of the digital twin model to the user layer, providing support for the interaction between the users and the digital twin model.

User layer. The user layer is composed of the project-related personnel. The user layer is the feedback object of the digital twin system. The user layer is based on the terminal devices, and through its displayed digital twin system platform interface, it can obtain various information about the steel structure construction process in real time and control events that occur during the construction process in a timely manner.

## 5. Case Analysis

In order to further illustrate the characteristics of the digital twin model for steel structure construction and to present its specific implementation method more clearly, case studies were conducted from a macro perspective and a single-application perspective, using the steel structure construction processes of the university park library project in Xiongan New Area and the reconstruction and expansion project of the Nanchong Gaoping airport as examples.

*5.1. University Park Library Project in Xiongan New Area*

In the construction process of the university park library project in Xiongan New Area, various information technologies and platforms were used to obtain data on the construction elements and create virtual models. According to the virtual models and obtained data, intelligent construction technologies—such as steel structure construction process simulation, real-time personnel management, and real-time environmental monitoring—were applied, as shown in Figure 7.

To obtain and transmit the physical space data, information such as the personnel's numbers, job types, and work status was entered into the smart construction site platform as inputs. In addition, the locations and attendance information of the personnel were collected through intelligent safety helmets and access control systems, and the information was transmitted to the smart construction site personnel management module through the network to achieve efficient statistics on the personnel management process. Regarding the mechanical equipment, a perception module embedded in the tower crane was used to monitor the height, torque, and other working status information of the tower crane in real time, transmitting it to the smart construction site platform to manage the operating status of the tower crane. Regarding the materials, a logistics tracking platform was used to view the transportation trajectory of the steel structural components in real time and obtain the entry information of the materials. Regarding the environment, on-site sensors were used to detect the temperature, wind speed, noise, and other environmental factors, obtaining real-time environmental information on-site and providing a reference for the construction process.

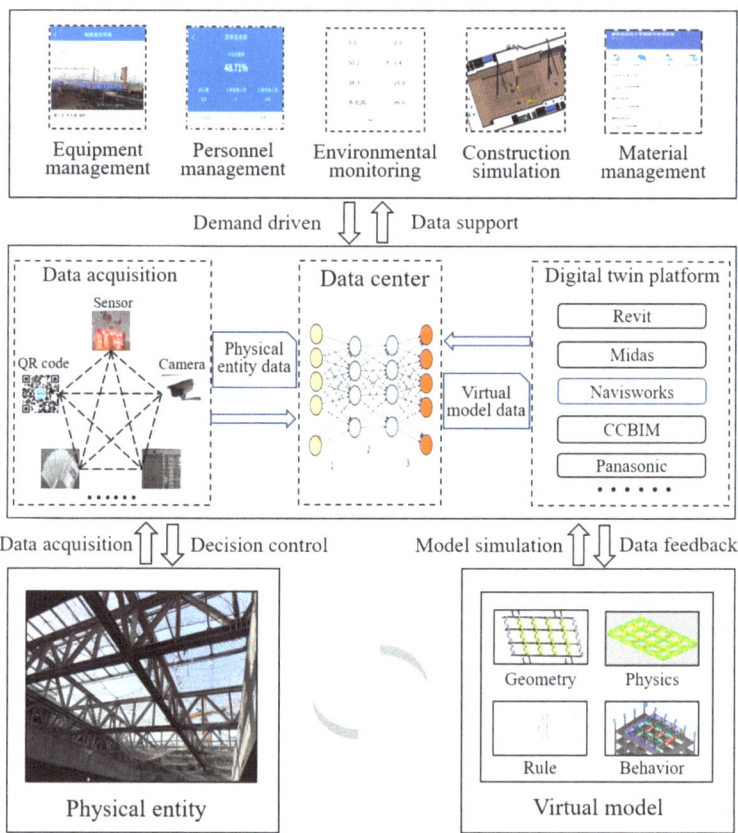

**Figure 7.** Application architecture of intelligent construction technology for steel structures based on digital twins.

With regard to the establishment of virtual models, in accordance with the information of architectural design drawings and the actual situation of the site, multiple software such as the BIM and finite element software were adopted to model the 3D virtual model of each professional design. The BIM model and finite element virtual model have the same geometric and physical properties as the physical entity. When modeling, the virtual model is constrained in line with the corresponding standards to form the rule model. Furthermore, the virtual model is integrated to drive the establishment of the behavior model through the needs of the construction process.

Through obtaining and transmitting physical entity data, constructing virtual models, and using networks and smart construction platforms to drive information exchange and the operation of a digital twin model, the establishment of digital twin models for steel structure construction processes can be achieved. Due to digital twin models, the construction and management process has become clearer and more direct, achieving information management of the personnel, machinery, and materials, and real-time monitoring of the environment during the construction process. In addition, quality and safety issues on-site can also be uploaded to virtual spaces through pictures and videos, enabling information-based management of the quality and safety aspects of the construction process. A digital twin model of the steel structure construction process can achieve the accurate, comprehensive, and rapid comprehension of various construction information, more effectively carry out collaborative management of the construction process, improve construction efficiency, reduce costs, and bring practical benefits to the process of construction projects.

*5.2. Reconstruction and Expansion Project of the Nanchong Gaoping Airport*

In the reconstruction and expansion project of the Nanchong Gaoping airport, the roof of Terminal T3 acquired a square pyramid grid structure with a maximum span of about 5 m and a maximum overhanging length of about 12 m. The digital twin model theory for steel structure construction processes was applied in the steel grid construction process of this project, as shown in Figure 8.

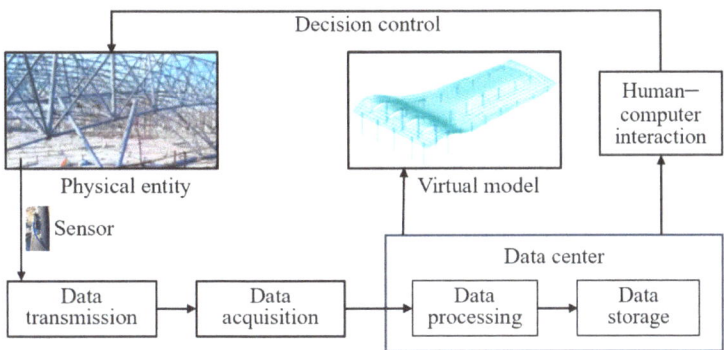

**Figure 8.** Example of application process.

Due to the long construction period of the steel grid structure in this project and the significant changes in the environmental temperature, the stress state of the steel structure was more significantly affected by temperature. Therefore, during the construction process, temperature and stress sensors were installed on the grid of the project to collect the stress and temperature data of the key steel components, which were transmitted to the platform. The virtual model was then modified based on the actual collected data. On the platform side, computers used the collected data to train and analyze machine learning algorithms. Through data training, the relationship between the temperature and stress of the key components of the steel grid structures was obtained, and then the impact of temperature changes on the stress of components could be predicted.

A BP neural network algorithm was adopted to process 600 sets of data to determine the relationship between temperature and stress. There were 480 sets of data in the training set and 120 sets of data in the testing set. A comparison between the predicted results on the neural network test set and the true monitoring values is shown in Figure 9, and some data are shown in Table 1. As shown in the figure, the predicted values (PVs) obtained from the BP neural network algorithm were highly consistent with the true values (TVs), indicating that the BP neural network established a reliable relationship between the temperature and stress during the steel structure construction and had high accuracy. By training machine learning algorithms on the temperature and stress data sets collected with sensors, it will be possible to accurately predict the impact of temperature changes on the stress of steel structural components in the future. Furthermore, the predicted results can be presented to relevant personnel to better guide the next construction step of the project, thereby forming closed-loop control of the steel structure construction process and ensuring safety during the construction process.

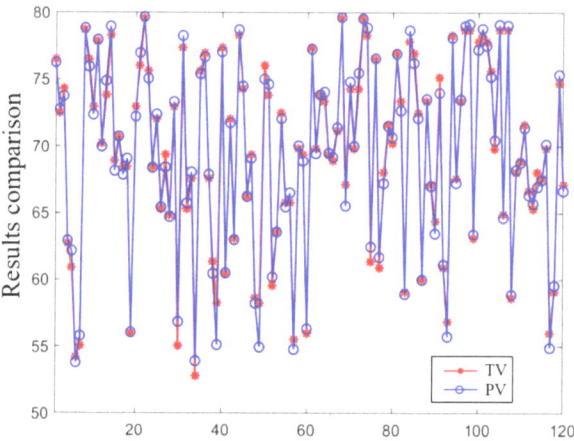

**Figure 9.** Comparison of prediction results.

**Table 1.** Temperatures and stress values.

| No. | Temperature /°C | Stress (TV) /MPa | PV /MPa | No. | Temperature/°C | Stress (TV) /MPa | PV /MPa |
|---|---|---|---|---|---|---|---|
| 1 | 17.105 | 79.584 | 79.590 | 13 | 29.246 | 65.117 | 65.052 |
| 2 | 18.373 | 77.823 | 77.935 | 14 | 30.217 | 64.469 | 64.097 |
| 3 | 19.043 | 77.823 | 77.040 | 15 | 31.867 | 62.252 | 62.468 |
| 4 | 20.106 | 76.941 | 75.609 | 16 | 32.415 | 60.916 | 61.919 |
| 5 | 21.229 | 74.282 | 74.110 | 17 | 33.495 | 60.470 | 60.822 |
| 6 | 22.359 | 72.947 | 72.644 | 18 | 34.066 | 61.362 | 60.231 |
| 7 | 23.556 | 71.608 | 71.157 | 19 | 35.342 | 59.577 | 58.882 |
| 8 | 24.368 | 69.817 | 70.194 | 20 | 36.040 | 58.682 | 58.126 |
| 9 | 25.229 | 69.817 | 69.214 | 21 | 37.223 | 59.577 | 56.816 |
| 10 | 26.113 | 69.368 | 68.247 | 22 | 38.647 | 56.887 | 55.195 |
| 11 | 27.426 | 67.117 | 66.874 | 23 | 39.336 | 54.634 | 54.395 |
| 12 | 28.305 | 66.665 | 65.986 | 24 | 40.714 | 54.182 | 52.774 |

## 6. Summary and Future Works

At present, practical problems, such as a low level of informatization and excessive reliance on experience, affect the construction process of steel structures. Traditional construction methods are not able to adapt to modern production methods. Therefore, there is an urgent need to achieve real-time, efficient, and accurate statistics, simulation, analysis, and prediction of construction processes to make the management of the construction of steel structures more efficient and decision making more scientific. In this context, the emergence and application of a large number of information technologies have provided new ideas for solving these problems.

Based on rapidly developing digital and information technology, this article proposed a digital twin model for the steel structure construction process, analyzing its connotations and characteristics. Furthermore, an operation method for the digital twin modeling of steel structure construction processes was proposed, including three stages: the acquisition and transmission of physical space data, the construction of virtual models, and information exchange in the digital twin model. Digital twin modeling of steel structure construction processes provides an intelligent method for steel structure construction, contributes different functions according to the different needs of the construction process, and reduces the influence of human factors in the construction process. Therefore, digital twin modeling could improve the accuracy of construction process decision making and achieve intelligent construction and management methods.

Using the proposed steel structure digital twin model and its operating method, the authors of this article took the steel structure of the university park library project in Xiongan New Area as an example and conducted a case analysis from a macro perspective. A construction system based on a digital twin model was built for this project, utilizing technologies such as BIM, the Internet of Things, and smart construction platforms and achieving good results in its construction and management efficiency, energy consumption control, and other aspects. Furthermore, taking the reconstruction and expansion project of the Nanchong Gaoping airport as an example, a case study was conducted from the perspective of a single-point application to illustrate the details of data collection and data processing in the digital twin model of a steel structure construction process.

Digital twin technology plays a pivotal role in achieving intelligent construction and management during the construction process. This paper came up with a digital twin model architecture for steel structure construction processes and delved into its establishment method. But for the time being, the application of digital twin technology in steel structure construction still confronts a multitude of challenges. For this reason, the next step should be guided by the specific requirements of the steel structure construction process, starting from the bottom technology and standard level, so as to explore how to collect, fuse, and process physical entity data in an all-round and real-time manner, further develop corresponding digital twin platform systems, integrate specific functional modules, and provide guidance for on-site construction. With further technological development, the application of digital twin technology in steel structure construction is expected to become increasingly comprehensive, thereby promoting the better development of steel structures.

**Author Contributions:** Conceptualization, Z.L.; methodology, S.L.; software, Z.L. and S.L.; validation, Z.L. and S.L.; writing—original draft preparation, S.L.; writing—review and editing, Z.L.; project administration, Z.L. All authors have read and agreed to the published version of the manuscript.

**Funding:** This research received no external funding.

**Data Availability Statement:** The data presented in this study are available upon request from the corresponding author. The data are not publicly available due to confidentiality.

**Acknowledgments:** The authors would like to thank the Beijing University of Technology for its support throughout the research project.

**Conflicts of Interest:** The authors declare no conflicts of interest. The funders had no role in the study's design; in the collection, analyses, or interpretation of data; in the writing of the manuscript; or in the decision to publish the results.

## References

1. Opoku, D.-G.J.; Perera, S.; Osei-Kyei, R.; Rashidi, M. Digital twin application in the construction industry: A literature review. *J. Build. Eng.* **2021**, *40*, 102726. [CrossRef]
2. Liu, Z.; Sun, X.; Shi, G. Summary of application of intelligent construction in civil engineering construction. *Constr. Technol.* **2021**, *50*, 40–53.
3. Zhang, J.; Chen, M.; Ballesteros-Pérez, P.; Ke, Y.; Gong, Z.; Ni, Q. A new framework to evaluate and optimize digital transformation policies in the construction industry: A China case study. *J. Build. Eng.* **2023**, *70*, 106388. [CrossRef]
4. Baduge, S.K.; Thilakarathna, S.; Perera, J.S.; Arashpour, M.; Sharafi, P.; Teodosio, B.; Shringi, A.; Mendis, P. Artificial intelligence and smart vision for building and construction 4.0: Machine and deep learning methods and applications. *Autom. Constr.* **2022**, *141*, 104440. [CrossRef]
5. Sepasgozar, S.M.E.; Khan, A.A.; Smith, K.; Romero, J.G.; Shen, X.; Shirowzhan, S.; Li, H.; Tahmasebinia, F. BIM and Digital Twin for Developing Convergence Technologies as Future of Digital Construction. *Buildings* **2023**, *13*, 441. [CrossRef]
6. Tuhaise, V.V.; Tah, J.H.M.; Abanda, F.H. Technologies for digital twin applications in construction. *Autom. Constr.* **2023**, *152*, 104931. [CrossRef]
7. Fan, Q.; Lin, P.; Wei, P.; Ning, Z.; Li, G. Closed-loop control theory of intelligence construction. *J. Tsinghua Univ. (Sci. Technol.)* **2021**, *61*, 660–670.
8. Mao, C.; Peng, Y. The Theoretical Framework and Core Logic of Intelligent Construction. *J. Eng. Manag.* **2020**, *34*, 1–6.
9. Niu, Y.; Anumba, C.; Lu, W. Taxonomy and deployment framework for emerging pervasive technologies in construction projects. *J. Constr. Eng. Manag.* **2019**, *145*, 04019028. [CrossRef]

10. Ghosh, A.; Edwards, D.J.; Hosseini, M.R. Patterns and trends in Internet of Things (IoT) research: Future applications in the construction industry. *Eng. Constr. Archit. Manag.* **2021**, *28*, 457–481. [CrossRef]
11. Chen, H.P.; Ying, K.C. Artificial Intelligence in the Construction Industry: Main Development Trajectories and Future Outlook. *Appl. Sci.* **2022**, *12*, 5832. [CrossRef]
12. Zabin, A.; González, V.A.; Zou, Y.; Amor, R. Applications of machine learning to BIM: A systematic literature review. *Adv. Eng. Inform.* **2022**, *51*, 101474. [CrossRef]
13. Tak, A.N.; Taghaddos, H.; Mousaei, A.; Bolourani, A.; Hermann, U. BIM-based 4D mobile crane simulation and onsite operation management. *Autom. Constr.* **2021**, *128*, 103766. [CrossRef]
14. Liu, H.; Cheng, J.C.; Gan, V.J.L.; Zhou, S. A knowledge model-based BIM framework for automatic code-compliant quantity take-off. *Autom. Constr.* **2022**, *133*, 104024. [CrossRef]
15. Lin, J.; Guo, J. BIM-based automatic compliance checking. *J. Tsinghua Univ. (Sci. Technol.)* **2020**, *60*, 873–879.
16. Yang, B.; Liu, B.; Xiao, J. Disassembly analysis and realization of steel frame structure based on BIM. *J. Build. Struct.* **2022**, *43*, 305–314.
17. Wang, Y.-G.; He, X.-J.; He, J.; Fan, C. Virtual trial assembly of steel structure based on BIM platform. *Autom. Constr.* **2022**, *141*, 104395. [CrossRef]
18. Wu, L.; Lu, W.; Xue, F.; Li, X.; Zhao, R.; Tang, M. Linking permissioned blockchain to Internet of Things (IoT)-BIM platform for off-site production management in modular construction. *Comput. Ind.* **2022**, *135*, 103573. [CrossRef]
19. Abioye, S.O.; Oyedele, L.O.; Akanbi, L.; Ajayi, A.; Delgado, J.M.D.; Bilal, M.; Akinade, O.O.; Ahmed, A. Artificial intelligence in the construction industry: A review of present status, opportunities and future challenges. *J. Build. Eng.* **2021**, *44*, 103299. [CrossRef]
20. Liu, J.; Cui, N.; Cheng, G.; Li, D.; Ma, X.; Liao, Y. Towards the automated virtual trial assembly of large and complex steel members using terrestrial laser scanning and BIM. *Eng. Struct.* **2023**, *291*, 116448. [CrossRef]
21. Schiavi, B.; Havard, V.; Beddiar, K.; Baudry, D. BIM data flow architecture with AR/VR technologies: Use cases in architecture, engineering and construction. *Autom. Constr.* **2022**, *134*, 104054. [CrossRef]
22. Ma, Z.; Ren, Y. Integrated application of BIM and GIS: An overview. *Procedia Eng.* **2017**, *196*, 1072–1079. [CrossRef]
23. Zhong, R.Y.; Peng, Y.; Xue, F.; Fang, J.; Zou, W.; Luo, H.; Ng, S.T.; Lu, W.; Shen, G.Q.P.; Huang, G.Q. Prefabricated construction enabled by the Internet-of-Things. *Autom. Constr.* **2017**, *76*, 59–70. [CrossRef]
24. Su, S.; Zhong, R.Y.; Jiang, Y.; Song, J.; Fu, Y.; Cao, H. Digital twin and its potential applications in construction industry: State-of-art review and a conceptual framework. *Adv. Eng. Inform.* **2023**, *57*, 102030. [CrossRef]
25. Sheng, J.; Zhang, Q.; Li, H.; Shen, S.; Ming, R.; Jiang, J.; Li, Q.; Su, G.; Sun, B.; Huang, C.; et al. Digital twin driven intelligent manufacturing for FPCB etching production line. *Comput. Ind. Eng.* **2023**, *186*, 109763. [CrossRef]
26. Dong, L.; Zhou, X.; Zhao, F.; He, S.; Lu, Z.; Feng, J. Key technologies for modeling and simulation of airframe digital twin. *Acta Aeronaut. Astronaut. Sin.* **2021**, *42*, 113–141.
27. Leng, J.; Wang, D.; Shen, W.; Li, X.; Liu, Q.; Chen, X. Digital twins-based smart manufacturing system design in Industry 4.0: A review. *J. Manuf. Syst.* **2021**, *60*, 119–137. [CrossRef]
28. Haleem, A.; Javaid, M.; Singh, R.P.; Suman, R. Exploring the revolution in healthcare systems through the applications of digital twin technology. *Biomed. Technol.* **2023**, *4*, 28–38. [CrossRef]
29. Cho, J.; Kim, C.; Lim, K.J.; Kim, J.; Ji, B.; Yeon, J. Web-based agricultural infrastructure digital twin system integrated with GIS and BIM concepts. *Comput. Electron. Agric.* **2023**, *215*, 108441. [CrossRef]
30. Bai, H.; Wang, Y. Digital power grid based on digital twin: Definition, structure and key technologies. *Energy Rep.* **2022**, *8*, 390–397. [CrossRef]
31. Li, Q.; Liu, J.; Li, J.; Zhang, C.; Guo, J.; Wang, X.; Ran, W. Digital twin of mine ecological environment: Connotation, framework and key technologies. *J. China Coal Soc.* **2023**, *48*, 3859–3873.
32. Tao, F.; Liu, W.; Zhang, M.; Hu, T.; Qi, Q.; Zhang, H.; Sui, F.; Wang, T.; Xu, H.; Huang, Z.; et al. Five dimension digital twin model and its ten applications. *Comput. Integr. Manuf. Syst.* **2019**, *25*, 1–18.
33. Tao, F.; Xiao, B.; Qi, Q.; Cheng, J.; Ji, P. Digital twin modeling. *J. Manuf. Syst.* **2022**, *64*, 372–389. [CrossRef]
34. Zhang, D.; Wang, Y.; Liao, S.; Lu, Y. Review of Digital Twin Construction Technology for Civil Engineering. *Constr. Technol.* **2023**, *52*, 1–12.
35. Liu, Z.; Liu, Z.S.; Sun, J.; Du, X. Intelligent construction methods and model experiments based on digital twins. *J. Build. Struct.* **2021**, *42*, 26–36.
36. Pan, Y.; Zhang, L. A BIM-data mining integrated digital twin framework for advanced project management. *Autom. Constr.* **2021**, *124*, 103564. [CrossRef]
37. Wang, X.; Wang, S.; Song, X.; Han, Y. IoT-based intelligent construction system for prefabricated buildings: Study of operating mechanism and implementation in China. *Appl. Sci.* **2020**, *10*, 6311. [CrossRef]
38. Zhao, Y.; Wang, N.; Liu, Z.; Mu, E. Construction theory for a building intelligent operation and maintenance system based on digital twins and machine learning. *Buildings* **2022**, *12*, 87. [CrossRef]
39. Torzoni, M.; Tezzele, M.; Mariani, S.; Manzoni, A.; Willcox, K.E. A digital twin framework for civil engineering structures. *Comput. Methods Appl. Mech. Eng.* **2024**, *418*, 116584. [CrossRef]

40. Yevu, S.K.; Owusu, E.K.; Chan, A.P.C.; Sepasgozar, S.M.E.; Kamat, V.R. Digital twin-enabled prefabrication supply chain for smart construction and carbon emissions evaluation in building projects. *J. Build. Eng.* **2023**, *78*, 107598. [CrossRef]
41. Wu, X.; Liu, J.; Chen, H.; Xu, W.; Liu, X. Digital Twin Frame System of Shield Tunneling System. *J. Inf. Technol. Civ. Eng. Archit.* **2023**, *15*, 105–110.
42. Qian, W.; Guo, Y.; Zhang, L.; Huang, S.; Genget, S. Towards discrete manufacturing workshop-oriented digital twin model: Modeling, verification and evolution. *J. Manuf. Syst.* **2023**, *71*, 188–205. [CrossRef]
43. Tao, F.; Zhang, H.; Qi, Q.; Xu, J.; Sun, Z.; Hu, T.; Liu, X.; Liu, T.; Guan, J.; Chen, C. Theory of digital twin modeling and its application. *J. Manuf. Syst.* **2021**, *27*, 1–15. [CrossRef]
44. Jiang, W.; Ding, L.; Zhou, C. Cyber physical system for safety management in smart construction site. *Eng. Constr. Archit. Manag.* **2021**, *3*, 788–808. [CrossRef]
45. Dihan, M.S.; Akash, A.I.; Tasneem, Z.; Das, P.; Das, S.K.; Islam, M.R.; Islam, M.M.; Badal, F.R.; Ali, M.F.; Ahamed, M.H. Digital Twin: Data Exploration, Architecture, Implementation and Future. *Heliyon* **2024**, *5*, e26503. [CrossRef] [PubMed]

**Disclaimer/Publisher's Note:** The statements, opinions and data contained in all publications are solely those of the individual author(s) and contributor(s) and not of MDPI and/or the editor(s). MDPI and/or the editor(s) disclaim responsibility for any injury to people or property resulting from any ideas, methods, instructions or products referred to in the content.

Article

# Seismic Performance of H-Shaped Steel Column with Replaceable Slip Friction Joints

Cheng-Yu Li [1,2,*], Fan Wang [1] and Ai-Zhu Zhu [3]

[1] School of Urban Construction, Wuhan University of Science and Technology, No. 947 Heping Avenue, Wuhan 430081, China
[2] Hubei Provincial Engineering Research Center of Urban Regeneration, Wuhan University of Science and Technology, No. 947 Heping Avenue, Wuhan 430081, China
[3] School of Civil and Hydraulic Engineering, Huazhong University of Science and Technology, No. 1037 Luoyu Road, Wuhan 430074, China
* Correspondence: lichengyu@wust.edu.cn; Tel.: +86-133-1714-6067

**Abstract:** Based on the concept of structural damage control, a beam-through steel frame system with continuous columns was constructed. Replaceable connectors were set at both ends of an H-shaped steel column to connect the beam with high-strength bolts. In this study, three specimens were designed and fabricated, that is, a standard H-shaped column, an H-shaped column with replaceable connectors at the bottom of the column, and an H-shaped column with replaceable connectors at both ends. Low-circumferential reciprocal loading tests were carried out to analyse the influence of the location of replaceable slip friction joints on the seismic performance of steel columns. Results showed that the H-shaped steel column with replaceable slip friction joints at both ends slipped during the loading process, as expected. The test hysteresis curve was full, and the skeleton curve did not drop significantly; thus, the column demonstrated satisfactory seismic performance. The steel column was not significantly damaged or deformed, and connectors could be reset and replaced after an earthquake to achieve post-earthquake repair. The effect of the thickness of the horizontal limbs of the connectors on the seismic performance of the H-shaped column with replaceable connectors at both ends was analysed using finite element simulation. The results revealed that the reasonable setting of the thickness of the horizontal limbs of the connectors can ensure the frictional energy dissipation capacity of the connectors and achieve the expected damage control.

**Keywords:** frictional energy dissipation; seismic performance; damage control; replaceable connector; column ends

## 1. Introduction

Modularized prefabricated steel structures have the advantages of short construction periods, less construction waste, low labor demand, and construction quality assurance [1–3]. In the modularized prefabricated steel structures, the use of beam-through type joints with the disconnection of the column at the floor can greatly improve the assembly efficiency of the structural system and the flexibility of spatial layout. At present, much research has been carried out on beam-through frame construction. Yao et al. [4] proposed a modified eccentrically braced frame system steel beam-through frames, aiming at improving energy dissipation capacity and seismic resistance. Du et al. [5] proposed a beam-through moment-resisting joint for H-section (wide-flange) beams and studied its seismic performance. Chen et al. [6] studied the tension-only concentrically braced beam-through frames.

In an ideal steel frame failure mode, seismic energy is typically dissipated by plastic hinges formed at the beam ends. However, owing to the randomness of seismic action and the uncertainty of the effect of the floor slab on a frame beam, the structure is difficult to completely avoid plastic hinges at the column ends, resulting in structural damage at a weak level [7]. Some researchers have shown that the vertical continuous stiffness contributes to the prevention of the formation of a weak layer failure mechanism. MacRae [8] introduced the concept of the continuous column, emphasising that continuous support stiffness at the column can prevent local collapse failure. Li et al. [9] proposed an energy-dissipative rocking column (EDRC) with beam-through configuration, which can reduce maximum inter-story drift and the drift concentration of low-rise buildings under earthquakes. Qu et al. [10] summarised several different forms of strong spine systems in steel buildings, showing that different forms of critical integral members can effectively distribute the lateral displacement of the structure under seismic action and avoid the weak layer damage in the structure.

Under earthquake action, the plastic hinge formed at the column end would lead to the axial shortening of the steel column, reduction of the bearing capacity, and failure of the weak layer of the structure, impacting the seismic stability of the structure [11–13]. Therefore, damage control should be conducted to contain the damage to repairable elements [14,15]. Frictional energy dissipation was widely used in damage control studies. Zhang et al. [16] proposed a new type of prefabricated cross-hinge column foot joint, for which the energy dissipation capacity is stable by the plastic deformation of LRECD and friction between plates. Liu [17,18] proposed a new type of site-bolted assembly joint and revealed that a slip of the bolts can significantly affect the node stiffness as well as the energy dissipation capacity of the joint. Zhang et al. [19] investigated the seismic performance of a steel rocking column-base joint equipped with an asymmetric friction connection (AFC). This joint can dissipate energy by frictional slipping instead of the yielding or buckling of the component and can be reused after a strong earthquake. Freddi et al. [20] conducted a study on an earthquake-resilient rocking damage-free steel column base, which uses friction devices to dissipate seismic energy. Chung et al. [21] proposed a special asymmetrical resistance friction damper (ARFD) for rocking column base.

Based on the theory of the column hinge energy dissipation mechanism, combined with the concepts of continuous column, slipping friction energy dissipation joints, and other new seismic design conceptions, the research team carried out a beam-through steel frame system with column ends slipping friction joints from the system level as shown in Figure 1. The plastic damage was transferred to the connectors and friction plates at the joints to achieve no or minimal damage to the main components. The joints are simple and easy to fabricate, assemble, and disassemble. The joints can be repaired quickly after an earthquake by replacing the connectors and friction plates. The seismic performance of H-shaped steel columns with replaceable slipping friction joints was tested and analysed.

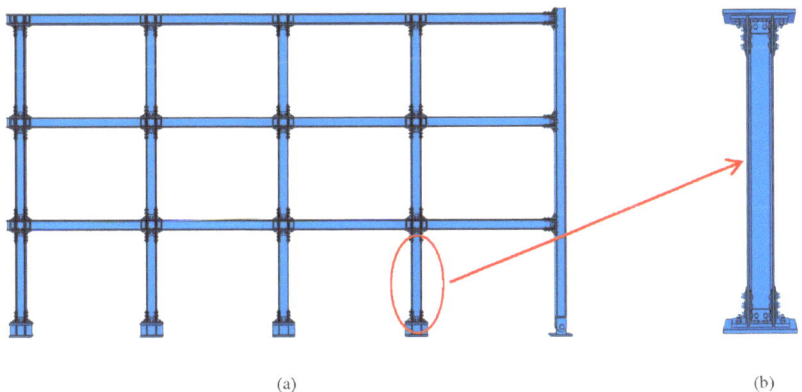

**Figure 1.** Test specimen model. (**a**) Continuous column frame structural system; (**b**) H-shaped column with replaceable slipping friction joints at both ends.

## 2. Construction and Working Principle

The joint specimen consists of an H-shaped steel column, two internal connectors, two external connectors, two web brass friction plates, two external flange brass friction plates, four internal flange brass friction plates, and several friction-type high-strength bolts, as shown in Figure 2. Long slotted holes and large round holes were created on the flange and web of the H-shaped steel column to allow for rotation. A 10 mm gap was left between the bottom end of the brass friction plates and the base plate to reduce the prying effect of the column end on the joint. In a small earthquake, the joints will not rotate. In a large earthquake, the steel column will rotate around one side of the flange, and the relative slipping between the steel column and brass friction plate will dissipate the seismic energy via slipping friction. The H-shaped steel column will basically remain elastic to achieve the objective of no energy loss.

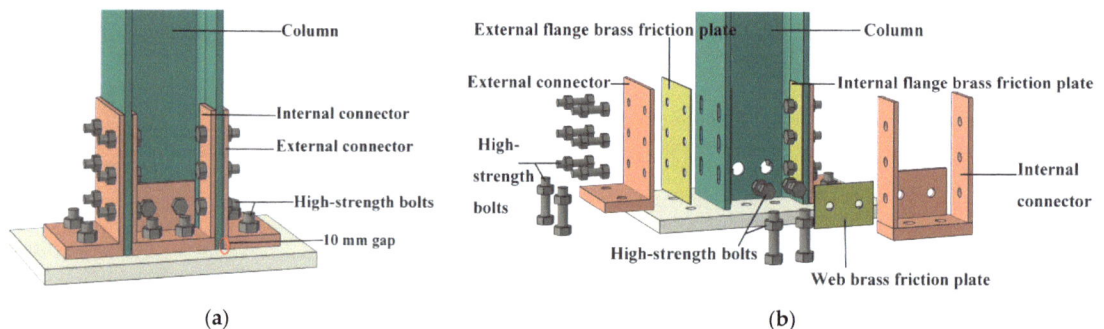

**Figure 2.** Replaceable slip friction joint. (**a**) The assembly joint; (**b**) components of the joint.

## 3. Overview of Experiment

### 3.1. Specimen Specification

Details of the specimen design are presented in Figures 3 and 4. Specimen C-1 is an ordinary H-shaped column used as a standard specimen to compare with other specimens. Specimen C-2 is an H-shaped column with a replaceable connector slip friction joint at the bottom of the column. Specimen C-3 is an H-shaped column with replaceable connector slip friction joints at both ends of the column. The influence of the joint location on the seismic performance of the steel column was analysed.

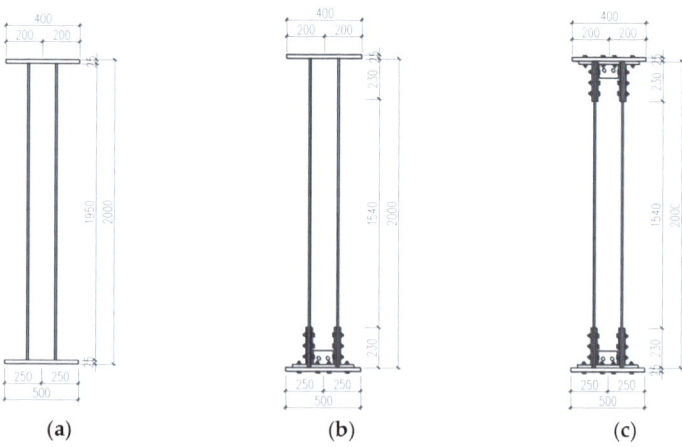

**Figure 3.** Test specimens (mm): (**a**) dimensions of C-1; (**b**) dimensions of C-2; (**c**) dimensions of C-3.

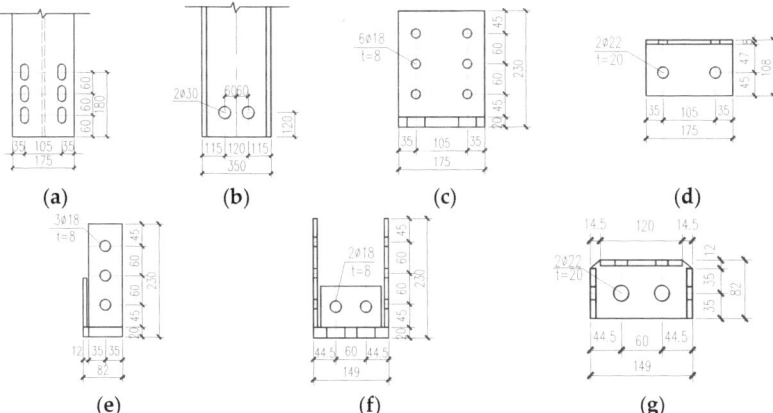

**Figure 4.** Specifications of the joint members (mm): (**a**) hole design of the flange; (**b**) hole design of the web; (**c**) holes on the vertical limb of the external connector; (**d**) holes on the horizontal limb of the external connector; (**e**) design of the vertical limb of the internal connector; (**f**) design of the internal connector; (**g**) design of the internal connector.

The steel column cross-sectional dimensions are HW 175 mm × 175 mm × 7.5 mm × 11 mm, with a column height of 2000 mm. Specifically, the H-shaped column and connectors were selected from Q355B (nominal yield stress is 355 MPa) steel, and a 2-mm-thick brass friction plate was set between the steel column and connectors. The contact surface was sandblasted, the vertical legs of the connectors were attached to the column with high-strength bolts with a strength grade of 10.9 (with nominal ultimate strengths 1000 MPa and the yield ratio equals 0.9) and nominal diameter of 16 mm, and the connectors' horizontal legs were attached to the base plate with bolts of the same strength but with a nominal diameter of 20 mm. Disc washers were used to prevent the bolts from loosening.

*3.2. Material Property Tests*

In accordance with the provisions of the room-temperature tensile test method for metallic materials (GB/T228-2021) [22], standard material property tests were conducted on the flanges and webs of the sections and joints, and the test results are reported in Table 1.

**Table 1.** Mechanical properties of steel materials from steel coupon tests.

| Sampling Position | Steel Type | $f_y$/MPa | $f_u$/MPa | δ |
| --- | --- | --- | --- | --- |
| Column flange | Q355B | 398.35 | 591.85 | 27% |
| Column web | Q355B | 435.40 | 606.89 | 25% |
| Connector horizontal leg | Q355B | 404.05 | 480.43 | 24% |
| Connector vertical leg | Q355B | 410.19 | 552.71 | 24% |

*3.3. Test Set-Up*

The test set-up is shown in Figure 5. The set-up was mainly composed of the reaction wall, a four-link rod, an actuator, a hydraulic jack, etc. The horizontal load of the specimen was provided by an actuator with a maximum limitation of 500 kN. The range of the actuator was ±150 mm. The vertical load was provided by a hydraulic jack with maximum limitation of 200 ton. A horizontal slipping device was placed between the reaction frame and the hydraulic jack. The friction coefficient was 0.01 to meet the lateral displacement and ensure that the specimen always maintained the axial stress state during the loading process.

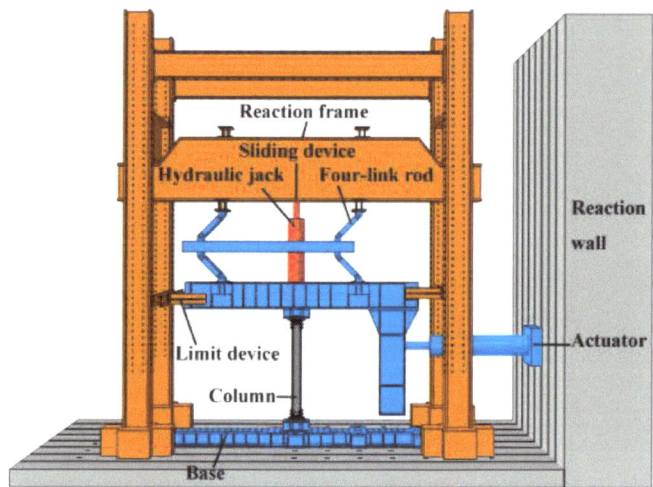

**Figure 5.** Test set-up.

*3.4. Loading Solutions*

Test loading solutions referred to the provisions of the American AISC seismic code [23], and the loading was controlled by the inter-story displacement angle. The loading solutions are depicted in Figure 6. The actual loading was conducted using the displacement corresponding to each inter-story displacement angle. The first three levels of loading were cycled six times each, and the fourth level of loading was cycled four times. Next, each level was cycled twice, and the loading was stopped at the ninth level (0.05 rad). The vertical load was applied using the hydraulic jack, and the corresponding column axial pressure ratio was taken as 0.2 [23–25]. Before the formal test, the specimens were pre-loaded to check whether the test device and measuring equipment were working properly.

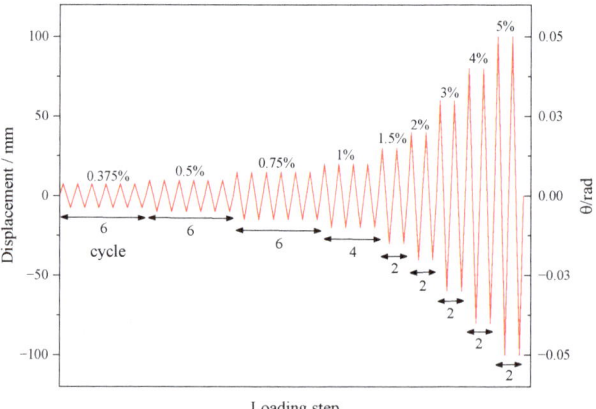

**Figure 6.** Test loading solutions.

*3.5. Strain Gauge and Displacement Metre Arrangement*

The displacement and strain gauges are presented in Figures 7 and 8, respectively. The strain gauges were arranged on the flange and web of the H-shaped steel columns, the horizontal and vertical legs of the connectors, and so on in order to measure the strain of the steel columns and connectors with high stress.

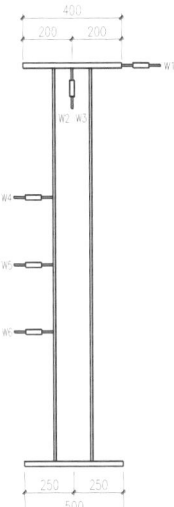

**Figure 7.** Displacement metre arrangement.

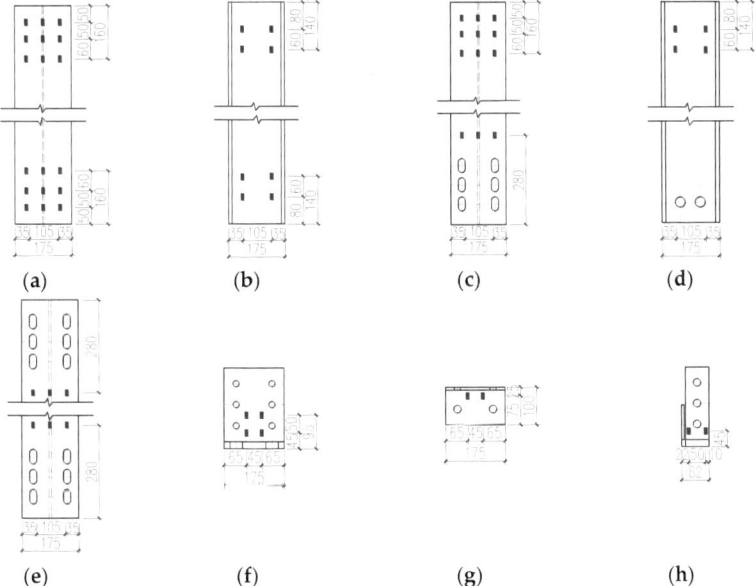

**Figure 8.** Strain gauge arrangement: (**a**) C-1 winged edge; (**b**) C-1 and C-3 webs; (**c**) C-2 winged edge; (**d**) C-2 web; (**e**) C-3 winged edge; (**f**) external connector vertical limb; (**g**) external connector horizontal limb; (**h**) internal connector vertical limb.

Displacement metre W1 was arranged at the loading position to measure the displacement of the end of the column. Displacement metres W2 and W3 were, respectively, arranged at the front and back of the midpoint of the column top to measure the axial shortening of the test piece. Displacement metres W4, W5, and W6 were arranged at the 1/3, 1/2, and 2/3 lengths of the test piece, respectively, in order to measure the displacement of the test piece along the horizontal loading direction.

## 4. Test Results and Analysis
### 4.1. Deformation Modes

The deformation modes of specimen C-1 are shown in Figure 9a–c. The steel column exhibited no obvious change under the first three levels of the loading. When the second cycle of the seventh level was 60 mm (0.03 rad), the top flange of the column showed slight buckling deformation. When the first cycle of the eighth stage was −80 mm (−0.04 rad), symmetric buckling deformation occurred on the left and right flanges of the column base, as shown in Figure 9c. When the load reached 80 mm (0.04 rad) in the second cycle of the eighth stage, buckling deformation was observed on the column base and column top web of the test specimen. It was loaded to the end of the first cycle of 100 mm (0.05 rad) at the ninth level, and then the test was stopped.

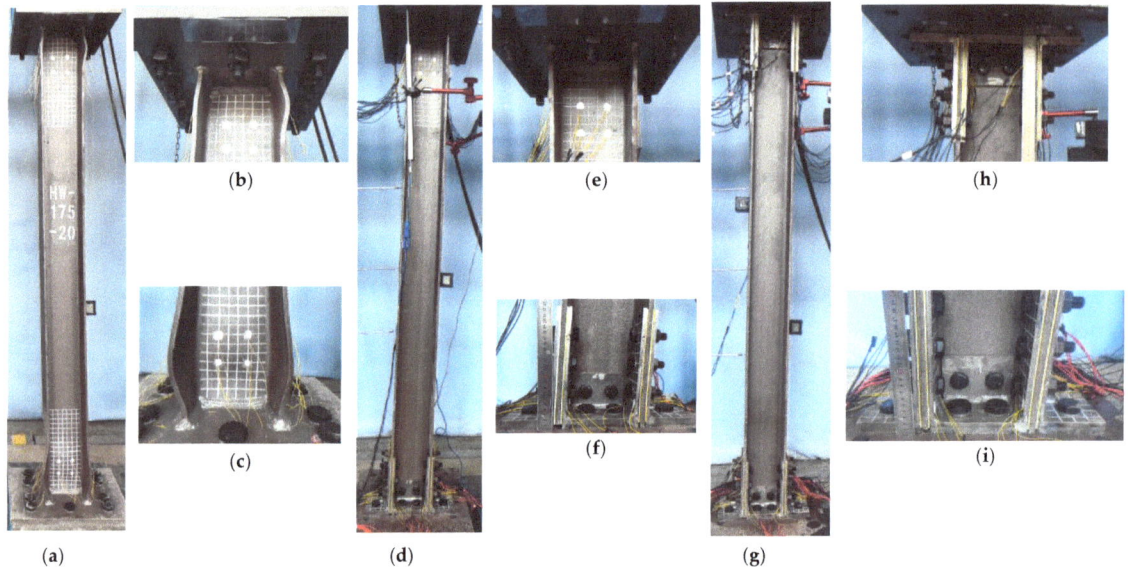

**Figure 9.** Deformation modes of specimens: (**a**) C-1 overall; (**b**) C-1 column top; (**c**) C-1 column base; (**d**) C-2 overall; (**e**) C-2 column top; (**f**) C-2 column base; (**g**) C-3 overall; (**h**) C-3 column top; (**i**) C-3 column base.

The deformation modes of specimen C-2 are shown in Figure 9d–f. The steel column exhibited no obvious change under the first two levels of the loading. When the horizontal displacement was loaded to 15 mm (0.0075 rad) in the first cycle of the third stage, slip rotation was observed on the column base joint. Loading was stopped until the second cycle of the ninth stage was −100 mm (−0.05 rad), and the tensile side of the column base flange was lifted approximately 11 mm, as shown in Figure 9f. After the test, the tensile side of the specimen was disassembled, as shown in Figure 10. Obvious bending deformation was observed between the column base flange and the vertical legs of the connectors, as shown in Figure 10a. The brass friction plates were obviously worn because the steel column was hard, yet the brass friction plates are soft. When the joint rotated owing to friction, the small bumps on the surface of the steel column were then embedded in the brass friction gaskets, 'furrow-like' scratches, which were finally manifested as abrasive wear [26], as shown in Figure 10b.

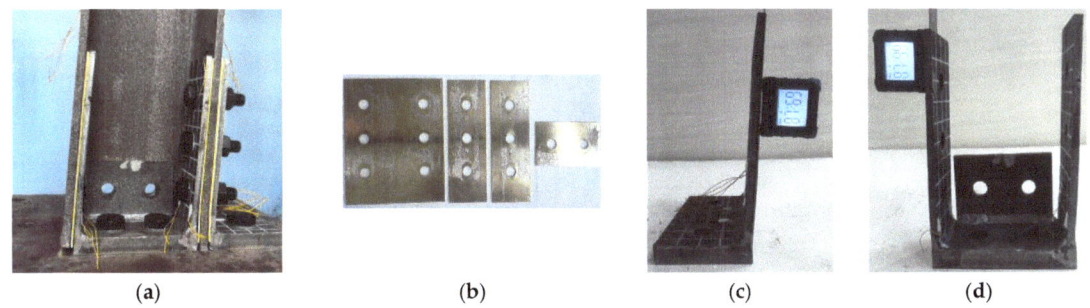

**Figure 10.** C-2 test piece disassembly diagram: (**a**) column base; (**b**) friction plates; (**c**) external connector; (**d**) internal connector.

The deformation modes of specimen C-3 are shown in Figure 9g–i. The steel column exhibited no obvious change under the first two levels of the loading. When the second cycle of the third stage was loaded to −15 mm (−0.0075 rad), the column top and base joints began to slip and rotate. Loading was stopped until the second cycle of the ninth stage was −100 mm (−0.05 rad). A lifting of about 8 mm was observed on the tensile side of the column base flange, as shown in Figure 9i. A lifting of about 5 mm was seen on the tensile side of the column top flange, as shown in Figure 9h. The steel column demonstrated no obvious deformation, as shown in Figure 9g. After the test, the tensile side of the specimen was disassembled, as shown in Figure 11. It was clearly observed that the steel column exhibited no damage, as shown in Figure 11a. The wear on the brass friction plates is similar to that on the brass friction plates of specimen C-2, and the vertical legs of the connectors were bent and deformed, as shown in Figure 11a,b.

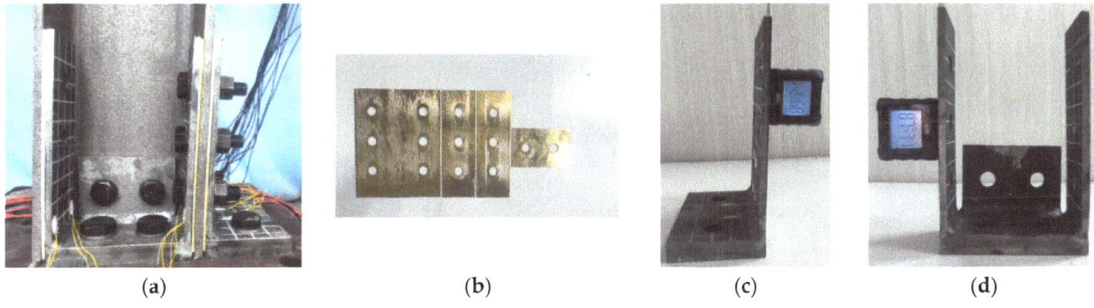

**Figure 11.** C-3 test piece disassembly diagram: (**a**) column base; (**b**) friction plates; (**c**) external connector; (**d**) internal connector.

Figure 9 reveals that serious buckling deformation occurred at both ends of specimen C-1 at the end of the loading. The joint of specimen C-2 slipped and rotated, and the flange of the column base exhibited slight buckling. Specimen C-3 exhibited no damage, and the joints at both ends slipped and rotated, which indicates that the slipping friction joints at both ends can effectively prevent and postpone the buckling of the steel column.

*4.2. Hysteresis Curves*

The hysteresis curves of the three specimens are presented in Figure 12. Specimen C-1 was loaded to the eighth level (0.04 rad), and the horizontal bearing capacity reached the maximum value. At the same cyclic loading level, the bearing capacity of the steel column showed slight degradation. The buckling form of the column base and top was not exactly the same, which led to asymmetry in the positive and negative directions of the hysteresis curve. The positive and negative directions of the hysteresis curve of specimen C-2 showed satisfactory symmetry. Owing to the friction 'vibration' of the joints in the slipping process, a slight 'jitter' phenomenon was observed in some sections of the hysteresis curve. Until the end of the test loading, the ultimate horizontal bearing capacity rose slowly and tended to be stable. The hysteresis curve of specimen C-3 is similar to that of specimen C-2. The positive and negative bearing capacities reached the peak value when the load reached 100 mm (0.05 rad). Owing to the increase in the friction 'vibration' during the test, the 'jitter' phenomenon in the hysteresis curve of specimen C-3 was more obvious than that in specimen C-2. At the end of the test, the horizontal bearing capacity gradually stabilised. At the same cyclic load level, the bearing capacity did not deteriorate.

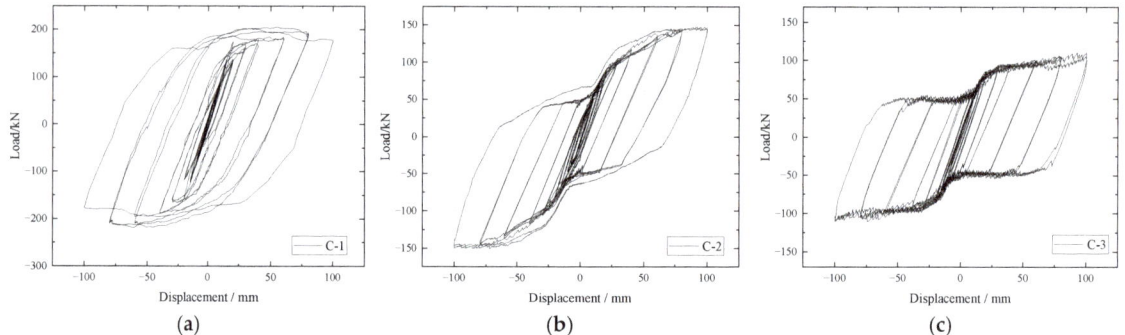

**Figure 12.** Test hysteresis curves: (**a**) C-1; (**b**) C-2; (**c**) C-3.

*4.3. Skeleton Curves*

Figure 13 shows the skeleton curves of the specimens. When specimen C-1 was loaded to 80 mm (0.04 rad), the peak load was reached. The positive peak load was 193.6 kN, and the negative peak load was −209.5 kN. The bearing capacity was reduced at the later phase of loading. After the slip rotation of the joint, the curve rising trend of specimen C-2 slowed gradually, and the bearing capacity tended to be stable in late loading. The positive load was stable at about 143.5 kN. The negative stability was 148.8 kN. After the slip rotation of specimen C-3, the rising trend of the curve slowed, and the subsequent horizontal bearing capacity tended to be stable. The positive load stabilised at about the load of 107.2 kN. The negative peak load stabilised at the load of 109.2 kN. The peak load value gradually increased in the sequence of specimen C-1, C-2, and C-3. This observation is related to the different mechanical behaviour observed at the top and bottom of steel column in these three specimens when the loading was completely finished. The top and bottom of the steel column in specimen C-1 entered the plastic phase. Part of the cross-section of the specimen C-2 entered the plastic phase at the end of the test. The two sides of steel column in specimen C-3 were still in the elastic domain at the end of loading.

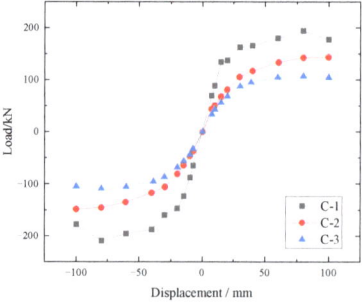

**Figure 13.** Skeleton curves.

## 4.4. Stiffness Degradation

The equivalent stiffness degradation factors for the three specimens during the loading are given in Figure 14. The stiffness degradation trend of the specimens was basically consistent. At the initial stage of the loading, specimen C-1 was in the elastic state, and the stiffness decreased linearly. When the specimen entered the elastic-plastic then plastic failure stages, the secant stiffness decline trend slowed gradually. Before the horizontal displacement of specimens C-2 and C-3 was loaded to 15 mm (0.0075 rad), the joints did not slip rotation, the steel column was in the elastic state, and the stiffness decline curve basically coincided. After the start of the slip rotation of the joints, friction energy consumption at the joints began, and the stiffness decline trend of the specimens increased. In the later test loading period, the friction energy consumption of the specimens stabilised gradually, and the slope of the secant stiffness curve decreased gradually.

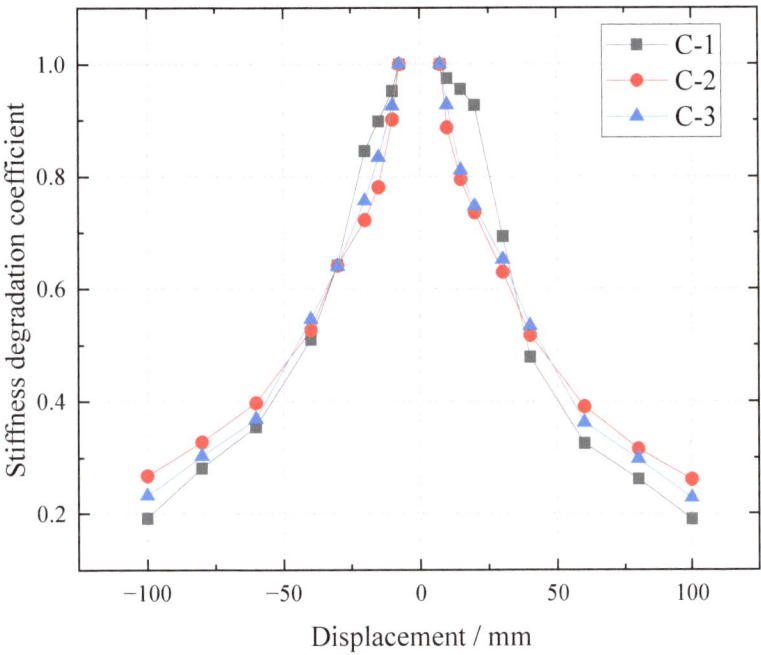

**Figure 14.** Stiffness degeneration curves.

## 4.5. Energy Consumption Performance

It can be seen from Figure 15 that the cumulative hysteretic energy of the three specimens increased as the loading displacement increased. In the first three stages of loading, the energy consumption of the three specimens was low and nearly the same. From the fourth stage of loading of 15 mm (0.0075 rad), the plastic energy consumption of specimen C-1 increased gradually and was much higher than that of specimens C-2 and C-3. Specimens C-2 and C-3 slipped and rotated from the joints at 15 mm (0.0075 rad) at the fourth level, and friction was involved in the energy consumption. Before loading to 40 mm (0.02 rad), the energy consumption of specimen C-3 was higher than that of specimen C-2 because specimen C-3 had more slipping friction joints than specimen C-2, which is conducive to friction energy consumption. When the load reached 60 mm (0.03 rad), the column base of specimen C-2 began to buckle, and the hysteretic energy consumption of specimen C-2 began to increase more than that of specimen C-3. As the loading continued, the energy consumption growth trend of the specimens accelerated.

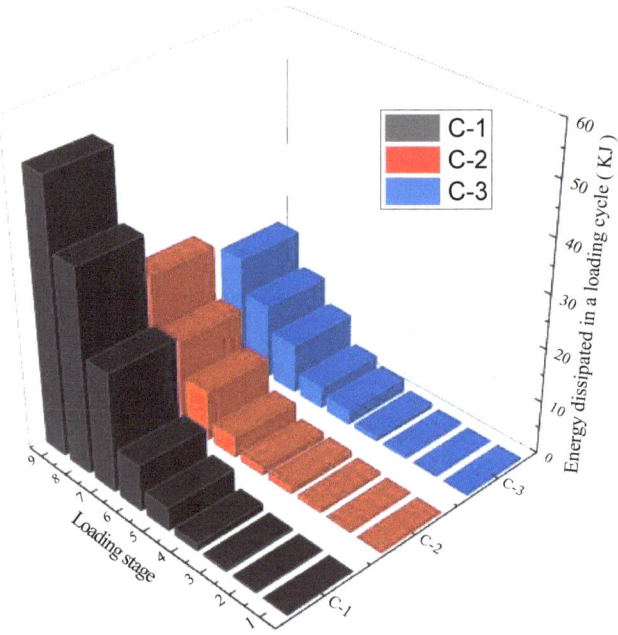

**Figure 15.** Hysteretic dissipated energy.

*4.6. Strain Analysis*

The strain curves of each specimen are shown in Figure 16. The arrangement of the strain gauges is depicted in Figure 8. The yield strain of the steel columns and connectors was 1934 με and 1961 με, respectively. It can be seen from Figure 16a that, when specimen C-2 was loaded to 20 mm (0.01 rad), the strain gauges on the external connectors of the column base joint yielded. When the load reached 40 mm (0.02 rad), the strain gauge on the internal connector at the column top flange and column base joint yielded. When the load reached 60 mm (0.03 rad), the strain gauge on the column top web yielded. At the end of the loading, the strain gauges on the column top and connectors of specimen C-2 yielded. It can be seen from Figure 16b that when specimen C-3 was loaded to 20 mm (0.01 rad), the strain gauges on the external connectors of the column top joint yielded. When the displacement reached 30 mm (0.015 rad), the strain gauges on the external connectors of the column base joint and internal connector of the column top joint yielded. When the load reached 60 mm (0.03 rad), the internal connector of the column base joint yielded. At the end of the loading, all the connectors of specimen C-3 yielded, and the measured point value on the steel column did not exceed 1,934 με, thereby indicating that the steel column was in the elastic state. In general, the strain distribution trend of the key components of each specimen was similar, and the position with a large amount of strain was located near the bottom plate of the vertical legs of both the internal and external connectors. Based on the comprehensive strain data, a reasonable design of the connector size can ensure that the steel column is in the elastic stage. This outcome shows that the slipping friction joints with replaceable connectors at both ends of the column play a satisfactory role in protecting the steel column and meet the requirements of structural function recovery after an earthquake.

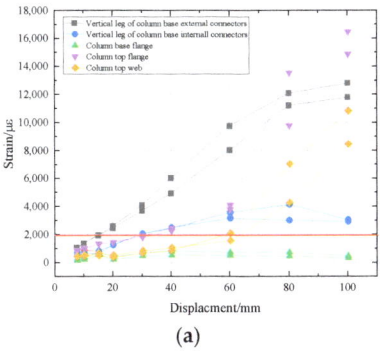
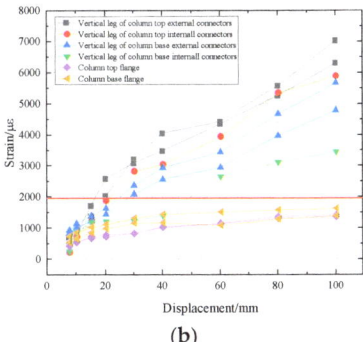

**Figure 16.** Strain curves: (**a**) C-2; (**b**) C-3.

## 5. Finite Element Analysis

The finite element software Abaqus was used to establish the finite element models of the specimens, as shown in Figure 17. In the models, C3D8I was used as the element type of all the components, and a structured grid technology was used for the joint model grid division. The mesh size for the plates with a large size, such as a column, was 30 mm, that for the replaceable connectors was 10 mm, and that for the high-strength bolts was 5 mm. At the same time, the grid of all the bolt hole areas was locally densified, and the number of elements on the circumference of each bolt hole was five. The welding part of the model adopted tie contact, and the other parts adopted face-to-face contact. A normal contact relationship is defined as hard contact, and the tangential contact relationship is defined as Coulomb friction contact. The friction coefficient obtained from the friction test was 0.45. The base plates were set as a rigid body to eliminate the influence of the deformation of the base plates on the performance of the joints during the loading process. The material constitutive model adopted the double broken line strengthening elastic–plastic model, and the material constitutive relationship was obtained from the material property test results. The boundary conditions of the finite element model were consistent with the test, and the sequence of the load application was consistent with that of the test. The bolt preload, vertical load, and horizontal load were applied to the model in turn.

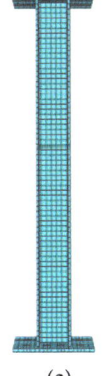
(**a**)
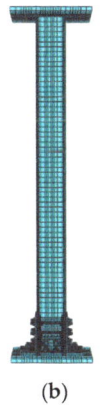
(**b**)

(**c**)

**Figure 17.** Finite element models of the specimens: (**a**) specimen C-1; (**b**) specimen C-2; (**c**) specimen C-3.

### 5.1. Collapse Mode Comparison of Specimens C-2 and C-3

A comparison of the test collapse modes and finite element simulations of specimens C-2 and C-3 is presented in Figures 18 and 19, respectively. It can be seen that the finite element simulations were consistent with the test results.

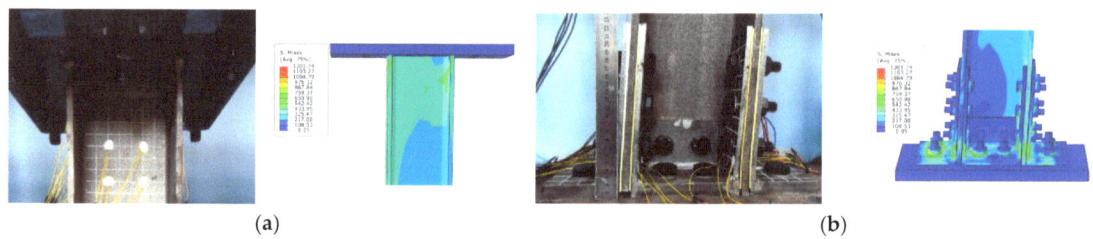

**Figure 18.** Comparison of test and simulation results of specimen C-2: (**a**) column top; (**b**) column base.

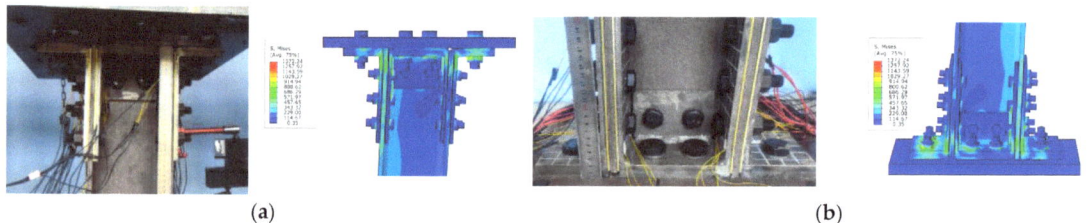

**Figure 19.** Comparison of test and simulation results of specimen C-3: (**a**) column top; (**b**) column base.

*5.2. Comparison of the Hysteresis Curves*

The results of the hysteresis curve comparison between the test and finite element simulation are shown in Figure 20. The finite element simulation results basically matched the test result curves, and the maximum error of the peak load was within 5%.

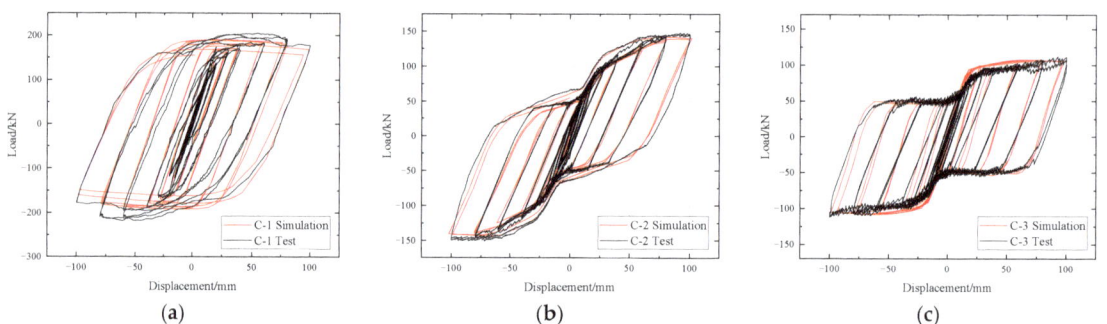

**Figure 20.** Comparison of specimen hysteresis curves: (**a**) C-1; (**b**) C-2; (**c**) C-3.

*5.3. Comparison of the Axial Shortening*

The axial shortening caused by the local buckling of the steel column base will have an extremely negative effect on the seismic stability of the structure. Figure 21 presents a comparison of the axial shortening of the specimens. As the number of loading stages increased, the axial shortening of the column end of the specimen C-1 accelerated and was approximately 4.84% of the column height at the end of the test. Specimens C-2 and C-3 demonstrated an axial shortening of approximately 2.6% and 0.018% of the total column height at the end of the test, respectively. It can be seen that the application of the slip friction joints at the end of the column can effectively suppress the axial shortening of the steel column.

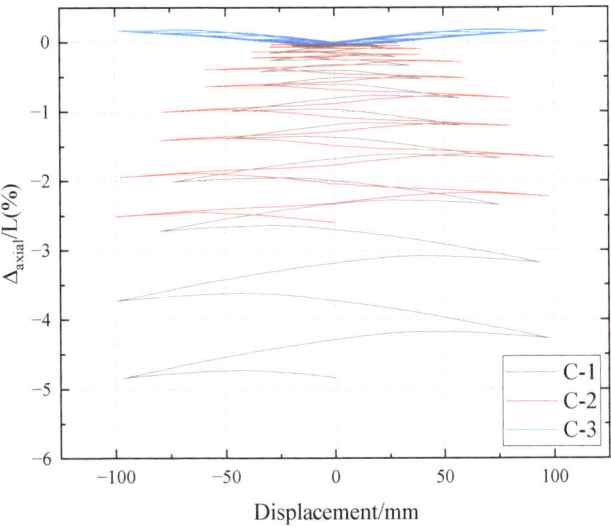

**Figure 21.** Comparison of axial shortening of specimens.

### 5.4. Comparison of the Strain of the Specimen C-3

Figure 22 illustrates the strain results obtained from the calculation of the finite element model of specimen C-3. The plastic strain was distributed mainly near the base plate of the vertical legs of the connectors, where the plastic strain of the external connectors was higher than that of the internal connector. Plastic strain also appeared at the top and base of the column, but its maximum PEEQ value was significantly lower than the maximum PEEQ value of the connectors. This result shows that the plastic damage accumulation occurred mainly on the connectors, which indicates that the slipping friction joints with replaceable connectors can effectively reduce the damage on the steel column and protect the main components.

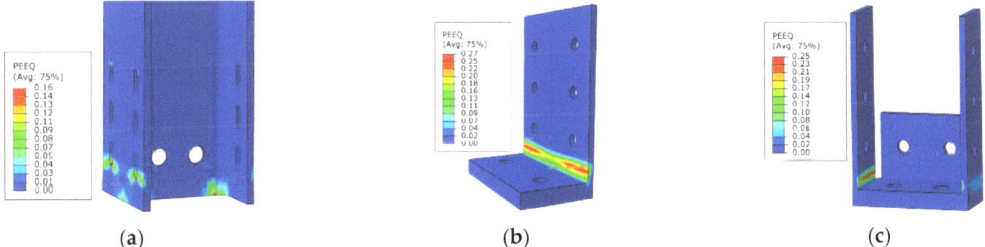

**Figure 22.** Strain analysis of specimen C-3: (**a**) column base; (**b**) external connector; (**c**) internal connecting piece.

### 5.5. Parametric Analysis

To examine the influence of the thickness of the horizontal legs of the connectors on the seismic performance of H-shaped steel columns with replaceable slipping friction joints at the column ends, six models were designed based on specimen C-3, and the specific parameters of the models are listed in Table 2. The simulated material properties were consistent with the test.

Table 2. Basic model parameters.

| Model | Column Section Size (mm) | Thickness of Horizontal Legs of Connectors (mm) |
|---|---|---|
| C-3 | | 20 |
| C-4 | | 8 |
| C-5 | HW 175 × 175 × 7.5 × 11 | 10 |
| C-6 | | 14 |
| C-7 | | 16 |
| C-8 | | 18 |

5.5.1. Hysteresis Performance and Energy Consumption

The hysteresis curves are presented in Figure 23, which shows that the hysteresis curves were all relatively full, with a symmetrical distribution in the positive and negative directions. As the thickness of the connector horizontal limbs increased, the calculated ultimate load-carrying capacity increased. This outcome indicates that the change in the horizontal limbs of the connectors has an effect on the hysteresis curves of the H-shaped columns with replaceable slip friction joints at the column ends.

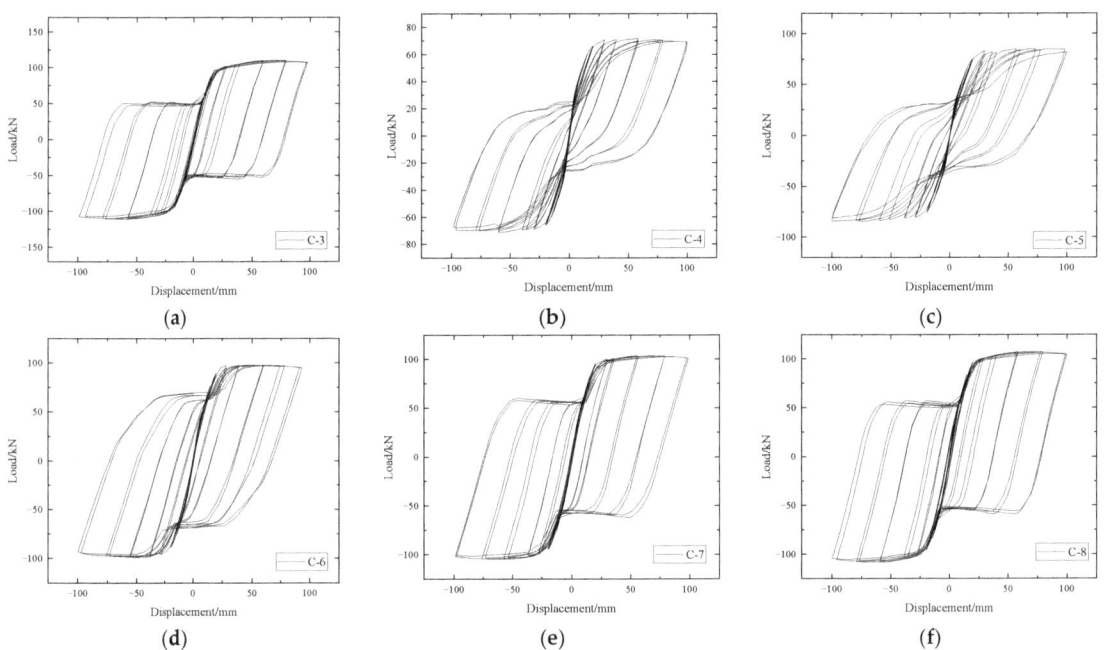

Figure 23. The calculated hysteretic curves: (a) model C-3; (b) model C-4; (c) model C-5; (d) model C-6; (e) model C-7; (f) model C-8.

The skeleton curves are shown in Figure 24, and the main performance indicators are reported in Table 3. It can be seen that, as the thickness of the connector horizontal limbs increased, the specimen bearing capacity gradually increased. The highest ultimate bearing capacity was demonstrated by model C-3, with a value of 110.11 kN. Compared with model C-3, the ultimate bearing capacity of models C-4, C-7, and C-8 was reduced by 34.96%, 6.33%, and 2.86%, respectively. It can be seen that the thickness of the connector horizontal limbs had a considerable influence on the ultimate bearing capacity of the H-shaped steel columns with slip friction joints with replaceable connectors.

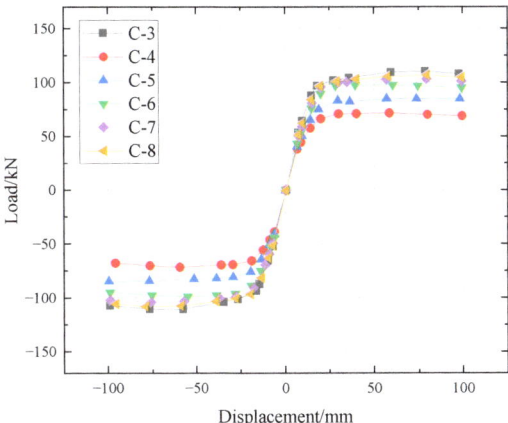

**Figure 24.** Skeleton curves of models.

**Table 3.** Primary performance indicators and energy dissipation indices during cyclic tests.

| Model | Py (kN) | Dy (mm) | Pmax (kN) | Dmax (kN) | Friction Energy Consumption (kN·m) | Total Energy Consumption (kN·m) | Proportion of Friction Energy Consumption (%) |
|---|---|---|---|---|---|---|---|
| C-3 | 97.62 | 19.64 | 110.11 | 78.51 | 113.34 | 125.02 | 90.66% |
| C-4 | 61.61 | 16.42 | 71.62 | 57.93 | 6.01 | 54.24 | 11.14% |
| C-5 | 74.27 | 18.59 | 84.99 | 56.59 | 8.70 | 62.18 | 13.99% |
| C-6 | 86.20 | 18.55 | 97.63 | 59.89 | 85.86 | 104.70 | 82.01% |
| C-7 | 93.32 | 19.10 | 103.13 | 78.91 | 100.94 | 114.25 | 88.35% |
| C-8 | 95.58 | 19.47 | 106.96 | 79.20 | 111.91 | 124.39 | 89.97% |

Figure 25 depicts the stiffness degradation curves of the models. The stiffness of the models increased as the thickness of the connector horizontal limbs increased. The stiffness degradation trend was generally the same for all models, with the stiffness degradation trend slowing as the thickness of the connector horizontal limbs increased in the later stages of the loading. This outcome indicates that the thickness of the connector horizontal limbs has an effect on the stiffness of the H-shaped columns with replaceable slip friction joints at the column ends.

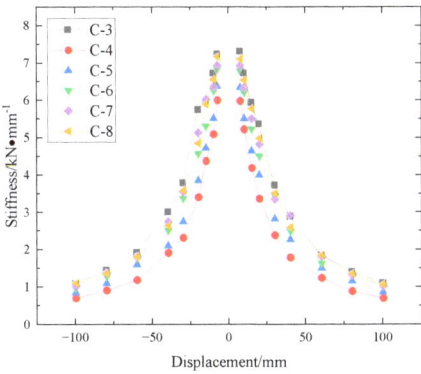

**Figure 25.** Stiffness degradation curves of models.

Figure 26 and Table 3 demonstrate the cumulative frictional energy dissipation and total energy dissipation of the models at each loading level. As the thickness of the connector horizontal limbs increased, the energy consumption gradually increased, and the frictional energy consumption ratio gradually increased. Because reducing the thickness of the connector horizontal limbs makes the connector and the column first slip together, and at the end of loading to a certain displacement, the steel column starts to slip relatively, the frictional energy consumption decreases. This outcome indicates that increasing the thickness of the connector horizontal limbs is beneficial to slip frictional energy consumption.

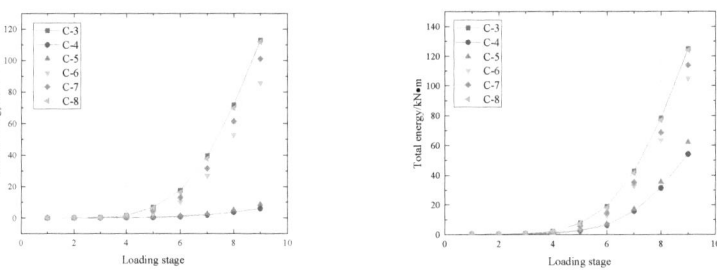

**Figure 26.** Hysteretic dissipated energy of models.

### 5.5.2. The Calculated Axial Shortening

By normalising the axial shortening relative to the column height L, the relationship curve between the axial shortening and chord angle was drawn, as shown in Figure 27. The residual axial shortening of the models decreased gradually as the thickness of the connector horizontal limbs increased. The possible reason is that, under the same axial pressure ratio, decreasing the thickness of the connector horizontal limbs makes the connectors and column co-slip section longer, and the joints and column are not completely reset after the loading, thereby resulting in a large residual axial shortening.

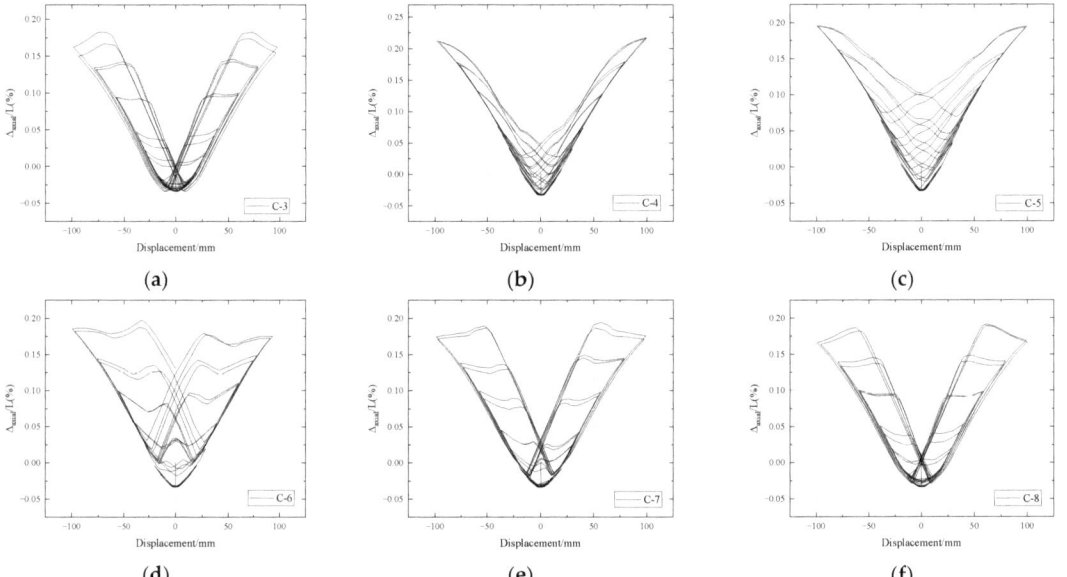

**Figure 27.** Comparison of calculated axial shortenings: (**a**) model C-3; (**b**) model C-4; (**c**) model C-5; (**d**) model C-6; (**e**) model C-7; (**f**) model C-8.

### 5.5.3. The Calculated Strain Analysis

Figure 28 presents the strain results obtained from the calculation of the finite element models. The strain was large near the base plate of the vertical legs of the connectors. The strain of the connectors increased gradually as the thickness of the connector horizontal limbs increased, but the strain of the column base flange of model C-3 was larger than that of the other models, as shown in Figure 28a, which indicates that the excessive thickness of the connector horizontal limbs causes damage to the main structure. The thickness of the connector horizontal limbs should be set reasonably to protect the main structure from damage.

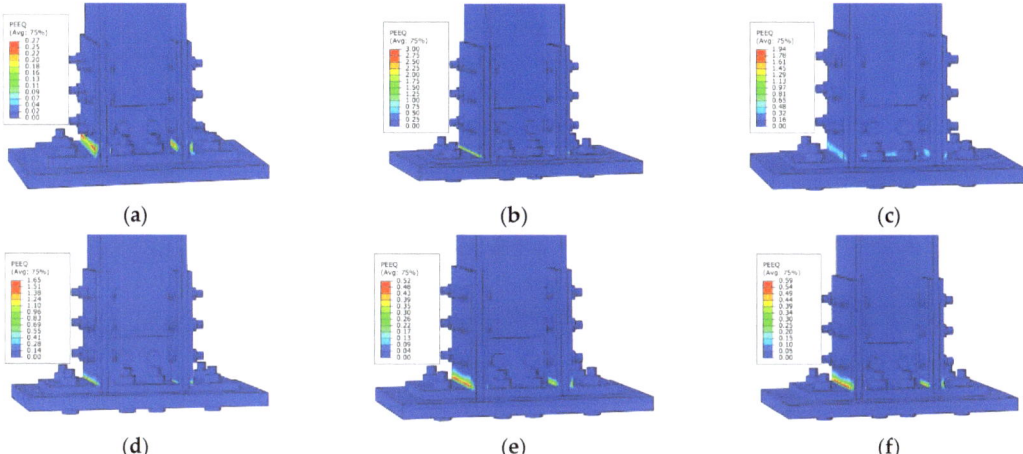

**Figure 28.** Calculated strain distribution of the column base: (**a**) model C-3; (**b**) model C-4; (**c**) model C-5; (**d**) model C-6; (**e**) model C-7; (**f**) model C-8 column.

The analysis of the hysteretic performance and energy dissipation capacity of the finite element models shows that, compared with model C-3 (20 mm), models C-7 (16 mm) and C-8 (18 mm) did not differ considerably in terms of their ultimate load-carrying capacity, stiffness degradation, and energy dissipation. By contrast, models C-4 (8 mm), C-5 (10 mm), and C-6 (14 mm) differed significantly from model C-3 in terms of their ultimate load-carrying capacity, initial stiffness, and cumulative frictional energy dissipation. The smaller thickness of the connector horizontal limbs caused the connectors and column co-slip section to become longer, which is not conducive to frictional energy dissipation. The excessive thickness of the connector horizontal limbs leads to damage transfer from the connectors to the steel column. For balance, the thickness of the connector horizontal limbs was set to 16 mm or 18 mm.

## 6. Conclusions

In this study, the seismic stability performance of an ordinary H-shaped steel column, a column with only one replaceable slip friction joint at the bottom, and a column with two replaceable joints at both ends were examined, and the following conclusions were obtained:

(1) When the standard H-shaped column was subjected to horizontal loading, severe buckling deformation occurred at the top and base of the column. Slight buckling deformation of the base flange was observed in the H-shaped steel column with a replaceable slipping friction joint at the column base. For the H-shaped column with replaceable slip friction joints at both ends, damage was concentrated on the vertical of the internal and external connectors near the base plate, while the steel column remained elastic.

(2) In comparison to the stable load bearing capacity of the H-shaped steel column with a replaceable slipping friction joint, significant degradation of the load bearing capacity of the standard H-shaped column was marked.

(3) It was found that the H-shaped column with replaceable slip friction joints at both ends consumed less energy than the standard H-shaped column. However, this energy loss can be offset by additional energy-consuming elements.

(4) The slip friction joints at the ends of the column can effectively reduce the axial shortening of the steel column and enhance the seismic stability of the structure.

(5) The finite element analysis was conducted on H-shaped columns with replaceable slip friction joints by taking into account the thickness of the connector horizontal limbs. The results showed that the thickness of the connector horizontal limbs is suggested to be less than twice the thickness of the connector vertical limbs; in this case, the connector improved the load-bearing capacity of the steel column and ensured the frictional energy dissipation of the joints. Additionally, it protected the main structure from damage and achieved the goal damage control. The frictional energy consumption of the models reached 85–90% of the total energy consumption, indicating that the energy is mainly consumed by friction at the members of the slip friction joints with replaceable connectors.

## 7. Outlook

The next step of this research route is to analyse the application of replaceable slip friction joints at column ends to a floor-by-floor assembled steel frame system to investigate its seismic performance.

**Author Contributions:** Conceptualization, C.-Y.L. and A.-Z.Z.; methodology, C.-Y.L. and A.-Z.Z.; software, F.W.; validation, C.-Y.L. and F.W.; formal analysis, C.-Y.L.; investigation, C.-Y.L. and A.-Z.Z.; resources, C.-Y.L.; data curation, C.-Y.L. and F.W.; writing-original draft, F.W.; writing-review and editing, C.-Y.L.; visualization, C.-Y.L.; supervision, C.-Y.L. and A.-Z.Z.; project administration, C.-Y.L.; funding acquisition, C.-Y.L. All authors have read and agreed to the published version of the manuscript.

**Funding:** This work was financially supported by the National Natural Science Foundation of China (No. 51878522).

**Data Availability Statement:** Data collected from the questionnaire survey and the data analysis results presented in the paper are available from the corresponding author by request.

**Conflicts of Interest:** The author(s) declare no potential conflict of interest with respect to the research, authorship, and/or publication of this article.

## References

1. Thai, H.-T.; Ngo, T.; Uy, B. A review on modular construction for high-rise buildings. *Structures* **2020**, *28*, 1265–1290. [CrossRef]
2. Wang, H.; Zhao, X.; Ma, G. Experimental study on seismic performance of column-column-beam joint in panelised steel-modular structure. *J. Constr. Steel Res.* **2022**, *192*, 107240. [CrossRef]
3. Deng, E.-F.; Zong, L.; Ding, Y.; Zhang, Z.; Zhang, J.-F.; Shi, F.-W.; Cai, L.-M.; Gao, S.-C. Seismic performance of mid-to-high rise modular steel construction—A critical review. *Thin-Walled Struct.* **2020**, *155*, 106924. [CrossRef]
4. Yao, Z.; Wang, W.; Fang, C.; Zhang, Z. An experimental study on eccentrically braced beam-through steel frames with replaceable shear links. *Eng. Struct.* **2020**, *206*, 110185. [CrossRef]
5. Du, H.; Zhao, P.; Wang, Y.; Sun, W. Seismic experimental assessment of beam-through beam-column connections for modular prefabricated steel moment frames. *J. Constr. Steel Res.* **2022**, *192*, 107208. [CrossRef]
6. Chen, Y.; Wang, W.; Chen, Y. Full-scale shake table tests of the tension-only concentrically braced steel beam-through frame. *J. Constr. Steel Res.* **2018**, *148*, 611–626. [CrossRef]
7. Zaghi, A.E.; Soroushian, S.; Itani, A.; Maragakis, E.M.; Pekcan, G.; Mehrraoufi, M. Impact of column-to-beam strength ratio on the seismic response of steel MRFs. *Bull. Earthq. Eng.* **2015**, *13*, 635–652. [CrossRef]
8. MacRae, G.A. The continuous column concept-development and use. In Proceedings of the Ninth Pacific Conference on Earthquake Engineering Building an Earthquake-Resilient Society, Auckland, New Zealand, 14–16 April 2011; pp. 14–16.
9. Li, Y.W.; Wang, Y.Z.; Wang, Y.B. Experimental and numerical study of beam-through energy-dissipative rocking columns for mitigating seismic responses. *J. Constr. Steel. Res.* **2022**, *189*, 107097. [CrossRef]

10. Qu, Z.; Gong, T.; Wang, X.; Li, Q.; Wang, T. Stiffness and strength demands for pin-supported walls in reinforced-concrete moment frames. *J. Constr. Steel. Res.* **2020**, *9*, 146. [CrossRef]
11. Macrae, G.A.; Urmson, C.R.; Walpole, W.R.; Moss, P.; Hyde, K.; Clifton, G.C. Axial shortening of steel columns in buildings subjected to earthquakes. *Bull. N. Z. Soc. Earthq. Eng.* **2009**, *42*, 275–287. [CrossRef]
12. Ibarra, L.F.; Medina, R.A.; Krawinkler, H. Hysteretic models that incorporate strength and stiffness deterioration. *Earthq. Eng. Struct. Dyn.* **2005**, *34*, 1489–1511. [CrossRef]
13. Lignos, D.G.; Hikino, T.; Matsuoka, Y.; Nakashima, M. Collapse assessment of steel moment frames based on e-defense full-scale shake table collapse tests. *J. Struct. Eng.* **2013**, *139*, 120–132. [CrossRef]
14. Lin, X.; Li, H.; He, L.; Zhang, L. Experimental study on seismic behavior of the damage-control steel plate fuses for beam-to-column connection. *Eng. Struct.* **2022**, *270*, 114862. [CrossRef]
15. Lin, X.; Chen, Y.; Yan, J.-B.; Hu, Y. Seismic behavior of welded beam-to-column joints of high-strength steel-moment frame with replaceable damage-control fuses. *J. Struct. Eng.* **2020**, *146*, 04020143. [CrossRef]
16. Zhang, A.-L.; Chen, X.; Jiang, Z.-Q.; Kang, Y.-T.; Yang, X.-F. Experiment on seismic behavior of earthquake-resilience prefabricated cross hinge column foot joint. *J. Constr. Steel Res.* **2022**, *189*, 107056. [CrossRef]
17. Liu, X.C.; Cui, F.Y.; Zhan, X.X.; Yu, C.; Jiang, Z.Q. Seismic performance of bolted connection of H-beam to HSS-column with web end-plate. *J. Constr. Steel Res.* **2019**, *156*, 167–181. [CrossRef]
18. Liu, X.; Yang, Z.; Wang, H.; Zhang, A.; Pu, S.; Chai, S.; Wu, L. Seismic performance of H-section beam to HSS column connection in prefabricated structures. *J. Constr. Steel Res.* **2017**, *138*, 1–16. [CrossRef]
19. Zhang, R.; Xie, J.-Y.; Chouery, K.E.; Liu, J.; Jia, L.-J.; Xiang, P.; Zhao, X.; Macrae, G.A.; Clifton, G.C.; Dhakal, R.P.; et al. Strong axis low-damage performance of rocking column-base joints with asymmetric friction connections. *J. Constr. Steel Res.* **2022**, *191*, 107175. [CrossRef]
20. Freddi, F.; Dimopoulos, C.A.; Karavasilis, T.L. Experimental evaluation of a rocking damage-free steel column base with friction devices. *J. Struct. Eng.* **2020**, *146*, 04020217. [CrossRef]
21. Chung, Y.L.; Du, L.J.; Pan, H.H. Performance evaluation of a rocking steel column base equipped with asymmetrical resistance friction damper. *Earthq. Struct.* **2019**, *17*, 49–61. [CrossRef]
22. *GB/T 228.1-2021*; Metallic Materials—Tensile Testing—Part 1: Method of Test at Room Temperature. National Standard of the People's Republic of China: Beijing, China, 2021. (In Chinese)
23. *ANSI/AISC 341-16*; Seismic Provisions for Structural Steel Buildings. American Institute of Steel Construction Inc.: Chicago, IL, USA, 2016.
24. Borzouie, J.; MacRae, G.A.; Chase, J.G.; Rodgers, G.W.; Clifton, G.C. Experimental studies on cyclic performance of column base strong axis–aligned asymmetric friction connections. *J. Struct. Eng.* **2016**, *142*, 04015078. [CrossRef]
25. Elettore, E.; Freddi, F.; Latour, M.; Rizzano, G. Design and analysis of a seismic resilient steel moment resisting frame equipped with damage-free self-centering column bases. *J. Constr. Steel Res.* **2021**, *179*, 106543. [CrossRef]
26. Kim, E.C.; Fan, K.; Jia, L.J. State-of-the-art review of symmetric and asymmetric friction connections: Seismic behavior and design methods. *Eng. Mech.* **2021**, *38*, 22–37. (In Chinese) [CrossRef]

Article

# Experimental Study and Finite Element Calculation of the Behavior of Special T-Shaped Composite Columns with Concrete-Filled Square Steel Tubulars under Eccentric Loads

Quan Li [1], Zhe Liu [1,2,*], Xuejun Zhou [1] and Zhen Wang [3]

[1] School of Civil Engineering, Shandong Jianzhu University, Jinan 250101, China
[2] Shandong Winbond Construction Group Co., Ltd., Weifang 262500, China
[3] School of Transportation & Civil Engineering, Shandong Jiaotong University, Jinan 250357, China
* Correspondence: liuzhe0624@126.com

**Abstract:** Special T-shaped composite columns with concrete-filled square steel tubulars have good restraint on internal concrete, are convenient to process, have a high bearing capacity and good mechanical properties, and can increase the aesthetics of the building and the utilization rate of indoor space. Theoretical analysis, experimental study, and numerical simulation of the eccentric compression performance of the special-shaped column are carried out. Taking the specimen length, eccentric distance, and eccentric direction as test parameters, nine specimens with different slenderness ratios were designed to carry out eccentric compression tests. The eccentric compression performance was numerically simulated and analyzed by the general finite element software ABAQUS. The results show that the short column mainly suffers section strength failure, while the middle and long columns mainly suffer bending instability failure without torsional deformation. The degree of influence of the test parameters decreases in turn according to the eccentric distance, eccentric direction, and length of the specimen; there is no weld cracking phenomenon, and the square steel pipes can work together. The finite element calculation results are in good agreement with the experimental and theoretical values.

**Keywords:** concrete-filled square steel tube; special T-shaped composite column; eccentric compression; mechanical properties; finite element calculation; experimental study

## 1. Introduction

There are many forms of special-shaped sections of CFSTs, mainly including ordinary special-shaped sections (Figure 1), special-shaped sections with restrained tie rods (Figure 2), special-shaped sections with built-in stiffeners (Figure 3), multi-chamber special-shaped sections (Figure 4), combined special-shaped sections (Figure 5), and lattice special-shaped sections (Figure 6). At present, the research on CFST special-shaped columns mainly focuses on their mechanical properties.

For ordinary special-shaped concrete-filled steel tubular columns, Shen et al. [1] and Lei et al. [2] studied the eccentric compression performance, hysteretic performance, and joint seismic performance of L-shaped and T-shaped CFST columns. The plastic deformation and energy dissipation capacity of the nodes are better, and a simplified formula for the bearing capacity of L-shaped and T-shaped CFST columns is proposed. Li et al. [3] and Zuo et al. [4] designed special-shaped columns with restrained bars, and studied the axial and bias performance of the components through axial compression and bias tests. The restrained bar changes the buckling mode of the steel tube, which can increase the bearing capacity of the CFST column and improve the ductility. Additionally, the calculation formula of the axial bearing capacity is established. Wang et al. [5] studied the hysteretic performance of T-shaped CFST columns with built-in stiffeners. Research shows that the width-to-thickness ratio mainly affects the sequence of peak loads and the decreasing trend of bearing capacity. Stiffeners can limit the deformation of weak parts, delay local buckling, and make the steel pipe and concrete work together. Tu et al. [6] conducted experimental research on the axial compression performance of multi-chamber CFST T-shaped CFST columns and found that the failure of medium and long columns is due to overall bending failure, and multi-chamber CFST columns can enhance the restraint of the section on the concrete. Du et al. [7], Cao et al. [8] and WANG et al. [9] conducted an experimental study on the axial compression and eccentric compression of T-shaped and L-shaped CFSTs. Research shows that the flexural performance and plastic deformation ability of the T-column with CFSTs are better, and the specimens mainly show three types of failure modes: shear failure, local bulging (or cracking), and bending instability. The axial compressive bearing capacity of the specimen has an obvious influence. The strength damage is mainly hoop specimens and welded short columns. The main damage mode of the welded slender column is bending instability damage. Rong et al. [10] and Zhou Ting et al. [11] designed lattice-type T-shaped, cross-shaped, L-shaped CFST composites with special-shaped columns to study their mechanical properties. The results show that the final failure form of the compression-bending specimen is the overall bending instability failure, the steel strength has an obvious effect on the compression-bending bearing capacity of the special-shaped column, and the affixed plate has a better restraint effect on the single-limb column.

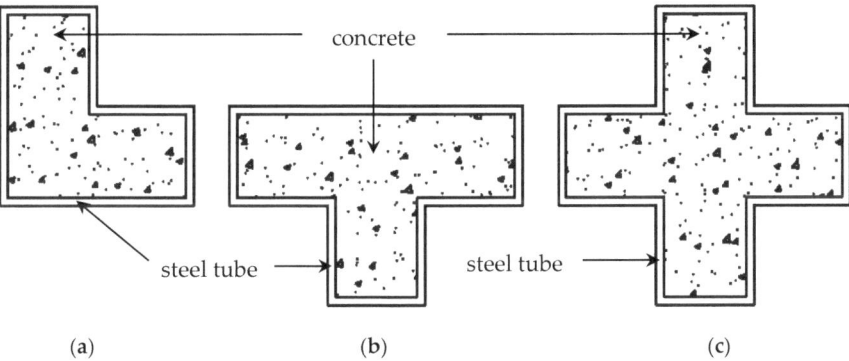

**Figure 1.** Ordinary special-shaped section: (**a**) L-shaped; (**b**) T-shaped; (**c**) cross.

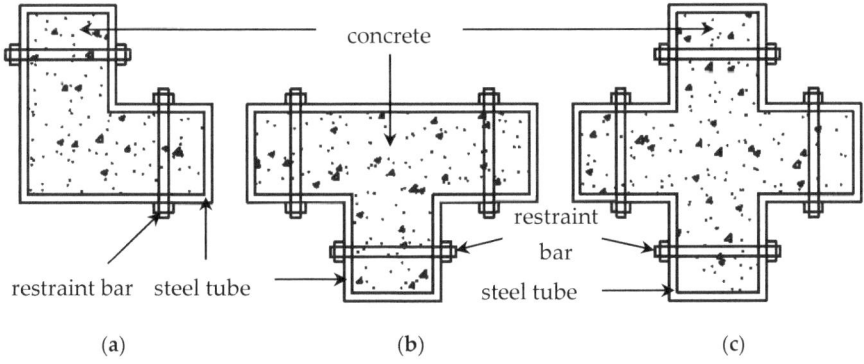

**Figure 2.** Profiled sections with restrained bars: (**a**) L-shaped; (**b**) T-shaped; (**c**) cross.

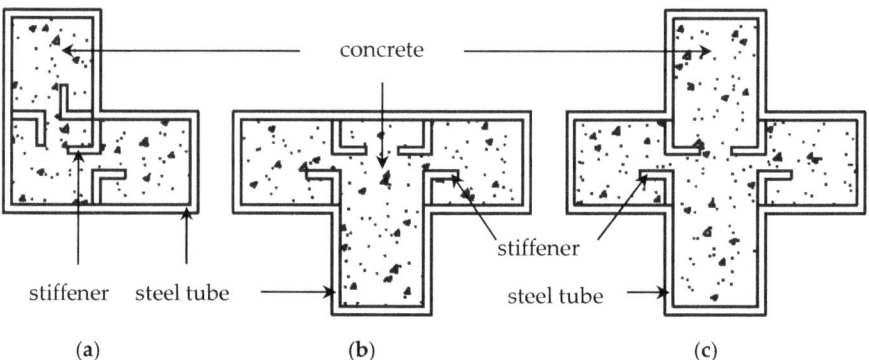

**Figure 3.** Profiled section with built-in stiffeners: (**a**) L-shaped; (**b**) T-shaped; (**c**) cross.

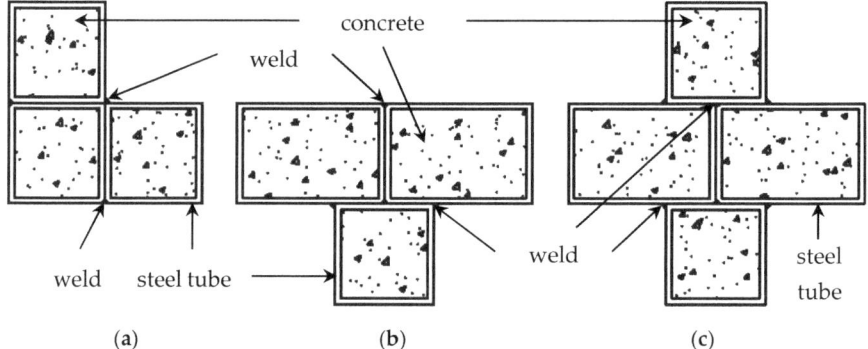

**Figure 4.** Multi-chamber profiled section: (**a**) L-shaped; (**b**) T-shaped; (**c**) cross.

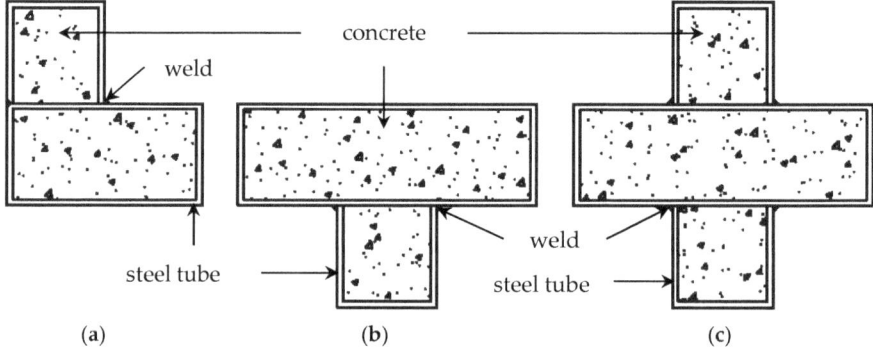

**Figure 5.** Combined special-shaped section: (**a**) L-shaped; (**b**) T-shaped; (**c**) cross.

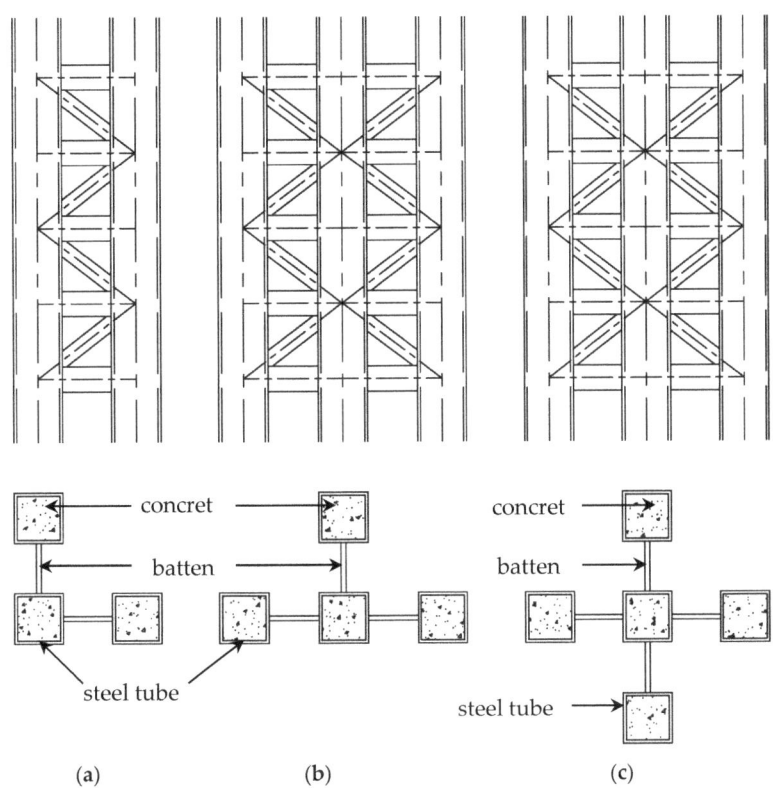

**Figure 6.** Lattice-shaped section: (**a**) L-shaped; (**b**) T-shaped; (**c**) cross.

Zeghiche, J. et al. [12], Ghannam S. [13], Ahiwale D. et al. [14], Achuthan, P. et al. [15], Umamaheswari, N. et al. [16] and Gupta, P. K. et al. [17] conducted axial and eccentric compression tests on CFST columns. It was found that the CFST columns were all damaged due to global buckling. The axial bearing capacity of CFST specimens with artificial sand is significantly improved. The axial and biased column bearing capacity test results of unidirectional bending are in good agreement with the calculation results of Eurocode 4. Phan h D. [18], Saleh, S. M. et al. [19], Jayalekshmi, S. et al. [20], Heman, A. M. et al. [21] and Bhartiya, R. [22] et al. conducted a finite element analysis on the axial compression performance of CFST columns. Studies have shown that increasing the concrete grade leads to a decrease in the ductility of the composite column. Steel yield strength and tube wall thickness contribute to ultimate strength. Restrained tie rods significantly increase the strength and ductility of the CFST column. Boukhalkhal S H et al. [23] found that CFST columns performed better in terms of ductility, plastic hinge distribution, and appearance order. Lazkani, A. [24], Tam, V. W. et al. [25], Ahmad, S. et al. [26], Mujdeci, A. et al. [27], Esmaeili Niari, S. et al. [28], De Azevedo et al. [29], Malathy, R. et al. [30] and Portolés, J. M. et al. [31] replaced the concrete filled in the steel tube with a different material. Studies have shown that expansion agents can improve the strength, ultimate strain, and ductility of recycled aggregate CFST columns. The bearing capacity of the concrete-filled rubber-filled steel tubular column section decreases with the increase in rubber content, but its ductility increases significantly. Adding 20% iron filings via sand weight increases the initial stiffness. The bearing capacity of recycled aggregate concrete-filled steel tubular columns is higher than that of ordinary columns. The impact of high-strength or ultra-high-strength concrete on axial compressive bearing capacity is more significant than that of eccentric compressive bearing capacity.

The inner corners of ordinary CFST columns with special-shaped sections are weak and cannot effectively constrain the corner concrete. There are many openings in the restraint tie rod which weaken the section of the steel pipe, cause a lot of stress concentration, and make the surface uneven. The built-in stiffening rib plate is inconvenient to process, the welding area is large, and the welding residual stress is large. Multi-chamber special-shaped steel pipes have different cross-sectional dimensions which are difficult to standardize and inflexible in layout. The long side of the combined special-shaped rectangular steel pipe is weak against the concrete. The special-shaped section of the lattice type is cumbersome in form, and the stress situation is complex, which is not convenient for analysis and calculation.

However, there is still a lack of relevant research on the mechanical properties of special-shaped CFST composite columns. After improving and optimizing the special-shaped section of CFSTs, a new type of special-shaped square CFST composite column is proposed. Figure 7 shows special-shaped columns with three cross-sections: L-shaped, T-shaped, and cross-shaped. The square steel tube concrete composite special-shaped column is directly processed and manufactured by the finished square steel tube. The welding forming is simple and convenient, the processing speed is fast, and it is easy to be produced in a factory. It can reduce the difficulty of on-site construction and ensure the quality of the welding seam, avoid the appearance of column edges and corners in the room, standardize the cross-section form, and make the layout flexible. The problem of deformation of the inner corner of the section has been improved. The surface is flat without protrusions and holes, reducing the weakening of the section by the opening. By reducing the aspect ratio of the section, the local stability of the steel tube and the restraining effect of the internal concrete are enhanced.

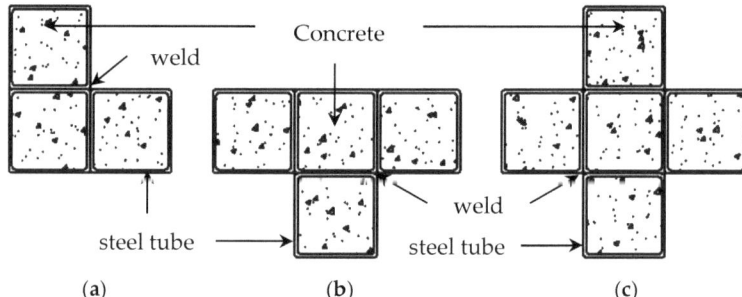

**Figure 7.** Cross-section of CFST composite special-shaped column: (**a**) L-shaped; (**b**) T-shaped; (**c**) cross.

## 2. Experimental Program

### 2.1. Specimen Design and Material Properties

In the T-shaped square steel tube concrete composite special-shaped column, the section size of the hollow square steel tube is 100 mm × 100 mm × 4 mm, as shown in Figure 8. The specimen is composed of CFST special-shaped column members and steel cover plates, and the T-shaped section is formed by four square steel pipes through four fillet welds, as shown in Figure 9. The design parameters of the nine specimens are shown in Table 1.

Table 2 shows the parameters of the steel samples, and the test results of the mechanical properties of the steel are shown in Table 3. The method of converting elastic modulus $E_c$ and concrete axial compressive strength $f_c$ adopts the calculation formula given in the modified stress–strain relationship of the concrete-filled steel tubular with different strength grades under uniaxial compression proposed by Ding et al. [32], where $f_c = 0.4 f_{cu}^{7/6}$, and $E_c = 9500 f_{cu}^{1/3}$. The test results of the mechanical properties of the concrete are shown in Table 4.

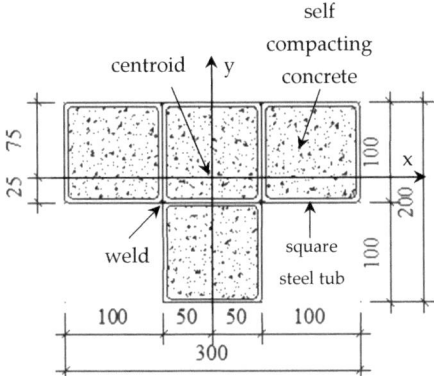

**Figure 8.** Section of T-shaped concrete-filled square steel tubular composite special-shaped column(mm).

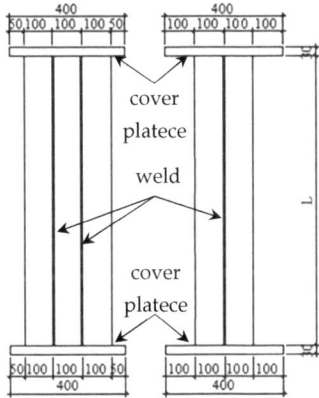

**Figure 9.** Design drawing of the test piece.

**Table 1.** Parameters of the test specimens.

| Specimen | t/mm | L/mm | e/mm | Eccentric Direction | λ |
|---|---|---|---|---|---|
| T-1 | 4 | 600 | 20 | x+ | 7 |
| T-2 | 4 | 600 | 40 | y+ | 10 |
| T-3 | 4 | 600 | 60 | y− | 10 |
| T-4 | 4 | 1500 | 20 | y+ | 25 |
| T-5 | 4 | 1500 | 40 | y− | 25 |
| T-6 | 4 | 1500 | 60 | x+ | 17 |
| T-7 | 4 | 1800 | 20 | y− | 29 |
| T-8 | 4 | 1800 | 40 | x+ | 20 |
| T-9 | 4 | 1800 | 60 | y+ | 29 |

Notes: $t$ denotes wall thickness of steel tube; $L$ denotes the length of test piece; $e$ denotes eccentricity; $\lambda$ denotes slenderness ratio. x+ means that the eccentric load action point is in the positive direction of the x-axis; y+ means that the eccentric load action point is in the positive direction of the y-axis; y− means that the eccentric load application point is in the negative direction of the y-axis. $\lambda_x$ and $\lambda_y$ are the slenderness ratios of the components around the x-axis and y-axis, respectively, $l = L/i$, where $i$ is the radius of gyration of the section and $L$ is the length of the test piece, $i = (I_s + I_c E_c/E_s)^{1/2}/(A_s + A_c f_c/f_s)^{1/2}$. The steel design strength grade of the test piece is Q235B, and the concrete design strength grade is C30. $f_s$ is the measured value of the yield strength of the steel; $f_c$ is the measured value of the axial compressive strength of the concrete; $I_s$ and $I_c$ are the section moment of inertia of steel and concrete, respectively; $A_s$ and $A_c$ are the cross-sectional areas of steel and concrete, respectively; $E_s$ and $E_c$ are the elastic moduli of steel and concrete, respectively.

Table 2. Parameters of material test specimens.

| Specimen | Number | $a_0$/mm | $b_0$/mm | $L_0$/mm | $L_c$/mm | $r$/mm | Collet Width | $L_t$/mm |
|---|---|---|---|---|---|---|---|---|
| 1–3 | 3 | 4 | 20 | 90 | 115 | 20 | 30 | 350 |

Notes: $a_0$ denotes thickness; $b_0$ denotes width; $L_0$ denotes original gauge length; $L_c$ denotes parallel length; $r$ denotes transition radius; $L_t$ denotes total length.

Table 3. Results of steel material properties test.

| Specimen | Thickness/mm | Width/mm | Yield Strength/MPa | Ultimate Strength/MPa | Elongation/% | Yield Strength Ratio |
|---|---|---|---|---|---|---|
| S1 | 4 | 20 | 335.38 | 423.77 | 18.26 | 0.791 |
| S2 | 4 | 20 | 349.63 | 421.13 | 20.87 | 0.830 |
| S3 | 4 | 20 | 348.00 | 427.75 | 19.13 | 0.814 |

Table 4. Results of concrete material properties test.

| Group | Number of Test Blocks | Size of Test Blocks/mm | $f_{cd}$/MPa | $f_{cu}$/MPa | $f_c$/MPa | $E_c$/MPa |
|---|---|---|---|---|---|---|
| 1 | 6 | 150 × 150 × 150 | 30 | 44.23 | 33.27 | 33,596.65 |
| 2 | 6 | 150 × 150 × 150 | 30 | 45.33 | 34.24 | 33,872.88 |

Notes: $f_{cd}$ denotes design value of concrete compressive strength; $f_{cu}$ denotes measured compressive strength of concrete cubes; $f_c$ denotes conversion value of concrete axial compressive strength; $E_c$ denotes conversion value of the elastic modulus of concrete.

### 2.2. Test Loading and Measurement

The column hinge is fixed on the end plate, and the boundary conditions at both ends of the specimen simulate the hinge. Figure 10 shows a schematic diagram of loading, and a 500 t pressure testing machine was used for bias testing.

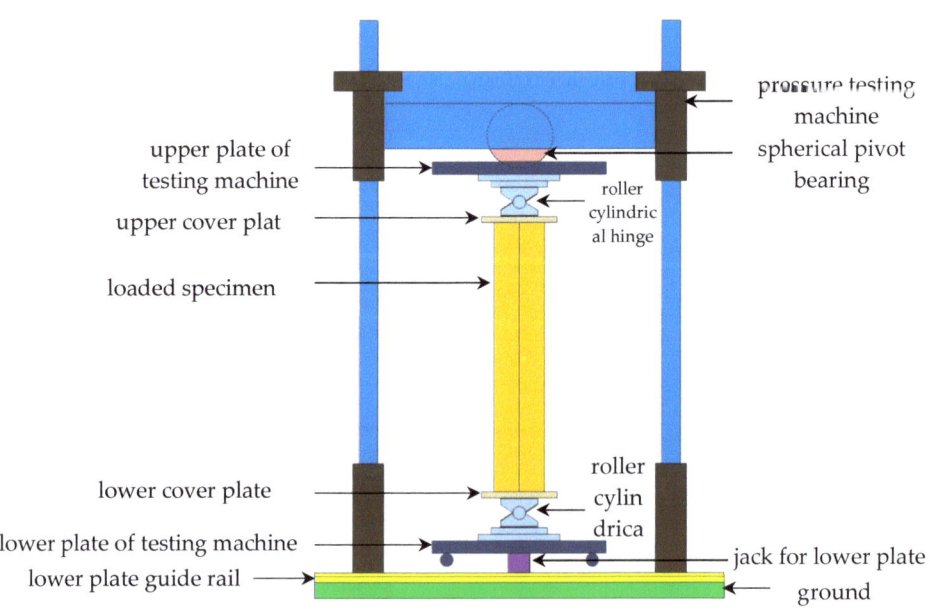

**Figure 10.** Test loading schematic.

The loading regime is shown in Figure 11. In a monotonic static load test, the loading is controlled by displacement. Take 1/10 of the calculated limit displacement as the loading displacement of each stage. When the load drops to 75% of the ultimate load, stop loading. Unloading adopts force control, and the unloading value of each stage is 1/5~1/20 of the ultimate load. Before the formal test, the specimen shall be preloaded according to 10% of the calculated ultimate load, and the formal loading shall be carried out after checking the state of the specimen and each measuring instrument.

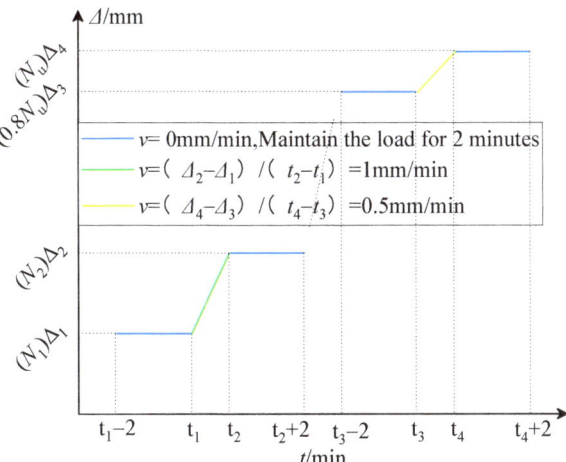

**Figure 11.** Test loading schematic.

Measure the vertical displacement value, the horizontal deflection value of the test piece, and the transverse and longitudinal strain of the steel pipe. Two displacement gauges are set at the lower and upper parts of the specimen to measure the axial displacement of the specimen. Along the height direction of the column, three displacement gauges are set at the quarter points on one side of the test piece to measure the horizontal deflection value of the test piece. Two displacement gauges were installed at the corners of the steel pipe along half of the height direction of the specimen to measure the torsional displacement of the specimen. At 1/2 of the height of the column, a strain (45° in three axes) is arranged on the exposed surface of each steel pipe to measure the longitudinal and transverse strain of the steel pipe. The location of the measuring points is shown in Figure 12.

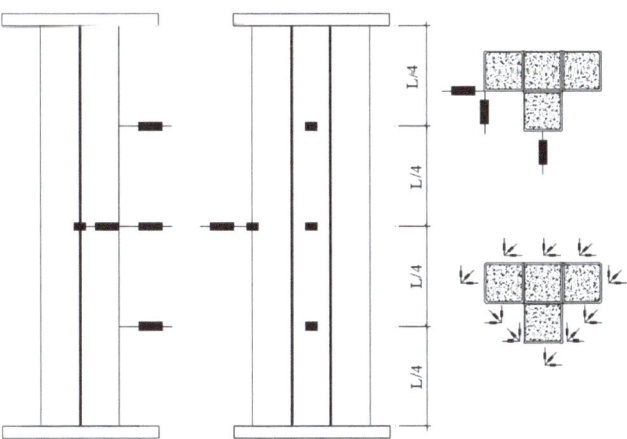

**Figure 12.** Test loading schematic.

## 3. Test Results and Discussion

### 3.1. General Observations and Failure Mode

The failure process of the three short-column specimens is roughly similar; the short-column specimen showed the failure mode of first bulging and then bending, showing the characteristics of strength failure. The short-column specimen did not undergo torsional deformation during the whole loading process. The weld in the short-column specimen did not show visible damage. The welds between the four square steel pipes did not crack, nor did the welds between the square steel pipes and the end plates, and all the welds showed no visible damage. This shows that the four square steel pipes can work together well and bear the force together. The failure process of some short column specimens is shown in Figures 13–15. The failure process of the six long-column specimens is generally similar; the long-column specimen presents a failure mode of bending first and then bulging, showing the characteristics of bending instability failure. There is no torsion phenomenon in the long column specimen during the whole loading process. The welds in the long column specimen also did not show visible damage, the welds between the four square steel pipes did not crack, the welds between the square steel pipe and the end plate did not crack, and all welds did not show visible damage. This shows that the four square steel pipes have good cooperative working performance. Figures 16–21 show the failure process of some long column specimens. The failure results of test pieces 1 to 9 are shown in Figure 22.

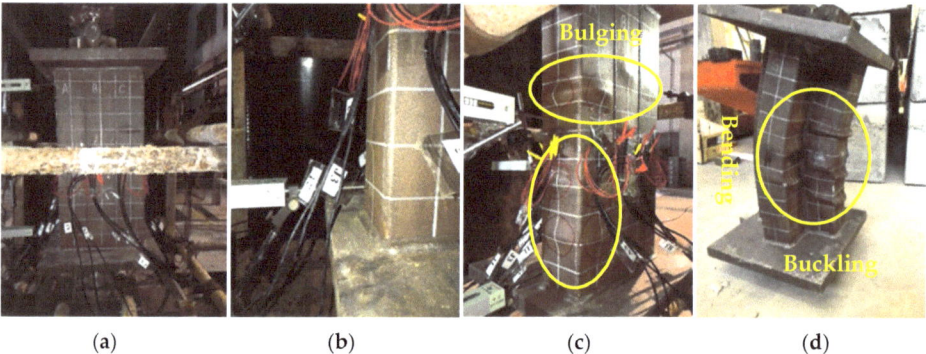

**Figure 13.** Failure process of specimen T-1: (**a**) Initial state; (**b**) Load status 1; (**c**) Load status 2; (**d**) Damage State.

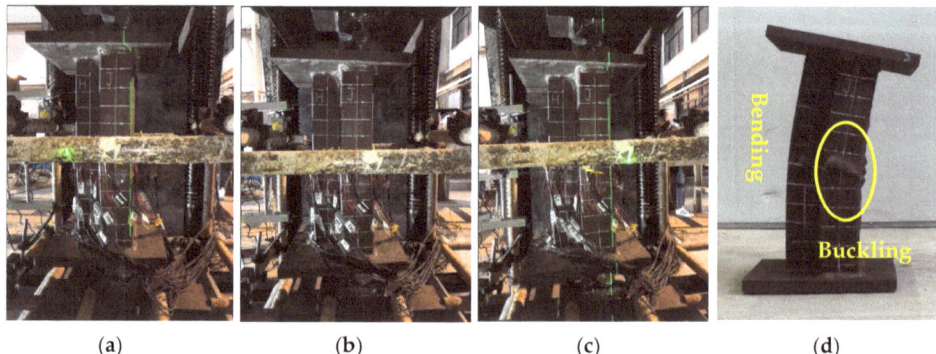

**Figure 14.** Failure process of specimen T-2: (**a**) Initial state; (**b**) Load status 1; (**c**) Load status 2; (**d**) Damage State.

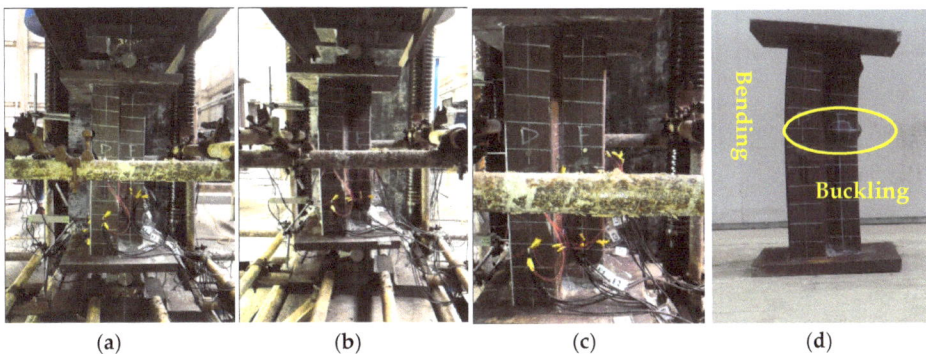

**Figure 15.** Failure process of specimen T-3: (**a**) Initial state; (**b**) Load status 1; (**c**) Load status 2; (**d**) Damage State.

**Figure 16.** Failure process of specimen T-4: (**a**) Initial state; (**b**) Load status 1; (**c**) Load status 2; (**d**) Damage State.

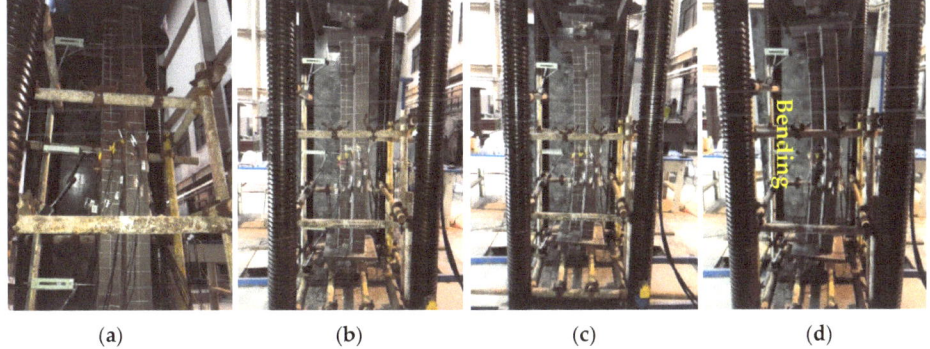

**Figure 17.** Failure process of specimen T-5: (**a**) Initial state; (**b**) Load status 1; (**c**) Load status 2; (**d**) Damage State.

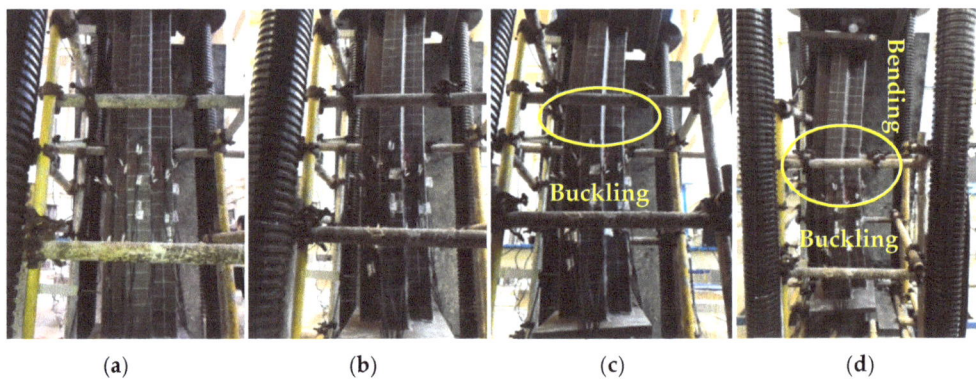

**Figure 18.** Failure process of specimen T-6: (**a**) Initial state; (**b**) Load status 1; (**c**) Load status 2; (**d**) Damage State.

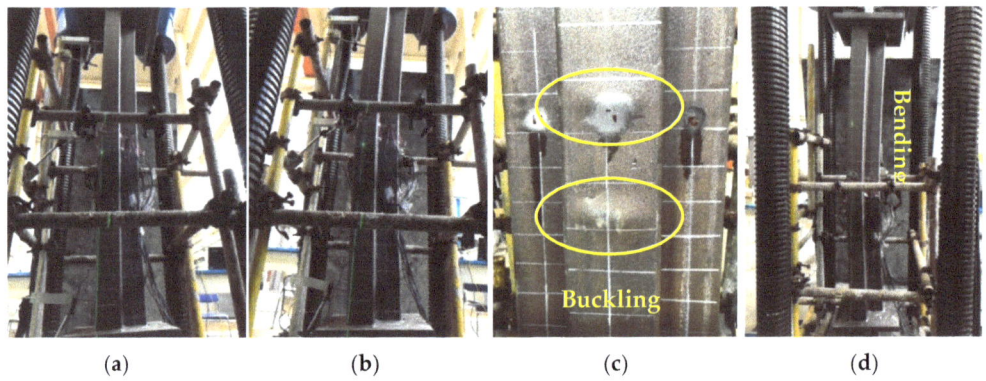

**Figure 19.** Failure process of specimen T-7: (**a**) Initial state; (**b**) Load status 1; (**c**) Load status 2; (**d**) Damage State.

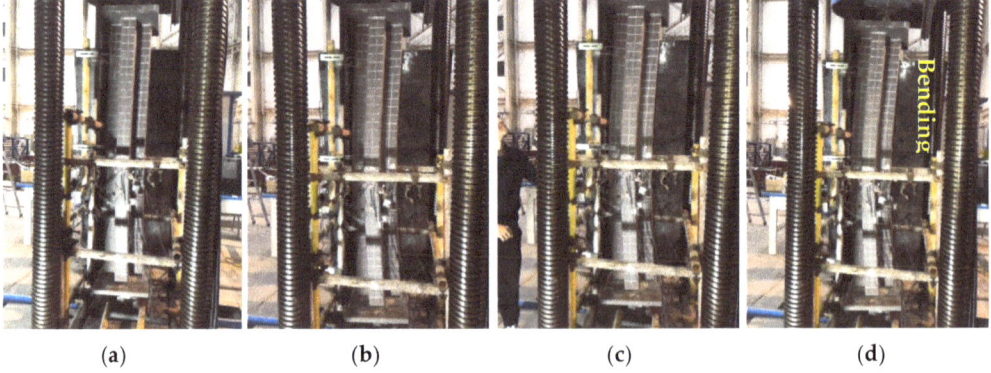

**Figure 20.** Failure process of specimen T-8: (**a**) Initial state; (**b**) Load status 1; (**c**) Load status 2; (**d**) Damage State.

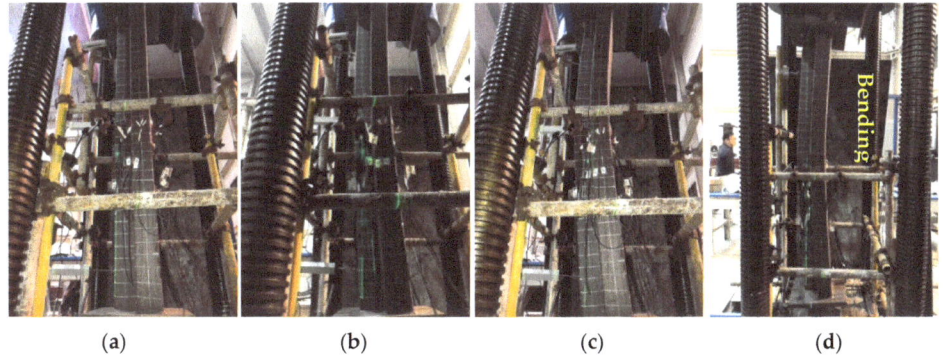

**Figure 21.** Failure process of specimen T-9: (**a**) Initial state; (**b**) Load status 1; (**c**) Load status 2; (**d**) Damage State.

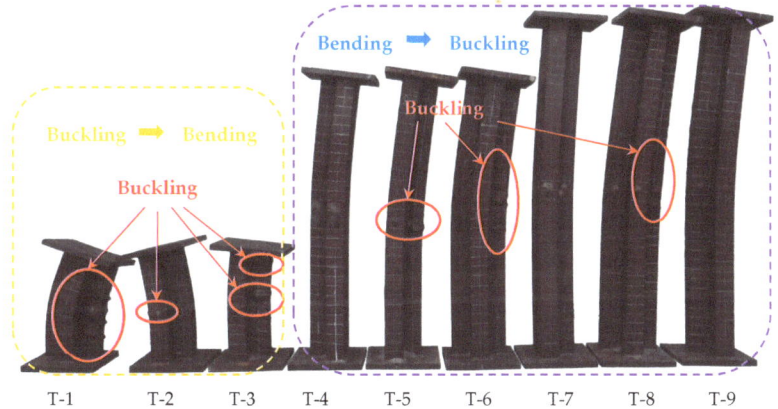

**Figure 22.** Failure results of test pieces 1 to 9.

### 3.2. The Ultimate Bearing Capacity of the Specimens

In Table 5, the eccentric compression test parameter levels of nine specimens and the test value $N_{ue}$ of ultimate bearing capacity are given. It can be seen from the table that when the slenderness ratio of the specimen is the same, the ultimate bearing capacity shows a decreasing trend with the increase in eccentricity. When the eccentric distance of the specimen is the same, and when the eccentric direction is on the asymmetric axis (x-axis) of the section, the ultimate bearing capacity of the specimen is relatively high.

**Table 5.** Results of concrete material properties test.

| Specimen | $t$/mm | $L$/mm | $e$/mm | Eccentric Direction | $\lambda$ | $N_{ue}$/kN |
|---|---|---|---|---|---|---|
| T-1 | 4 | 600 | 20 | x+ | 7 | 3058.00 |
| T-2 | 4 | 600 | 40 | y+ | 10 | 2290.90 |
| T-3 | 4 | 600 | 60 | Y− | 10 | 1898.70 |
| T-4 | 4 | 1500 | 20 | y+ | 25 | 2409.70 |
| T-5 | 4 | 1500 | 40 | y− | 25 | 1859.50 |
| T-6 | 4 | 1500 | 60 | x+ | 17 | 2036.30 |
| T-7 | 4 | 1800 | 20 | y− | 29 | 2459.50 |
| T-8 | 4 | 1800 | 40 | x+ | 20 | 2340.00 |
| T-9 | 4 | 1800 | 60 | y+ | 29 | 1534.30 |

Notes: $t$ denotes wall thickness of steel tube; $L$ denotes the length of test piece; $e$ denotes eccentricity; $\lambda$ denotes slenderness ratio; $N_{ue}$ denotes test value of the ultimate load.

## 3.3. Load–Strain Curve

Figure 23 shows the correlation curve between the steel strain and the load N at the edge of the compression zone and the tension zone for 1/2 of the column height. It can be seen from the curve that: (1) In the early stage of loading, the longitudinal direction of the edge fibers during the compression and tension process of the strain increase linearly with increasing load. (2) From the beginning of loading to before the limit load, the entire section of the specimen is compressed. When the steel in the compression zone reaches the yield strain, the surface of the steel pipe wall appears with bulging deformation. After that, tensile strain occurs in the tension zone, and the specimen gradually reaches the limit. (3) When the specimen reaches the ultimate bearing capacity, the stress of the steel pipe in the tensile and compressive zone of the specimen reaches its peak at the same time, which proves that the cooperative working performance of the specimen is good. With the increase in strain, the bearing capacity of the specimen shows a gentle decline, and the specimen shows good ductility. (4) During the loading process of the test, the strain in the compression position is larger than that in the tensile position, and the specimen shows a relatively good ductility. Destruction begins when the pressurized area begins to drop out of work.

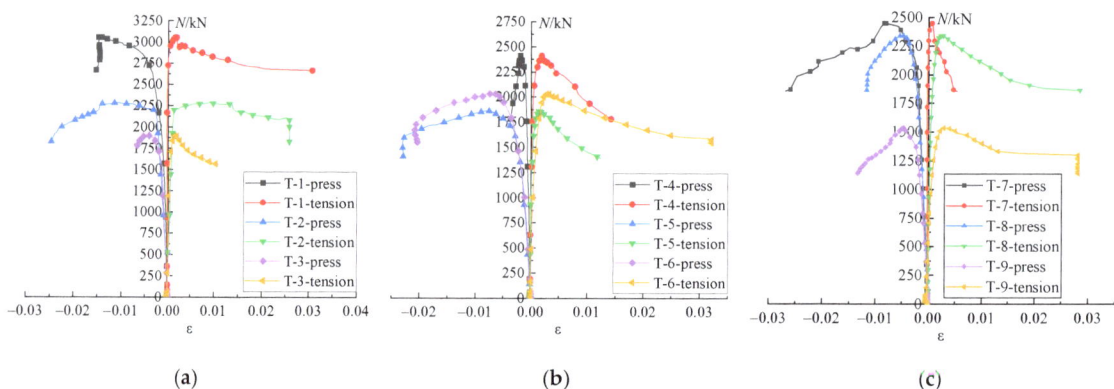

**Figure 23.** Load–strain curves of specimens 1 to 9: (**a**) load–strain curves of specimens 1 to 3; (**b**) load–strain curves of specimens 4 to 6; (**c**) load–strain curves of specimens 7 to 9.

## 3.4. Load–Deflection Curve

Figure 24 shows the N–w relationship curve of specimens No. 1 to No. 9. It can be seen from Figure 24 that at the initial stage of loading of the specimen, the deflection and load show a linear correlation. As the load continues to increase, the horizontal deflection of the column mid-section increases linearly. When approaching the ultimate load, the deflection increases rapidly, and the specimen exhibits obvious bending deformation. When the specimen reaches the ultimate load, the horizontal deflection of the middle of the short column is smaller than that of the middle of the long column.

## 3.5. Strain Distribution of Section in the Column

Figure 25 shows the distribution curve of the section strain along the height of the T-2, T-5, and T-7 columns at different loading stages. It can be seen from the relationship diagram that: (1) Before the specimen reaches the ultimate load, when the specimen is bent and deformed, the distribution of the strain along the height of the middle section of the column basically conforms to the assumption of the plane section, and it can be considered that the deformation of the plane section is maintained. (2) After the specimen reaches the ultimate bearing capacity, the tension area of the middle section of the column still maintains the plane section deformation, but the section deformation of the compression area is no longer consistent with the assumption of the plane section. (3) With the increase in eccentricity, the neutral axis begins to gradually shift to the direction of the centroid due to the influence of the second-order effect. (4) After the specimen reaches the ultimate bearing capacity, due to the damage of the compression area, the compression position begins to withdraw from work, and the position of the neutralization axis gradually moves towards the centroid of the section.

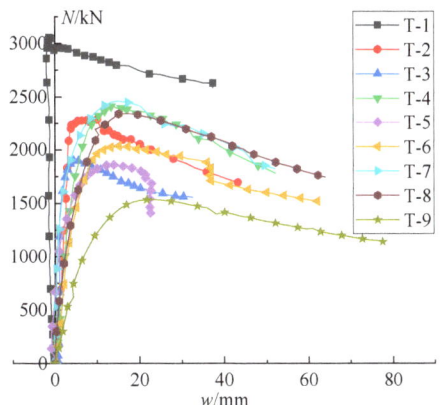

**Figure 24.** Load–deflection curves of specimens 1 to 9.

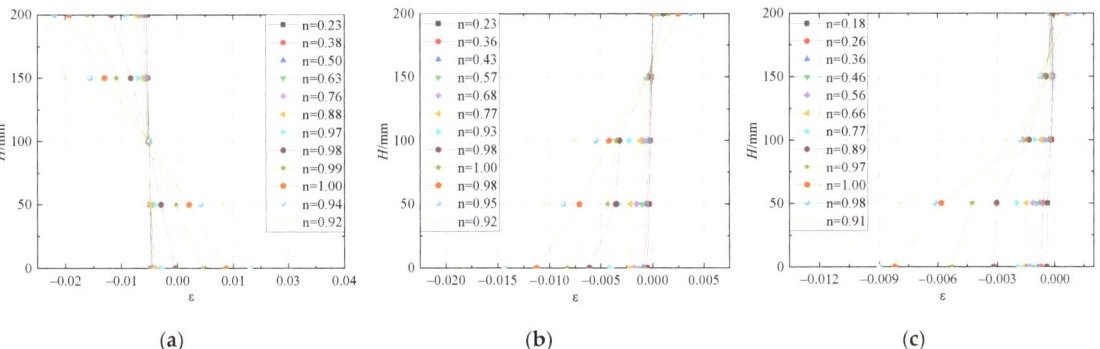

**Figure 25.** Strain distribution of the middle section of the pieces: (**a**) strain distribution in the column section of No. 2 specimen (e = 40 mm); (**b**) strain distribution in the column section of No. 5 specimen (e = 40 mm); (**c**) strain distribution in the column section of No. 7 specimen (e = 40 mm).

*3.6. Analysis of Test Parameters*

Tables 6–8 are the results of the orthogonal analysis of the test parameters. Through the orthogonal analysis, we can see that: (1) The intuitive analysis of the test results shows the influence of the three test parameters on the eccentric compressive bearing capacity of the T-shaped square concrete-filled steel tube special-shaped column: B (eccentric distance) > C (eccentric direction) > A (length). (2) The range analysis results show that the eccentric distance is the most influential factor on the pressure performance of the eccentricity, followed by the eccentric direction and the length of the specimen The degree is relatively small. (3) The results of variance analysis can show that the fitting results of the general linear models are good, and the results of the variance analysis are also reliable. Among the three test parameters, B (eccentric distance) and C (eccentric direction) have a greater influence on the test value.

Table 6. Analysis of test results.

| Specimen | L/mm | e/mm | Eccentric Direction | $N_{ue}$/kN |
|---|---|---|---|---|
| T-1 | 600 | 20 | x+ | 3058.00 |
| T-2 | 600 | 40 | y+ | 2290.90 |
| T-3 | 600 | 60 | y− | 1898.70 |
| T-4 | 1500 | 20 | y+ | 2409.70 |
| T-5 | 1500 | 40 | y− | 1859.50 |
| T-6 | 1500 | 60 | x+ | 2036.30 |
| T-7 | 1800 | 20 | Y− | 2459.50 |
| T-8 | 1800 | 40 | x+ | 2340.00 |
| T-9 | 1800 | 60 | y+ | 1534.30 |
| K1 | 2415.867 | 2642.4 | 2478.1 | — |
| K2 | 2101.833 | 2163.467 | 2078.3 | — |
| K3 | 2111.267 | 1823.1 | 2072.567 | — |
| Range | 314.0333 | 819.3 | 405.5333 | — |
| Rank | 3 | 1 | 2 | 4 |

Notes: L denotes the length of the test piece; e denotes eccentricity; $N_{ue}$ denotes the test value of ultimate load; K1, K2, and K3 are the average values of the test results of each parameter at the three-parameter levels.

Table 7. Mean response analysis of test results.

| Parameter Level | L/mm | e/mm | Eccentric Direction | Empty Column |
|---|---|---|---|---|
| 1 | 2416 | 2642 | 2478 | 2151 |
| 2 | 2102 | 2163 | 2078 | 2262 |
| 3 | 2111 | 1823 | 2073 | 2216 |
| Delta | 314 | 819 | 406 | 112 |
| Rank | 3 | 1 | 2 | 4 |

Notes: L denotes the length of the test piece; e denotes eccentricity; $N_{ue}$ denotes the test value of ultimate load; 1, 2, and 3 represent different parameter values of each factor at three parameter levels, respectively.

Table 8. Analysis of variance of test results.

| Parameter | Degrees of Freedom | Adj SS | Adj MS | Value of F | Value of P |
|---|---|---|---|---|---|
| Length | 2 | 191,487 | 95,744 | 10.14 | 0.090 |
| Eccentricity | 2 | 101,6479 | 508,240 | 53.83 | 0.018 |
| Eccentric direction | 2 | 324,330 | 162,165 | 17.18 | 0.055 |
| Error | 2 | 18,882 | 9441 | — | — |
| Total | 8 | 1,551,178 | — | — | — |
| S = 97.1644 | R-sq = 98.78% | R-sq(adjusted) = 95.13% | 406 | 112 | — |

Notes: Adj SS denotes corrected sum of squares; Adj MS denotes corrected mean square; F denotes the ratio of the between-level variance to the within-level variance of the parameter; S denotes the difference between data value and fitting value; R-sq denotes goodness of fit, which is the ratio of the regression sum of squares to the total deviation sum of squares; R-sq(adjusted) denotes modified goodness of fit.

Figure 26 shows the changing trend of the influence of various factors on the eccentric compressive bearing capacity of the T-shaped CFST composite special-shaped column. With the increase in the eccentric distance, the bearing capacity of the eccentric compression specimen decreases significantly, and with the increase in the length of the specimen and the change in the eccentric direction, the change degree of the eccentric compression specimen is similar. The influence is the largest, followed by the eccentric direction, and finally the length of the specimen.

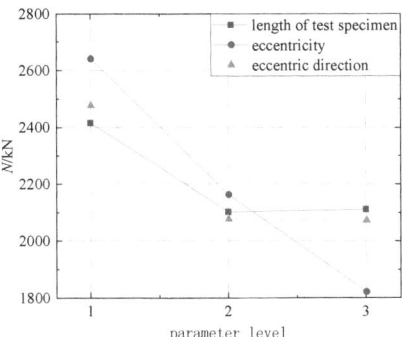

**Figure 26.** Graph of the influence of test parameters.

### 3.7. Calculation of Bearing Capacity

At present, there is no unified design and calculation method for CFST special-shaped columns in the domestic and foreign codes and regulations about CFST. This paper refers to the AISC-LRFD (1999) [33] code of the United States, BS 5400 (1979) [34], the code formulated by the British Standards Association, Eurocode 4 (1994) [35], the code formulated by the European Standards Association, AIJ (1997) [36], the code of the Architectural Society of Japan, the specification for the design and construction of concrete-filled steel tubular structures (CECS 28:90) [37] of China, and the technical specification for concrete-filled steel tube structures (DBJ/t13-51-2010) [38] of Fujian Province of China. Using the calculation formula on the bearing capacity of concrete-filled steel tubular composite columns, the ratio of the calculated value $N_u$ to the test value $N_{ue}$ is shown in Table 9. Through the comparison of the calculation results of various codes and regulations, it can be found that the calculated values of DBJ/t13-51-2010 and AIJ are the most consistent with the test values, but the dispersion of AIJ is higher than that of DBJ/t13-51-2010; the calculated value of Eurocode 4 is in good agreement with the test value, but slightly worse than DBJ/t13-51-2010 and AIJ, and also BS 5400. The calculated value of CECS is generally consistent with the test value, and the calculated result is unsafe; the calculated value of the AISC specification is in the lowest agreement with the test value, and the calculated result is too safe. It can be seen that using the DBJ/T13-51-2010 specification of the unified theory proposed by Zhong [39], the calculation of the eccentric compressive bearing capacity of the T-shaped square concrete-filled steel tubular composite special-shaped column is in the best agreement with the test results.

**Table 9.** The comparison between the calculated value and the test value of the test piece's eccentric bearing capacity.

| Specimen | $t$/mm | $L$/mm | $e$/mm | $\lambda$ | AISC $\eta$ | DBJ $\eta$ | BS5400 $\eta$ | EC4 $\eta$ | AIJ $\eta$ | CECS $\eta$ |
|---|---|---|---|---|---|---|---|---|---|---|
| T-1 | 4 | 600 | 20 | 7 | 0.718 | 1.018 | 0.821 | 0.904 | 0.948 | 1.149 |
| T-2 | 4 | 600 | 40 | 10 | 0.764 | 1.043 | 0.916 | 1.050 | 1.006 | 1.208 |
| T-3 | 4 | 600 | 60 | 10 | 0.760 | 1.035 | 0.956 | 0.844 | 1.011 | 1.202 |
| T-4 | 4 | 1500 | 20 | 25 | 0.922 | 1.033 | 0.976 | 1.096 | 1.059 | 1.190 |
| T-5 | 4 | 1500 | 40 | 25 | 0.941 | 0.974 | 1.042 | 1.165 | 1.109 | 1.270 |
| T-6 | 4 | 1500 | 60 | 17 | 0.693 | 0.994 | 0.838 | 0.786 | 0.861 | 1.014 |
| T-7 | 4 | 1800 | 20 | 29 | 0.903 | 0.999 | 0.935 | 1.057 | 0.985 | 1.105 |
| T-8 | 4 | 1800 | 40 | 20 | 0.734 | 1.035 | 0.846 | 1.040 | 0.880 | 0.957 |
| T-9 | 4 | 1800 | 60 | 29 | 0.941 | 0.921 | 1.043 | 0.946 | 1.084 | 1.269 |
| $\mu$ | — | — | — | — | 0.820 | 1.006 | 0.930 | 0.987 | 0.994 | 1.151 |
| $\sigma$ | — | — | — | — | 0.098 | 0.037 | 0.079 | 0.118 | 0.081 | 0.102 |

Notes: $t$ denotes wall thickness of the steel tube; $L$ denotes the length of test piece; $e$ denotes eccentricity; $\lambda$ denotes slenderness ratio; $\mu$ denotes mean; $\sigma$ denotes standard deviation; $N_u$ denotes calculated value of ultimate bearing capacity; $N_{ue}$ denotes test value of ultimate bearing capacity; $\eta$ denotes $N_u/N_{ue}$.

## 4. Finite Element Modeling and Validation

### 4.1. Finite Element Modeling

According to the Mises yield criterion, obey the isotropic strengthening criterion, follow the corresponding flow law, and select the plastic model provided by ABAQUS for modeling and calculation. The square steel tube adopts the shell element (S4R), and the core concrete part adopts the non-coordinated eight-node linear hexahedron solid element (C3D8I). The contact friction coefficient of the steel is 0.3, and the friction coefficient between the steel and concrete is 0.6. Welds are simulated using binding constraints. Figure 27 shows each component unit and grid division.

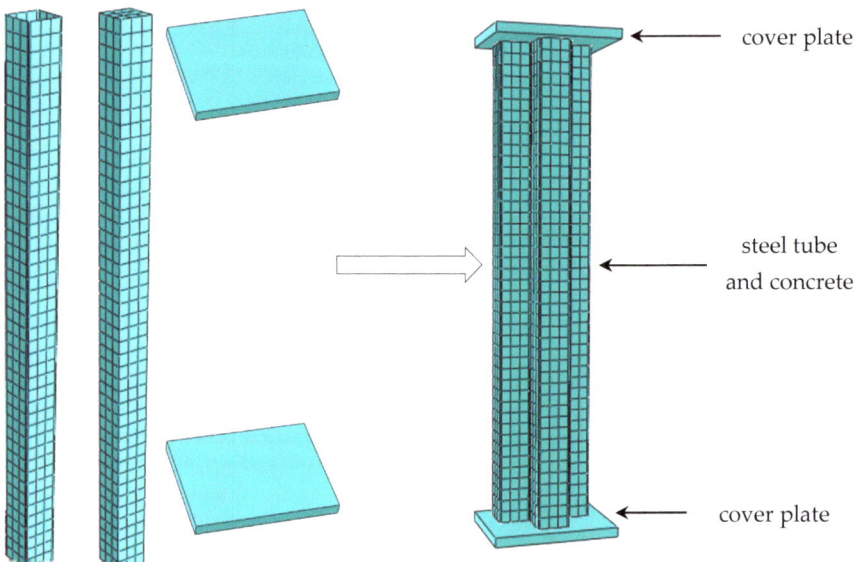

**Figure 27.** Elements and meshing of components.

Using the steel constitutive model proposed by Ding et al. [40], the simplified model of the constitutive relation is shown in Figure 28. Mathematical expressions such as Formula (1) are used.

$$\sigma_i = \begin{cases} E_s \varepsilon_i & (\varepsilon_i \leq \varepsilon_y) \\ f_s & (\varepsilon_y < \varepsilon_i \leq \varepsilon_{st}) \\ f_s + \zeta E_s(\varepsilon_i - \varepsilon_{st}) & (\varepsilon_{st} < \varepsilon_i \leq \varepsilon_u) \\ f_u & (\varepsilon_u < \varepsilon_i) \end{cases} \quad (1)$$

where $\zeta = 1/216$; $i$ = the equivalent stress of the steel; $E_s$ = the elastic modulus of the steel, taking $E_s = 2.06 \times 10^5$ MPa; $\varepsilon_i$ = the equivalent strain of the steel; $\varepsilon_y$ = the strain of the steel when it yields; $f_s$ = the yield strength of steel; $\varepsilon_{st}$ = the strain when the steel is strengthened; $\varepsilon_{st} = 12\,\varepsilon_y$; $\varepsilon_u$ = the strain when the steel reaches the ultimate strength; $\varepsilon_u = 120\,\varepsilon_y$; and $f_u$ = the ultimate strength of the steel, taking $f_u = 1.5 f_s$.

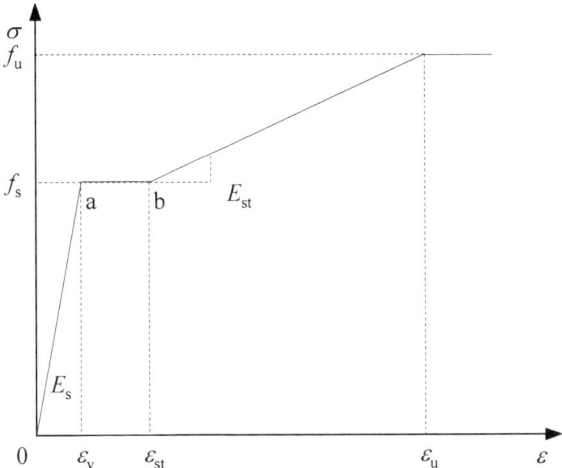

**Figure 28.** Constitutive relation model for steel.

The plastic damage model is used for concrete. The constitutive relation of constrained concrete under compression adopts the modified stress–strain relation of CFST with different strength grades proposed in the literature [40] under uniaxial compression, and the mathematical expression is shown in Formula (2).

$$y = \begin{cases} \frac{A_1 x + (B_1 - 1)x^2}{1 + (A_1 - 2)x + B_1 x^2} & (x \leq 1) \\ \frac{x}{\alpha_1 (x-1)^2 + x} & (x > 1) \end{cases} \quad (2)$$

where $x = \varepsilon/\varepsilon_c$; $y = \sigma/f_c$; $\varepsilon_c$ = the peak compressive strain of concrete; $\varepsilon_c = 383 f_{cu}^{7/18} \times 10^{-6}$; $A_1$ = the ratio of concrete elastic modulus to peak secant modulus; $A_1 = 9.1 f_{cu}^{-4/9}$; and $B_1$ = a physical quantity related to the attenuation of the elastic modulus of the ascending curve. Before the ascending segment $\sigma = 0.4 f_c$, the curve approximates a straight line. At this time, $B_1 = 1.6(A_1 - 1)^2$; $\alpha_1$ is a parameter related to the descending section of the stress–strain curve of concrete under uniaxial compression. For the core concrete under the constraint of steel pipe, $\alpha_1 = f_c^{0.1}/(1.2 \sqrt{1 + \xi})$, $\xi = A_s f_y/(A_c f_c)$. In the nonlinear finite element analysis of CFST using ABAQUS, good calculation results can be obtained by taking $\alpha_1 = 0.15$; $f_{cu}$ = the compressive strength of the concrete cube; $A_s$ and $f_y$ are the cross-sectional area of the steel pipe and the yield strength of the steel; and $A_c$ and $f_c$ are the cross-sectional area of the concrete and the compressive strength of the concrete axis, where $f_c = 0.4 f_{cu}^{7/6}$.

Constrained concrete plastic damage coefficient $D$ is calculated according to Formula (3), $D_0$ is the damage value of concrete at peak stress; $D_0 = 2.1 - 0.4\ln(f_{cu} + 41)$; for uniaxial compression, the strain $\varepsilon_p$ is the peak compression value strain $\varepsilon_c$; $\varepsilon_c = 383 f_{cu}^{7/18} \times 10^{-6}$; $c_1$, $c_2$ and $c_3$ are calculation parameters; $c_1 = 0.56 - 0.004 f_{cu}$; $c_2 = 1.17 + 4.34 \times 10^{-5} f_{cu}^{2.8}$; and $c_3 = 0.32 + 0.3\ln(f_{cu} - 10)$. Figure 29 shows the constitutive relation curve of concrete.

$$D = \begin{cases} \left[1 - (1 - \varepsilon/\varepsilon_p)^{c_1}\right] D_0 & (\varepsilon \leq \varepsilon_p) \\ 1 - \frac{1 - D_0}{c_2(1 - D_0)(\varepsilon/\varepsilon_p - 1)^{c_3} + 1} & (\varepsilon > \varepsilon_p) \end{cases} \quad (3)$$

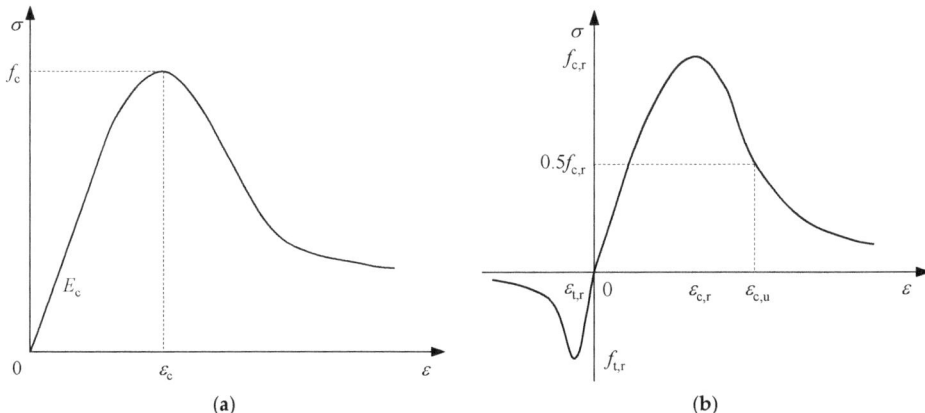

**Figure 29.** Stress–strain curve of concrete: (**a**) uniaxial compressive stress–strain curves for confined concrete; (**b**) uniaxial tensile and compressive stress–strain curves of unconstrained concrete.

The stress–strain relationship of tensile concrete adopts the constitutive curve provided in appendix C of the code for design of concrete structures (GB 50010-2010) [41]. The mathematical expression is as shown in Formula (4); $d_t$ is the uniaxial tensile damage evolution parameter of concrete; $E_c$ is the elastic modulus of concrete, calculated according to $E_c = 9500 f_{cu}^{1/3}$; $\alpha_t$ is the falling section parameter of the concrete uniaxial tensile stress–strain curve, which is taken according to C.2.3 in GB 50010-2010; $\varepsilon_{t,r}$ is the peak tensile strain of concrete corresponding to the representative value of uniaxial tensile strength, which is taken according to C.2.3 in GB 50010-2010; $f_{t,r}$ is the representative value of concrete uniaxial tensile strength, which is taken according to the test results.

$$\sigma = (1 - d_t)E_c\varepsilon \tag{4}$$

$$d_t = \begin{cases} 1 - \rho_t\left[1.2 - 0.2x^5\right] & (x \leq 1) \\ 1 - \dfrac{\rho_t}{\alpha_t(x-1)^{1.7}+x} & (x > 1) \end{cases} \tag{5}$$

$$x = \frac{\varepsilon}{\varepsilon_{t,r}} \tag{6}$$

$$\rho_t = \frac{f_{t,r}}{E_c\varepsilon_{t,r}} \tag{7}$$

*4.2. Reliability Verification of FEM*

Figures 30–38 show the overall stress distribution of No. 1 to No. 9 specimens and the comparison between the failure phenomenon of the finite element model and the experimental phenomenon. From left to right are the failure phenomenon of the test, the failure phenomenon of the finite element model, the failure phenomenon of the steel pipe in the finite element model, and the failure phenomenon of the core concrete in the finite element model.

The failure process and overall stress distribution of the T-1 to T-3 specimen models are shown in Figures 30–32. During the whole loading process, the compression zone begins to yield first. As the load increases, the yield surface gradually expands, and the plastic zone expands. Finally, the surface of the steel tube on the compression side is severely deformed by bulging, followed by bending. The finite element analysis results are in good agreement with the test results.

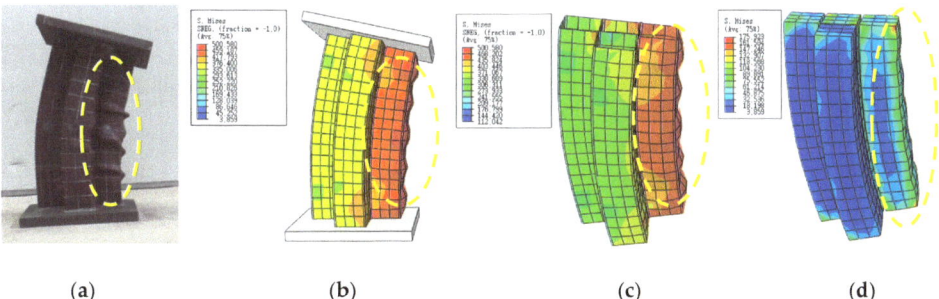

**Figure 30.** Stress distribution and failure phenomenon of finite element model of T-1 specimen: (**a**) Test failure mode; (**b**) Numerical calculation of failure mode; (**c**) Failure modes of steel tube; (**d**) Failure modes of concrete.

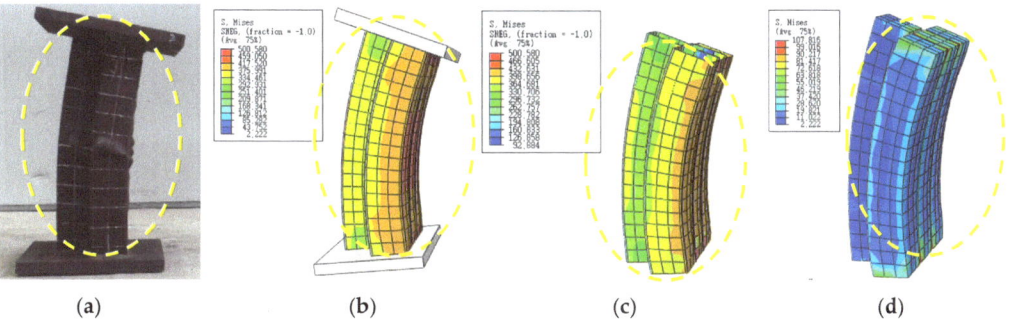

**Figure 31.** Stress distribution and failure phenomenon of finite element model of T-2 specimen: (**a**) Test failure mode; (**b**) Numerical calculation of failure mode; (**c**) Failure modes of steel tube; (**d**) Failure modes of concrete.

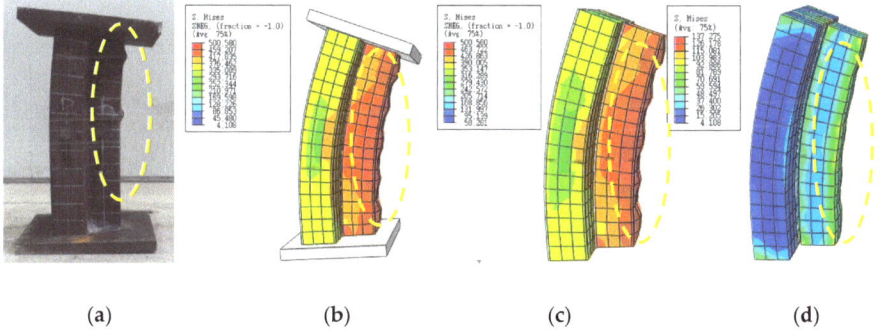

**Figure 32.** Stress distribution and failure phenomenon of finite element model of T-3 specimen: (**a**) Test failure mode; (**b**) Numerical calculation of failure mode; (**c**) Failure modes of steel tube; (**d**) Failure modes of concrete.

The failure process and overall stress distribution of the specimens T-4 to T-9 are shown in Figures 33–38. During the whole loading process, the stress in the compression zone increases the fastest; it first enters the plastic development stage, and the surface of the compression side has bulging deformation. Finally, it was damaged due to bending instability, and the finite element analysis results were in good agreement with the experimental results.

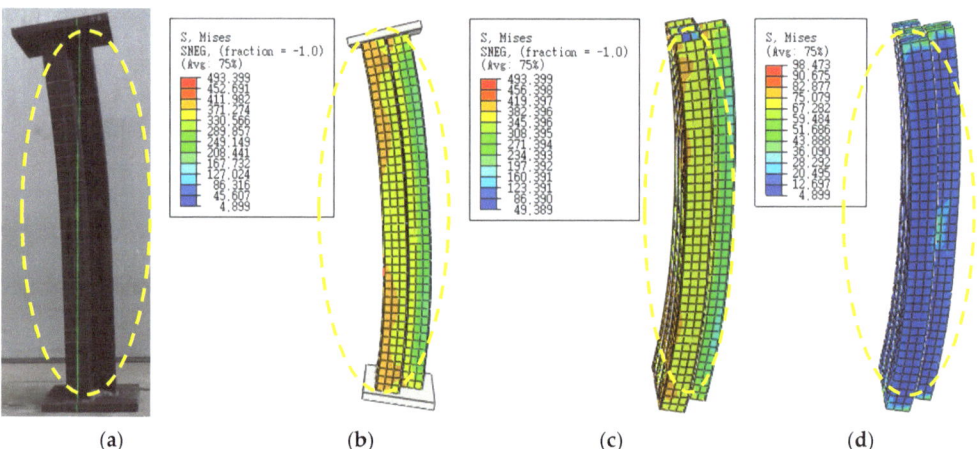

(a)  (b)  (c)  (d)

**Figure 33.** Stress distribution and failure phenomenon of finite element model of T-4 specimen: (**a**) Test failure mode; (**b**) Numerical calculation of failure mode; (**c**) Failure modes of steel tube; (**d**) Failure modes of concrete.

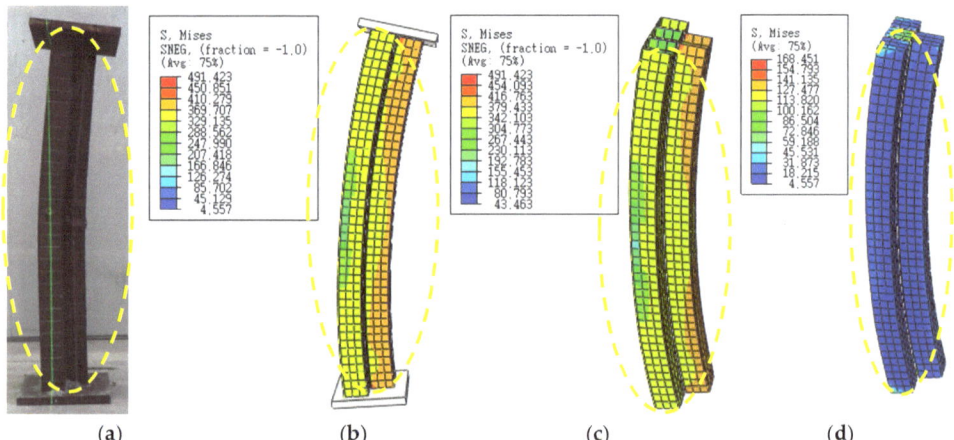

(a)  (b)  (c)  (d)

**Figure 34.** Stress distribution and failure phenomenon of finite element model of T-5 specimen: (**a**) Test failure mode; (**b**) Numerical calculation of failure mode; (**c**) Failure modes of steel tube; (**d**) Failure modes of concrete.

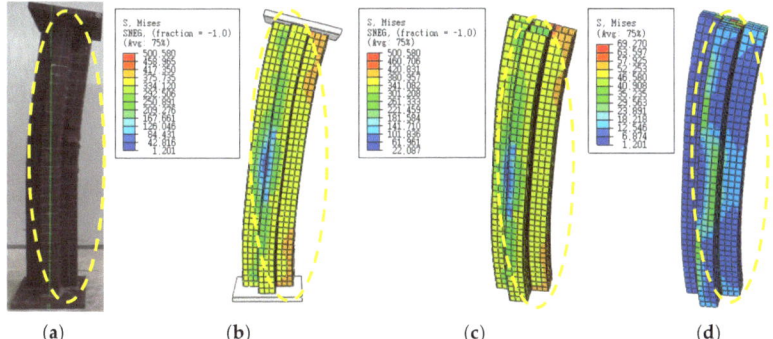

**Figure 35.** Stress distribution and failure phenomenon of finite element model of T-6 specimen: (**a**) Test failure mode; (**b**) Numerical calculation of failure mode; (**c**) Failure modes of steel tube; (**d**) Failure modes of concrete.

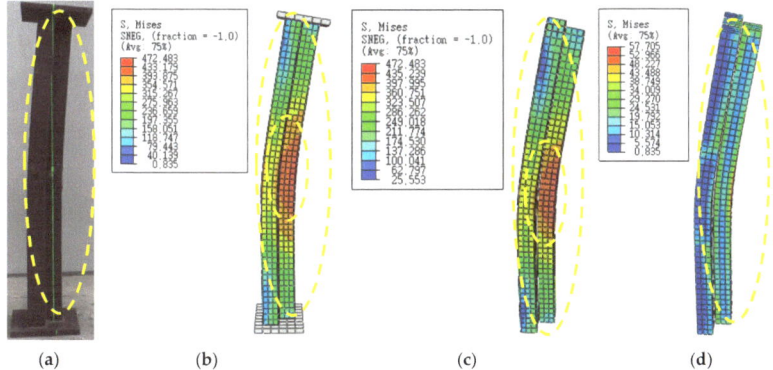

**Figure 36.** Stress distribution and failure phenomenon of finite element model of T-7 specimen: (**a**) Test failure mode; (**b**) Numerical calculation of failure mode; (**c**) Failure modes of steel tube; (**d**) Failure modes of concrete.

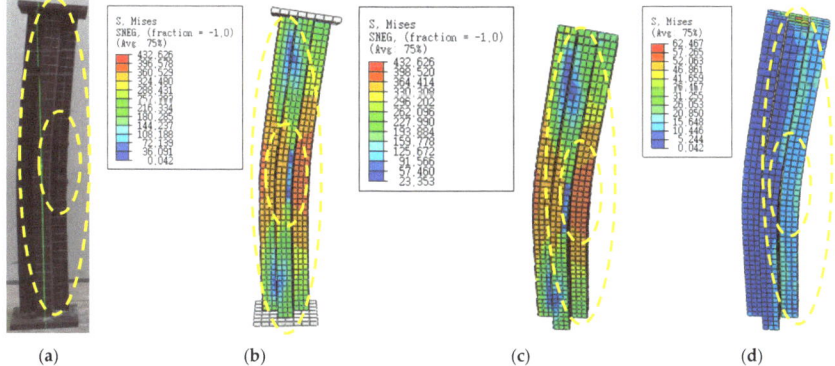

**Figure 37.** Stress distribution and failure phenomenon of finite element model of T-8 specimen: (**a**) Test failure mode; (**b**) Numerical calculation of failure mode; (**c**) Failure modes of steel tube; (**d**) Failure modes of concrete.

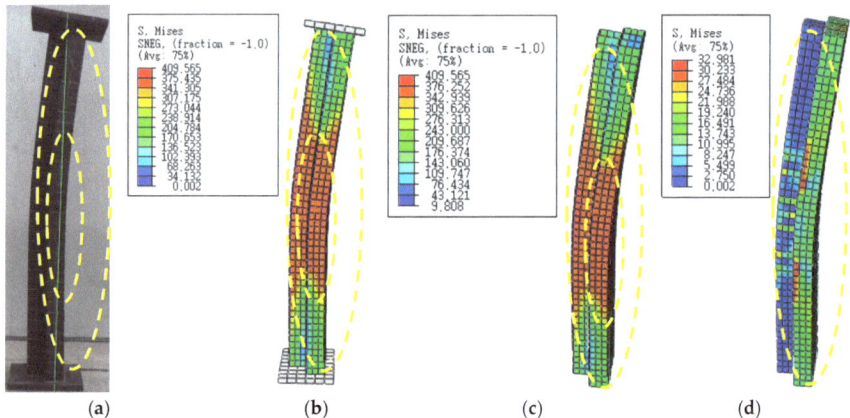

(a)        (b)        (c)        (d)

**Figure 38.** Stress distribution and failure phenomenon of finite element model of T-9 specimen: (**a**) Test failure mode; (**b**) Numerical calculation of failure mode; (**c**) Failure modes of steel tube; (**d**) Failure modes of concrete.

The ultimate bearing capacity values and corresponding parameters of specimens 1–9 obtained through finite element analysis calculations are listed in Table 10. The ratio between the calculated value of finite element simulation and the test value is calculated in the table.

**Table 10.** Ultimate bearing capacity of T-shaped concrete-filled square steel tubular composite special-shaped column under eccentric compression.

| Specimen | L/mm | e/mm | Eccentric Direction | λ | $N_{uf}$/kN | $N_{ue}$/kN | $N_{uf}/N_{ue}$ |
|---|---|---|---|---|---|---|---|
| T-1 | 600 | 20 | x+ | 7 | 3042.57 | 3058.00 | 0.99 |
| T-2 | 600 | 40 | y+ | 10 | 2348.86 | 2290.90 | 1.03 |
| T-3 | 600 | 60 | y− | 10 | 1818.53 | 1898.70 | 0.96 |
| T-4 | 1500 | 20 | y+ | 25 | 2593.20 | 2409.70 | 1.07 |
| T-5 | 1500 | 40 | y− | 25 | 1943.16 | 1859.50 | 1.04 |
| T-6 | 1500 | 60 | x+ | 17 | 1925.75 | 2036.30 | 0.95 |
| T-7 | 1800 | 20 | y− | 29 | 2358.61 | 2459.50 | 0.96 |
| T-8 | 1800 | 40 | x+ | 20 | 2205.27 | 2340.00 | 0.94 |
| T-9 | 1800 | 60 | y+ | 29 | 1574.10 | 1534.30 | 1.03 |

Notes: $L$ denotes the length of the test piece; $e$ denotes eccentricity; $\lambda$ denotes slenderness ratio; $N_{uf}$ denotes the simulated value of bearing capacity; $N_{ue}$ denotes the test value of the ultimate load. The steel strength grade of the test piece is Q235B, the concrete strength grade is C30, and the wall thickness of the steel pipe is 4 mm.

### 4.3. Load–Strain Curve of FEM

Figure 39 shows the comparison between the load–strain of the nine specimen models and the test results, Ei represents the test result of the i-th specimen, and FEi represents the finite element calculation result of the i-th specimen. Through the test and the finite element load–strain curve, it can be found that in the elastic stage, the longitudinal strain of the steel pipe increases gradually with the increase in load. After entering the plastic stage, the strain growth accelerates, the steel deforms greatly, and the bearing capacity of the component decreases slowly. The experimental results are in good agreement with the finite element calculation results.

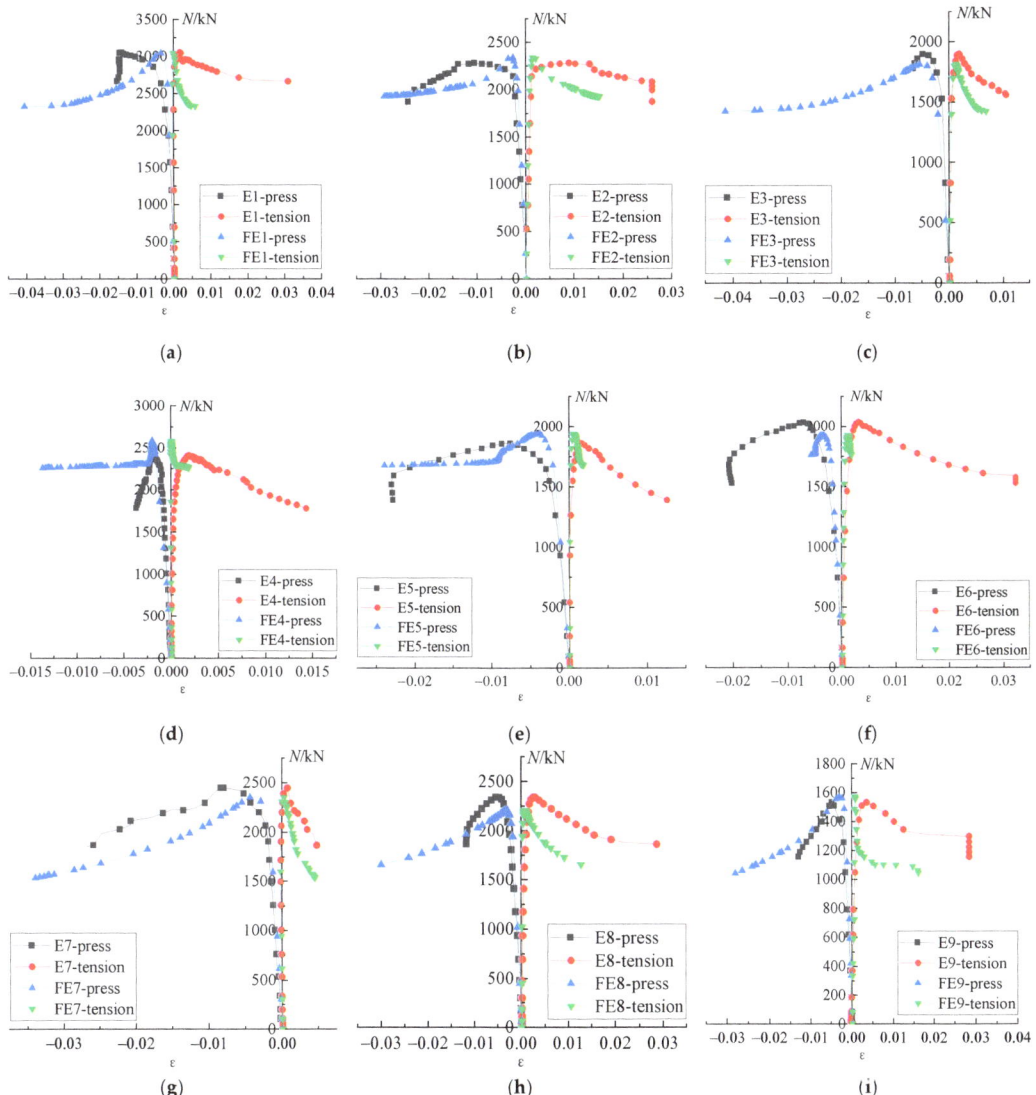

**Figure 39.** Load–strain curve of FEM: (**a**) load–strain curve of T-1; (**b**) load–strain curve of T-2; (**c**) load–strain curve of T-3; (**d**) load–strain curve of T-4; (**e**) load–strain curve of T-5; (**f**) load–strain curve of T-6; (**g**) load–strain curve of T-7; (**h**) load–strain curve of T-8; (**i**) load–strain curve of T-9.

*4.4. Load–Deflection Curve of FEM*

Figure 40 shows the finite element calculation results and test results of the load N and the horizontal deflection w of the T-1 to T-9 specimens. Ei represents the experimental value of the $i$-th specimen, and FEi represents the finite element calculation value of the $i$-th specimen. Before the specimen reaches the ultimate load, the horizontal deflection of the specimen is small. After reaching the ultimate load, the horizontal deflection of the specimen gradually increased with the decrease in load; after reaching the ultimate load, the specimen showed good ductility; the finite element calculation curve was in good agreement with the experimental curve.

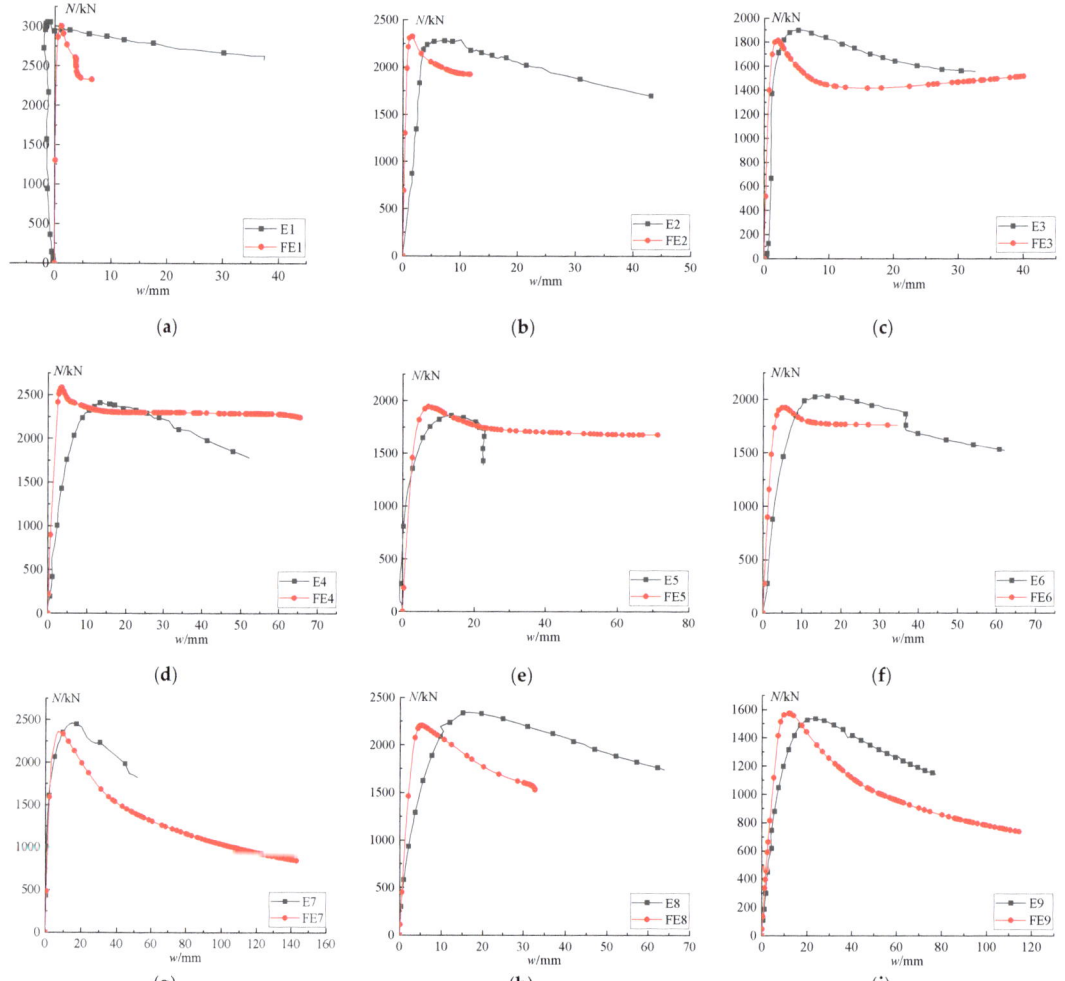

**Figure 40.** Load–deflection curve of FEM: (**a**) load–deflection curve of T-1; (**b**) load–deflection curve of T-2; (**c**) load–deflection curve of T-3; (**d**) load–deflection curve of T-4; (**e**) load–deflection curve of T-5; (**f**) load–deflection curve of T-6; (**g**) load–deflection curve of T-7; (**h**) load–deflection curve of T-8; (**i**) load–deflection curve of T-9.

## 5. Conclusions

The effects of specimen length, eccentric distance, and eccentric direction on the eccentric compression performance of T-shaped concrete-filled square steel tubular composite special-shaped columns are studied through an eccentric compression test, and the calculated values in the code are compared with the experimental values. The numerical analysis model of a T-shaped concrete-filled square steel tubular composite special-shaped column is established by using the general finite element numerical analysis program, ABAQUS. The modeling calculation of nine specimens in the test is carried out to verify the test results and theoretical analysis results.

1. The failure mode of the T-shaped short column specimen is mainly strength failure, and the long column specimen is mainly bending instability failure. The ultimate bearing capacity of the short column under eccentric compression is higher than

that of the long column. The bending deformation of the specimen is similar to the sinusoidal half wave curve, and there is no torsional deformation. In the process of the eccentric compression failure of the T-shaped concrete-filled square steel tubular composite special-shaped column, the strain in the compression area is large, and the steel pipe wall in the compression area first begins to yield and enters the plastic stage, resulting in large bulging deformation and bending deformation.
2. During the stress process of the specimen, the strain distribution on the section in the middle of the column is consistent with the plane section assumption. The compression area yields before the tension area. The deformation of tensile and compressive stress areas is relatively coordinated, the cooperative working performance of all parts of the specimen is good, and the specimen has good ductility.
3. The eccentricity has the greatest influence on the mechanical properties of the specimen under bias pressure, followed by the eccentricity direction, and finally the specimen length. The influence of eccentricity and eccentricity direction on the mechanical properties of the specimen under bias pressure is more significant than the specimen length.
4. The finite element calculation results are in good agreement with the experimental results. The simulated value of ultimate bearing capacity is basically consistent with the test value, and the failure mode of the finite element specimen model is also consistent with the test. The finite element calculation model of the T-shaped concrete-filled square steel tubular composite special-shaped column has good reliability and can be used as the basis of theoretical calculation and analysis.
5. Comparing the calculation results and test results of six codes at home and abroad, it is found that the calculated values of the concrete-filled steel tubular bearing capacity formula recommended by DBJ / T13-51-2010 and AIJ are in good agreement with the test values, but the calculation results of DBJ / T13-51-2010 are less discrete.

**Author Contributions:** Q.L., methodology, conceptualization, writing—review and editing; Z.L., writing—review and editing, funding acquisition; X.Z., methodology, conceptualization, writing—review and editing, funding acquisition; Z.W., writing—review and editing. All authors have read and agreed to the published version of the manuscript.

**Funding:** This research was supported by the Major Scientific and Technological Innovation Projects of Shandong Province, grant number 2021CXGC011204; the Natural Science Foundation of Shandong Province, grant number ZR2020QE247; the Research and development project of Housing and UrbanRural Development of Shandong Province, grant number 2021-K5-14 and the Research Fund for the Doctoral Program of Shandong Jianzhu University, grant number X19035Z.

**Institutional Review Board Statement:** Not applicable.

**Informed Consent Statement:** Not applicable.

**Data Availability Statement:** The data presented in this study are available on request from the authors.

**Conflicts of Interest:** The authors declare no conflict of interest.

# References

1. Shen, Z.; Lin, Z.; Luo, J.; Zhang, J.; Li, Y. Hysteretic behaviors of steel frames with concrete-filled L-shaped steel tubular columns. In Proceedings of the 3rd International Forum on New Progress in Structural Engineering, Shanghai, China, 4–6 November 2009.
2. Lei, M.; Shen, Z.; Li, Y.; Luo, J. Analysis of behavior of concrete-filled T-shaped steel tube tall column subjected to uniaxial eccentric load. *J. Tongji Univ.* **2016**, *44*, 207–212. [CrossRef]
3. Li, Z.; Cai, J.; Tan, Z.; Chen, D. Experimental study on mechanical properties of concrete filled anisotropic steel tubular columns with restrained tie rods. In Proceedings of the 10th National Academic Conference on Structural Engineering, Nanjing, China, 20–24 October 2001.
4. Zuo, Z.; Cai, J.; Zhu, C. Experimental research on L-shape CFT stub columns with binding bars subjected to eccentric compression. *J. Southeast Univ.* **2010**, *40*, 346–351. [CrossRef]

5. Wang, Y.; Yang, Y.; Zhang, S.; Liu, J. Experimental research on seismic behavior of T-shaped concrete-filled steel tube columns. In Proceedings of the 30th Anniversary of the Founding of the Journal of Building Structures and the Symposium on Basic Theory and Innovation of Building Structures, Shanghai, China, 28–31 May 2010. [CrossRef]
6. Tu, Y.; Liu, L.; Ye, Y. Study on the properties of multi-cell T-shaped concrete-filled steel tubular intermediate long columns under axial load. *China Civ. Eng. J.* **2012**, *45*, 27–35. [CrossRef]
7. Du, G.; Xu, L.; Xu, H.; Wen, F. Study on composite T-shaped concrete filled steel tubular columns under eccentric compression. *J. Build. Struct.* **2010**, *31*, 72–77. [CrossRef]
8. Cao, B.; Dai, S.; Huang, J. Experimental study on axial compressive behavior of improved composite T-shaped concrete-filled steel tubular columns. *J. Build. Struct.* **2014**, *35*, 36–43. [CrossRef]
9. Wang, Z.; Liu, Z.; Zhou, X. Experimental Investigation of Special-Shaped Concrete-Filled Square Steel Tube Composite Columns with Steel Hoops under Axial Loads. *Materials* **2022**, *15*, 4179. [CrossRef] [PubMed]
10. Rong, B. *Theoretical Analysis and Experimental Study on Concrete Filled Square Steel Tubular Composite Special-Shaped Columns*; Tianjin University: Tianjin, China, 2009. [CrossRef]
11. Zhou, T.; Xu, M.; Chen, Z.; Li, Y. Experimental study on biaxial eccentric compression stability of L-shaped special-shaped columns composed of concrete-filled square steel tube connected by steel plates. *Build. Struct.* **2018**, *48*, 82–86. [CrossRef]
12. Zeghiche, J.; Chaoui, K. An experimental behaviour of concrete-filled steel tubular columns. *J. Constr. Steel Res.* **2005**, *61*, 53–66. [CrossRef]
13. Ghannam, S. Buckling of Concrete-Filled steel tubular slender columns. *Int. J. Res. Civ. Eng. Archit. Des.* **2015**, *3*, 41–47.
14. Ahiwale, D.; Khartode, R.; Bhapkar, A.; Narule, G.; Sharma, K. Influence of compressive load on concrete filled steel tubular column with variable thickness. *Innov. Infrastruct. Solut.* **2021**, *6*, 23. [CrossRef]
15. Achuthan, P.; Prabhu, G.G.; Vimal Arokiaraj, G.G.; Sivanantham, P.A.; Suthagar, S. Axial Compression Performance of Concrete-Filled Steel Tubular Columns with Different D/t Ratios. *Adv. Mater. Sci. Eng.* **2022**, *2022*, 9170525. [CrossRef]
16. Umamaheswari, N.; Arul Jayachandran, S. Experimental Investigation on Uniaxial Compressive Behaviour of Square Concrete Filled Steel Tubular Columns. In *Advances in Structural Engineering*; Springer: New Delhi, India, 2015; pp. 2087–2101. [CrossRef]
17. Gupta, P.K.; Sarda, S.M.; Kumar, M.S. Experimental and computational study of concrete filled steel tubular columns under axial loads. *J. Constr. Steel Res.* **2007**, *63*, 182–193. [CrossRef]
18. Phan, H.D. Numerical analysis of seismic behavior of square concrete filled steel tubular columns. *J. Sci. Technol. Civ. Eng.* **2021**, *15*, 127–140. [CrossRef]
19. Saleh, S.M.; İhsan, A.L.A. Strength and behaviour assessment of axially loaded concrete filled steel tubular stub columns. *Turk. J. Eng.* **2021**, *5*, 154–164. [CrossRef]
20. Jayalekshmi, S.; Sankar Jegadesh, J.S. Finite Element Analysis and Codal Recommendations of Concrete Filled Steel Tubular Columns. *J. Inst. Eng. Ser. A* **2016**, *97*, 33–41. [CrossRef]
21. Heman, A.M.; Roshni, K.G. Numerical Study on Concrete-Filled Steel Tubes with Diagonal Binding Ribs and Longitudinal Stiffeners. In *Recent Advances in Computational and Experimental Mechanics, Vol II*; Springer: Singapore, 2022; pp. 15–24. [CrossRef]
22. Bhartiya, R.; Sahoo, D.R. Prediction of axial compression behavior of rectangular RCFST columns with confining ties. *J. Constr. Steel Res.* **2021**, *186*, 106920. [CrossRef]
23. Boukhalkhal, S.H.; Neves, L.F.D.C.; Madi, W. Dynamic behavior of concrete filled steel tubular columns. *Int. J. Struct. Integr.* **2019**, *10*, 244–264. [CrossRef]
24. Lazkani, A. Behavior of Expansive Concrete-Filled Steel Tubular (Ecfst) Columns under Axial Loadings. 2016. Available online: https://scholarworks.uaeu.ac.ae/all_theses/316 (accessed on 23 September 2022).
25. Tam, V.W.Y.; Tao, Z.; Evangelista, A. Performance of recycled aggregate concrete filled steel tubular (RACFST) stub columns with expansive agent. *Constr. Build. Mater.* **2021**, *272*, 121627. [CrossRef]
26. Ahmad, S.; Kumar, K.; Kumar, A. Axial behaviour of steel tubes filled with concrete incorporating high-volume rubber. *Innov. Infrastruct. Solut.* **2022**, *7*, 148. [CrossRef]
27. Mujdeci, A.; Bompa, D.; Elghazouli, A. Structural performance of composite steel rubberised concrete members under combined loading conditions. *Ce/Papers* **2021**, *4*, 641–647. [CrossRef]
28. Esmaeili Niari, S.; Yaghoubi, S.; Akrami, V. Experimental study on the behavior of steel tubular columns filled with concrete containing iron filings. *J. Struct. Constr. Eng.* **2022**, *9*, 8.
29. de Azevedo, V.D.S.; de Lima, L.R.; Vellasco, P.C.D.S.; Tavares, M.E.D.N.; Chan, T.M. Experimental investigation on recycled aggregate concrete filled steel tubular stub columns under axial compression. *J. Constr. Steel Res.* **2021**, *187*, 106930. [CrossRef]
30. Malathy, R.; Mohanraj, E.K.; Kandasamy, S. Comparative study on behaviour of concrete-filled steel tubular columns using recycled aggregates. In *Excellence in Concrete Construction through Innovation*; CRC Press: Boca Raton, FL, USA, 2008; pp. 469–474. [CrossRef]
31. Portolés, J.M.; Serra, E.; Romero, M.L. Influence of ultra-high strength infill in slender concrete-filled steel tubular columns. *J. Constr. Steel Res.* **2013**, *86*, 107–114. [CrossRef]
32. Ding, F.; Ying, X.; Zhou, L.; Yu, Z. Unified calculation method and its application in determining the uniaxial mechanical properties of concrete. *Front. Archit. Civ. Eng. China* **2011**, *5*, 381–393. [CrossRef]
33. AISC. *Specification for Structural Steel Buildings*; American Institute of Steel Construction Inc.: Chicago, CA, USA, 1999.

34. *BS 5400-5*; Steel, Concrete and Composite Bridges, Part5: Code of Practice for Design of Composite Bridges. British Standards Institutions: London, UK, 1979.
35. *DD ENV 1994-1-1*; Eurocode 4: Design of Composite Steel and Concrete Structures. Part 1.1: General Rules and Rules for Buildings. European Committee for Standardization: Brussels, Belgium, 1994.
36. AIJ. *Recommendations for Design and Construction of Concrete Filled Steel Tubular Structures*; Architectural Institute of Japan: Tokyo, Japan, 1997.
37. *GB 50011-2010*; Specification for Design and Construction of Concrete-Filled Steel Tubular Structures. China Planning Press: Beijing, China, 2010. (In Chinese)
38. *DBJ/T13-51-2010*; Technical Specification for Concrete Filled Steel Tube Structure. Fujian Housing and Urban-Rural Development Department: Fuzhou, China, 2010. (In Chinese)
39. Zhong, S. *The Concrete-Filled Steel Tubular Structures*; Tsinghua University Press: Beijing, China, 2003. (In Chinese)
40. Ding, F.; Liu, J.; Liu, X.; Yu, Z.; Li, D. Mechanical behavior of circular and square concrete filled steel tube columns under local compression. *Thin-Walled Struct.* **2015**, *94*, 155–166. [CrossRef]
41. *GB50011-2010*; Code for Seismic Design of Buildings. China Architecture & Building Press: Beijing, China, 2010. (In Chinese)

Article

# Seismic Behavior of UHPC-Filled Rectangular Steel Tube Columns Incorporating Local Buckling

Yanxiang Yan [1], Yu Yan [2,*], Yansong Wang [2], Heng Cai [3] and Yaorui Zhu [1]

[1] School of Civil Engineering, Hubei Engineering University, Xiaogan 432000, China; yyxtm@163.com (Y.Y.)
[2] School of Urban Design, Wuhan University, Wuhan 430072, China
[3] School of Civil Engineering, Hubei Polytechnic University, Huangshi 435003, China
* Correspondence: yanyudw@163.com

**Abstract:** This paper presents a numerical study on the static behavior and cyclic behavior of UHPC-filled steel tube (UHPCFST) columns. A novel fiber element model is developed based on the effective distribution width method to consider the influence of local buckling. The parameters of the descending branch of the stress–strain curve of constrained concrete have been modified and proposed according to the existing experimental results. Thereafter, the impact parameter analysis of the seismic performance of UHPCFST columns under the pseudo static load is conducted, and the strength of steel and UHPC, width–thickness ratio, length–diameter ratio and axial compression ratio are considered. The results indicate that the proposed fiber element model can accurately predict the static and cyclic nonlinear behaviors of the UHPCFST columns. The bearing capacity and the post-peak ductility of UHPCFST columns can be overestimated, such as neglecting the local buckling of the steel tube, which will lead to the insecurity of structures.

**Keywords:** UHPCFST columns; fiber model; static behavior; cyclic behavior; local buckling

Citation: Yan, Y.; Yan, Y.; Wang, Y.; Cai, H.; Zhu, Y. Seismic Behavior of UHPC-Filled Rectangular Steel Tube Columns Incorporating Local Buckling. *Buildings* **2023**, *13*, 1028. https://doi.org/10.3390/buildings13041028

Academic Editor: Giuseppina Uva

Received: 14 February 2023
Revised: 11 April 2023
Accepted: 12 April 2023
Published: 13 April 2023

Copyright: © 2023 by the authors. Licensee MDPI, Basel, Switzerland. This article is an open access article distributed under the terms and conditions of the Creative Commons Attribution (CC BY) license (https://creativecommons.org/licenses/by/4.0/).

## 1. Introduction

Concrete-filled steel tube (CFST) columns possess the advantages of high bearing capacity, large stiffness and excellent ductility [1], and are often used as the vertical and horizontal load-bearing structure members in bridges and high-rise building structures, as shown in Figure 1. In the past few decades, many numerical calculation methods have been proposed in order to estimate the static performance, cyclic behavior, as well as the fire resistance behavior of CFSTs, such as existing 3D finite element methods, secondary development based on existing numerical software ABAQUS and OpenSees, and the fiber element model. Compared with the three-dimensional finite element method, the fiber model has been considered a highly efficient algorithm in the state of only uniaxial compression, especially for nonlinear calculations of complicated engineering structures. For CFSTs, the fiber element model can predict their static behaviors, including axial compression behavior [2,3] of stub columns, axial compression behavior and eccentric compression behavior [4–7] of slender columns, as well as pushover analysis [8]. In addition, it can also be used for evaluating the fire resistance behavior [9], as well as the hysteresis behavior [3,7,8,10] of CFSTs. Generally, there have been mainly two methods to handle the local buckling of steel tubes in the fiber element model: the first method is to modify the yield stress, the stress–strain skeleton curve and the hysteretic criterion of steel in advance, according to the sectional width to thickness ratio [3,7,10]. Another method is to introduce the concept of effective distribution width that is calculated according to the sectional stress state [2,4–6]. At present, there is still relatively little research on the cyclic behavior of CFSTs, with local buckling considered by using the fiber element model [3,4,7,10]. In addition, once the local buckling occurs, the partial areas nearby the web are out of work, and the phenomenon of redistribution of the stress in the section occurs, leading to the stress borne by the web being transferred to the flange. On the other hand, by modifying the stress–strain skeleton curve, as well as the hysteretic criterion of steel in advance, can not really reflect the actual stress in the section and the behavior of local buckling [3,7,10].

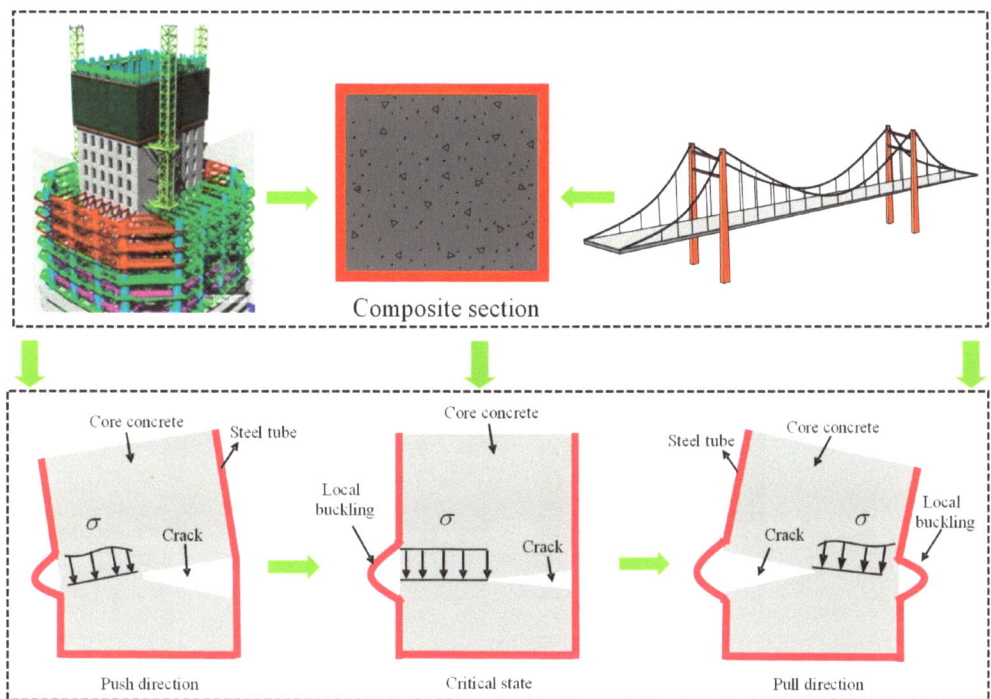

**Figure 1.** Application of CFSTs in structural engineering and its local buckling effects.

As modern structures develop toward super-high rise, possessing heavy load bearing capacity and durability, ultra-high performance concrete (UHPC), regarded as an excellent cementitious composite rather than the ordinary concrete [11], has been gradually used in civil engineering because of its ultra-high compressive strength, high tensile strength and high elastic modulus, along with the strain hardening behavior [12–16]. To further improve the performance of CFSTs, the UHPC is filled into steel tubes to form UHPCFST members, which consequently contribute to the reduction of the member size and the self-weight of the structure, as well as the increase in available space in buildings under the same load conditions. In addition, the brittleness of UHPC is also avoided and its bearing capacity, as well as ductility, is further improved.

There is still relatively little research on the axial compression performance of rectangular UHPCFST stub columns at present, whilst research on the hysteresis performance of UHPCFST columns is even fewer. The reinforcement effect of the steel tubes on the core UHPC is not so strong as that of the ordinary concrete due to its ultra-high compressive strength and inherent brittleness of UHPC, and the local buckling of steel tubes is still inevitably submerged under the combined action of axial compression and cyclic loading. In this work, a fiber element model is proposed to assess the axial compression behavior and cyclic behavior of UHPCFST columns, and the local buckling is considered based on the redefined effective distribution width rather than modifying the stress–strain skeleton curve of steel. The parametric analysis is performed based on the verified model, where the effects of the yield strength of steel, the UHPC strength, length–diameter ratio, as well as the axial compression ratio on the hysteretic performance of UHPCFST columns are extensively discussed. What is more, the effects of the steel tube local buckling on the bearing capacity and ductility of UHPCFST columns are also analysed.

## 2. Fiber Element Model

In the present work, the sections of the UHPCFST columns are divided into lots of small fiber elements, as shown in Figure 2. To simplify the calculation model, the following assumptions are adopted [1]:

(1) Plane-section assumption.
(2) The strains are the same in each individual fiber of the same height of the cross-section.
(3) The bond-slip at the interface between the two materials is neglected.
(4) The lateral deflection curve of the member presents the sine curve with half a wave.

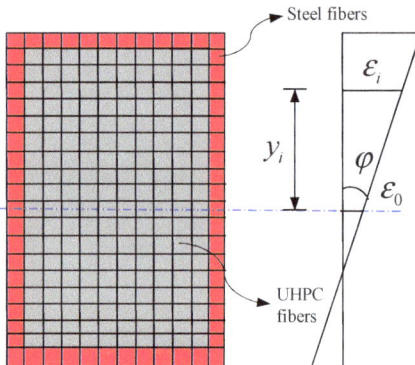

**Figure 2.** Fiber model cross-section.

It is obvious that the first assumption, that the plane sections remain plane after flexural deformation, has been proven by lots of experiments. When the fibers in the section are discretized finely enough, the errors caused by the second assumption are very small and can be neglected. Considered that there will be large gap at the interface of the two materials when the local buckling of the steel tubes occurs (shown in Figure 1), the slippage between the two materials is neglected. Based on the above assumptions, the central strain of the fiber is given by Equation (1):

$$\varepsilon_i = \varepsilon_0 + \varphi y_i, \tag{1}$$

where $\varepsilon_0$ ($\mu\varepsilon$) is the strain at the center fiber of the cross-section, $y_i$ (mm) is the distance from the center of the $i$ fiber to the center of the cross-section, and $\varphi$ ($\mu\varepsilon$/mm) is the curvature of the cross-section. Hence, according to the stress–strain relationships and loading history of the materials, the internal forces, such as the axial compression force $N_{in}$ (N) and the bending moment $M_{in}$ (N.mm), are given by Equations (2) and (3):

$$N_{in} = \sum_{i=1}^{k} \sigma_{ci} A_{ci} + \sum_{i=1}^{m} \sigma_{si} A_{si} \tag{2}$$

$$M_{in} = \sum_{i=1}^{k} \sigma_{ci} A_{ci} y_i + \sum_{i=1}^{m} \sigma_{si} A_{si} y_k, \tag{3}$$

where $\sigma_{ci}$ (N/mm$^2$) and $\sigma_{si}$ (N/mm$^2$) are the stress of UHPC and steel, $A_{ci}$ (mm$^2$) and $A_{si}$ (mm$^2$) are the area of UHPC fiber and steel fiber, and $k$ and $m$ are the fiber numbers of UHPC and steel.

The fourth assumption is reasonable for the members with both ends hinged, as shown in Figure 3a, which can be utilized for the calculation of UHPCFST members under axial compression or eccentric compression. Figure 3b,c are the simplified calculation of reverse bending point of columns under the different restrict boundary. As for the frame column in Figure 3b with both ends fixed and a lateral displacement of one end, the inflection point is in the middle of the column. Therefore, from the inflection point to the fixed end, it can be simplified as a cantilever member with a geometric length L, as shown in Figure 3c. If the influence of lateral load on the lateral deflection curve can be ignored, the cantilever member can be equivalent to the members with both ends hinged, as shown in Figure 3a.

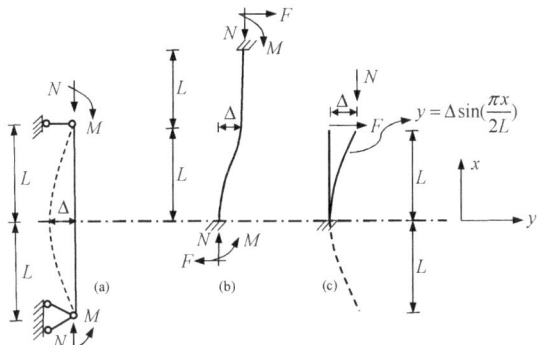

**Figure 3.** Mechanical models of the UHPCFST members.

According to the fourth assumption, the relationship between lateral displacement and sectional curvature can be given by Equation (4):

$$\varphi = \frac{\Delta \pi^2}{4L^2}, \tag{4}$$

where $\Delta$ (mm) is the lateral displacement, and $L$ (mm) represents the effective length of the UHPCFST column.

*2.1. Constitutive Model of Materials*

2.1.1. Concrete

There are various forms of stress–strain models for constrained concrete [17,18], and the constitutive relationship of constrained UHPC is the basis for the numerical research on the seismic performance of UHPC-filled rectangular high strength steel tube columns in this paper. For the rectangular section, the constitutive model of the constrained concrete is shown in Figure 4a, which incorporates the skeleton curves and the hysteretic rules. The skeleton curve of constrained concrete proposed by Han [1] is used in this work and the formulas are given by Equations (5)–(7):

$$f = f_{cc}[2(\varepsilon/\varepsilon_{cc}) - (\varepsilon/\varepsilon_{cc})^2] \text{ for } \varepsilon \leq \varepsilon_{cc} \tag{5}$$

$$f = f_{cc}(\varepsilon/\varepsilon_{cc})/[\beta(\varepsilon/\varepsilon_{cc})^\eta + \varepsilon/\varepsilon_{cc}] \text{ for } \varepsilon \geq \varepsilon_{cc} \tag{6}$$

$$\eta = 1.6 + 1.5/(\varepsilon/\varepsilon_{cc}), \ \beta = f_c^{0.1}/(\gamma\sqrt{\xi}+1) \ (\xi \leq 3) \tag{7}$$

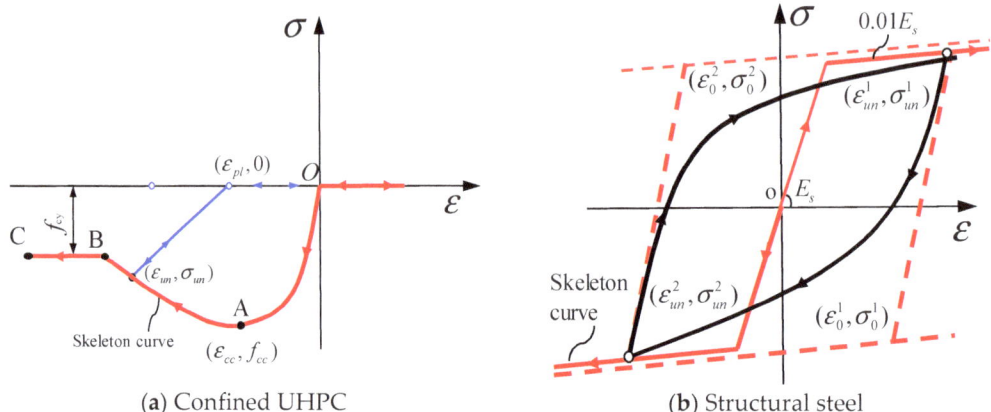

(**a**) Confined UHPC  (**b**) Structural steel

**Figure 4.** The constitutive models of the two materials.

In Equations (5)–(7), $\beta$, $\gamma$ and $\eta$ are the parameters to determine the descending branch, and $\xi$ is the confinement index of steel tube. $\varepsilon_{cc}$ ($\mu\varepsilon$) and $f_{cc}$ (MPa) are the compressive peak strain and stress of the confined concrete, respectively. Although Han's model considers the reinforcing effect of steel tubes on the core concrete, it is only appropriate for normal concrete and high-strength concrete with an $f_c$ (MPa) ranging from 24 MPa to 80 MPa. Le'geron and Paultre [19] (2003) proposed the peak stress $f_{cc}$ and the peak strain $\varepsilon_{cc}$ of normal and ultra-high strength confined concrete, with an $f_c$ ranging from 27 MPa to 124 MPa according to a great quantity of experimental results, and they are given by Equations (8) and (9):

$$f_{cc} = f_c[1 + 2.4(I_e)^{0.7}] \tag{8}$$

$$\varepsilon_{cc} = \varepsilon_c[1 + 35(I_e)^{1.2}], \tag{9}$$

where $I_e$ is the equivalent effective confinement index at the peak strength, which is given by Le'geron and Paultre [19], $\varepsilon_c$ ($\mu\varepsilon$) is the peak compressive strain of unconfined UHPC which has been given by An and Fehling [20], as shown by Equation (10):

$$\varepsilon_c = 0.00083 f_c^{0.276} \tag{10}$$

Considering that the tensile strength of the ultra-high-performance concrete is much smaller than its compressive strength, the contribution of UHPC in the tensile zone to the internal force of the section can be ignored [21].

The hysteretic criterion includes the unloading branch and the reloading branch. The residual plastic strains at the zero-stress point, proposed by Mander et al. [22], is adopted in the present work, and it is given as Equations (11) and (12):

$$\varepsilon_{pl} = \varepsilon_{un} - \frac{(\varepsilon_{un} + \varepsilon_a)\sigma_{un}}{\sigma_{un} + E_c\varepsilon_a} \tag{11}$$

$$\varepsilon_a = \max\left(\frac{\varepsilon_{cc}}{\varepsilon_{cc} + \varepsilon_{un}}, \frac{0.09\varepsilon_{un}}{\varepsilon_{cc}}\right), \tag{12}$$

where $\varepsilon_{un}$ ($\mu\varepsilon$) and $\sigma_{un}$ (MPa) are the strains and stress at the unloading point, respectively, $\varepsilon_{pl}$ ($\mu\varepsilon$) is the residual plastic strain, $E_c$ (MPa) is the elastic modulus of UHPC. Considering that the unloading branch and reloading branch suggested by Mander are too complicated, the simplified model is adopted. It is assumed that the unloading branch and the reloading branch are both straight lines between the unloading points and residual plastic strain points. They are given by Equations (13) and (14):

$$f = E_r(\varepsilon - \varepsilon_{pl}) \tag{13}$$

$$E_r = \frac{\sigma_{un}}{\varepsilon_{un} - \varepsilon_{pl}}, \tag{14}$$

where $E_r$ (MPa) and $f$ (MPa) are the stiffness and stress of the unloading stage.

2.1.2. Steel

In the present work, the bilinear hardening model with a hardening stiffness of $0.01 E_s$ for the stress–strain skeleton curve of the steel is adopted. The uniaxial hysteretic constitute model for the steel, proposed by Menegotto and Paolo [23], as shown in Figure 4b, is also adopted in the present work.

A lot of previous research indicates that for CFSTs, the local buckling of steel tubes is one of the significant factors affecting the bearing capacity and the ductility [3,7,10], especially for thin-walled steel tubes of which the local buckling is very serious. Therefore, the sectional width–thickness ratios are limited in current provision codes [24–26] to avoid local buckling to some extent. As already known, after the local buckling of the steel tube, there is a stress redistribution phenomenon in the cross-section immediately, which will lead to the stress transmission path of steel tubes, with local buckling in the web being transferred to the flange.

The concept of the effective width, shown in Figure 5 is usually used to describe the post-local buckling behavior of thin-walled steel tubes. The effective width and the elastical critical local buckling strength of steel tubes for CFSTs proposed by Liang and Uy [27,28] are adopted in this work, which are given by Equations (15) and (16):

$$b_e/b_0 = 0.675(\sigma_{cr}/f_y)^{1/3} \tag{15}$$

$$\frac{\sigma_{cr}}{f_y} = 0.5507 + 5.132 \times 10^{-3}(\frac{b_0}{t}) - 9.869 \times 10^{-5}(\frac{b_0}{t})^2 + 1.198 \times 10^{-7}(\frac{b_0}{t})^3, \tag{16}$$

where $b_e$ is the total of effective width, $b_0$ is the unsupported width in the section, $t$ is the thickness of the steel tube, $\sigma_{cr}$ is the elastic critical local buckling strength of the steel tubes, which only relies on the width–thickness ratio of the steel tube and yield strength of the steel. During the loading stages, the ineffective width $b_i$ gradually increases from zero to the maximum value $(b-b_e)$. As a consequence, it can be expressed by Equation (17):

$$b_i = (\frac{\sigma_1 - \sigma_{cr}}{f_y - \sigma_{cr}})(b - b_e) \tag{17}$$

In the calculation, the maximum compressive stress $\sigma_1$ at the edge of the cross-section flange is firstly obtained, which is greater than $\sigma_{cr}$. Then, the ineffective width can be calculated according to Equation (17) and the stresses of the steel fibers within it can be updated as zero until they reach the maximum ineffective width.

It should be noted that since the UHPCFST columns are subjected to combined axial compression and lateral cyclic loading, the stresses of the steel tube and core UHPC are not only depended on the strains, but also depended on the loading history when cyclic behavior is computed.

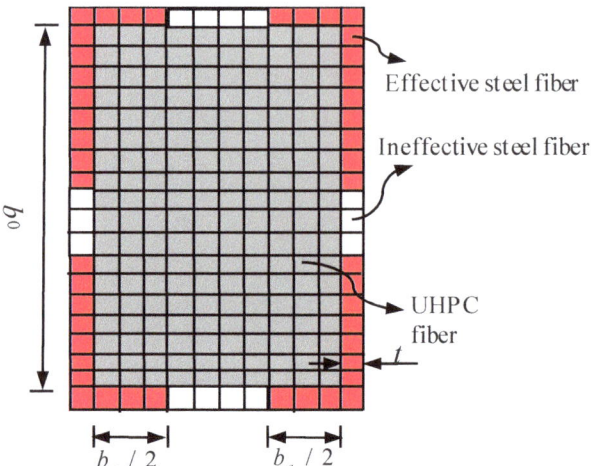

**Figure 5.** The effective distribution width of the steel tube.

## 3. Model Verification

In the present work, the computational process of stub UHPCFST columns under axial compression has been referred to by Ahmed et al. [2,4]. On the other hand, for the predication of cyclic behavior, the UHPCFST member is regarded as a cantilever column subjected to the combined action of axial compression and lateral cyclic loading. Considering the second-order effect of vertical axial compression load on the top of the column, the lateral load can be expressed as Equation (18):

$$F = (M - N\Delta)/L, \tag{18}$$

where $M$ is the calculated bending moment at the bottom of the column and $N$ is the pre-applied axial compression force. The calculated steps of the cyclic behavior for UHPCFST columns are detailed in Figure 6.

The calculated steps of cyclic behavior for UHPCFST columns are as follows:

(1) Input data.
(2) Discretize section into fibers and obtain the coordinates.
(3) Gradually increase the displacement and calculate sectional curvature according to Equation (4).
(4) Assume the strain at the neutral axis and calculate the fiber stress $\sigma_{ci}$ and $\sigma_{si}$ according to loading history.
(5) Judge whether the local buckling of steel tubes occurs and calculate the ineffective width; then, update the stress.
(6) Compute internal force according to Equations (2) and (3), including $M_{in}$ and $N_{in}$.
(7) Judge whether the axial compression load satisfies the equilibrium condition $|N_{in} - N| < 10^{-2}$. If not, return to step (4) until the equilibrium condition is satisfied.
(8) Compute the lateral load according to Equation (18).
(9) Repeat steps (3–8) until the maximum lateral displacement is achieved.
(10) Plot $F$-$\Delta$ hysteretic curves.

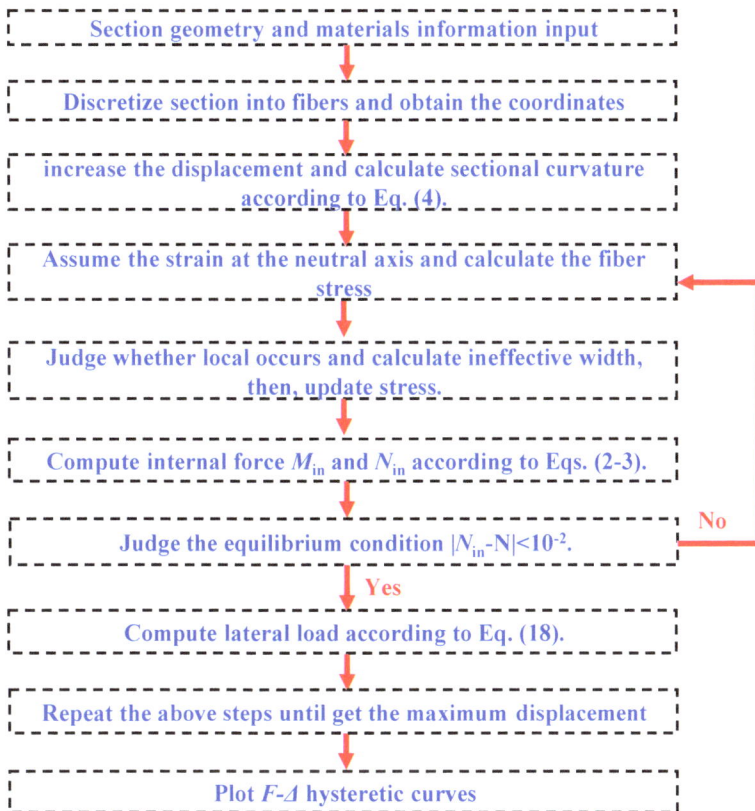

**Figure 6.** The flowchart of the hysteresis curve calculation.

### 3.1. Stub UHPCFST Columns under Axial Compressive Load

The axial compression behavior is important for UHPCFST columns on the account of the axial compression load–strain ($N$-$\varepsilon$) curves, showing information of axial compressive stiffness, the ultimate bearing capacity, as well as the residual bearing capacity. Chen et al. [29] and Yan et al. [30] investigated some stub rectangular UHPCFST columns under axial compressive load by experiments. The length of the stub columns were 300 mm, with the dimensions of 100 (mm) × 100 (mm). The strength of the steel tube and the core UHPC, as well as the steel tube thickness of each column varied. The details of the specimens are summarized in Table 1. The specimens are simply supported at both ends, and the axial displacement is imposed to the boundary of the column end.

**Table 1.** Details of stub rectangular UHPCFST specimens under axial compressive load.

| Origin | Specimen Name | $B \times h$ (mm) | $t$ (mm) | $L$ (mm) | $f_y$ (MPa) | $f_c$ (MPa) | $N_c$ (kN) | $N_t$ (kN) | $N_c/N_t$ |
|---|---|---|---|---|---|---|---|---|---|
| | SS1-2 | 100 × 100 | 2.03 | 300 | 348.7 | 113.2 | 1340 | 1406 | 0.95 |
| | SS1-3 | 100 × 100 | 2.05 | 300 | 348.7 | 130.8 | 1503 | 1575 | 0.95 |
| Chen et al. | SS2-2 | 100 × 100 | 3.83 | 300 | 306.7 | 113.2 | 1454 | 1544 | 0.94 |
| [29] | SS2-3 | 100 × 100 | 3.79 | 300 | 306.7 | 130.8 | 1595 | 1676 | 0.95 |
| | SS3-2 | 100 × 100 | 7.59 | 300 | 371.6 | 113.2 | 1921 | 1976 | 0.97 |
| | SS3-3 | 100 × 100 | 7.63 | 300 | 371.6 | 130.8 | 2069 | 2051 | 1.01 |

**Table 1.** Cont.

| Origin | Specimen Name | $B \times h$ (mm) | $t$ (mm) | $L$ (mm) | $f_y$ (MPa) | $f_c$ (MPa) | $N_c$ (kN) | $N_t$ (kN) | $N_c/N_t$ |
|---|---|---|---|---|---|---|---|---|---|
| Yan et al. [30] | S1-5-100 | 100 × 100 | 4.9 | 300 | 668.8 | 89.2 | 2038 | 1800 | 1.13 |
| | S2-5-110 | 100 × 100 | 4.9 | 300 | 668.8 | 100.3 | 2128 | 2004 | 1.06 |
| | S3-6-110 | 100 × 100 | 5.8 | 300 | 646.2 | 100.3 | 2274 | 2220 | 1.02 |
| | S4-6-120 | 100 × 100 | 5.8 | 300 | 646.2 | 111.3 | 2364 | 2391 | 0.99 |
| | S5-6-140 | 100 × 100 | 5.8 | 300 | 646.2 | 128.1 | 2484 | 2573 | 0.97 |
| | S6-7-100 | 100 × 100 | 6.8 | 300 | 599.5 | 89.2 | 2262 | 2209 | 1.02 |
| | S7-7-110 | 100 × 100 | 6.8 | 300 | 599.5 | 100.3 | 2345 | 2295 | 1.02 |
| | S8-7-120 | 100 × 100 | 6.8 | 300 | 599.5 | 111.3 | 2427 | 2369 | 1.02 |
| | S9-7-140 | 100 × 100 | 6.8 | 300 | 599.5 | 128.1 | 2552 | 2492 | 1.02 |
| | S10-10-100 | 100 × 100 | 10 | 300 | 458.6 | 89.2 | 2305 | 2206 | 1.04 |
| | S11-10-120 | 100 × 100 | 10 | 300 | 458.6 | 111.3 | 2449 | 2298 | 1.07 |
| | S12-10-140 | 100 × 100 | 10 | 300 | 458.6 | 128.1 | 2558 | 2499 | 1.04 |
| | S13-14-100 | 100 × 100 | 14.2 | 300 | 468.6 | 89.2 | 2867 | 3107 | 0.92 |
| | S14-14-120 | 100 × 100 | 14.2 | 300 | 468.6 | 111.3 | 2933 | 3120 | 0.94 |
| | S15-14-140 | 100 × 100 | 14.2 | 300 | 468.6 | 128.1 | 2986 | 3274 | 0.91 |
| | S16-18-140 | 100 × 100 | 18.5 | 300 | 444.6 | 128.1 | 3382 | 3441 | 0.98 |

Note: $N_c$ is the calculated axial bearing capacity in the present work, $N_t$ is the test results, and the mix ratio of UHPC for experimental and numerical calculations can be found in relevant literature.

The full axial compression load–strain ($N$-$\varepsilon$) curves of specimen SS2-2 with different $\gamma$ values are shown in Figure 7. The result of the experiment is also plotted in Figure 7. It can be easily concluded that the ascending branch of the full $N$-$\varepsilon$ curve can be well predicted by Han's model, whilst it is inaccurate for the descending branch. It is obvious that the residual bearing capacity and the post-peak ductility of the stub UHPCFST column are greatly underestimated by Han's model. Therefore, the descending branch of the stress–strain curve of concrete in Han's model needs to be revised. The parameter $\gamma$ in Equation (7) is a key factor to affect the post-peak ductility and residual stress of concrete, and it is taken as 1.2 in Han's model. In the present work, the fiber element result is compared with the test result by adjusting the value of $\gamma$ ($\gamma$ = 1.2, 2, 3, 4) of the stub UHPCFST column. It is found that when $\gamma$ value is taken as 3, the descending branch predicted by the fiber model is in good agreement with the experimental results, and it can well predict the post-peak ductility and the residual bearing capacity of the stub UHPCFST columns. It can be also seen from Figure 8 and Table 1 that the bearing capacities calculated by the fiber model are shown to agree with test results. Except for specimen S1-5-100, the errors between them are within the range of 10%, whilst for specimen S1-5-100, the error between the fiber model and the test result is 13%. This may be due to the uncertainty of the actual strength of UHPC.

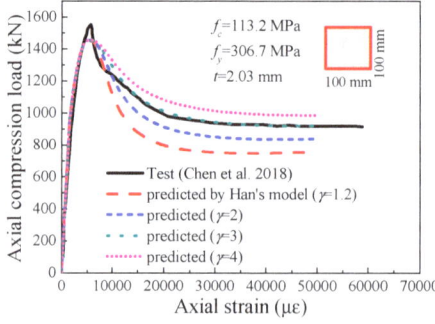

**Figure 7.** Full $N$-$\varepsilon$ curves of specimen SS2-2 with different $\gamma$ values [29].

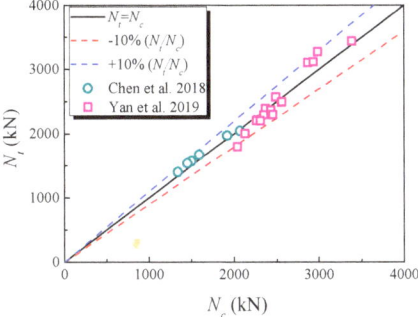

**Figure 8.** Comparisons of fiber model with test data [29,30].

The full N-ε curves of partial specimens predicated by the fiber model in the present work ($\gamma$ = 3) are plotted in Figures 9 and 10. As illustrated in Figures 9 and 10, the calculations of the fiber model are in good agreement with the test results. In addition, for the strengthening effect of the high-strength steel and the constraint enhancement effect of the steel tubes on the core UHPC, the residual bearing capacity decreases slowly after reaching peak value, and subsequently remains basically constant, which illustrates that the favorable post-peak ductility and the residual bearing capacity of UHPCFST columns are showed.

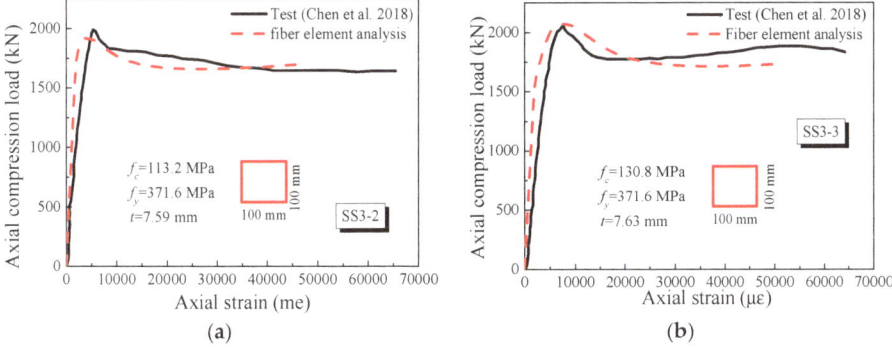

**Figure 9.** Calculations for the UHPCFST specimen columns SS3-2 and SS3-3 [29].

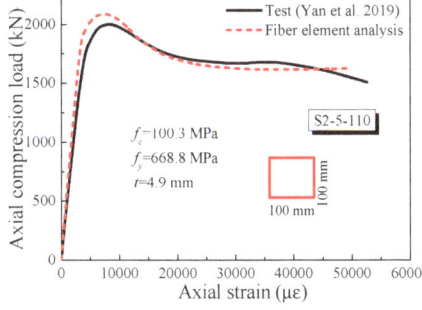 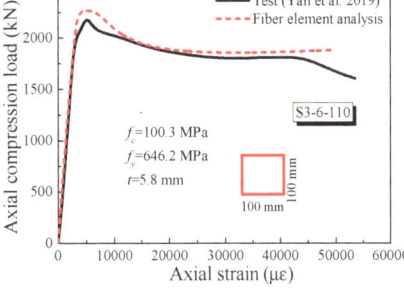

**Figure 10.** *Cont.*

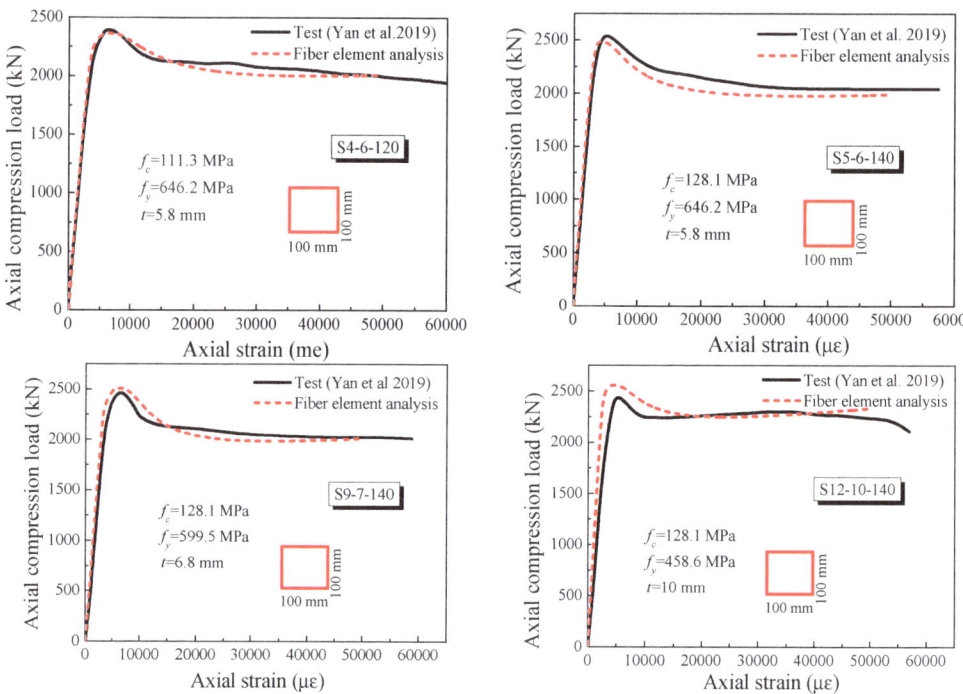

**Figure 10.** Calculations for the UHPCFST specimen column [30].

### 3.2. UHPCFST Columns under Cyclic Loading

The cyclic load testing is an effective means of evaluating the seismic performance of structures and members. So far, there is limited research on the cyclic behaviors of UHPCFST columns. The seismic performance of the UHPCFST columns under combined axial compression and cyclic lateral loading has been investigated by Xu et al. [31] and Cai et al. [32]. The details of the specimens are summarized in Table 2. The lateral load–displacement skeleton curves of the positive direction of the UHPCFST columns with local buckling considered or not considered are showed in Figure 11, and the corresponding test results are also plotted in Figure 11. As illustrated in Figure 11, the local buckling has a significant impact on the bearing capacity and the ductility of the UHPCFST columns. The larger bearing capacity as well as stiffness (after local buckling occuring) of The UHPCFST columns will be provided if local buckling is neglected. In addition, neglecting the local buckling will greatly overestimate the post-peak ductility of the UHPCFST columns. The reason for this result is that the compressive strength of UHPC is far higher than normal concrete, and the partial area of the cross-section will be out of work when the local buckling of steel tubes occurs, which consequently weakens the restraining effect of steel tubes on the core UHPC and results in a significant reduction of post-peak ductility. The descending branch of the lateral load–displacement curves in Figure 11 are more steeper if the local buckling is considered, and the post-peak ductility is worse, which is closer to the test results.

Table 2. Details of the UHPCFST specimens under the cyclic load.

| Source | Specimen Name | $B \times h$ (mm) | $t$ (mm) | $L$ (mm) | $f_y$ (MPa) | $f_{cu}$ (MPa) | $n$ | $N$ (kN) | $P_c$ (kN) | $P_t$ (kN) | $P_c/P_t$ |
|---|---|---|---|---|---|---|---|---|---|---|---|
| Xu et al. [31] | SpeUTH4 | 250 × 250 | 4 | 1250 | 360 | 152.6 | 0.24 | 1736 | 275 | 288 | 1.05 |
| | SpeUTH5 | 250 × 250 | 5 | 1250 | 360 | 155.4 | 0.24 | 1798 | 307 | 331 | 1.08 |
| | SpeUTH6 | 250 × 250 | 6 | 1250 | 360 | 152.2 | 0.24 | 1854 | 357 | 369 | 1.03 |
| | SpeUCR12 | 250 × 250 | 5 | 1250 | 360 | 150.4 | 0.12 | 899 | 272 | 294 | 1.08 |
| | SpeUCR36 | 250 × 250 | 5 | 1250 | 360 | 151.3 | 0.36 | 2697 | 360 | 352 | 0.98 |
| Cai et al. [32] | S-10-0.2-1.5 | 100 × 150 | 10 | 800 | 460 | 140 | 0.2 | 690 | 139 | 143 | 0.97 |
| | S-10-0.4-1.5 | 100 × 150 | 10 | 800 | 460 | 140 | 0.4 | 1380 | 116 | 110 | 1.05 |
| | S-10-0.2-2 | 100 × 200 | 10 | 900 | 460 | 140 | 0.2 | 884 | 169 | 173 | 0.98 |

Note: '$n$' is the axial compression ratio, '$N$' is the constant axial compression load, '$P_c$' is the calculated bearing capacity in the present work, and '$P_t$' is the averaged value of test results in the push and pull directions.

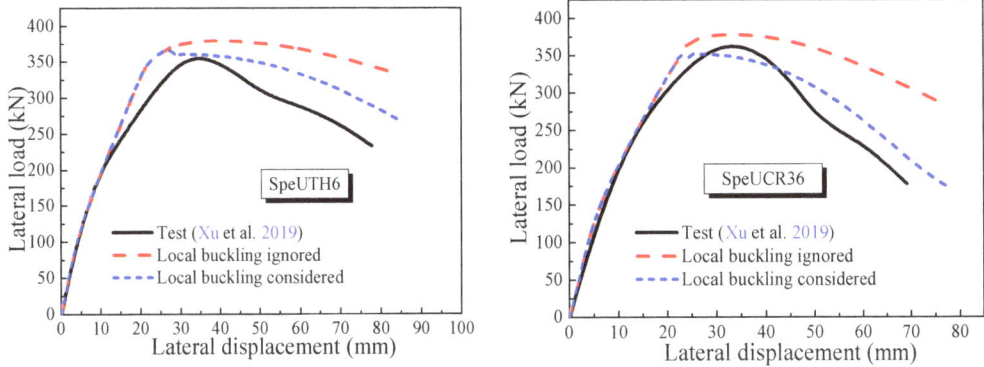

Figure 11. Calculations of the UHPCFST specimens SpeUTH6 and SpeUCR36 [31].

The lateral load–displacement hysteretic curves of the test, and which were predicted by the fiber element model with the local buckling considered, are shown in Figure 12. The skeleton curve, without considering the influence of local buckling, is also plotted in Figure 12. As illustrated in Figure 12, similarly taking no account the local buckling of steel tubes overestimates the bearing capacity and post-peak ductility of UHPCFST columns under cyclic loading, which will lead to the insecurity of structures. The bearing capacities of specimens named S-10-0.2-1.5 and S-10-0.4-1.5 are overestimated by 3.2% and 11.8%, respectively, and this phenomenon tends to be increased with the increase in the axial compression ratio. In this work, the bearing capacities and the post peak ductility with local buckling considered are in good agreement with experimental results. The errors of the maximum bearing capacity between the fiber model and the test results in Table 2 are within the range of 10%. However, for the unloading branch and reloading branch, there are a few differences in the local area between the fiber model and the test results. This may be attributed to the fact that the UHPCFST columns are ideal consolidation models (one end fixed to the ground) on the ground in the fiber model, whilst this is not the case in the experiment.

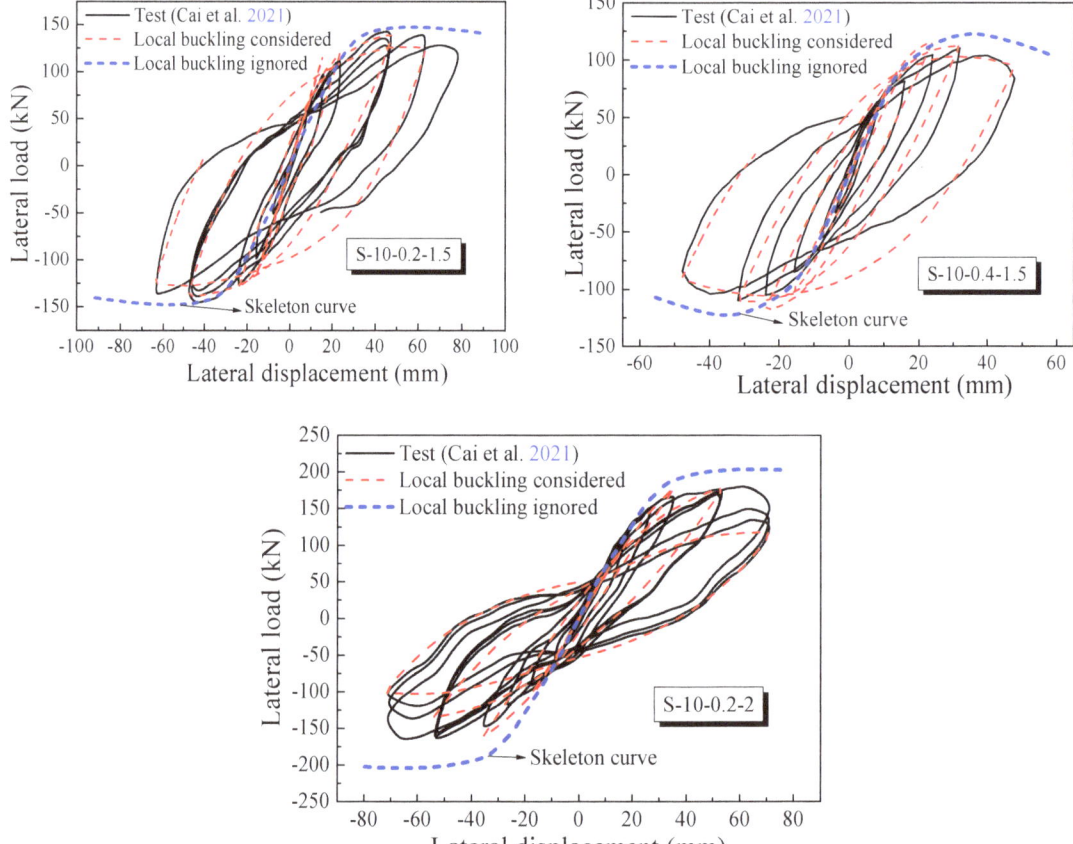

**Figure 12.** Calculations of the UHPFST specimens S-10-0.2-1.5, S-10-0.4-1.5 and S-10-0.2-2 [32].

The effective confinement effect of steel tubes on the core UHPC is the basis for UHPCFST members to fully exploit the potential of the two materials; therefore, the adverse effect of the local buckling of steel tubes should be reasonably considered in the seismic design, which is particularly important.

## 4. Parametric Analysis

In order to further reveal the impact of some parameters on the seismic performance of the UHPCFST columns, the yield strength of steel ($f_y$ = 345 MPa, 460 MPa, 560 MPa), compressive strength of UHPC ($f_{cu}$ = 100 MPa, 120 MPa, 140 MPa), length–diameter ratio ($\lambda$ = 23.1, 34.6, 46.2) and axial compression ratio ($n$ = 0.3, 0.4, 0.5) are comprehensively considered to conduct parametric analysis. Based on the previously validated fiber model, the parameters of the columns for numerical analysis are summarized in Table 3. The bearing capacity, stiffness degradation and cumulative dissipated energy are the main indicators to evaluate the seismic performance of the columns and the structures. The definition of the secant stiffness in this article is as follows:

$$K = F_i / \Delta_i, \tag{19}$$

where $\Delta_i$ is the peak displacement in each hysteresis loop and $F_i$ is the lateral load corresponding to the $\Delta_i$. The hysteretic curves are plotted in Figure 13, and the bearing capacity, cumulative dissipated energy, as well as lateral stiffness degradation, including initial stiffness (at 0.5% drift ratio level), are shown in Figures 14–17. In Figure 13, the blue line represents the skeleton curve of the quasi-static test of the column.

**Table 3.** The parameters of the columns for numerical analysis.

| Specimen | $f_y$ (MPa) | $f_{cu}$ (MPa) | $L$ (mm) | $B \times h$ (mm) | $t$ (mm) | $\lambda$ | $w$ | $n$ | $N$ (kN) |
|---|---|---|---|---|---|---|---|---|---|
| S1 | 345 | 100 | 1000 | 150 × 150 | 5 | 23.1 | 30 | 0.3 | 823 |
| S2 | 460 | 100 | 1000 | 150 × 150 | 5 | 23.1 | 30 | 0.3 | 924 |
| S3 | 560 | 100 | 1000 | 150 × 150 | 5 | 23.1 | 30 | 0.3 | 1010 |
| S4 | 345 | 120 | 1000 | 150 × 150 | 5 | 23.1 | 30 | 0.3 | 965 |
| S5 | 345 | 140 | 1000 | 150 × 150 | 5 | 23.1 | 30 | 0.3 | 1053 |
| S6 | 345 | 100 | 1500 | 150 × 150 | 5 | 34.6 | 30 | 0.3 | 823 |
| S7 | 345 | 100 | 2000 | 150 × 150 | 5 | 46.2 | 30 | 0.3 | 823 |
| S8 | 345 | 100 | 1000 | 150 × 150 | 5 | 23.1 | 30 | 0.4 | 1098 |
| S9 | 345 | 100 | 1000 | 150 × 150 | 5 | 23.1 | 30 | 0.5 | 1372 |

Note: '$\lambda$' is the length–diameter ratio and '$w$' is the width–thickness ratio. Converting the cube strength of 100 MPa, 120 MPa and 140 MPa to prism strength, they are respectively 89.1 MPa, 111.3 MPa and 128.1 MPa.

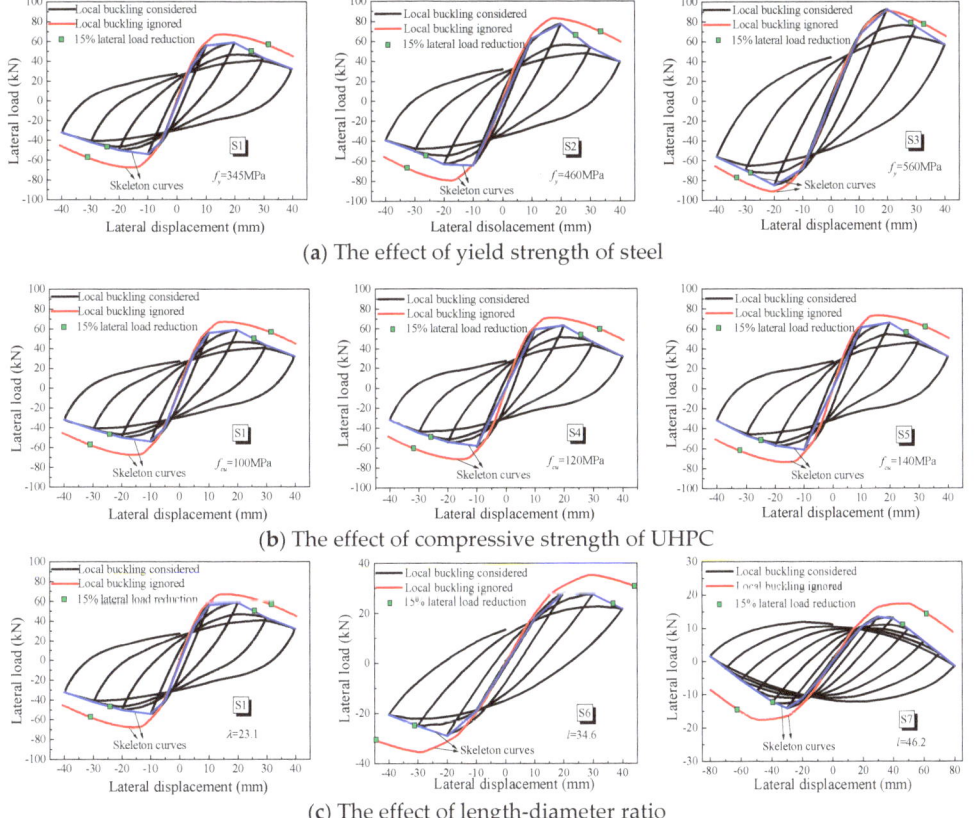

(a) The effect of yield strength of steel

(b) The effect of compressive strength of UHPC

(c) The effect of length-diameter ratio

**Figure 13.** Cont.

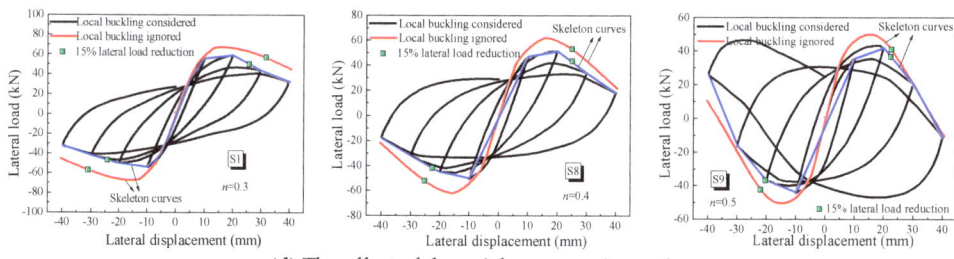

(d) The effect of the axial compression ratio.

Figure 13. The effects of parameters on hysteretic curves.

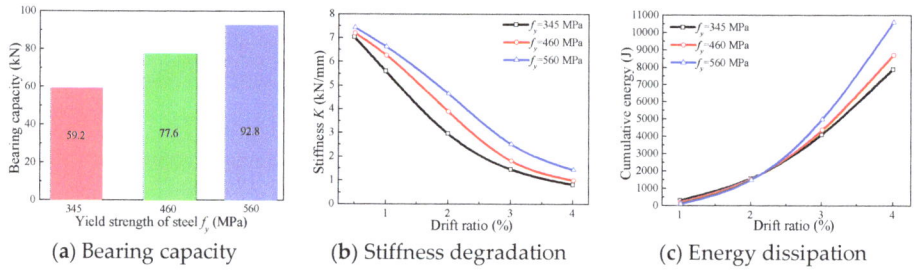

(a) Bearing capacity     (b) Stiffness degradation     (c) Energy dissipation

Figure 14. The effect of the yield strength of steel.

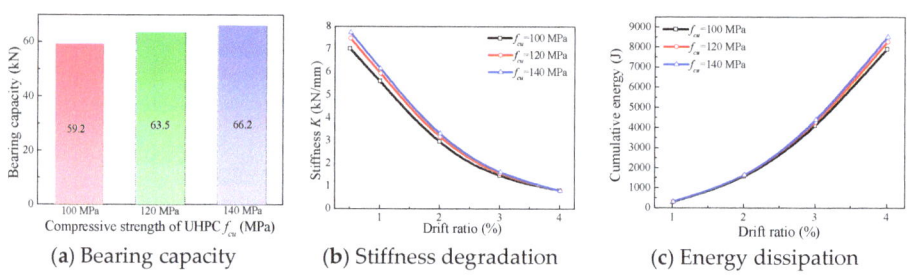

(a) Bearing capacity     (b) Stiffness degradation     (c) Energy dissipation

Figure 15. The effect of the compressive strength of UHPC.

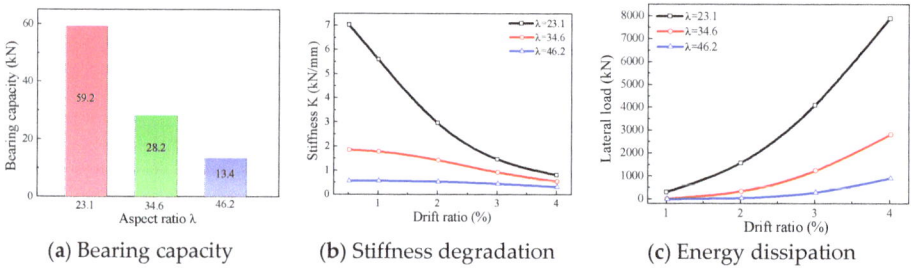

(a) Bearing capacity     (b) Stiffness degradation     (c) Energy dissipation

Figure 16. The effect of the length–diameter ratio.

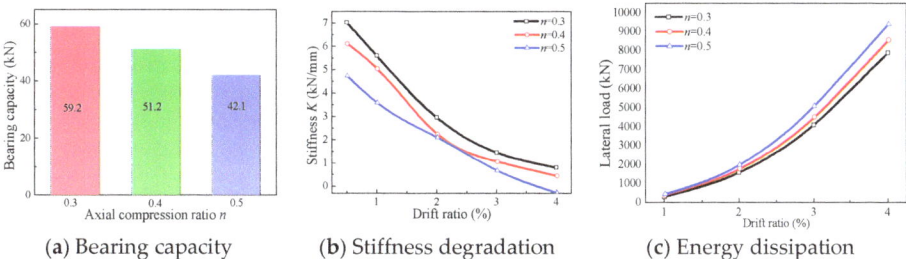

(a) Bearing capacity  (b) Stiffness degradation  (c) Energy dissipation

**Figure 17.** The effect of the axial compression ratio.

### 4.1. The Effect of the Strength of Steel

As illustrated in Figures 13a and 14, the bearing capacity, lateral stiffness and cumulative dissipated energy of UHPCFST columns are both increased with the increase in the yield strength of steel. As expected, the bearing capacity and the post-peak ductility could be overestimated, neglecting the local buckling of the steel tube. The bearing capacities of UHPCFST columns are overestimated by 13.7%, 7% and 2.1% if the yield strength of steel is 345 MPa, 460 MPa and 560 MPa, respectively. The errors caused by local buckling are gradually decreased. This is mainly on the account that the steel with higher yield strength possess higher critical local buckling stress. However, the accuracy of post-peak ductility estimation is still not improved.

### 4.2. The Effect of the UHPC Strength

In Figures 13b and 15, the bearing capacity, the lateral stiffness and the cumulative dissipated energy capacity of UHPCFST columns are only slightly increased with the compressive strength of UHPC increasing from 100 MPa to 140 MPa, which indicates that it is inappropriate to promote the seismic performance of UHPCFST columns by increasing the compressive strength of UHPC. Moreover, the error caused by the local buckling does not seem to be increased with the increase in compressive strength.

### 4.3. The Effect of the Length–Diameter Ratio

From Figures 13c and 16, it can be seen that the length–diameter ratio has a significant influence on the seismic performance of UHPCFST columns. The bearing capacity, lateral stiffness and cumulative dissipated energy of the UHPCFST columns have significant negative correlations with the length–diameter ratio. Specimen S1, with a length–diameter ratio of 23.1, possesses plumper hysteretic curves, larger bearing capacity, as well as cumulative dissipated energy; whilst for specimens S6 and S7 with larger length–diameter ratios, although the residual deformation is small, the pinching effects of hysteresis curves are pretty serious and the energy dissipation capacity is worse. In addition, as the length–diameter ratio increases, not considering the local buckling of the steel tube will further increase the overestimation of the bearing capacity and post-peak ductility of the UHPCFST columns. Therefore, slender columns should be avoided in seismic design, or reasonable lateral support should be laid out to decrease the shear span.

### 4.4. The Effect of the Axial Compression Ratio

The axial compression ratio is one of the major factors to influence the seismic performance of UHPCFST columns. As shown in Figures 13d and 17, the bearing capacity and lateral stiffness of the UHPCFST columns are both decreased with the increment of the axial compression ratio. Specimen S9, with a higher axial compression ratio of 0.5, experiences great lateral stiffness degradation, with the drift ratio ranging from 1 to 3%, and it even shows negative stiffness when the drift ratio reaches 4%, which is closely related to the second-order effect of the vertical load at the top of the columns. As the axial compression ratio increases, the cumulative dissipated energy is slightly increased. It should be noted that when the axial compression ratio reaches 0.5, neglecting the local buckling causes an overestimation of the maximum value rather than the post-peak ductility, the descending branch of the skeleton curve with the local buckling ignored agrees well with the hysteretic curve. This is mainly attributed to a more severe second-order effect of axial compressive load–lateral displacement under the high axial compression ratio.

While analysis of the influencing factors is reported, relatively fewer studies reported mostly the seismic performance of the UHPCFST columns comprising various supplementary columns of a large aspect ratio ($h/t \geq 50$) and high strength steel ($f_y \geq 560$ MPa). Of particular importance, there is relatively little research on analyzing the parameters affecting the seismic performance under the large axial compression ratios ($n \geq 0.6$). It is also shown that there is an urgent need to conduct research on the seismic performance of concrete-filled thin-walled steel tube columns composed of ultra-high performance concrete ($f_{cu} \geq 160$ Mpa) and high-strength steel ($f_y \geq 560$ MPa) under high axial compression ratios ($n \geq 0.6$).

## 5. Conclusions

In the present work, a fiber element model of the UHPCFST columns is developed to investigate the static behavior and hysteretic behavior of UHPCFST columns, where the effect of the local buckling of the steel tubes is considered based on the effective distribution width. The correctness and reliability of the fiber element model are verified by lots of experiments. Then, the parametric analysis is presented for discussing the influence of the yield strength of the steel, the strength of UHPC, the length–diameter ratio and the axial compression ratio on the seismic performance of UHPCFST columns. On the basis of the results and discussions presented in the paper, the main conclusions are summarized as follows:

(1) For the stress–strain model for the confined UHPC, satisfactory results are obtained when the parameter $\gamma$ is taken as 3.0.
(2) The proposed fiber element model can predict the nonlinear static and cyclic behavior of UHPCFST columns well.
(3) Neglecting the local buckling of the thin-walled steel tubes can bring about the overestimation of the bearing capacity and the post-peak ductility of UHPCFST columns.
(4) The errors caused by the local buckling of the steel tube are increased with the increasing in the length–diameter ratio. The errors in terms of bearing capacity, induced by the local buckling, are decreased with the increasing of the yield strength of steel. A higher axial compression ratio causes an overestimation of the maximum value rather than the post-peak ductility.

**Author Contributions:** Conceptualization, Y.W. and Y.Y. (Yanxiang Yan).; methodology, H.C.; software, H.C.; validation, Y.W. and Y.Y. (Yanxiang Yan); formal analysis, H.C.; investigation, Y.Y. (Yu Yan); resources, Y.Y. (Yanxiang Yan); data curation, Y.Z.; writing—original draft preparation, Y.Y. (Yu Yan); writing—review and editing, Y.Y. (Yanxiang Yan); visualization, Y.Y. (Yu Yan); supervision, Y.Y. (Yanxiang Yan); project administration, Y.Y. (Yanxiang Yan); funding acquisition, Y.W. All authors have read and agreed to the published version of the manuscript.

**Funding:** This research was funded by the Natural Science Foundation of Xiaogan City Hubei Province [XGKJ2022010099], the College Students Innovations Special Project of Hubei Engineering University [DC2022037], and the National Natural Science Foundation of China [51508421].

**Data Availability Statement:** All data is in editable origin images and will no longer be provided separately.

**Acknowledgments:** Many thanks to Lihua Xu from Wuhan University for providing the research conditions and foundations.

**Conflicts of Interest:** The authors declare no conflict of interest.

## References

1. Han, L.H. *Concrete Filled Steel Tubular Structures from Theory to Practices*; Science Press: Beijing, China, 2016.
2. Ahmed, M.; Liang, Q.Q.; Patel, V.I. Nonlinear analysis of rectangular concrete-filled double steel tubular short columns incorporating local buckling. *Eng. Struct.* **2018**, *175*, 13–26. [CrossRef]
3. Zubydan, A.H.; ElSabbagh, A.I. Monotonic and cyclic behavior of concrete-filled steel-tube beam-columns considering local buckling effect. *Thin-Walled Struct.* **2011**, *49*, 465–481. [CrossRef]
4. Ahmed, M.; Liang, Q.Q.; Patel, V.I.; Hadi, M.N.S. Nonlinear analysis of square concrete-filled double steel tubular slender columns incorporating preload effects. *Eng. Struct.* **2020**, *207*, 110272. [CrossRef]
5. Vrcelj, Z.; Uy, B. Strength of slender concrete-filled steel box columns incorporating local buckling. *J. Constr. Steel. Res.* **2002**, *58*, 275–300. [CrossRef]
6. Uy, B. Strength of concrete filled steel box columns incorporating local buckling. *J. Struct. Eng.* **2000**, *126*, 341–352. [CrossRef]
7. Valipour, H.R.; Foster, S.J. Nonlinear static and cyclic analysis of concrete-filled steel columns. *J. Constr. Steel. Res.* **2010**, *66*, 793–802. [CrossRef]
8. Varma, A.H.; Ricles, J.M.; Sause, R. Seismic behavior and modeling of high-strength composite concrete-filled steel tube (CFT) beam–columns. *J. Constr. Steel. Res.* **2002**, *58*, 725–758. [CrossRef]
9. Kamila, G.M.; Liang, Q.Q.; Hadi, M.N.S. Fiber element simulation of interaction behavior of local and global buckling in axially loaded rectangular concrete-filled steel tubular slender columns under fire exposure. *Thin-Walled Struct.* **2019**, *145*, 106403. [CrossRef]
10. Chung, K.; Chung, J.; Choib, S. Prediction of pre- and post-peak behavior of concrete-filled square steel tube columns under cyclic loads using fiber element method. *Thin-Walled Struct.* **2007**, *45*, 747–758. [CrossRef]
11. Richard, P.; Cheyrezy, M. Composition of reactive powder concretes. *Cem. Concr. Res.* **1995**, *25*, 1501–1511. [CrossRef]
12. Xu, L.Y.; Huang, B.T.; Lao, J.C. Tensile over-saturated cracking of Ultra-high-strength engineered cementitious composites (UHS-ECC) with artificial geopolymer aggregates. *Cem. Concr. Comp.* **2023**, *136*, 104896. [CrossRef]
13. Su, Y.; Wu, C.Q.; Li, J. Development of novel ultra-high performance concrete: From material to structure. *Constr. Build. Mater.* **2017**, *135*, 517–528. [CrossRef]
14. Deng, E.F.; Zhang, Z.; Zhang, C.X. Experimental study on flexural behavior of UHPC wet joint in prefabricated multi-girder bridge. *Eng. Struct.* **2023**, *275*, 115314. [CrossRef]
15. Kang, S.T.; Chio, J.I.; Koh, K.T. Hybrid effects of steel fiber and microfiber on the tensile behavior of ultra-high performance concrete. *Compos. Struct.* **2016**, *145*, 37–42. [CrossRef]
16. Park, S.H.; Kim, D.J.; Ryu, G.S. Tensile behavior of ultra high performance hybrid fiber reinforced concrete. *Cem. Concr. Compos.* **2012**, *34*, 172–184. [CrossRef]
17. Montuori, R.; Piluso, V.; Tisi, A. Ultimate behavior of FRP wrapped sections under axial force and bending: Influence of stress-strain confinement model. *Compos. Part B-Eng.* **2013**, *54*, 85–96. [CrossRef]
18. Cavaleri, L.; Trapani, F.D.; Ferrotto, M.F. Stress-strain models for normal and high strength confined concrete: Test and comparison of literature models reliability in reproducing experimental results. *Ing. Sismica-ital.* **2017**, *34*, 114–137.
19. Le´geron, F.; Paultre, P. Uniaxial confinement model for normal- and high-strength concrete columns. *J. Struct. Eng.* **2003**, *129*, 241–252. [CrossRef]
20. An, L.H.; Fehling, E. Assessment of stress-strain model for UHPC confined by steel tube stub columns. *Struct. Eng. Mech.* **2017**, *63*, 371–384.
21. Li, G.C.; Liu, D.; Yang, Z.J.; Zhang, C.Y. Flexural behavior of high strength concrete filled high strength square steel tube. *J. Constr. Steel. Res.* **2017**, *128*, 732–744. [CrossRef]
22. Mander, J.B.; Priestly, M.N.J.; Park, R. Theoretical stress–strain model for confined concrete. *J. Struct. Eng.* **1988**, *114*, 1804–1826. [CrossRef]
23. Menegotto, M.; Paolo, E. Method of analysis for cyclically loaded R.C. plane frames including change in geometry and non-elastic behavior of elements under combines normal force and bending. In Proceedings of the IABSE Symposium on Resistance and Ultimate Deformability of Structures, Lisbon, Portugal, 12–14 September 1973; pp. 15–22.
24. AIJ. *Recommendations for Design and Construction of Concrete Filled Steel Tubular Structures*; Architectural Institute of Japan: Tokyo, Japan, 2001.
25. AISC. *Load and Resistance Factor Design (LRFD) Specification for Structural Steel Buildings*; American Institute of Steel Construction: Chicago, IL, USA, 1999.
26. EC4. *Design of Composite Steel and Concrete Structures*; European Committee for Standardization: Brussels, Belgium, 2004.
27. Liang, Q.Q.; Uy, B.; Liew, J.Y.R. Local buckling of steel plates in concrete filled thin-walled steel tubular beam-columns. *J. Constr. Steel. Res.* **2007**, *63*, 396–405. [CrossRef]
28. Liang, Q.Q.; Uy, B. Theoretical study on the post-local buckling of steel plates in concrete filled thin-walled steel box columns. *Comput. Struct.* **2000**, *75*, 479–490. [CrossRef]
29. Chen, S.M.; Zhang, R.; Jia, L.J. Structural behavior of UHPC filled steel tube columns under axial loading. *Thin-Walled Struct.* **2018**, *130*, 550–563. [CrossRef]
30. Yan, Y.X.; Xu, L.H.; Li, B. Axial behavior of ultra-high performance concrete (UHPC) filled stocky steel tubes with square sections. *J. Constr. Steel. Res.* **2019**, *158*, 417–428. [CrossRef]

31. Xu, S.C.; Wu, C.Q.; Liu, Z.X. Experimental investigation on the cyclic behaviors of ultra-high performance steel fiber reinforced concrete filled thin-walled steel tubular columns. *Thin-Walled Struct.* **2019**, *140*, 1–20. [CrossRef]
32. Cai, H.; Xu, L.H.; Chi, Y. Seismic performance of rectangular ultra-high performance concrete filled steel tube (UHPCFST) columns. *Compos. Struct.* **2021**, *259*, 113242. [CrossRef]

**Disclaimer/Publisher's Note:** The statements, opinions and data contained in all publications are solely those of the individual author(s) and contributor(s) and not of MDPI and/or the editor(s). MDPI and/or the editor(s) disclaim responsibility for any injury to people or property resulting from any ideas, methods, instructions or products referred to in the content.

*Article*

# Behavior of Concrete-Filled U-Shaped Steel Beam to CFSST Column Connections

Yan Lin [1,2,*], Zhijie Zhao [1], Xuhui Gao [1], Zhen Wang [3] and Shuang Qu [1,2]

1. School of Civil Engineering, Shandong Jianzhu University, Jinan 250101, China
2. Key Laboratory of Building Structural Retrofitting and Underground Space Engineering, Shandong Jianzhu University, Ministry of Education, Jinan 250101, China
3. College of Transportation and Civil Engineering, Shandong Jiaotong University, Jinan 250351, China
* Correspondence: linyan123@sdjzu.edu.cn

**Abstract:** Two new types of connection between concrete-filled U-shaped steel (CFUS) beams and concrete-filled square steel tube (CFSST) columns were presented in this study, including rebar-sleeve with internal diaphragm connection and rebar-through with internal diaphragm connection. Based on the experiments of the rebar-plate with internal diaphragm connections between CFUS beams and CFSST columns under cyclic loading, the nonlinear finite element models of the tested specimens were developed and validated by comparing them with the experimental results. The numerical results were in agreement with the experimental results in terms of failure modes, stress distribution, and load-displacement skeleton curves. Based on the FEA results, the mechanical behavior of the two new types of connection were comprehensively discussed and compared. Furthermore, this parametric study was conducted for the rebar-sleeve with internal diaphragm connection to investigate the effect of specific parameters on the capacity of the connection. The parameters included: The thickness of U-shaped steel, the ratio of longitudinal reinforcement in the concrete slab, the strength of concrete in the beam, the strength of the U-shaped steel, and the thickness of the internal diaphragm. The results indicate that the thickness of the U-shaped steel ($t_b$), the ratio of the longitudinal reinforcement in concrete slab ($\rho$), and the strength of the U-shaped steel have significant effects on the loading capacity of the connection—the loading capacity increases by about 20% when $t_b$ increases from 6 mm to 8 mm, increases by about 45% when $\rho$ increases from 1.5% to 4.8% under negative P, and increases by about 20% when the steel yield strength ($f_y$) increases from 235 Mpa to 420 Mpa.

**Keywords:** behavior; concrete-filled U-shaped steel (CFUS) beam; concrete-filled square steel tubular (CFSST) column; finite element model

**Citation:** Lin, Y.; Zhao, Z.; Gao, X.; Wang, Z.; Qu, S. Behavior of Concrete-Filled U-Shaped Steel Beam to CFSST Column Connections. *Buildings* **2023**, *13*, 517. https://doi.org/10.3390/buildings13020517

Academic Editors: André Rafael Dias Martins and Harry Far

Received: 29 December 2022
Revised: 20 January 2023
Accepted: 2 February 2023
Published: 14 February 2023

**Copyright:** © 2023 by the authors. Licensee MDPI, Basel, Switzerland. This article is an open access article distributed under the terms and conditions of the Creative Commons Attribution (CC BY) license (https://creativecommons.org/licenses/by/4.0/).

## 1. Introduction

Concrete-filled square steel tubular (CFSST) columns have been widely used in bridges and buildings due to their higher bearing capacity, higher stiffness, and better seismic performance. Furthermore, the square tube not only serves as formwork for casting concrete, but also offers convenience for beam–column connections [1].

Over the past few years, some types of profiled composite beams have been proposed and explored for better structural properties and constructability. Oehlers [2,3] and Uy and Bradford [4,5] developed composite profiled beams consisting of profiled steel sheets and in-filled concrete. They performed tests to investigate the flexural capacity and deflection of the beam. Chen et al. [6] proposed the checked steel-encased concrete beam and conducted tests to study the bending and slipping performance of the beam. Recently, the concrete-filled U-shaped steel (CFUS) beam (as shown in Figure 1) was gaining popularity in engineering practices. This beam consists of U-shaped steel, T-shaped concrete, and shear connectors, where the U-shaped steel is fabricated using cold forming or the welding of steel plates. The CFUS beam has the merits of higher strength, stiffness, and ductility compared to the steel or reinforced concrete beam. Indeed, the in-filled concrete in the

U-shaped steel beam not only prevents the local buckling of the web and flange of the U-shaped steel, but also decreases the thermal effect and enhances fire resistance [7]. In addition, the U-shaped steel serves as the formwork for casting concrete, shortening the construction cost as well as the construction period.

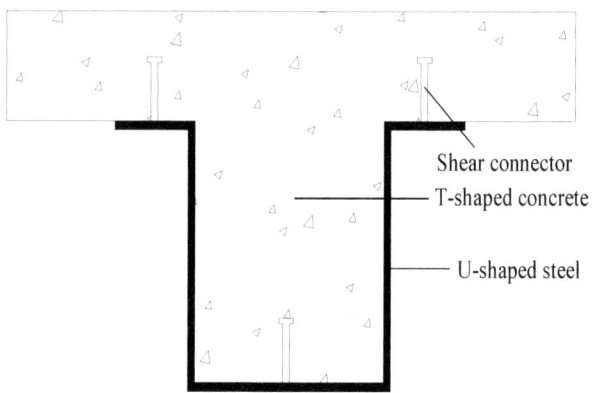

**Figure 1.** Concrete-filled U-shaped steel (CFUS) beam.

Over the past several years, the majority of connections between CFSST columns and steel beams or CFSST columns and conventional composite beams composed of H-shaped steel and concrete slab have been developed and applied in practice engineering. Some research has been carried out to investigate the structural behavior of these connections, such as that of Parvaria et al., Liu et al., Xue et al., Fan et al., and Zhang et al. [8–12].

Recently, research on the connections for CFUS beams and columns has been conducted. Kim et al. [13] investigated the behavior of CFUS beam to CES (concrete-encased steel) column connections. The results indicate that the in-filled concrete was effective in preventing premature local buckling of the web and flange plates. Moreover, the specimens showed good earthquake resistance which was in accordance with the AISC 341-05 specification. Park et al. [14] tested two connections consisting of CFUS beams and RC columns under cyclic loading. All specimens exhibited higher strength, better ductility, and energy dissipation capacity. Lee et al. [15] conducted an experimental study on the seismic performance of CFUS beams to H-shaped steel column connections with band plates. This study indicated that the specimens had higher loading bearing and deformation capacity. Hwang et al. [16] investigated the seismic behavior of connections between CFUS beams and PSRC (prefabricated steel-reinforced concrete) columns. Based on the test results, the shear strength of connections was evaluated. Ding et al. [17] investigated an optimized connection consisting of U-shaped steel beams and CFSST columns. The results showed that the bearing capacity and seismic performance of the specimens were improved. Chen et al. [18] conducted an experimental test on H-shaped steel beam and square steel tubular column connections with the column thickened near the connection zone. This study indicated that the thickness of the column near the connection zone had a notable effect on the plastic deformation ability.

It appears that most of the past research has focused on the connections of CFUS beams to RC, H-shaped steel, or CES columns. The CFUS beam to CFFST column connection details are not well established and their behaviors are not understood. The lack of this research will prevent the use of the structural system composed of CFUS beams and CFFST columns in practice. Therefore, it is necessary to develop new types of CFUS beam to CFFST column connections and study their behaviors.

In this study, two new types of connections composed of CFUS beams and CFFST columns were proposed, including rebar-through with internal diaphragm connection (i.e., the RT connection) and rebar-sleeve with internal diaphragm connection (i.e., the RS connection). Based on the experimental results of three specimens of the rebar-plate with internal diaphragm connection (i.e., the RP connection) between the CFUS beam and the CFSST column under cyclic loading, the nonlinear finite element analyses of the test specimens were conducted and compared to validate the feasibility of this model in simulating the behavior of the composite connections. Furthermore, on the basis of the validated FEA model, the stress distributions of two new types of connections were comprehensively analyzed and compared to study their load-transfer mechanisms. Subsequently, a parametric study was conducted. The parameters included: the thickness of the U-shaped steel, the ratio of the longitudinal reinforcement in concrete slab, the strength of the concrete in beams, the strength of the U-shaped steel, and the thickness of the internal diaphragm.

## 2. Connection Details

Figure 2 depicts the details of the RS connection composed of the CFUS beam and the CFSST column. In this type of connection, there are two internal diaphragms welded to the inside of the steel tube—one of them corresponding to the bottom plate of the U-shaped steel beam location, and the other one corresponding to the position of the longitudinal rebars in the beam. The bottom plate of the U-shaped beam is welded directly to the steel tube wall by a full penetration weld. The webs and the extending flanges of the U-shaped beam are attached to the wall of the steel tube by double fillet welds. The longitudinal rebars in the beam are cut off and connected to the column by sleeves that are welded to the tube wall. In order to ensure the quality of concrete pouring in the connection, the pouring holes and the vent holes should be provided in the upper and lower diaphragms. Moreover, the cope holes should be provided in the bottom plate of the U-shaped steel beam to ensure the quality of welding.

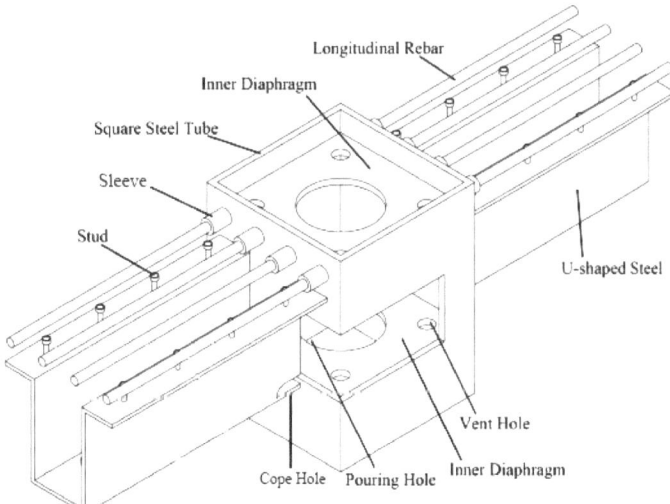

**Figure 2.** RS connection.

Figure 3 depicts the details of the RT connection composed of the CFUS beam and the CFSST column. In this connection, the longitudinal rebars in the beam are passed through the column through the holes drilled on the face of the tube wall, and there is no upper internal diaphragm in the tube. The connection details between the U-shaped steel beam and the steel tube wall are the same as those of the RS connection described above.

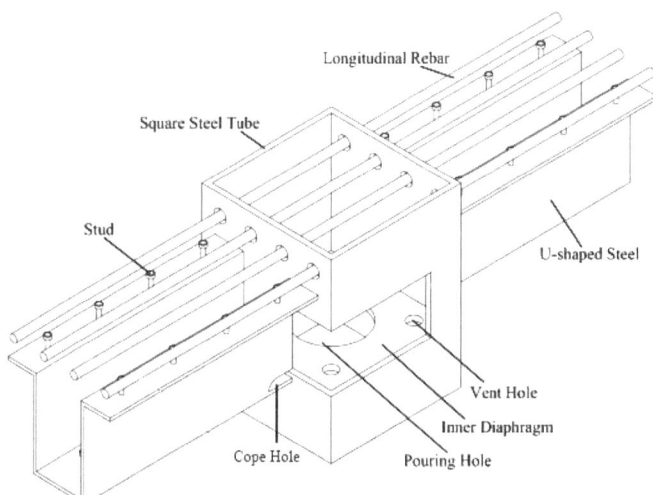

**Figure 3.** RT connection.

## 3. Experimental Program

### 3.1. Design and Production of the Specimens

A total of three specimens of the RP connections between the CFUS beams and the CFSST columns were designed and produced, consisting of C-1, C-2, and C-3. Figure 4 depicts the details of the RP connection. In this type of connection, the longitudinal rebars in each beam were cut off and welded to the upper exterior diaphragm plate set around the steel tube column, and the connection details between the U-shaped steel beam and the steel tube wall were the same as those of an RS or RT connection. For the specimens, the main design variables were the thickness of the square steel tube and the concrete strength in the beam. All the specimens were cruciform-shaped specimens and were approximately 1/2 scale relative to the element sizes needed for the prototype frame. Table 1 shows the dimensions and parameters of the specimens. The $b_c \times b_c \times t_c$ of the steel tube in Table 1 represents the section size of the tube, where $b_c$ is the width of the column and $t_c$ is the thickness of the tube. The $h_w \times b \times b_1 \times t_b$ in Table 1 represents the section size of the U-shaped steel beam, where $h_w$ is the height of the U-shaped steel beam, $b$ is the width of the bottom plate, $b_1$ is the width of extending flanges, and $t_b$ is the thickness of the U-shaped steel beam. Figure 5 shows the connection details and the dimensions of the specimens.

**Table 1.** Size of specimens.

| Specimen | Column<br>Steel Tube<br>$b_c \times b_c \times t_c$ | Beam<br>U-Shaped Steel<br>$h_w \times b \times b_1 \times t_b$ | Negative Rebar | Internal Diaphragm | | | Axial Load Ratio | The Vertical Load Values |
|---|---|---|---|---|---|---|---|---|
| | | | | Width | Length | Thickness | | |
| C-1 | 250 × 250 × 10 | 160 × 120 × 50 × 6 | 4D14 | 230 | 230 | 10 | 0.2 | 800 KN |
| C-2 | 250 × 250 × 8 | 160 × 120 × 50 × 6 | 4D14 | 234 | 234 | 10 | 0.2 | 800 KN |
| C-3 | 250 × 250 × 10 | 160 × 120 × 50 × 6 | 4D14 | 230 | 230 | 10 | 0.2 | 800 KN |

Note: Unit in this table is mm.

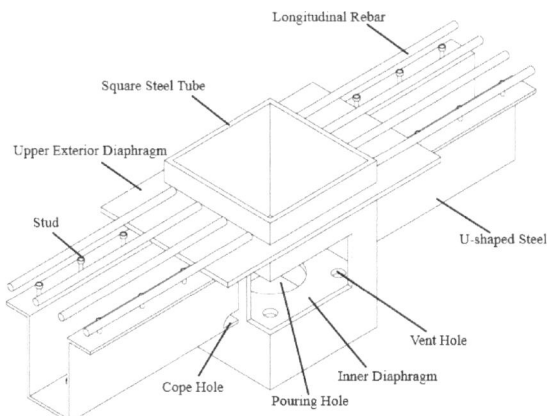

**Figure 4.** RP connection.

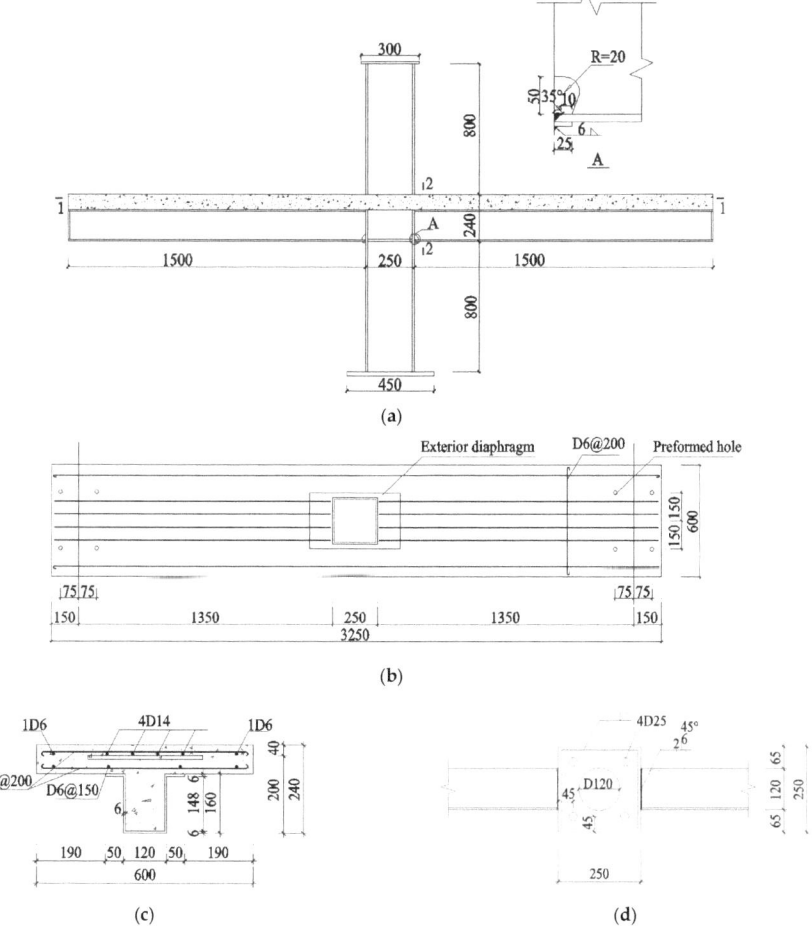

**Figure 5.** Details and dimensions of specimens: (**a**) the whole specimen; (**b**) section 1-1 of specimen C-1; (**c**) section 2-2 of specimen C-1; (**d**) inner diaphragm.

The cold-formed square steel tube was used for the column. The U-shaped steel beam was fabricated using the cold-forming steel plate. Q235B steel with the nominal strength of 235 Mpa was used for all of the steel elements in the three specimens. Concrete with the nominal compressive cubic strength of 40 Mpa was used in the column, and concrete with the nominal compressive cubic strength of 30 Mpa (C-1, C-2) and 20 Mpa (C-3) were used in the beam and slab. Hot-rolled ribbed rebar (HRB) with a nominal yield strength of 335 Mpa was used as the longitudinal rebars in the concrete slab, and hot-rolled plain rebar (HPB) with a nominal yield strength of 235 Mpa was used as the transverse distribution rebar in the slab. In order to achieve full strength and stiffness of the CFUS beam, the shear studs with a diameter of 13 mm were welded onto the bottom plate and the top extending flanges of the U-shaped steel beam. A full penetration weld was used to connect the bottom plate of the U-shaped steel and the steel tube wall, where the welding pad was used during welding and removed after welding to improve the quality of welds. All of the steel members were fabricated in the steel factory, and the subsequent works were carried out at the structural laboratory of Shandong Jianzhu University, such as binding and welding the rebars, and casting and curing the concrete.

Material properties of steel and concrete used for the specimens are given in Tables 2 and 3.

Table 2. Material properties of steel.

| Type | Thickness (mm) | Yield Strength $f_y$ (MPa) | Ultimate Strength $f_u$ (MPa) | Elastic Modulus ($10^5$ MPa) | Elongation δ (%) |
|---|---|---|---|---|---|
| Steel tube | 8 | 312 | 455 | 1.99 | 35 |
| | 10 | 330 | 435 | 2.03 | 34.5 |
| U-shaped steel beam | 6 | 285 | 423 | 1.97 | 31 |
| Diaphragm | 10 | 370 | 445 | 2.09 | 31.5 |

Table 3. Material properties of concrete.

| Grade | Mix Proportion (kg/m³) | | | Cube Compressive Strength (MPa) |
|---|---|---|---|---|
| | Cement | Sand | Gravel | |
| C20 | 336 | 640 | 1172 | 21.9 |
| C30 | 360 | 609 | 1220 | 29.3 |
| C40 | 420 | 523 | 1280 | 42.6 |

*3.2. Test Setup and Loading Procedure*

Figure 6a shows a schematic of the test setup. Axial loads were applied to the top of the column to simulate gravity loading. The two ends of the beam were subjected to equal and opposite vertical cyclic loads to simulate the seismic loading. The method of loading cycle was determined in accordance with the requirements of JGJ 101–96 [19]. The column's bottom end was fastened to the spherical pin support connected with the ground, which was allowed to rotate in the plane of loading but was constrained from movement. The crossing braces were provided at the top of the column to prevent lateral moving of the column. Meanwhile, the pin joints were used at the connection between the braces and the column wall to allow the top end of the column to rotate. The vertical axial load was applied using a hydraulic jack with 2000 kN capacity. The hydraulic jack was attached to a short column which was connected to the reaction frame. The vertical reversed cyclic loads at the beam ends were applied by the MTS actuators attached to the reaction frame with a 500 kN capacity. Figure 6b shows the loading site.

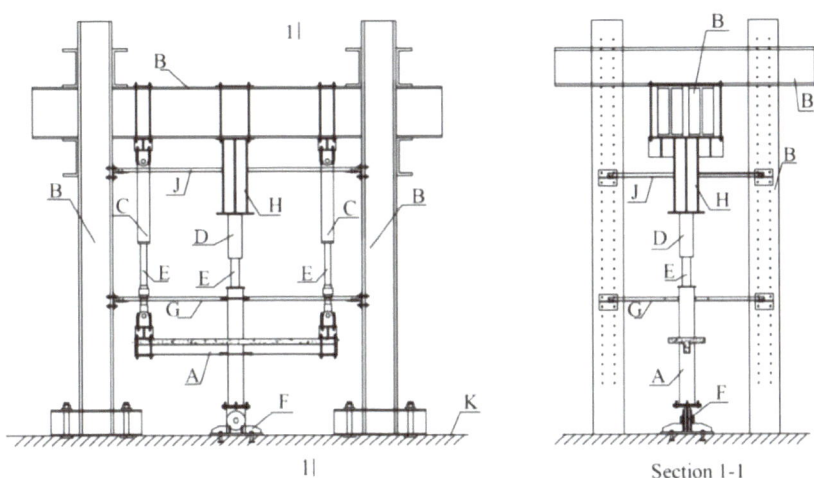

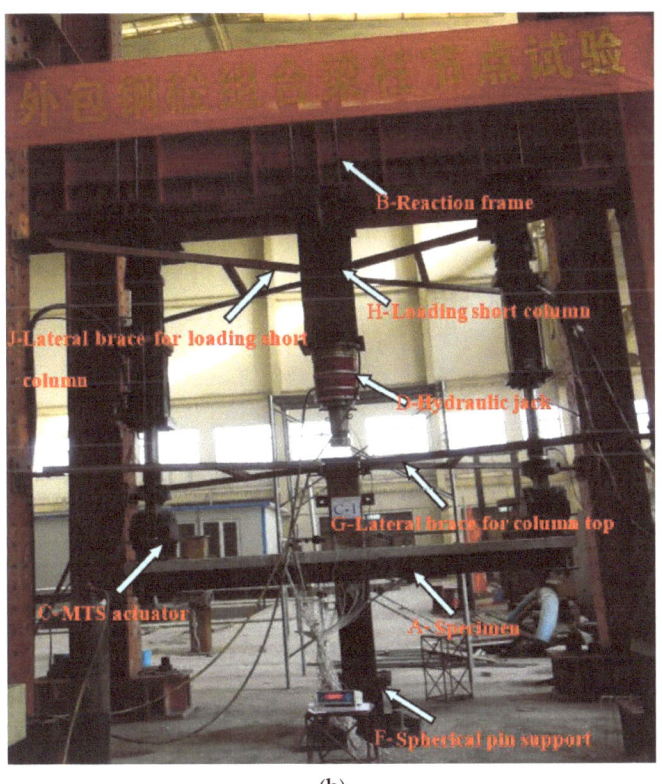

**Figure 6.** Test setup: (**a**) the schematic of the test setup; (**b**) test loading site.

The displacement-control method was used in the loading procedure. The axial load was first imposed on the top of the column until it reached the value of the axial load ratio—as shown in Table 1—and then remained constant throughout the whole test. The vertical cyclic loads were then applied at the ends of the beams until failure. The loading cycle was repeated only once at each control point of $0.25\Delta_y$, $0.5\Delta_y$, and $0.75\Delta_y$, and then repeated three times at each control point of $\Delta_y$, $2\Delta_y$, $3\Delta_y$, $4\Delta_y$, etc., where $\Delta_y$ represents the displacement of the beam end corresponding to the yield load estimated from the finite element analysis. The test was terminated in any of the following cases: (1) The load capacity dropped to less than 85% of the peak load. (2) The concrete of the slab adjacent to the column was crushed. (3) The bottom plate of the U-shaped steel beam in the heat affect zone fractured completely.

### 3.3. Experimental Results

All of the specimens exhibited the same behavior in terms of failure mode. When the maximum load was reached, the fracture occurred in the bottom plate and the webs of the U-shaped steel adjacent to the weld connecting between the steel tube and the bottom plate of the beam, and the was concrete crushed in the compression slab near the tube (as shown in following Figures). For all of the specimens, the deformation of the column in the connection zone was small, and no slip between the T-shaped concrete and the U-shaped steel was found up to the point of failure in all the specimens.

The P–Δ hysteretic curves of three specimens are given in Figure 7, where P is the load imposed onto the end of the beam and Δ is the corresponding displacement. The positive load in Figure 7 means that the bottom plate of the composite beam is in tension and the concrete slab is in compression.

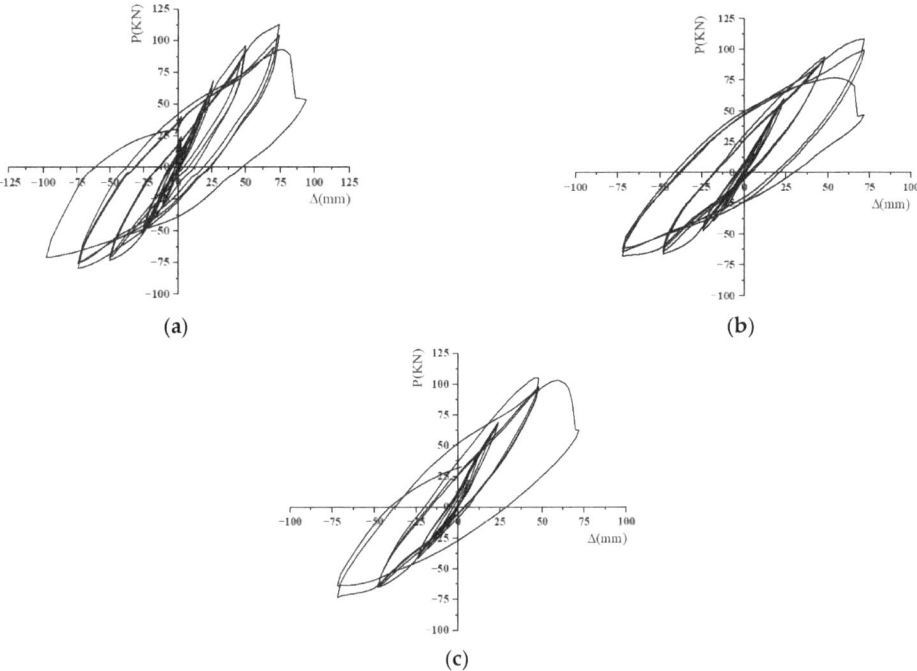

**Figure 7.** P-Δ hysteretic curves of specimens: (**a**) specimen C-1; (**b**) specimen C-2; (**c**) specimen C-3.

It is indicated that the hysteretic curves of all the specimens were plump and had a shuttle shape without significant pinching, which exhibited better energy dissipation, higher deformation, and better ductility. In addition, the hysteretic curves of all the specimens were obviously asymmetrical due to the effect of the composition of the concrete slab of the beam, where the areas of hysteretic loops under positive moment were larger than those under negative moment.

## 4. Finite Element Model

### 4.1. Material Modeling

The concrete damage plasticity model provided by ABAQUS is applied to simulate the concrete where the stress–strain relationship can be selected according to whether the concrete is confined. The stress–strain constitutive model of confined concrete proposed by Han et al. [20] is used for in-filled concrete in the square steel tube, and the stress–strain relationship presented by GB50010-2010 [21] is adapted to simulate the normal concrete for the composite beam, as shown in Figure 8 ($\sigma_c$ = stress of concrete and $\varepsilon_c$ = strain of concrete). In the concrete constitution, the damage variables of concrete are defined according to the theory proposed by Du et al. [22]. Five parameters are used to describe the concrete yield function and plastic flow procedure, i.e., the dilation angle ($\psi$) is 30°, the eccentricity ($\varepsilon$) is 0.1, the ratio of initial equiaxial compressive yield stress to initial uniaxial compressive yield stress ($f_{b0}/f_{c0}$) is 1.16, the ratio of the second stress invariant on the tensile meridian ($K$) is 0.6667, and the viscosity parameter ($\mu$) is 0.005.

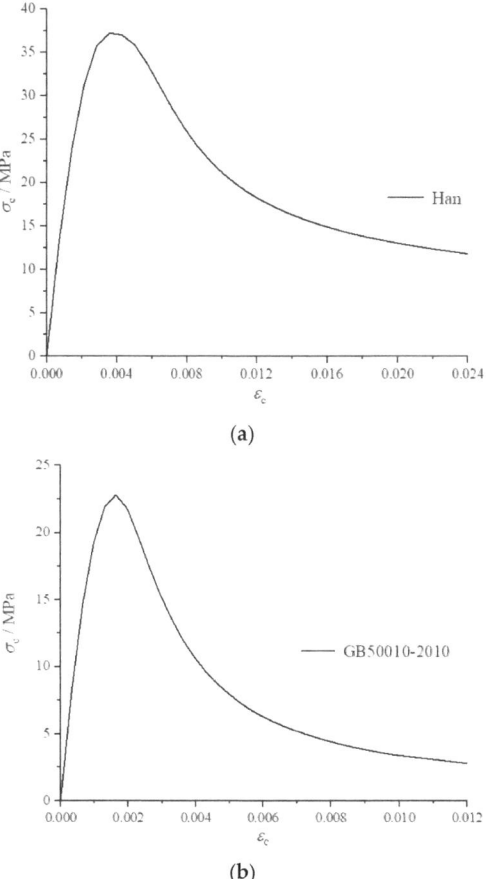

**Figure 8.** Stress–strain curves: (**a**) stress–strain relation model used for in-filled concrete in the square steel tube; (**b**) stress–strain relation model used for the normal concrete of the composite beam.

The bilinear stress–strain curve is used to model the steel and reinforcement. This curve is composed of two segments. The first segment is the elastic segment with the yield strength ($f_y$) and the modulus of elasticity ($E_s$) as shown in Table 2. The second part is the elastoplastic part, where the hardening modulus is usually taken to be 0.01 of the elastic modulus ($E_{s0} = 0.01\ E_s$). The Poisson's ratio is set to 0.3.

### 4.2. Finite Element Type and Mesh

The results of the FEA with various element types show that the three-dimensional eight nodes solid element with reduced integration (C3D8R) exhibits the most effective results when modeling for the concrete, steel tube, U-shaped steel beam, diaphragm, and reinforcement. Therefore, the C3D8R element is used for all components in the connection. In order to obtain a more regular element shape, the structured meshing technique is applied, and different mesh densities are adopted for different parts—the grid nodes are relatively dense near the panel zone, while the grid can be relatively sparse away from the panel zone. The three-layer mesh along the thickness of the steel plate is suggested by Ozkilic [23]. However, the results of the FEA with different layers of mesh show that these have a light effect on the numerical results for connections composed of CFUS beams and CFSST columns in our studies. In addition, multilayers of mesh result in the non-convergence of calculation. Therefore, one layer is meshed along the thickness of the steel plate in the analysis.

Due to the fact that there is no relative movement between the steel tube and the concrete inside it during the whole loading cycle, the interaction between them is simulated by adopting the 'TIE' command. Due to the same reason, the 'TIE' is also selected to model the interaction between the U-shaped steel and the concrete inside the beam, as well as the rebars and the steel members (external plates of RP connection and sleeves of RS connection). The contact between the steel tube wall and the concrete at the end of the beam is set up with the 'hard' contact in the normal direction and the 'Coulomb friction model' contact (the friction coefficient of 0.25) in the tangential direction. In addition, for the three types of connections, the rebar elements and concrete elements are all connected by adopting the embedded element technique.

### 4.3. Boundary and Loading Conditions

A rigid block is set on the bottom of the column to model a rigid base. All the degrees of freedom at the middle line of the bottom block except the rotation about the x axis are constrained to simulate hinge support. The displacements in the x and y directions and the rotations about the y and z axes of the middle line at the top of the column are restrained. In order to prevent the lateral flexural-torsional buckling of a beam, the displacements out of the plane at the beam ends are constrained.

In the FE analysis, the loading procedure is divided into two stages. In the first stage, the degrees of freedom in the z direction for all of the nodes on the top of the column are coupled, and then an axial concentrated load is imposed on the principal node and kept constant during the whole procedure. In the second stage, the vertical degrees of freedom for the nodes at the beam ends are coupled, and then the cyclic loads are applied to the principal node in the form of displacement. For all the connections, the displacements applied at the beam ends are the same. Figure 9 shows the boundary conditions scheme and the finite element models of three types of connections.

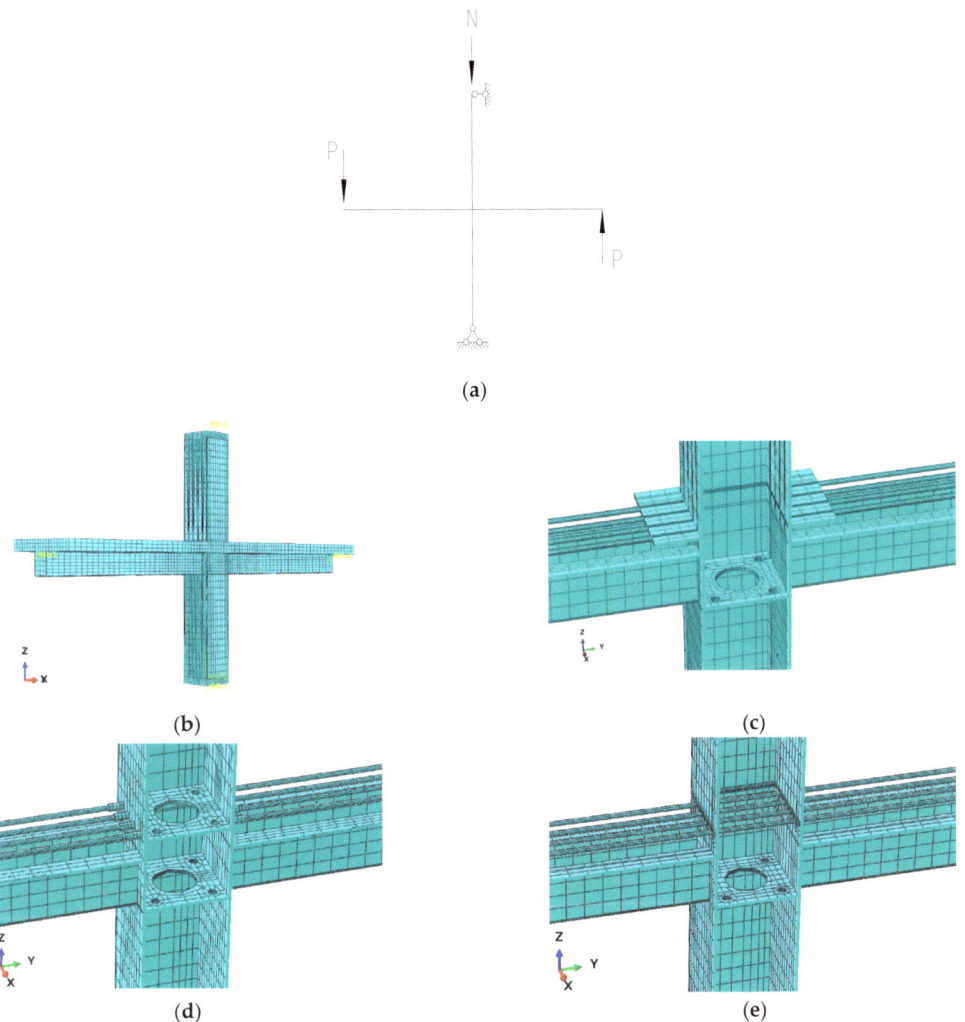

**Figure 9.** Boundary conditions scheme and finite element models: (**a**) boundary conditions scheme; (**b**) the whole model; (**c**) RP connection; (**d**) RS connection; (**e**) RT connection.

## 5. Numerical Results

### 5.1. Verification of FEA Model

#### 5.1.1. Failure Mode

In order to verify the feasibility and accuracy of the developed finite element model in Section 4, the finite element analyses under cyclic load of the three tested specimens are conducted and the numerical results are compared to those from the experiments.

Due to the fact that the failure mode of each specimen is similar, only the failure mode of specimen C-1 is used to compare with the experimental results. The stress contour is used to simulate the fracture between the U-shaped steel beam and the tube wall in the FE model. The PEEQ contour is used to simulate the crushing of concrete in the FE model. Figure 10 shows the comparison of tested and simulated failure modes of specimen C-1.

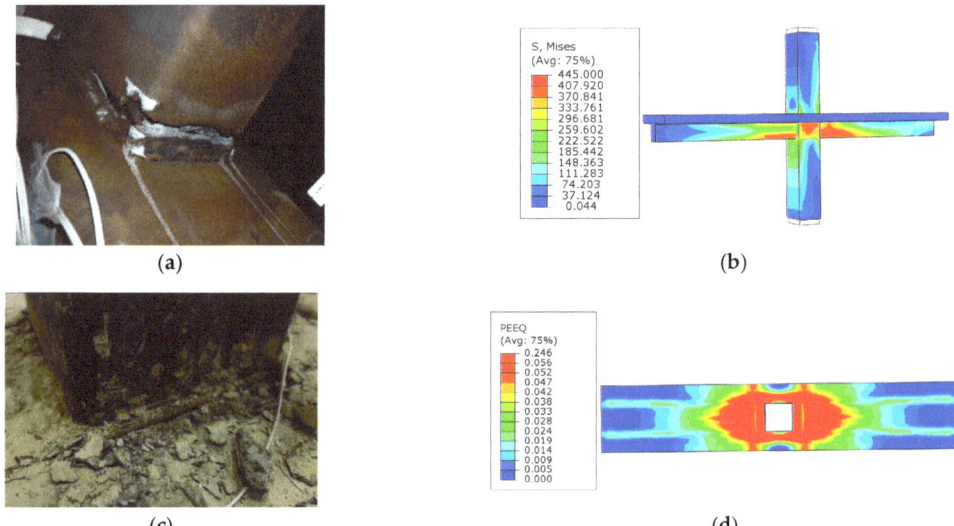

**Figure 10.** Comparison of tested and simulated failure modes of specimen C-1: (**a**) fracture of the bottom plate of U-shaped beam; (**b**) von Mises stress contour in the connection; (**c**) concrete crushing in the slab; (**d**) PEEQ contour in the concrete slab.

From Figure 10, it can be seen that the stress in the region adjacent to the connection between the bottom plate of the U-shaped steel beam and the tube wall has reached the ultimate strength of steel, which indicates that the fracture occurred here. The red part in Figure 10d is the most severe concrete damage area, which means that the concrete slab near the column in this area is crushed. Meanwhile, the stress in the region far away from the connection zone is much smaller than the corresponding yield strength of the material. Therefore, the numerical results are consistent with the experimental results.

5.1.2. Load Versus Displacement Curves

The comparison between the skeleton curves obtained from the finite element analysis and the experimental results for the specimens are shown in Figure 11.

It can be found that the load-displacement curves obtained by the numerical simulations are in reasonable agreement with those obtained by the experiments. However, the loading capacity and the stiffness of the connection from the finite element analysis are higher than the experimental results. There are some reasons for this: (1) The initial geometrical imperfection and the initial residual stress are neglected in the finite element model. (2) The boundary and loading conditions applied in the FEA model are more ideal than when compared with the test setup. (3) The material constitutive relationship used in the FE analysis is a little different from the actual one used. (4) The damage degree of concrete based on the damage variables in the finite element model is less than that in the test. (5) For the test, the fracture in the bottom plate and the webs of the U-shaped steel adjacent to the welding line led to unloading—it is difficult to simulate this fracture in the numerical models; therefore, there is no unloading branch of the skeleton curves in the numerical analysis. Although the factors described above cause the differences between the numerical results and the experimental results, these differences are in the allowable range. In conclusion, the numerical results are in reasonable agreement with the experimental results in terms of the failure modes and the skeleton curves. Therefore, FE analysis is dependable to conduct further study. In addition, on the basis of the simulation method of the validated FEA model of RP connection, the finite element models of the RS and RT connections are dependable to conduct the stress analysis and parametric analysis because the material modeling, the element type and mesh, the interaction, as well as the boundary and loading condition of the RS and RT connections are identical to those of RP connections—in spite of the different connection details of the longitudinal rebars in beams.

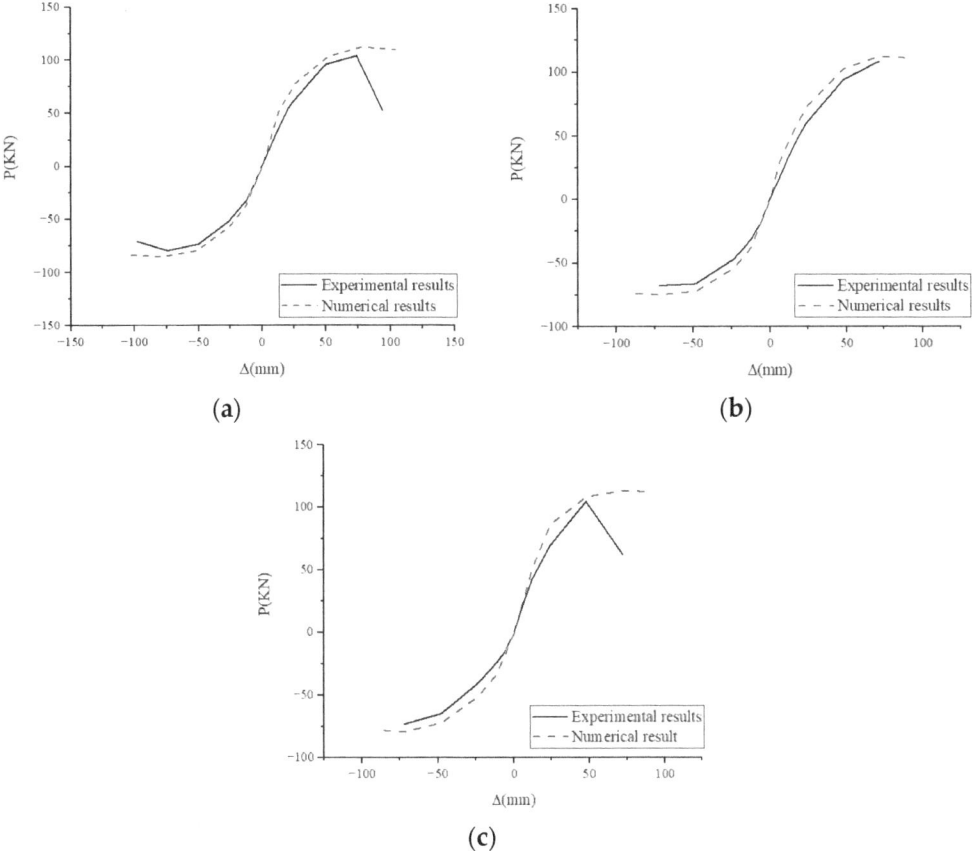

**Figure 11.** Comparison of skeleton curves of three specimens: (**a**) specimen C-1; (**b**) specimen C-2; (**c**) specimen C-3.

### 5.2. Stress Analysis

The stress distributions of the various components of the RS connection and the RT connection are comprehensively investigated and compared to identify the mechanical characteristics. The geometry and material properties of both specimens are similar to those of the experimental specimen C-1.

#### 5.2.1. Stress Analysis of the End of Bottom Plate for U-Shaped Steel Beam and the Internal Diaphragm

The von Mises stress contours of the end of the bottom plate of the U-shaped steel beam and the internal diaphragm at the yield state for the RS connection and the RT connection are shown in Figure 12.

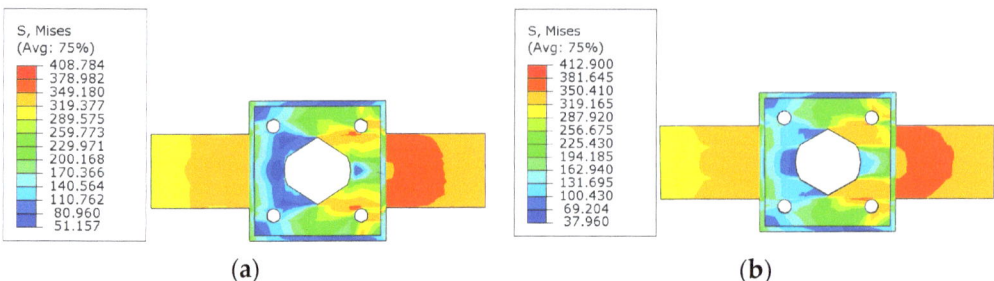

(a)    (b)

**Figure 12.** Von Mises stress contours of the end of bottom plate of U-shaped steel beam and the internal diaphragm at the yield state: (**a**) RS connection; (**b**) RT connection.

It can be seen that the stress in the compressive portion (the left side) is much less than that in the tensile portion (the right side) due to the effect of in-filled concrete in the beam and column for each connection. Furthermore, the stress in most regions of the internal diaphragm is much smaller except that the stress in the tensile region adjacent to the line connecting the center of the pouring hole to the center of the vent hole approaches or exceeds the yield strength of steel.

5.2.2. Stress Analysis of Steel Tube in the Connection Zone

Figure 13 shows the von Mises stress contours in the webs of the steel tube in the connection zone at the yield state for the RS connection and the RT connection.

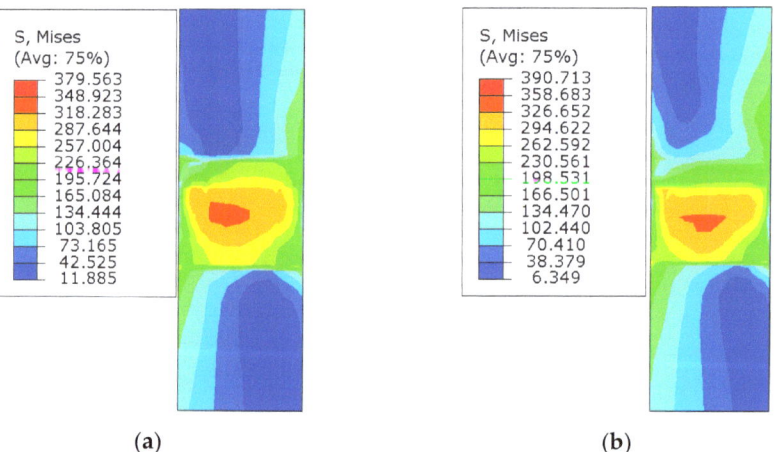

(a)    (b)

**Figure 13.** Von Mises stress contours in the webs of steel tube in connection zone at the yield state: (**a**) RS connection; (**b**) RT connection.

It can be seen that the stress is the largest in the center part of the panel zone and decreases gradually from the center to the outside for each connection. Compared with the RT connection, the stress distribution in the webs of the steel tube adjacent to the upper internal diaphragm of the RS connection is relatively uniform and the stress level in this region is lower. This is mainly due to the fact that the upper internal diaphragm in the RS connection provides support for the column, which limits the out-of-plane deformation of the column webs, resulting in the relatively uniform stress distribution and the decrement of stress in this region.

Figures 14 and 15 depict the von Mises stress contours of the left and right flange of the steel tube in the connection zone at the yield state. The upper part of the left flange given in Figure 14 is in tension and the lower part is in compression. This is because the left flange is connected with the composite beam under a negative moment. The right flange given in Figure 15 is connected with the beam under a positive moment. Consequently, the upper part of the flange is in compression and the lower part is in tension.

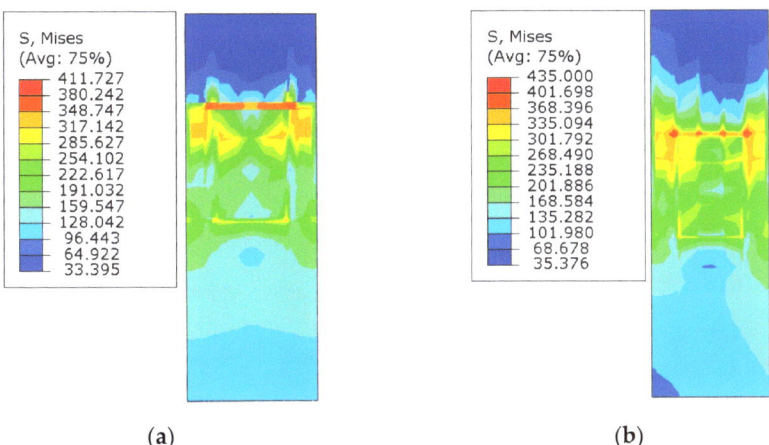

**Figure 14.** Von Mises stress contours of the left flange of steel tube in the connection zone: (**a**) RS connection; (**b**) RT connection.

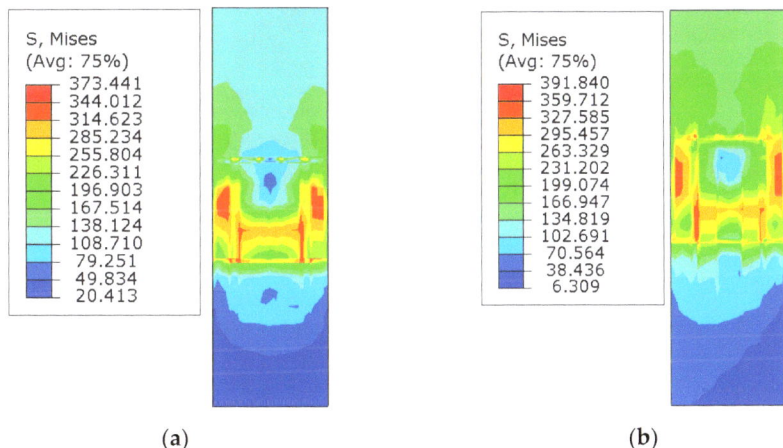

**Figure 15.** Von Mises stress contours of the right flange of steel tube in the connection zone: (**a**) RS connection; (**b**) RT connection.

From Figures 14 and 15, it can be found that:

1. For each specimen, the stress in the compressive region of the steel tube flange of the connection zone is smaller than that in the tensile region, due to the fact that the concrete in the beam participates in transferring the compressive force and thus increases the loading area of the flange and reduces the stress level in the compressive region. In addition, the concrete in the steel tube is closely compacted under compression, preventing the deformation of the tube wall, which contributes to reduced stress in this region. For the tensile region, however, the tensile forces are mainly transferred to the flange of the steel tube through the steel plate or rebar in the composite beam, resulting in higher stress.

2. For the RS connection, the stress in the left and right flanges of the tube adjacent to the concrete slab is smaller than that of the RT connection due to the fact that there are some holes on the surface of the tube to let the longitudinal rebars pass through, resulting in stress concentration in this region. Furthermore, the upper interior diaphragm of the RS connection can not only transfer the force in the longitudinal rebars but also provide extra support for the steel tube, which constrains the deformation of the column flange and hence reduces the stress in this region.

5.2.3. Stress Analysis of Concrete in Connection Zone

Figure 16 depicts the principal compressive stress $\sigma_3$ contours of the concrete in the connection zone for the RS connection and the RT connection at the yield state.

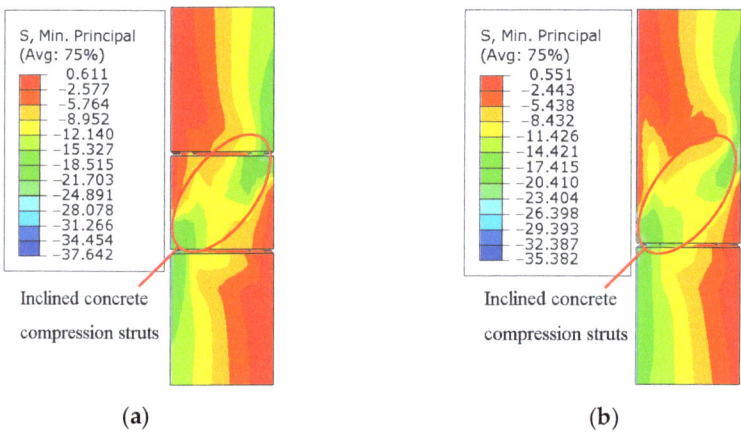

**Figure 16.** Principal compressive stress $\sigma_3$ contours of the concrete in connection zone at the yield state: (**a**) RS connection; (**b**) RT connection.

It can be seen that the inclined concrete compression strut has been formed along the diagonal line of the connection zone for each connection, and the principal compressive stress in the inclined concrete strut increases gradually from the center to the ends. Compared to the RT connection, the inclined concrete compression strut of the RS connection exhibits better behavior with a regular shape and higher stress level. This is mainly due to the fact that the upper and bottom internal diaphragm of the RS connection formed a confined space within the steel tube which gives a strong restraining effect on its internal concrete, and thus increases the main compressive stress of the concrete and develops the concrete material properties.

5.2.4. Stress Analysis of Rebars

Figure 17 shows the longitudinal stress distribution of rebars in the concrete slab for the RS connection and the RT connection at the yield state.

It can be seen that the maximum stress in both the continuous rebars and cutting rebars of the composite beam occurred near the tube wall, and the stress decreased as it moved away from the tube wall. For both specimens, the stress in the compressive region of the longitudinal rebars is significantly less than that in the tensile region. This indicates that the horizontal forces in the tensile slab are mainly resisted by the longitudinal rebars due to the lower concrete tensile strength, whereas the horizontal forces in the compressive slab are resisted by the longitudinal rebars and concrete together.

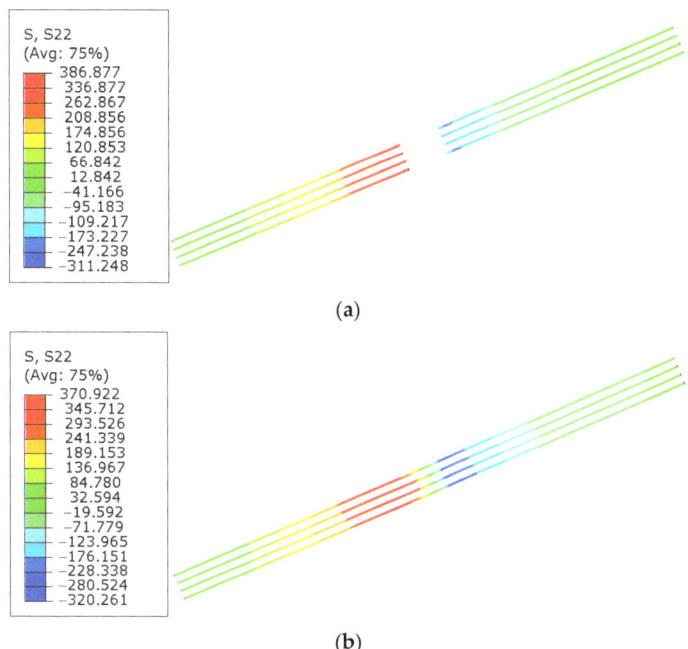

**Figure 17.** Longitudinal stress distribution of rebars in concrete slab at the yield state: (**a**) RS connection; (**b**) RT connection.

5.2.5. Stress Development of Steel Components

The stress development of the steel components in each connection is similar. Therefore, the RS connection is taken as an example to discuss the stress development of the steel components during the whole loading procedure. Figure 18 shows the von Mises stress contours of the RS connection under different states, including axial load on the column state, the yield state, and the ultimate state.

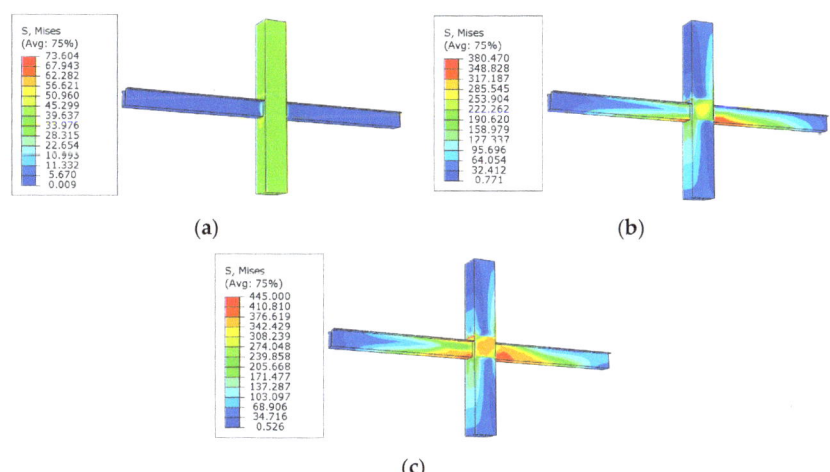

**Figure 18.** Development of von Mises stress of steel components: (**a**) von Mises stress contours of steel components subjected to axial load on the column; (**b**) von Mises stress contours of steel components at the yield state; (**c**) von Mises stress contours of steel components at the ultimate state.

When there is only the axial load imposed on the ends of the column, the stress is small and uniform in most regions of the steel tube, and the initial stress appears in the steel beam adjacent to the steel tube. The maximum stress is located in the region near the junction between the tensile bottom plate of the steel beam and the column after the vertical loads are applied at the beam ends. Consequently, the stress in this region reaches the yield strength of steel with the increase of the vertical loads. As the specimen is at the ultimate state, the stress in the bottom plate of the U-shaped steel beam near the connection zone has significantly exceeded the yield strength, especially for the tensile plate. However, the stress in the components that are far away from the connection zone is much smaller than the yield strength of the corresponding material.

## 6. Parametric Analysis

On the basis of the RS connection, parametric studies are conducted to investigate the influences of some parameters on the behavior of the connection between CFUS beams and CFSST columns. These parameters include: The thickness of the U-shaped steel, the ratio of the longitudinal rebar in the concrete slab, the strength of the concrete in the beam, the strength of the U-shaped steel, and the thickness of the internal diaphragm. All the specimens are designed to satisfy the seismic principle of 'strong column–weak beam and strong connection–weak members'. This is accomplished by limiting the beam-to-column linear stiffness ratio to less than 0.6, and the beam-to-column flexural capacity ratio to no more than 0.8 [24,25], resulting in failing at the beam ends for the connections.

### 6.1. Effects of Thickness of U-Shaped Steel

The comparison of load-displacement curves with different thicknesses of the U-shaped steel are shown in Figure 19. It can be seen that the loading capacity of the connection increases obviously with the increases in the thickness of the U-shaped steel under both positive and negative P, and that the increase of the loading capacity under positive P is bigger than that under negative P. In addition, the increased amplitude of loading capacity for the connection decreases with the increases of $t_b$. The loading capacity increases by about 20% when $t_b$ increases from 6 mm to 8 mm, while it increases only about 10% with $t_b$ from 10 mm to 12 mm. It can be concluded that the loading capacity of the connection is substantially improved when $t_b$ is increased within a certain range.

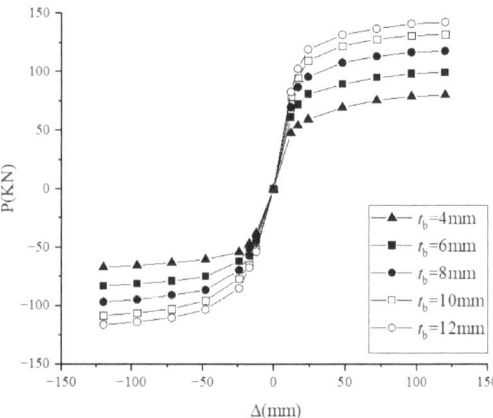

Figure 19. Thickness of U-shaped steel.

### 6.2. Effects of Ratio of Longitudinal Rebar in Concrete Slab

The comparisons of load-displacement curves with different ratios of the longitudinal rebars ($\rho$) are shown in Figure 20. It can be seen that the ratio of the longitudinal rebars has a notable effect on the loading capacity of the connection—especially under negative P. The loading capacity is increased by about 45% when $\rho$ is increased from 1.5% to 4.8% under negative P. However, the loading capacity only increased by about 15% when $\rho$ increased from 1.5% to 4.8% under positive P.

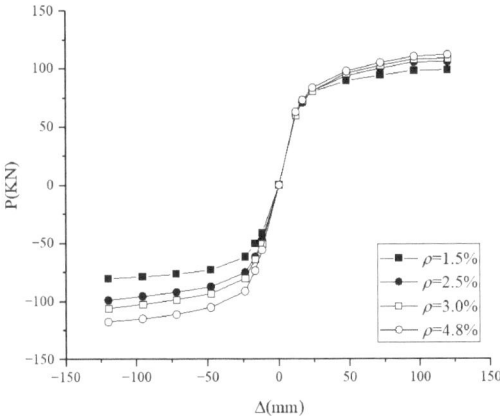

**Figure 20.** Ratio of longitudinal rebar in concrete slab.

### 6.3. Effects of Strength of Concrete in Beam

The comparisons of load-displacement curves with different strengths of concrete in the beam are shown in Figure 21. The strength of concrete in the beam has little effect on the loading capacity of the connection. The loading capacity under positive P is increased by about 10% when the concrete strength ($f_{cu}$) increased from 30 MPa to 60 MPa. However, the loading capacity under negative P faintly increases.

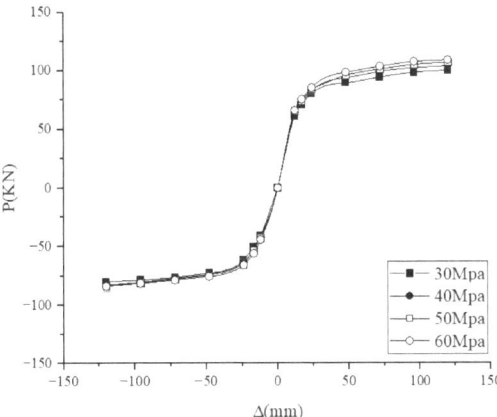

**Figure 21.** Strength of concrete in beam.

### 6.4. Effects of Strength of U-Shaped Steel

The comparisons of load-displacement curves with different strengths of the U-shaped steel are shown in Figure 22. The strength of the U-shaped steel has a definite effect on the loading capacity of the connection under both positive and negative P. The loading capacity is increased by about 20% when the steel yield strength ($f_y$) increased from 235 Mpa to 420 Mpa.

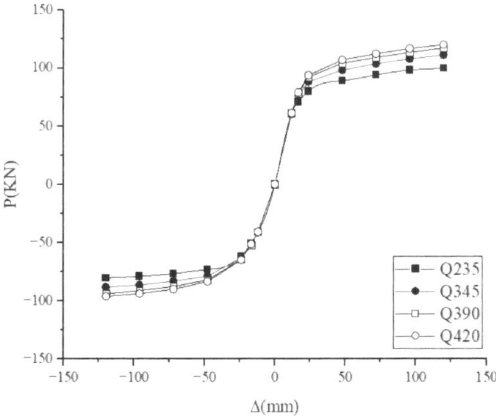

**Figure 22.** Strength of U-shaped steel.

*6.5. Effects of Thickness of Internal Diaphragm*

The comparisons of load-displacement curves with different thicknesses of the internal diaphragm ($h$) are shown in Figure 23. It can be seen that the thickness of the internal diaphragm has a slight influence on the loading capacity of the connection under both positive and negative P. The loading capacity hardly increases with an increase in $h$. This is due to all of the specimens meeting the seismic design principle of strong columns and weak beams, strong junctions and weak components. Therefore, the loading capacity of the connection is mainly dependent on that of the beam ends for the specimens that failed at the beam end.

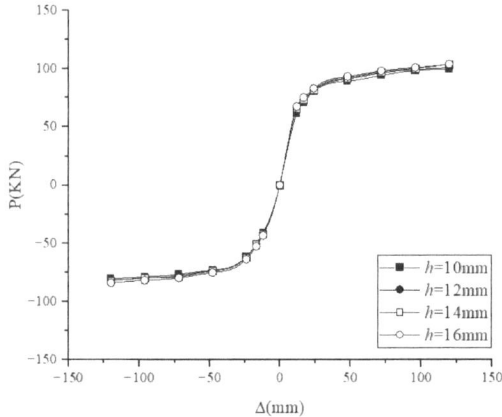

**Figure 23.** Thickness of internal diaphragm.

### 7. Conclusions

This paper presents two new types of connection details between CFUS beams and CFFST columns. The nonlinear FEA of connections is conducted using the validated model by the experimental results. The stress distribution of two new types of connections is discussed. Furthermore, the parametric studies are conducted to investigate the effects of some parameters, including the thickness of the U-shaped steel, the ratio of the longitudinal rebar in the concrete slab, the strength of concrete in the beam, the strength of the U-shaped steel, and the thickness of the internal diaphragm on the performances of the connections. The conclusions can be summarized as follows:

1. The numerical results are in agreement with the experimental results, which indicate that the developed finite element model could be used to analyze the behavior of the composite connection with proper precision.
2. The stress analysis shows that the stress in the tensile bottom plate of the U-shaped steel beam near the connection zone has reached the ultimate strength of the steel, while the stress in the components that are far away from the panel zone is much smaller when the RS and RT connection fail. Furthermore, for the RS connection, the stress comparison shows that not only the stress distribution in the flanges and webs of the steel tube near the junction is more uniform, but also the inclined concrete compression struts in the panel zone exhibit better behavior due to the upper internal diaphragm.
3. The parametric analysis indicates that the thickness of the U-shaped steel, the ratio of the longitudinal reinforcement in the concrete slab, and the strength of the U-shaped steel have a notable effect on the loading capacity of the connection, while the strength of concrete in the beam and the thickness of the internal diaphragm has a lighter effect on that.
4. Based on the parameter analysis results of the connections and construction practicability, the bearing capacity of connections can be improved by increasing the ratio of the longitudinal reinforcement in the concrete slab and the thickness of the U-shaped steel in practical engineering when the structural requirements of reinforcement and the design conditions of strong column and weak beam are met.

**Author Contributions:** Conceptualization, methodology, resources, and funding acquisition, Y.L.; formal analysis and investigation, Z.Z. and X.G.; data curation, Z.Z.; writing—original draft preparation, Y.L. and Z.Z.; writing—review and editing, S.Q. and Z.W. All authors have read and agreed to the published version of the manuscript.

**Funding:** This research was funded by the National Key Research and Development Program (SQ2020YFF0426523), the Research and Innovation Team Supported by the Ministry of Education (IRT13075), the Science and Technology Project of the Ministry of Housing and Urban-Rural Development (2019-k-073), and the Doctoral Foundation of Shandong Jianzhu University (Z0320).

**Acknowledgments:** All of the specimens were fabricated by Jincheng Steel Structure Company in the Shandong Province. The numerical calculations in this paper have been done on the supercomputing system in Shandong Jianzhu University. The authors appreciate this help.

**Conflicts of Interest:** The authors declare no conflict of interest.

# References

1. Nie, J.G.; Tao, M.X.; Huang, Y.; Tian, S.M.; Chen, G. Research advances of steel-concrete composite structural systems. *J. Build. Struct.* **2010**, *31*, 71–80. (In Chinese)
2. Oehlers, D.J. Composite profiled beams. *J. Struct. Eng.* **1993**, *119*, 1085–1100. [CrossRef]
3. Oehlers, D.J.; Wright, H.D.; Burnet, M.J. Flexural strength of profiled beams. *J. Struct. Eng.* **1994**, *120*, 378–393. [CrossRef]
4. Uy, B.; Bradford, M.A. Ductility of profiled composite beams. Part I: Experimental study. *J. Struct. Eng.* **1995**, *121*, 876–882. [CrossRef]
5. Uy, B.; Bradford, M.A. Ductility of profiled composite beams. Part II: Analytical study. *J. Struct. Eng.* **1995**, *121*, 883–889. [CrossRef]
6. Chen, L.H.; Li, S.T.; Zhang, H.Y.; Wu, X.F. Experimental study on mechanical performance of checked steel-encased concrete composite beam. *J. Constr. Steel. Res.* **2018**, *143*, 223–232. [CrossRef]
7. Keo, P.; Lepourry, C.; Somja, H.; Palas, F. Behavior of a new shear connector for U-shaped steel-concrete hybrid beams. *J. Constr. Steel. Res.* **2018**, *145*, 153–166. [CrossRef]
8. Parvaria, A.; Zahraib, S.M.; Mirhosseinia, S.M. Numerical and experimental study on the behavior of drilled flange steel beam to CFT column connections. *J. Struct.* **2020**, *28*, 726–740. [CrossRef]
9. Liu, H.Q.; Liu, Y.Z.; Huo, J.S. Cyclic behaviour of a novel steel beam-to-prefabricated CFST column connection with threaded sleeve bolts. *J. Struct.* **2021**, *34*, 615–629. [CrossRef]
10. Xue, J.Y.; Li, H.C.; Chen, X. Experimental research on seismic damage of T-shaped CFST column to steel beam joints. *J. Struct.* **2022**, *38*, 1380–1396. [CrossRef]

11. Fan, J.C.; Zhao, J.H.; Zhu, Q. Seismic behavior and analytical model for a fully bolted joint between CFDST columns and steel beams. *J. Struct.* **2022**, *42*, 515–530. [CrossRef]
12. Zhang, A.L.; Li, C.H.; Liu, X.C. Seismic performance of joint for H-beam to CFST column with field-bolted flange-splicing. *J. Constr. Steel. Res.* **2022**, *196*, 107375. [CrossRef]
13. Kim, S.B.; Ham, J.T.; Lee, C.N.; Kim, S.S. Study on the structural behavior of TSC beam-to-SRC column connection. *J. Archit. Inst. Korea* **2006**, *22*, 55–62. (In Korean)
14. Park, H.G.; Hwang, H.J.; Lee, C.H.; Park, C.H.; Lee, C.N. Cyclic loading test for concrete-filled U-shaped steel beam-RC column connections. *J. Eng. Struct.* **2012**, *36*, 325–336. [CrossRef]
15. Lee, C.H. Cyclic seismic testing of composite concrete filled U-shaped steel beam to H-shaped column connections. *J. Struct. Eng.* **2013**, *139*, 360–378. [CrossRef]
16. Hwang, H.J. Cyclic loading test for beam-column connections of concrete-filled U-shaped steel beams and concrete-encased steel angle columns. *J. Struct. Eng.* **2015**, *141*, 04015020-1–04015020-12. [CrossRef]
17. Ding, X.B.; Yang, F. Experimental investigation and finite element analysis of concrete-filled square steel tubular column to cold bending U-shaped steel beam joint. *J. Ind. Constr.* **2019**, *49*, 153–159. (In Chinese)
18. Chen, L.H.; Chen, K.; Xia, D.R. Experiment study on seismic performance of H-shaped steel beam joint to square tubular column connection by joint field column wall reinforcement. *J. Build. Struct.* **2021**, *51*, 9–16. (In Chinese)
19. *JGJ 101-96*; Specification for Seismic Test of Buildings. China Architecture and Building Press: Beijing, China, 1996.
20. Han, L.H. *Concrete-Filled Steel Tubular Structures*; Science Press: Beijing, China, 2016.
21. *GB 50010-2010*; Code for Design of Concrete Structures. China Building Industry Press: Beijing, China, 2010.
22. Du, G.F.; Bie, X.M. Study on constitutive model of shear performance in panel zone of connections composed of CFSSTCs and steel-concrete composite beams with external diaphragms. *J. Eng. Struct.* **2018**, *155*, 178–191. [CrossRef]
23. Ozkilic, Y.O. Cyclic and monotonic performance of stiffened extended end-plate connections with large-sized bolts and thin end-plates. *J. Bull. Earthq. Eng.* **2022**, *20*, 7441–7475. [CrossRef]
24. Li, W.; Han, L.H. Seismic performance of CFST column-to-steel beam joints with RC slab: Analysis. *J. Constr. Steel. Res.* **2011**, *67*, 127–139. [CrossRef]
25. Nie, J.G.; Qin, K.; Cai, C.S. Seismic behavior of connections composed of CFSSTCS and steel-concrete composite beams-finite element analysis. *J. Constr. Steel. Res.* **2008**, *64*, 680–688. [CrossRef]

**Disclaimer/Publisher's Note:** The statements, opinions and data contained in all publications are solely those of the individual author(s) and contributor(s) and not of MDPI and/or the editor(s). MDPI and/or the editor(s) disclaim responsibility for any injury to people or property resulting from any ideas, methods, instructions or products referred to in the content.

Article

# Experimental Study on Flexural Performance of Precast Prestressed Concrete Beams with Fiber Reinforcement

Jingjing Zhang [1], Chao Liu [1], Jianning Wang [2,3,*], Xuguang Feng [4] and Huanqin Liu [1]

[1] School of Architectural Engineering, North China Institute of Aerospace Engineering, Langfang 065000, China; zjj1990@nciae.edu.cn (J.Z.)
[2] China National Machinery Industry Co., Ltd., Beijing 100080, China
[3] Department of Civil Engineering, Tsinghua University, Beijing 100084, China
[4] China Academy of Building Research, Beijing 100013, China
* Correspondence: wangjianninghebut@163.com

**Abstract:** Fiber-reinforced concrete (FRC) has good toughness and a gentle stress–strain softening section, which can improve the inherent defects of concrete material such as high brittleness, easy cracking, and poor fracture toughness. In this paper, carbon fiber, aramid fiber and mixed fiber are introduced to enhance the performance of precast prestressed concrete beams (PPCB). The effects of different fiber types and adding rate on mechanical properties of FRC were studied via axial compression test and four-point bending test. Based on the flexural performance test of precast FRC beams, the failure form and the improvement degree of flexural ability of the beams were analyzed. Moreover, the load–deflection curve and the quantified ductility index obtained by the test were discussed, and the law of the improvement effect of fiber type on flexural property was revealed. The results show that the optimal addition rate of fiber is 0.6%. In addition, the addition of fiber significantly increased the cracking load and ultimate bearing capacity of the test beam, whereby the average increase in cracking load and ultimate bearing capacity was 40% and 20%, respectively. At the same time, the ductility of the beam is obviously enhanced by the action of fibers, among which the hybrid fiber has the best effect. Specifically, the ductility coefficient analysis verifies that aramid fiber plays an important role in improving the ductility of the components.

**Keywords:** precast prestressed concrete beam (PPCB); fiber-reinforced concrete (FRC); fiber prestressed concrete beam (FPCB); flexural performance

**Citation:** Zhang, J.; Liu, C.; Wang, J.; Feng, X.; Liu, H. Experimental Study on Flexural Performance of Precast Prestressed Concrete Beams with Fiber Reinforcement. *Buildings* **2023**, *13*, 1982. https://doi.org/10.3390/buildings13081982

Academic Editor: Ahmed Senouci

Received: 12 July 2023
Revised: 24 July 2023
Accepted: 1 August 2023
Published: 3 August 2023

**Copyright:** © 2023 by the authors. Licensee MDPI, Basel, Switzerland. This article is an open access article distributed under the terms and conditions of the Creative Commons Attribution (CC BY) license (https://creativecommons.org/licenses/by/4.0/).

## 1. Introduction

In recent years, China's transportation industry has achieved historic milestones. By the end of 2022, the total length of the comprehensive transportation network had exceeded 6 million kilometers, ranking first globally in both high-speed rail and expressway mileage [1]. Bridges play a vital role as key nodes in transportation infrastructure, and the safety of their structures is crucial for the normal functioning of cities and the coordinated development of regional economies. According to incomplete statistics, the total number of road and railway bridges in China exceeds 1 million, thus establishing China's status as a bridge construction country, of which prestressed concrete bridges account for a considerable proportion [2,3].

With the advancement and widespread adoption of prefabricated construction technology, the prefabricated construction technique for bridge structures has seen rapid development in China [4]. In this innovative approach, raw materials such as steel and concrete are transported to prefabrication plants, where components forming the main structure are produced on assembly lines. Furthermore, the manufactured components undergo maintenance and storage in the prefabrication area until they are transported to the construction site as per the production plan and lifted into position to complete the construction of the main structure. Overall, the construction process resembles assembling blocks, enabling the factory prefabrication and standardization of bridge construction [5]. Compared to traditional cast-in-place methods, prefabricated construction offers advantages such as faster construction speed, reduced on-site personnel, and higher project quality. The construction process no longer requires rebar binding and wet concrete operations, resulting in minimal generation of construction waste, significantly reduced construction noise and dust pollution, and substantial time savings [6,7]. Additionally, the substantial reduction in the number of construction workers, construction waste, and carbon emissions contributes directly to the goals of achieving carbon peak and carbon neutrality [8]. Therefore, in the context of China's strong advocacy and development of green and environmentally friendly prefabricated construction technology, the prefabrication and industrialization of prestressed concrete bridges have experienced rapid growth [9].

Concrete materials possess inherent drawbacks such as high brittleness, susceptibility to cracking, low tensile strength, and poor fracture toughness. Previous studies indicate that more than half of the prestressed concrete bridges face problems such as concrete surface cracking and reinforcement corrosion due to increased traffic and ongoing harmful environmental impacts. When significant cracks manifest in prestressed concrete structures, the concrete cover in some bridges undergoes detachment, thereby exposing and corroding the reinforcements, which severely compromises the safety of the bridge structures. Consequently, the issue of cracking defects in prestressed concrete bridges remains a focal point of engineering research.

However, fiber materials with high strength and toughness properties can effectively address the limitations of concrete materials [10,11]. The combination of concrete and fibers facilitates the maximization of their respective advantages, resulting in the development of fiber-reinforced concrete (FRC) with enhanced toughness and ductility [12,13]. In recent years, carbon fiber, aramid fiber, polyethylene fiber, and basalt fiber are the four fiber types that have developed most rapidly, and they have become the main raw materials for improving concrete performance, among which carbon fiber and aramid fiber are the most widely used [14,15]. Considerable progress has been made in the research of FRC, including material mix design, mechanical properties, and load-bearing characteristics. Ayub et al. [16] investigated the mechanical properties of short-cut basalt FRC with a fiber volume fraction of 3%, and they observed a significant improvement in the flexural performance of concrete after adding basalt fibers. Lee et al. [17] found that although both steel fiber and glass fiber have a certain degree of improvement in flexural toughness, the effect of steel fiber is better. Specifically, after the bending strength reaches its peak, there is still about 30% of the bearing capacity, and this gradually decreases until it is completely destroyed. Nie et al. [18] observed that aramid fiber presented better properties than carbon fiber to improve the mechanical performance of cement mortars. Avanaki et al. [19,20] carried out a study on the seismic performance of FRC tunnel segments, and they discussed the influence of different steel FRC composite materials on the bending response of segment joints under earthquake via numerical and experimental methods. Halvaei et al. [21] introduced carbon textiles and chopped carbon fibers as reinforcing materials of engineered cementitious composite (ECC). Wille et al. [22] proposed a new tensile device and carried out uniaxial tensile properties tests of ultra-high performance fiber-reinforced concrete (UHP-FRC) considering different volume fractions. Deng et al. [23] conducted four-point bending tests on 16 groups of ductile FRC specimens, finding that the flexural strength and bending toughness of the specimens gradually increased with an increase in fiber dosage. Wang et al. [24] examined the influence of carbon fiber length and stirrup ratio on the flexural capacity of carbon FRC beams. The results showed that carbon fiber effectively improved the brittle failure of the concrete beams, and as the carbon fiber length increased, the deflection at failure of the beams also increased, while the stirrup ratio had minimal impact on the deflection and strain of carbon FRC beams. Li [25] performed flexural performance tests on six PVA-FRC beams and conducted a detailed analysis of the effects of fiber volume fraction on the cracking load, ultimate load, and flexural stiffness of the concrete beams. Considering the excellent intrinsic strength, micro-fibrillated surface characteristics, and interfacial properties of aramid fibers, the research by Qiao et al. [26] indicated that aramid fibers exhibit superior crack resistance compared to polypropylene fibers. Meanwhile, aramid fibers have a positive impact on reinforcement and toughening under low water–cement ratio conditions. The improvement in flexural strength in high-fiber-content ECC using aramid fibers is significantly better than that achieved by PVA fibers, albeit with a slightly smaller deflection. Additionally, the employment of multiple types of hybrid fibers is currently a prominent research focus in FRC. When two or more types of fibers are added, the mechanical strength of concrete is further enhanced compared to single fiber reinforcement. Krūmiņš et al. [27] conducted four-point bending tests on hybrid FRC and observed an overall improvement in the performance of the concrete beams.

The present study investigates the influence of different types and proportions of carbon fiber, aramid fiber, and hybrid fibers on the basic mechanical properties of concrete specimens. The conducted tests include axial compressive tests and three-point bending tests. By studying the effect of fiber type and dosage on the properties of FRC, the flexure properties of precast prestressed concrete beam (PPCB) are further studied on the basis of selecting the best dosage ratio. The load-bearing process, failure modes, and crack propagation patterns of PPCB are systematically analyzed. The research findings provide important references for enhancing the performance and structural safety and durability of existing bridge structures.

## 2. Mechanical Properties of FRC

### 2.1. Material Properties

Carbon fiber (CF) has high strength and light weight, and is a good reinforcement material, which is widely used in anti-seepage [28] and anti-cracking projects [29]. Similarly, aramid fiber (AF) is an excellent toughening material with a high specific strength, large specific modulus, and high temperature resistance [30]. Therefore, CF and AF are selected as the main research objects in this paper for improving the toughness and crack resistance of concrete. As shown in Figure 1, CF and AF are produced by Nanjing Mankat Technology Co., Ltd. of Nanjing, China and Zhejiang Xuantai New Materials Co., Ltd. of Tongxiang, China, respectively. The short-cut fiber length is 1.2 mm, and the mechanical properties of the two short-cut fiber materials are shown in Table 1.

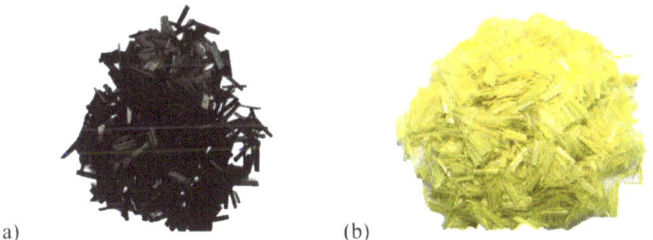

(a) (b)

**Figure 1.** The short-cut fibers used in the test: (**a**) CF, (**b**) AF.

**Table 1.** Mechanical properties of fiber materials.

| Fiber Type | Density (kg/m$^3$) | Cut Length (mm) | Diameter (μm) | Tensile Strength (MPa) | Tensile Modulus (GPa) | Elongation (%) |
|---|---|---|---|---|---|---|
| Carbon fiber (CF) | 1750 | 12 | 8 | 3530 | 240 | 1.5 |
| Aramid fiber (AF) | 1440 | 12 | 12 | 3150 | 80 | 3.6 |

### 2.2. Experimental Design

Compressive strength and flexural strength are important mechanical properties of cement-based materials. FRC has good toughness under compression and bending, and the influence of different fiber content on the mechanical properties of FRC is obvious. In order to obtain the best performance of FRC, it is necessary to carry out a basic mechanical study on the FRC test block to determine the optimal fiber content. The basic mechanical properties of FRC include axial compressive strength and flexural strength. During the test, CF represents the carbon fiber test block, AF refers to the aramid fiber test block, and CAF is the carbon and aramid 1:1 mixed fiber test block. The basic mechanical properties tests of FRC were carried out in the laboratory of Beijing University of Technology. The relevant test procedures were carried out according to the provisions of the "Standard for test methods of concrete physical and mechanical properties" (GB/T 50081-2019) [31].

A total of 77 groups (3 in each group) of prismatic blocks were set up in the experiment. Among them, 29 groups of 150 × 150 × 300 mm test blocks were used for compressive test, and 29 groups of 150 × 150 × 300 mm specimens were used for elastic modulus test. In addition, the bending test used 19 groups of 100 × 100 × 400 mm blocks, equaling a total of 57 blocks.

### 2.3. Axial Compressive Strength

There are three test blocks in each group in the test, and the test block whose compressive strength is closest to the average value and whose failure phenomenon is representative is selected for analysis, as shown in Figure 2.

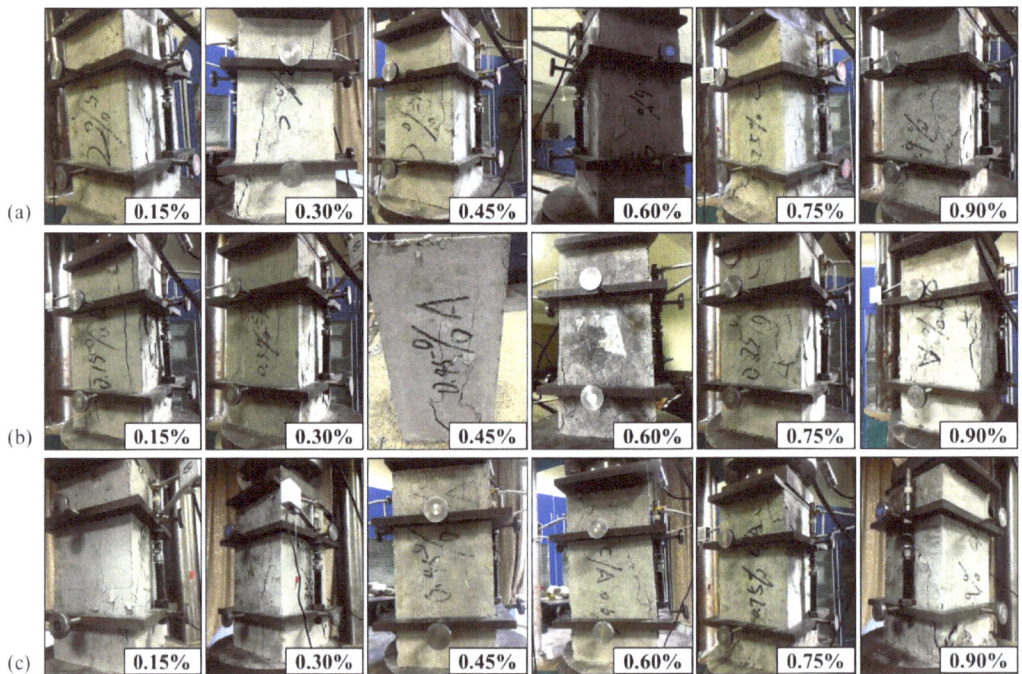

**Figure 2.** Compression failure of concrete test blocks reinforced with different fibers: (**a**) CF, (**b**) AF, (**c**) CAF.

As can be seen from Figure 2, the failure process of FRC is obviously different from that of ordinary concrete. X-type cracks appear in the section of ordinary concrete prismatic test block when it is compressed, and concrete collapse and sudden reduction in strength occur when it reaches peak load, which is a typical brittle failure. During the compression process of the fiber concrete test block, due to the cracking resistance and toughening effect of the fiber, the compressive toughness increases significantly. When the load reaches about 40% of the ultimate load, vertical micro-cracks appear in the middle of the specimen. With the increase in the load, the cracks extend to both ends, and new vertical cracks appear around the specimen. Failure of the test block was declared, with no spalling of concrete. The failure modes observed from this test are similar to those investigated by Huang et al. [10], which clearly indicated the action of the FRC.

The compressive strength results of the test block are shown in Table 2. Combined with the analysis of the failure phenomenon of the test block, when the fiber content is small, the compressive strength is slightly improved, and the brittleness property is greatly improved. When the fiber content is increased to 0.6%, the compressive strength is the largest improvement, and the ductility property is improved compared with that of the 0.3% doped block. However, when the content is increased to 0.9%, the compressive strength of the test block is decreased. The reason for this result is that excessive fiber content leads to clumping, forming weak points and reducing ductility. Therefore, when the fiber content is 0.6%, the FRC performance is better played.

Table 2. Axial compressive strength $f_{ck}$ of concrete test block (unit: MPa).

| Fiber Type | Fiber Content (%) | | | | | | |
|---|---|---|---|---|---|---|---|
| | 0.00 | 0.15 | 0.30 | 0.45 | 0.60 | 0.75 | 0.90 |
| CF | 40.4 | 39.2 | 39.3 | 40.5 | 41.9 | 38.8 | 37.8 |
| AF | 40.4 | 38.7 | 39.5 | 40.9 | 44.3 | 39.4 | 36.9 |
| CAF | 40.4 | 39.7 | 39.4 | 40.6 | 42.4 | 41.2 | 40.5 |

*2.4. Flexural Performance*

2.4.1. Flexural Strength

For the FRC bending performance, 100 × 100 × 400 mm beams are used, the calculated span is 300 mm, and the supports are located 50 mm from each end, and the test device and loading results are shown in Figure 3. During the loading process of the FRC test block, many micro-cracks are produced across the pure bend section, with the width of one main crack increasing; then, the load gradually decreases, and failure is declared, and although the deflection of the test block is large, the crack does not penetrate it, as shown in Figure 3c; and the test block can still maintain good integrity. As a control group, the failure of the ordinary concrete test block occurred very suddenly, accompanied by a "bang", the loading point on one side of the test block suddenly broke into two segments, and the load curve displayed by the system dropped sharply.

**Figure 3.** Loading and failure diagram of bending test: (**a**) loading diagram, (**b**) failure pattern of plain concrete; (**c**) failure pattern of FRC.

According to the "Standard for Test Methods for Physical and Mechanical Properties of Concrete" [31], the flexural strength of FRC test blocks under different fiber types and fiber content is calculated, as shown in Table 3. It can be seen from the table that when the fiber addition amount is small, the bending strength of the test block is basically unchanged, and when the addition rate is greater than 0.45%, the bending strength of the test block is greatly improved, and the increase is about 20%. The trend is similar to that of previous studies [10]. Among them, carbon fiber has the greatest effect of improving the flexural strength, followed by hybrid fiber (CAF).

**Table 3.** Flexural strength $f_p$ of concrete test block (unit: MPa).

| Fiber Type | Fiber Content (%) | | | | | | |
|---|---|---|---|---|---|---|---|
| | 0.00 | 0.15 | 0.30 | 0.45 | 0.60 | 0.75 | 0.90 |
| CF | 5.82 | 5.80 | 5.62 | 5.92 | 7.26 | 6.49 | 7.00 |
| AF | 5.82 | 5.72 | 5.94 | 5.89 | 6.18 | 5.85 | 5.94 |
| CAF | 5.82 | 5.81 | 6.32 | 6.64 | 7.00 | 6.52 | 6.25 |

The curves of load and deflection with loading time are shown in Figure 4. It can be seen from the curve that carbon fiber still shows a certain brittleness when the content is low; that is, the falling section of the curve is relatively steep. When the block load is reduced to half of the ultimate load, the deflection value of the AF block is the largest, followed by CAF, which shows that aramid fiber plays an important role in improving the toughness of concrete.

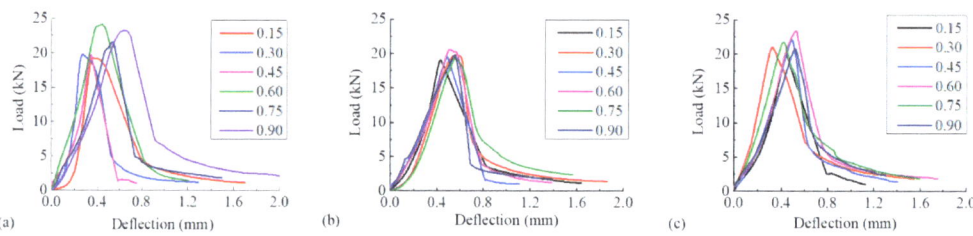

**Figure 4.** The load–deflection curve of FRC: (**a**) CF, (**b**) AF, (**c**) CAF.

2.4.2. Flexural Toughness (FT)

Due to the large human error in the judgment of initial crack deflection, Banthia et al. [32] proposed a toughness analysis method bounded by peak load, which divided the load–deflection curve area into two parts, pre-peak ($E_{pre}$) and post-peak ($E_{post,m}$), and considered the energy consumption of fiber concrete during deformation with specific deflection ($L/m$) as the variable. The proposed resilience indicator $PCS_m$ is defined as follows:

$$PCS_m = \frac{E_{post,m} \, L}{\left(\frac{L}{m} - \delta\right) bh^2} \quad (1)$$

where $E_{post,m}$ is the area surrounded by the load–deflection curve after peak loading; $L$ is the span of the beam (take 300 mm); $\delta$ is the deflection value corresponding to the peak load; $b$ and $h$ are the width and height of the beam section, respectively; and $L/m$ is defined as the deflection corresponding to the load falling to 20% of the peak load.

According to Equation (1), the flexural toughness index $PCS_m$ of the FRC test block is calculated as shown in Table 4. On the whole, the flexural toughness of FRC test block is significantly improved compared with that of the ordinary concrete test block, the improvement effect of aramid fiber on the toughness of concrete test block is more obvious, and the maximum increase range is 235%. The degree of improvement in mixed fibers was secondary, reflecting the positive effect of mixing the two fibers.

**Table 4.** Flexural toughness $PCS_m$ of concrete test block.

| Fiber Type | Fiber Content (%) | | | | | | |
|---|---|---|---|---|---|---|---|
| | 0.00 | 0.15 | 0.30 | 0.45 | 0.60 | 0.75 | 0.90 |
| CF | 1.07 | 0.86 | 0.73 | 1.15 | 2.86 | 2.44 | 2.56 |
| AF | 1.07 | 1.59 | 2.53 | 2.39 | 2.73 | 2.53 | 3.59 |
| CAF | 1.07 | 1.68 | 1.32 | 2.63 | 3.37 | 2.04 | 2.95 |

## 3. Experimental Program of FPCB

### 3.1. Element Design

According to the results of the mechanical properties of the FRC test block, 0.6% was selected as the optimal fiber addition rate, and the bending performance of the fiber concrete test beam was tested. All test members are simple support beams, rectangular sections are 200 mm × 180 mm, the total length of the beam is 4 m, and the calculated span diameter is 3.7 m. The upper, middle, and lower ends of the beam are equipped with 2φ6 non-prestressed steel bars, all test beams are equipped with stirrups of No. 12 iron wire φ2.8@100, and the stirrups within 500 mm at each end of the beam are encrypted to φ2.8@50. The ordinary steel bar used in the component is HPB300, and the prestressed steel bar adopts φ7 prestressed steel wire, and its tensile stress is 0.73 times the standard value of tensile strength and the maximum tensile value does not exceed 1.05 times, and the material parameters of the steel bar are shown in Table 5. The detailed reinforcement details of the PPCB are shown in Figure 5, and the production process of the components is shown in Figure 6.

**Table 5.** Mechanical properties of rebar materials.

| Rebar Type | Diameter (mm) | Yield Strength (MPa) | Ultimate Strength (MPa) | Elongation (%) |
|---|---|---|---|---|
| Regular rebar | 6 | 312 | 407 | 25 |
| Prestressing tendon | 7 | 1410 | 1603 | 4.2 |

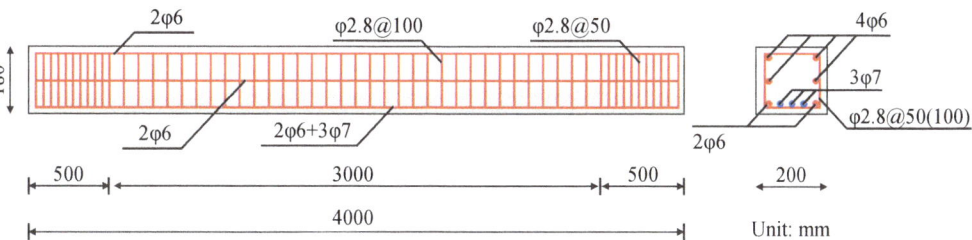

**Figure 5.** Dimensions and reinforcement of PPCB.

**Figure 6.** Preparation of PPCB: (**a**) lashing of rebar, (**b**) tensioning prestressed tendons, (**c**) concreting; (**d**) steam curing.

### 3.2. Load Equipment and System

The schematic diagram of the test loading and the location of the measurement points are shown in Figure 7. The test adopts the three-point loading method, a total of 4 test beams, including 1 ordinary concrete prestressed beam for the control test, and 3 concrete beams mixed with different fibers. During the test, L represents the prototype scaled test beam, CL is the carbon fiber test beam, AL is the aramid fiber test beam, and CAL refers to the carbon and aramid 1:1 mixed fiber test beam. The loading test adopts a hierarchical loading system, and before the cracks of the test beam, 3 kN is loaded in each stage, and data acquisition and crack observation are started after each stage is loaded for 10 min. When loaded to 80% of the calculated value of cracking load, the loading of each stage is changed to 1 kN; after the cracking of the test beam, it is changed to 3 kN per stage for loading; and, when the load reaches 80% of the calculated value of the bending bearing capacity, the displacement control is used to obtain the accurate ultimate bearing capacity, maximum deflection, and maximum crack width.

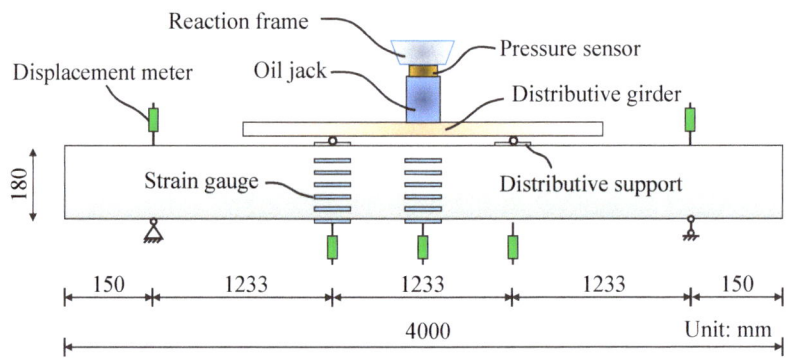

**Figure 7.** Sensor used in the test.

## 4. Experimental Results and Discussion

### 4.1. Failure Pattern

For the prototype beam L, the first crack appeared near the loading point when the load was increased to 12 kN. As the load increased, new cracks continued to form, and when loaded to 24 kN, the cracks were essentially continuous. Among them, the first major crack developed at the fastest rate, and the deflection of the beam increased significantly. Finally, when the load reached 38.7 kN, the tension reinforcement yielded, the surface concrete spalled, and the test beam failed. The failure modes of the PPCB test beams are shown in Figure 8. The test process showed that the first crack appeared in the beams when the loads reached 17 kN, 16 kN, and 16.5 kN, respectively. As the loading continued, the number of cracks increased. Unlike the prototype beam, when loaded to 80% of the ultimate load, the crack quantity in the FRC-enhanced beams stabilized, and the crack height was smaller than that of the prototype beam L. Among them, the crack development in beam CL was the slowest, with the fewest cracks, only 15. The final failure mode was the crushing of the upper concrete and crack overloading. Beam AL had an increased range and number of cracks compared to beam CL, showing good ductility. Even after the crack width exceeded the limit, the beam deflection continued to increase until the reinforcement yielded, without concrete crushing. Beam CAL exhibited a positive hybrid effect, with a significant redistribution of stresses after cracking. The crack distribution was the widest, and the crack spacing and width were the smallest, and in the end, it produced 21 cracks.

Table 6 presents the cracking load, yielding load, and ultimate load, as well as the converted section bending moments for the four test beams under static loading. From Table 6, it can be observed that the cracking load, yielding load, and ultimate load of FRC beams have all increased, with minimum increases of 30%, 14%, and 12%, respectively. This indicates that the use of fibers has greatly improved the drawbacks of concrete, such as brittleness and susceptibility to cracking. Carbon fiber has the largest influence on the cracking load and flexural performance of the test beams, followed by hybrid fibers.

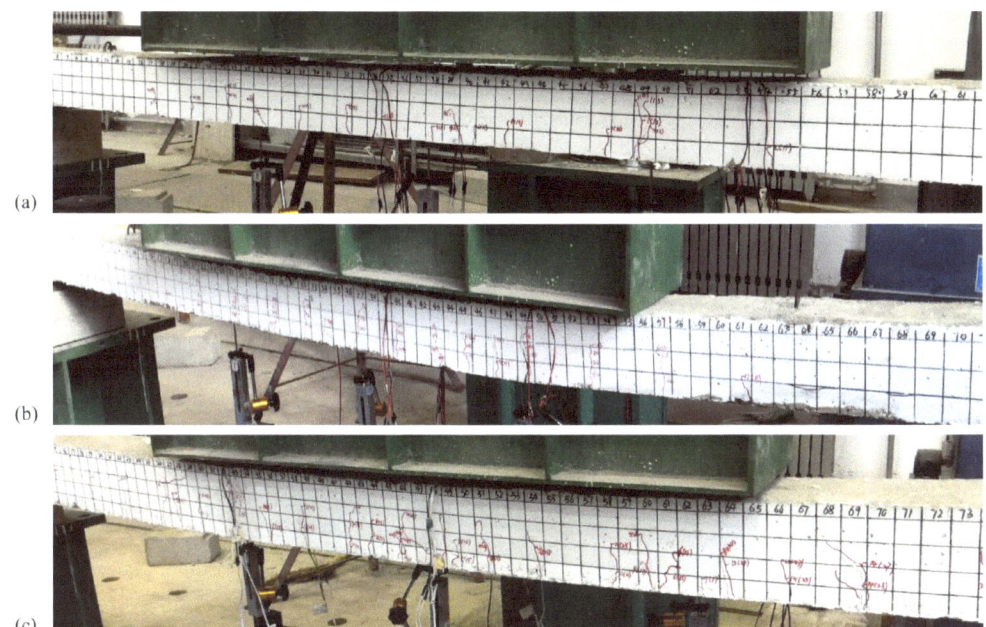

**Figure 8.** Failure diagram of prefabricated beams: (**a**) CL, (**b**) AL, (**c**) CAL.

**Table 6.** Flexural test results.

| Beam Type | Cracking Load $F_{cr}$ (kN) | Cracking Moment $M_{cr}$ (kN·m) | Yield Load $F_y$ (kN) | Yield Moment $M_y$ (kN·m) | Ultimate Load $F_u$ (kN) | Ultimate Moment $M_u$ (kN·m) |
|---|---|---|---|---|---|---|
| L | 12.0 | 7.4 | 30.9 | 19.09 | 38.8 | 23.9 |
| CL | 17.0 | 10.5 | 41.6 | 25.64 | 49.0 | 30.2 |
| AL | 16.1 | 9.9 | 35.3 | 21.78 | 43.5 | 26.8 |
| CAL | 16.5 | 10.2 | 38.3 | 23.61 | 44.9 | 27.7 |

### 4.2. Strain Results of Concrete

During the bending test, concrete strains along the height of the cross-section at the mid-span were measured for the four test beams. Figure 9 shows the development of concrete strains at different load levels before failure. It should be noted that due to the gradual increase in load during the test, the strains at the bottom of the beam exceeded the limit tensile value and caused damage to the strain gauges, resulting in missing data.

Figure 9a for beam L, it can be observed that the strain and load of the concrete at the mid-span cross-section are directly proportional. Under the first two load levels, the stress–strain curve of the concrete cross-section is linear, and the neutral axis of the test beam continuously shifts upward as the load increases, in accordance with the assumption of a plane section. In the initial loading stage, the neutral axis of prototype beam L is around 80 mm. As the load increases, the tension zone of the concrete develops cracks and gradually becomes inactive, causing the height of the compressed zone to decrease and the neutral axis to move upward. When the test beam is close to failure, the neutral axis reaches around 110 mm, with a significant upward shift. At the point of imminent failure, cracks develop rapidly, resulting in damage to the strain gauge at the bottom of the compressed zone, leading to missing strain values for the last two load levels.

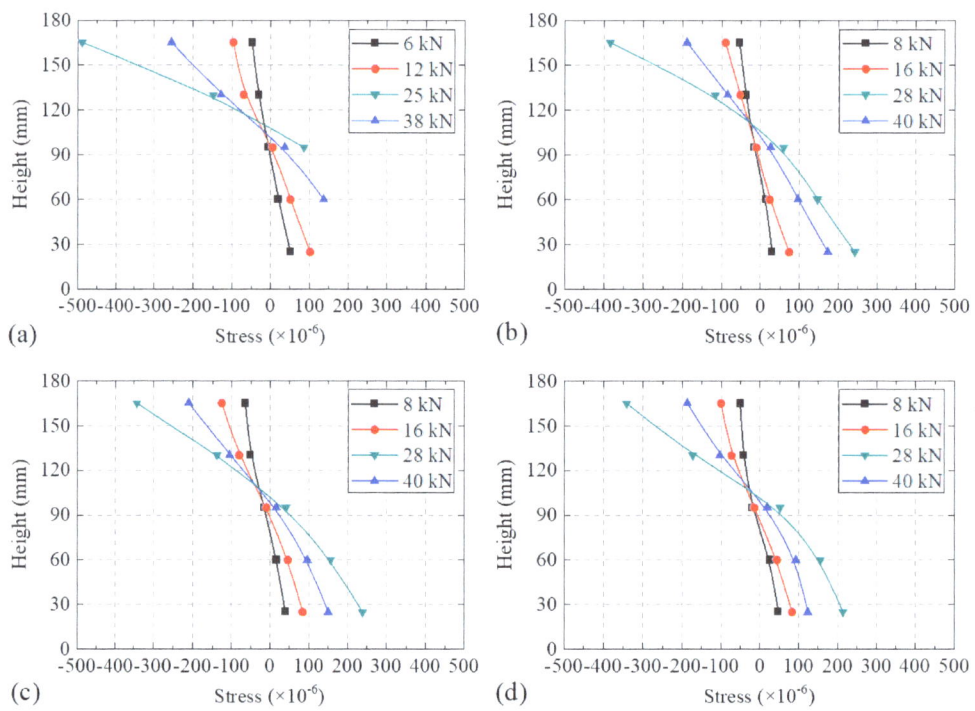

**Figure 9.** Variation in concrete strain with height in mid-span section: (**a**) L, (**b**) CL, (**c**) AL, (**d**) CAL.

Figure 9b–d show that under the various load levels, the concrete strains of the FRC-enhanced beams along the cross-section height generally follow the assumption of a plane section. Before the concrete cracks, the position of the neutral axis is around 80 mm, and as the load continues to increase, the concrete gradually cracks, causing the neutral axis to move upward. Near the point of failure, the neutral axis is around 102 mm, slightly lower compared to beam L. Among the beams, the neutral axis of beam CL has the slowest upward movement, followed by beam CAL. Additionally, the inclusion of carbon fiber, aramid fiber, and hybrid fibers results in smaller concrete strains compared to ordinary concrete strains under the same load. This indicates that the fibers in the concrete act as micro-reinforcement, sharing the load with the internal reinforcement of the beam. It not only improves the ultimate load-carrying capacity of the test beams but also effectively delays the occurrence and development of cracks.

### 4.3. Strain Results of Rebar

In the rebar strain analysis, it is noted that the steel reinforcement in the bending members is the main load-bearing component. For the partially prestressed concrete beams with a low reinforcement ratio, once the mild steel reinforcement yields, it indicates that the beam is approaching failure. Therefore, it is necessary to analyze the load–rebar strain relationship and investigate the influence of different treatment methods on the flexural performance of partially prestressed concrete beams. Figure 10 shows the strain curves of mild steel reinforcement and prestressed steel reinforcement in PPCB.

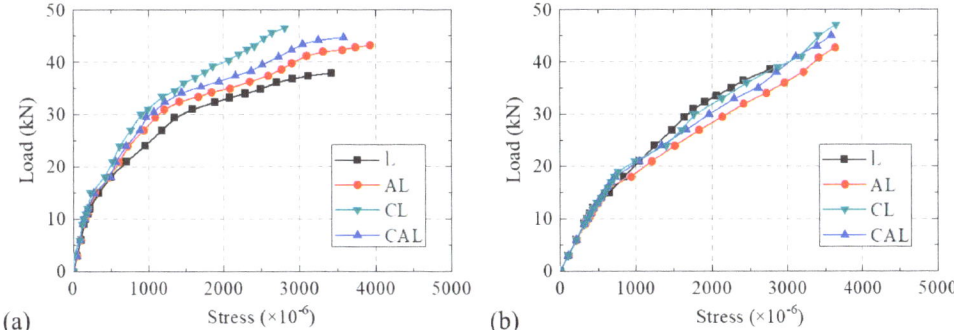

**Figure 10.** The load–rebar strain curves of FRC beams. (**a**) Ordinary steel reinforcement, (**b**) prestressed steel reinforcement.

From Figure 10a, it can be observed that the strain curves of mild steel reinforcement overlap and exhibit linear growth before concrete cracking, with a relatively slow increase in strain. This is because before cracking, the steel reinforcement and concrete jointly bear the sectional stress, with the concrete bearing the majority of the stress. After concrete cracking, the strain of mild steel reinforcement in Beam L increases rapidly due to the concrete no longer contributing to the load-carrying capacity, and the stress is solely transferred to the steel reinforcement. In contrast, the strain increment of steel reinforcement in beams CL, AL, and CAL is smaller than that of the prototype beam after concrete cracking. This is attributed to the inhibition of crack propagation by nearby fibers, partially offsetting the stress concentration. As the load continues to increase, fibers are pulled out or broken, resulting in significantly smaller slopes of the strain curves for beams CL, AL, and CAL compared to the pre-cracking phase, with similar trends among them. When the tensile reinforcement reaches yield, the steel reinforcement in beams AL and CAL yields later than that in beam L, while in beam CL, the cracks have already exceeded the permissible limit before steel reinforcement yielding due to its higher stiffness. Under the same load, beam CL exhibits the smallest strain in mild steel reinforcement, beam AL shows the largest strain, and beam CAL, with hybrid fibers, falls between the two, indicating a positive hybrid effect. The analysis suggests that fibers provide a certain tensile resistance in concrete, thus enhancing the flexural performance of concrete beams.

In this study, the pre-tensioning method was used for prestressing the steel reinforcement, which resulted in initial strain in the prestressed steel reinforcement before the experiment. Therefore, the strain increment was analyzed in this section. Figure 10b indicates that the prestressed steel reinforcement did not reach yield until the failure of the test beams. Before concrete cracking, the strain values of the prestressed steel reinforcement did not differ significantly and exhibited a linear relationship. After cracking, stress redistribution occurred, with the prestressed steel reinforcement bearing more load and thus experiencing increased strain. Under the same load, the prestressed steel reinforcement strain in beam L was greater than that in the FRC beam. This can be attributed to the bridging effect of fibers, which impedes crack propagation and facilitates energy transfer between fibers and concrete, resulting in a more balanced stress distribution between the mild steel reinforcement and prestressed reinforcement.

### 4.4. Load–Deflection Curve

The line displacement along the axis perpendicular to the cross-section, known as deflection, during bending deformation reflects the deformation capacity of the test beam under load. Figure 11 shows the load–deflection curve for PPCB.

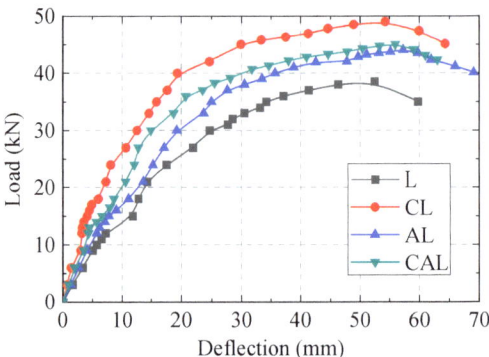

**Figure 11.** Load–deflection curve.

From the curve, the turning points of the test beam's cracking load, yield load, and ultimate load can be observed, indicating that the failure process of the test beam can be roughly divided into three stages: Stage I: Loading until concrete cracking. The load–deflection curve of the test beam shows linear growth, indicating that the test beam is operating in the full cross-section and exhibiting maximum stiffness, corresponding to the elastic working stage. Stage II: Working with cracks. After reaching the cracking load, the first crack appears in the pure bending zone, leading to a decrease in stiffness and a change in the load–deflection curve, with a turning point. Beyond the turning point, the load–deflection curve continues to increase until the reinforcement yields. Stage III: Reinforcement yielding until beam failure. After reinforcement yielding, the load-bearing capacity of the test beam increases slightly, crack propagation accelerates, and deflection significantly increases.

During the initial loading stage, when the load is relatively small, the test beam does not exhibit cracks, and the deflection change is not significant, following a linear increase. This indicates elastic deformation characteristics of the test beam. As the load increases, the test beam L is the first to crack. Under the same loading conditions, the deflection of FRC test beams is significantly smaller than that of the prototype beam. This is because the fibers exhibit excellent resistance to bending and crack prevention, and the fiber extraction and fracture process dissipate some energy, delaying the yielding of the reinforcement and improving the ultimate load-carrying capacity of the test beam. Under the same loading conditions, the deflection sequence from largest to smallest for FRC beams is as follows: AL, CAL, CL. This is due to carbon fibers significantly improving the brittleness of concrete and enhancing its stiffness, while aramid fibers improve the ductility of concrete. When combined, they fully exploit their respective advantages when incorporated into the concrete.

Ductility refers to the ability of a structure, member, or section to deform from initial yield to maximum bearing capacity without a significant reduction in bearing capacity. It reflects the deformation ability of the structure. The deformation ability of the structure with poor ductility will lead to sudden failure, so it is particularly important to analyze the ductility of test beams. The deflection ductility coefficient is used in this paper as $\mu_1 = f_\mu / f_y$, where $f_\mu$ and $f_y$ represent the ultimate deflection and yield deflection of the test beam, respectively.

The ductility coefficient of test beams result is shown in Table 7. It can be seen from Table 7 that compared with the L beam, the ductility of the other fiber-reinforced beams except the CL-P beam is improved to varying degrees, and the elongation of the fiber concrete beams is larger. Compared with the effect of different fiber types, it can be seen that aramid fiber has a greater effect on beam ductility than carbon fiber, and the hybrid positive effect of the two fibers can be fully reflected by ductility values of the CAL beam.

Table 7. The ductility coefficient of test beams.

| Beam Type | $f_y$/mm | $f_u$/mm | $\mu_1$ |
|---|---|---|---|
| L | 37.1 | 59.80 | 1.61 |
| CL | 29.87 | 54.30 | 1.82 |
| AL | 27.61 | 57.34 | 2.08 |
| CAL | 27.52 | 56.05 | 2.04 |

For FRC beams, the ductility of AL beam is greatly improved by 29% due to the good toughness of aramid fibers. Meanwhile, the high strength of carbon fiber makes the ductility of CL beam minimally improved. Hybrid fibers combine the characteristics of the two fibers to achieve a complementary effect, and the ductility of CAL beam is improved by 26.7% compared with that of the prototype beams. It shows the positive effect of fiber mixing.

## 5. Conclusions

In order to study the flexural performance of fiber-reinforced prestressed reinforced concrete beams, the load–deflection curves, the strain between reinforcement and concrete, and the ductility properties of the beams under bending load were analyzed via test methods. The following conclusions were obtained:

(1) The addition of fiber significantly increased the cracking load and ultimate bearing capacity of the test beam, with the cracking load increasing on average by 40% and ultimate bearing capacity by 20%. When the ordinary prestressed concrete test beam is damaged, the concrete in the compression zone will crush and fall off, while the FRC beam will maintain good integrity when it is damaged.

(2) The deflection corresponding to the ultimate load of the fiber prestressed concrete beam is higher than that of the ordinary prestressed concrete beam, and according to the analysis of the ductility coefficient, the addition of fiber not only improves the bearing capacity of the test beam, but also improves the ductility of the beam body. Among the fiber concrete beams, beam AL has the best ductility, so it can be seen that aramid fiber plays an important role in improving the ductility of the component.

(3) The short-chopped carbon fiber and aramid fiber as reinforcement materials can effectively improve the compressive strength and flexural performance of concrete, and they can be used to improve the technology of precast concrete bridge members, thereby increasing the service life of bridge structures. It should be noted that further tests and numerical analyses are still needed to verify the reliability of the overall mechanical properties of complex structures.

**Author Contributions:** Conceptualization, J.Z. and J.W.; Methodology, X.F.; Investigation, C.L. and H.L.; Resources, H.L.; Data curation, C.L.; Writing—original draft, J.Z. and X.F.; Writing—review & editing, J.Z. and J.W.; Funding acquisition, J.W. All authors have read and agreed to the published version of the manuscript.

**Funding:** The authors wish to acknowledge the research funding provided by the Doctoral Research Fund (BKY-2020-27) and Science and Technology Research Project by Hebei Provincial Department of Education (ZC2023175), the Construction of Scientific and Technological Research Project by Hebei Department of Housing and Urban-Rural Development (2023-2156), the SINOMACH Youth Science and Technology Fund (QNJJ-PY-2022-02), and the Young Elite Scientists Sponsorship Program (BYESS2023432). All statements, results, and conclusions are those of the researchers and do not necessarily reflect the views of these foundations.

**Data Availability Statement:** The data presented in this study are available on request from the authors.

**Acknowledgments:** The authors also sincerely thank the anonymous reviewers for their insightful comments and suggestions.

## References

1. Ministry of Transport. *Statistical Bulletin on Development of Transport Industry in 2022*; China Communications News; China Railway: Beijing, China, 2023; 06:002.
2. Zhuo, W.D.; Li, C.C.; Sun, Z.X.; Xiao, Z.R.; Lin, Z.T.; Huang, X.Y. Static performance test of sectional precast prestressed concrete cap beams. *J. Tongji Univ.* **2022**, *50*, 1752–1760.
3. Gao, C.; Zong, Z.H.; Lou, F.; Yuan, S.J.; Lin, J. Model test of explosion load on deck of prestressed concrete continuous beam bridge. *China J. Highw. Transp.* **2022**, *35*, 106–114.
4. Shi, X.A.; Rong, X.; Nan, L.; Wang, L.D.; Zhang, J.X. A new steel-joint precast concrete frame structure: The design, key construction techniques, and building energy efficiency. *Buildings* **2022**, *12*, 1974. [CrossRef]
5. Ferdous, W.; Bai, Y.; Ngo, T.D.; Manalo, A.; Mendis, P. New advancements, challenges and opportunities of multi-storey modular buildings—A state-of-the-art review. *Eng. Struct.* **2019**, *183*, 883–893. [CrossRef]
6. Jaillon, L.; Poon, C.S.; Chiang, Y.H. Quantifying the waste reduction potential of using prefabrication in building construction in Hong Kong. *Waste Manag.* **2009**, *29*, 309–320. [CrossRef]
7. Osmani, M.; Glass, J.; Price, A. Architect and contractor attitudes to waste minimization. *Waste Resour. Manag.* **2006**, *159*, 65–72.
8. Liu, M.; Jia, S.; Liu, X. Evaluation of mitigation potential of GHG emissions from the construction of prefabricated subway station. *J. Clean. Prod.* **2019**, *236*, 117700. [CrossRef]
9. Fang, A.; Zhu, M. Analysis of production technology and energy consumption index of different prefabricated component production lines. *Concrete* **2021**, *1*, 127–131.
10. Huang, H.; Yuan, Y.J.; Zhang, W.; Zhu, L. Property assessment of high-performance concrete containing three types of fibers. *Int. J. Concr. Struct. Mater.* **2021**, *15*, 39. [CrossRef]
11. Han, B.; Zhang, L.; Zhang, C.; Wang, Y.; Yu, X.; Ou, J. Reinforcement effect and mechanism of carbon fibers to mechanical and electrically conductive properties of cement-based materials. *Constr. Build. Mater.* **2016**, *125*, 479–486. [CrossRef]
12. Li, Z.X.; Li, D.H.; Bian, L.B.; Feng, Y.C.; Zhang, Y.Q.; Yu, H.Y. The effect of chopped aramid fiber content on strength and pore structure of cement-based composites. *Mater. Rep.* **2021**, *35*, 638–641.
13. Nguyen, H.; Carvelli, V.; Fujii, T.; Okubo, K. Cement mortar reinforced with reclaimed carbon fibres, CFRP waste or prepreg carbon waste. *Constr. Build. Mater.* **2016**, *126*, 321–331. [CrossRef]
14. Li, Y.F.; Wang, H.F.; Syu, J.Y.; Ramanathan, G.K.; Tsai, Y.K.; Lok, M.H. Mechanical properties of aramid/carbon hybrid fiber-reinforced concrete. *Materials* **2021**, *14*, 5881. [CrossRef]
15. Feng, Y.C.; Li, D.H.; Bian, L.B.; Li, Z.X.; Zhang, Y.Q. Study on mechanical properties and impact properties of aramid fiber reinforced cement-based composites. *Mater. Rep.* **2021**, *35*, 634–637+654.
16. Ayub, T.; Shafiq, N.; Nuruddin, M.F. Effect of chopped basalt fibers on the mechanical properties and microstructure of high performance fiber reinforced concrete. *Adv. Mater. Sci. Eng.* **2014**, *2014*, 587686. [CrossRef]
17. Lee, M.G.; Wang, W.C.; Wang, Y.C.; Hsieh, Y.C.; Lin, Y.C. Mechanical properties of high-strength pervious concrete with steel fiber or glass fiber. *Buildings* **2022**, *12*, 620. [CrossRef]
18. Nie, L.; Xu, J.; Luo, X.; Chen, H.; Chang, S.; Wang, T.; Liu, G. Study of aramid and carbon fibers on the tensile properties of early strength cement mortar. *IOP Conf. Ser. Earth Environ. Sci.* **2019**, *267*, 032009. [CrossRef]
19. Avanaki, M.J.; Hoseini, A.; Vahdani, S.; de la Fuente, A. Numerical-aided design of fiber reinforced concrete tunnel segment joints subjected to seismic loads. *Constr. Build. Mater.* **2018**, *170*, 40–54. [CrossRef]
20. Avanaki, M.J. Response modification factors for seismic design of steel Fiber Reinforced Concrete segmental tunnels. *Constr. Build. Mater.* **2019**, *211*, 1042–1049. [CrossRef]
21. Halvaei, M.; Jamshidi, M.; Latifi, M.; Ejtemaei, M. Effects of volume fraction and length of carbon short fibers on flexural properties of carbon textile reinforced engineered cementitious composites (ECCs); an experimental and computational study. *Constr. Build. Mater.* **2020**, *245*, 118394. [CrossRef]
22. Wille, K.; El-Tawil, S.; Naaman, A.E. Properties of strain hardening ultra high performance fiber reinforced concrete (UHP-FRC) under direct tensile loading. *Cem. Concr. Compos.* **2014**, *48*, 55–66. [CrossRef]
23. Deng, M.K.; Sun, H.Z.; Liang, X.W.; Jing, W.B. Experimental study on flexural performance of ductile fiber reinforced concrete. *Ind. Constr.* **2014**, *44*, 85–90.
24. Wang, X.C.; Liu, H.T. Experimental study on flexural properties of carbon fiber concrete flexural members. *Concrete* **2013**, *8*, 129–132+139.
25. Li, X. *Study on Flexural Performance of PVA Fiber Concrete Beam*; Hubei University of Technology: Wuhan, China, 2012.
26. Qiao, Y.J.; Yang, Z.Q.; Liu, J.Z.; Xu, D.G.; Li, L.; Zhou, H.X. Application of high performance aramid fiber in cement-based composites. *Concrete* **2015**, *1*, 94–97.
27. Krūmiņš, J.; Zesers, A. Experimental investigation of the fracture of hybrid-fiber-reinforced concrete. *Mech. Compos. Mater.* **2015**, *51*, 25–32. [CrossRef]
28. Rangelov, M.; Nassiri, S.; Haselbach, L.; Englund, K. Using carbon fiber composites for reinforcing pervious concrete. *Constr. Build. Mater.* **2016**, *126*, 875–885. [CrossRef]

29. Dong, Z.J.; Dang, F.N.; Gao, J. Experimental study on the flexural behavior of connected precast concrete square piles. *Adv. Civ. Eng.* **2023**, *2023*, 2731841. [CrossRef]
30. Alwis, K.; Burgoyne, C.J. Statistical lifetime predictions for aramid fibers. *J. Compos. Constr.* **2005**, *9*, 106–116. [CrossRef]
31. *GB/T 50081-2019*; Standard for Test Methods of Concrete Physical and Mechanical Properties. Chinese Ministry of Housing and Urban-Rural Development: Beijing, China, 2019.
32. Banthia, N.; Trottier, J.F. Test methods for flexural toughness characterization of fiber reinforced concrete: Some concerns and a proposition. *ACI Mater. J.* **1995**, *92*, 48–57.

**Disclaimer/Publisher's Note:** The statements, opinions and data contained in all publications are solely those of the individual author(s) and contributor(s) and not of MDPI and/or the editor(s). MDPI and/or the editor(s) disclaim responsibility for any injury to people or property resulting from any ideas, methods, instructions or products referred to in the content.

MDPI AG
Grosspeteranlage 5
4052 Basel
Switzerland
Tel.: +41 61 683 77 34

*Buildings* Editorial Office
E-mail: buildings@mdpi.com
www.mdpi.com/journal/buildings

Disclaimer/Publisher's Note: The title and front matter of this reprint are at the discretion of the Guest Editors. The publisher is not responsible for their content or any associated concerns. The statements, opinions and data contained in all individual articles are solely those of the individual Editors and contributors and not of MDPI. MDPI disclaims responsibility for any injury to people or property resulting from any ideas, methods, instructions or products referred to in the content.

www.ingramcontent.com/pod-product-compliance
Lightning Source LLC
LaVergne TN
LVHW072334090526
838202LV00019B/2418